# Early Hominid Activities
## at Olduvai

# FOUNDATIONS OF HUMAN BEHAVIOR

*An Aldine de Gruyter Series of Texts and Monographs*

Edited by
### Sarah Blaffer Hrdy, *University of California, Davis*
### Richard W. Wrangham, *University of Michigan*

# Early Hominid Activities
## at Olduvai

Richard Potts

**Smithsonian Institution**

**ALDINE DE GRUYTER**

New York

## About The Author

**Richard Potts** is Associate Curator of Anthropology, National Museum of Natural History, Smithsonian Institution, Washington, D.C. He is currently directing new excavations at Olorgesailie and other early human sites in Kenya, and has been a major contributor to numerous journals and books.

ALDINE DE GRUYTER
A Division of Walter de Gruyter, Inc.
200 Saw Mill River Road
Hawthorne, New York 10532

Library of Congress Cataloging-in-Publication Data
Potts, Richard, 1953–
    Early hominid activities at Olduvai / Richard Potts.
      p.   cm. — (Foundations of human behavior)
    Bibliography: p.
    Includes index.
    ISBN 0-202-01176-3 (pbk.)
    1. Paleolithic period, Lower—Tanzania—Olduvai Gorge.   2. Animal remains (Archaeology)—Tanzania—Olduvai Gorge.   3. Olduvai Gorge (Tanzania)—Antiquities.   4. Tanzania—Antiquities.   I. Title. II. Series.
    GN772.42.T34P67   1988                              88-14791
    967.8—dc19                                              CIP

Printed in the United States of America
10 9 8 7 6 5 4 3 2 1

# Contents

Preface

## Part III. Hominid Behavior and Paleoecology

# Preface

Olduvai Gorge is an extraordinary place, and the objects found in it take the imagination back to an extraordinary time in our evolutionary history. This volume presents a personal study, which began in 1977, of the fossil animals and stone tools excavated from the oldest strata of Olduvai. It also presents a series of developing debates about living, dynamic realms of the Plio-Pleistocene and the methods by which such realms are interpreted from the dead, static things studied by paleoanthropologists and geologists.

Scientific and public views on human evolution have been powerfully influenced by the discoveries at Olduvai by Mary and Louis Leakey. In some circles, less notice has been given to the slower, painstaking excavation, description, and analysis of fossils and stone tools which has yielded, in my view, the most significant information about the early hominids of Olduvai. These aspects comprise Mary Leakey's research at Olduvai from 1959 to 1985; her volume (Leakey, 1971) which describes in detail the excavations and stone artifacts from Bed I is a landmark publication in the field of early human archeology. Richard Hay's research on the overall geology of Olduvai must also be singled out for its innovative blend of detailed field and laboratory work on the all-important context of the Olduvai sites (Hay, 1976). The publications by Leakey and by Hay comprise the foundation for the present research on hominid activities at Olduvai.

In 1976, Alan Walker suggested I carry out further study of the faunal remains, stone artifacts, and geology of the oldest excavated sites in the Gorge and examine these sites from the perspective of taphonomy and hominid behavior. In retrospect, this suggestion may have rescued me from the upsets and frustrations of arguments about hominid phylogenetic trees and anatomical traits, areas I saw myself entering as a young graduate student. Yet it drew me into perhaps the more daunting, less tangible world of ancient behavior and ecological settings—that of the tool makers of Bed I Olduvai. The writings of Glynn Isaac already argued influentially that excavated sites held important information about early hominid behavior and adaptation. It seemed exciting to try to determine what activities coincided with the home base sites that were widely acknowledged to have existed at Olduvai almost 2 million years ago. As the examination and analysis of the remains developed, a more fundamental question emerged: Why does a collection of stone artifacts and the bones from numerous animals necessarily signify a home base?

That dynamic world that existed almost 2 million years ago in a small region of eastern Africa included hominids, at least two species and possibly more. At least one of these species made tools, durable indicators not only of a degree of technological skill but also of the very fact that hominids were active in the vicinity of that final resting place for tools, the archeological site. Just as much a part of that setting, and certainly as pervasive, was a wide range of environmental and geological processes. Other animals, such as herbivores and carnivores, interacted with hominids and with the artifacts they happened to leave on successive landscapes. Sedimentation and burial are obviously paramount in the preservation of any information about hominids and the environments they inhabited; it is thus important not to lose sight of the fact that most of what is stirring and significant in paleoanthropology (including interpretation of fossil and archeological finds and chronology) hinges on geological processes and their interaction with the paleobiological and behavioral realm. This study of Olduvai was carried out to try to comprehend such interactions, to show how they are evidenced in the static fossil record and, thereby, to try to elucidate more clearly than previously the behaviors attributable to tool-making hominids at Olduvai.

During the initial public presentation of this research (Potts, 1980) and in the few years that followed (Potts, 1982), several other, important studies of the archeological sites of Bed I Olduvai were underway and were beginning to be published. These include the studies by Pat Shipman, Henry Bunn, and Lewis Binford. As discussed briefly in this book, there have been some intriguing convergences and divergences of interpretation among these and other researchers, including myself, since 1981. Indeed, two trends in thinking about early archeological sites and early hominid activities may be recognized: recognition of the importance of scavenging, and critique of the home base interpretation of early archeological sites, particularly those at Olduvai. As we will see, not all researchers agree with these revised interpretations. Ultimately, it is crucial that revised ideas or trends in interpretation be based not upon current sensitivities or intuitions, for example, a desire to do away with the "Man the Hunter" image of human ancestors, but on methods or criteria for discerning in the fossil record the activities that typify home bases, hunting, scavenging, and other aspects of hominid behavior.

Turning now to the many people who helped this study along, my first word of gratitude is to Mary Leakey for permission to study the Olduvai material. This research would not have been possible without her pioneering excavation, dedicated organization of bone and artifact materials, and hospitality during my stay at Olduvai. By her invitation, I was also able to visit Olduvai in 1986 to study the faunal remains excavated from

Long K, a site located at the top of Bed I. Long K was not part of the original plans for this book. Yet during the writing, the analysis of this site proved so intriguing as to warrant inclusion of the fresh results in chapters concerning animal bone accumulation at Olduvai.

I gratefully acknowledge research permission from the governments of Kenya and Tanzania; and permission, advice, and help from R.E. Leakey and the National Museums of Kenya; A.A. Mturi; F. Masao and the National Museum of Tanzania; and J. de Vos, D.A. Hooijer, and the Rijksmuseum van Natuurlijke Historie, Leiden.

The inspiration and intellectual contributions of many individuals have given vitality to this study. In particular, I sincerely thank Alan Walker, Erik Trinkaus, Pat Shipman, David Pilbeam, Glynn Isaac, and Andrew Hill for discussing my first analyses and ideas about Olduvai. Invaluable discussions, especially in the field in East Africa, were had with Anna K. Behrensmeyer, Henry Bunn, Ian Findlater, Jack Harris, Peter Jones, Ellen Kroll, Kathy Schick, and Nick Toth. During my few years teaching at Yale University, Alison Richard and Robert Dewar sharpened my writing and thinking about early hominids, and I feel this research has benefited greatly from their input. In addition to continued exchange with many of these people, more recently John Gurche, Alison Brooks, John Yellen, Kathleen Gordon, and Robert Blumenschine have also kindly shared their time and curiosity in discussing with me evidence and interpretations about the Olduvai sites.

During the preparation of this manuscript many people gave their time and assistance to help make it better than it might have been. In particular, I thank Elizabeth Bailey, Ralph Chapman, Anne Cooksey, Ann Dentry, John Nissenbaum, Marion Schwartz, Thalassa Skinner, Agnes Stix, and Lawan Tyson. Illustrations were done by Jennifer Clark, Jill Perry, Marcia Bakry, Shelley Bougan, and Pua Ford. Louise DeMars offered the original drawings of the symbols seen on the cover. Others who helped during earlier phases of this research were Hazel Potgeiter, Linda Perez, Jaime Taafe, Richard Landau, Barbara Benn, and Katherine Wolf. I also thank Trev Leger and the excellent collaborators at Aldine for their patience and care in the production of this book.

I gratefully acknowledge funding for this research primarily from the National Science Foundation (BNS-7819174), the Boise Fund (University of Oxford), Harvard University, Yale University, and the Smithsonian Institution.

This book is dedicated to my family and to the memory of a dear friend, Thomas C. O'Connor.

*Richard Potts*

# Part I

Bed I Olduvai: A Case Study in
Paleoanthropological Inference

# Introduction

Evidence from the earliest archeological sites has played a dominant role in ideas about the evolution of human behavior. On the basis of present evidence, early hominids from the Plio–Pleistocene, 1.5 to 2.5 million years ago (Ma), were the first to make stone tools. Tools and the sites where they are found have drawn the attention of paleoanthropologists and the public alike, for they suggest a time and a place for the origins of several distinctively human traits. The manufacture of tools has long been considered a product of manipulative skill and mental facility that is special to humans. The earliest human artifacts made from stone signify an incipient technology and the ability to enter hard or tough plant foods or to open up an animal's carcass. The implication, according to traditional views, is that these early hominids performed economic functions that once characterized all humans, the ability to hunt and to gather food. Moreover, continuity in the shape of the earliest known tools over long periods of time appears to embody the essence of cultural learning, the passing of information across generations, and a unique medium for maintaining a way of life.

Probably more than the discoveries from any other paleoanthropological site, the finds from Olduvai Gorge, Tanzania, have helped to shape ideas about the origins of these human behaviors. The first discoveries at Olduvai, between 1931 and 1959 by Drs. Louis and Mary Leakey, showed what very early stone tools looked like and what species of animals were contemporary with the hominid toolmakers. From 1959 through the early 1960s, fossils provided the first glimpses of those hominids. Actually, more than one species was found: the large-toothed robust australopithecine (*Australopithecus boisei*); the more lightly built and larger brained *Homo habilis*; and *Homo erectus*, the still larger brained successor to *H. habilis*. Fossils of both robust *Australopithecus* and *H. habilis* were found in the oldest sedimentary layers of Olduvai. On the basis of consistent spatial associations between stone artifacts and the remains of *H. habilis*, a case has been made that this species was the earliest toolmaker at Olduvai (Leakey, 1971). Although the idea is partly based on an assumption that the first stone toolmaker had a relatively large brain, it is now generally believed, though by no means proved, that early *Homo* rather than *Australopithecus* was responsible for the earliest stone tools throughout East Africa.

Research at Olduvai was directed not only toward discovering the maker of stone tools. In fact, the technology and overall activity patterns of the hominids were the primary focus of intensive excavations led by Mary Leakey during the early 1960s. Leakey's excavations concentrated on the two geologic units at the base of the Gorge, named Beds I and II. Certain layers of fine-grain sediment within Bed I, in particular, contained clusters of stone artifacts and the broken, fossilized bones of numerous animals. These sites—such as FLK "Zinj," where the first Plio–Pleistocene fossil of *Australopithecus* in East Africa was found—occurred in a zone of sediments laid down on the border of an ancient lake that no longer exists. The expansions and contractions of this lake were portrayed as gradual, undisturbing to the artifacts and bones deposited along its margin. This kind of geologic setting suggested to Leakey that the sites in Bed I were areas where hominids had brought stone tools and had eaten the meat of animals represented by bones. The animal bones found with the artifacts thus became especially important to interpretations of the Olduvai sites. Because of the presumed importance of these bones to the diet of hominids, excavations of dense concentrations of fossils and stone tools were called "living sites" (Leakey, 1971). Other paleoanthropologists working in East Africa, especially J. Desmond Clark and Glynn Isaac, came to the same conclusion and referred to the Olduvai sites as traces of early hominid campsites (Clark, 1970; Isaac, 1969, 1971). The layers of Bed I were dated approximately 1.75 million years old (Ma). Thus, the sites were nearly four times older than the earliest archeological sites previously known. The finds from Olduvai had pushed back the evidence for early hominid activities to almost 2 million years ago.

About 12 years ago, it became clear that the initial view of the Olduvai sites as areas of hominid activity, specifically campsites, needed reevaluation. There were two main reasons for this. First, researchers began to pay a great deal of attention to the ways by which stone artifacts and animal bones become deposited and modified. Studies of carcasses in modern habitats and in ancient deposits showed that a number of geological and environmental processes can affect bones in ways that may mimic the accumulation and preservation of such remains at archeological sites. Thus, while it once seemed straightforward to assume that the Olduvai sites preserved the undisturbed traces of hominid activity, it ultimately became necessary to test this idea rigorously (Isaac, 1983a).

A second motivation for reassessing the Olduvai sites was the increasing emphasis on both the differences and similarities between early hominids and modern humans. The campsite, or home base, interpretation of the Olduvai sites emphasizes the similarities of hominids to modern hunting and gathering peoples. However, the hominids of Bed I at Olduvai lived about 1.5 million years before the earliest *Homo sapiens* and possibly 100,000 years before the oldest known *Homo erectus*. Thus, it appears far too limiting to reconstruct the adaptations of the hominids at Olduvai by considering only behaviors observable in humans today. To apply present-day human analogies in a sweeping manner to ancient hominids essentially eliminates any question about behavioral evolution. Such questions must consider the possible antecedents to modern human behavior. Numerous archeologists have considered early hominid life to have been quite similar to that of modern hunter–gatherers, whereas others (e.g., Gould, 1980) state that the conditions of life before modern *Homo sapiens* were "fundamentally different from what they are today." In an evolutionary perspective this point becomes the object of study rather than the major assumption.

With these reasons in mind, a personal study of the excavated remains from Bed I Olduvai was carried out. In this volume I will discuss mainly six levels excavated and originally described by Leakey (1971). Since a thorough account of these levels is provided in the next chapter, a brief description will suffice here. In five of the levels stone artifacts and animal bones were preserved, while only faunal remains occurred in the sixth. The remains were found in both thin and thick layers of sediment (approximately 9–68 cm thick) and concentrated in areas about 10–20 m in diameter. Each of these levels and the debris they contained are referred to as *sites*, representing distinct events or periods of bone, artifact, and sediment accumulation. A wide range of species have been identified from the fossilized bones, especially large mammals that ranged in size from gazelle (over 12 kg) to elephant. Most of the faunal remains were broken before burial and fossilization occurred. Stone artifacts from the five tool-bearing sites are diverse in size, shape, and raw material. They include pieces modified by percussion flaking (core tools), small flakes known as debitage, pieces apparently modified solely by their use as implements (utilized material), and unmodified rocks obtained from outcrops in the ancient Olduvai region (manuports).

What do these fossil bones and stone artifacts buried at Olduvai indicate about early hominids? Do they provide clues about hominid activity and adaptations to ancient environments? If so, what were these activities and adaptations? How did they compare with the behaviors of ancestral hominoids and of later humans? These general questions about the Olduvai sites are of greatest interest to students of human evolution.

There are four major aspects of this study. First, it is crucial to test the idea that the artifact and bone concentrations of Bed I represent primary areas of hominid activity. Second, based on an assessment of how the Olduvai sites were formed, the paleoecology of ancient Olduvai will then be explored. Reconstruction of the ecological settings in which hominids lived provides a necessary background for considering the possible adaptations of early hominids at Olduvai and why they may have developed. In this regard, the large mammal communities that existed at Olduvai are an important context for understanding the possible ecological roles played by these hominids.

It will be shown that several geological, biological, and behavioral agents or processes were involved in the formation of the Olduvai sites. Yet for the five levels containing artifacts and fauna, hominids were an important, and probably the primary, collector of these materials. A third goal of this study, thus, will be to assess what kinds of hominid activities led to the accumulation of animal bones and stone artifacts. Particularly interesting questions concern whether hominids hunted or scavenged for meat and other useful animal tissues, and how the transport of stone material and of bones were related to one another. In other words, how did hominid activities result in the creation of sites in the first place?

Finally, the traditional interpretation of the Olduvai sites as campsites, or home bases, will be examined. The home base hypothesis, explained in the following section, ties together many crucial elements of human behavioral evolution and, thus, it is one of the most significant and elaborate statements about the lives of human ancestors.

There appears to be little room to doubt that the development of home bases was important to the course of human evolution. However, the view expressed here is that the earliest hominid sites at Olduvai were not home bases but were antecedent to them. Although there is evidence for variations in climate and in the specific makeup of animal communities during the deposition of Bed I, throughout this period hominids collected stone materials and left them at specified locations. Parts of animal carcasses, obtained most likely by a combination of scavenging and hunting, were brought over a period of time to these places where stone material and tools were accumulated. These "stone caches," I suggest, were areas for processing food—at least parts of animal carcasses—and the attraction of carnivores to these sites prohibited their use by hominids as the primary areas of social activity, that is, as home bases in the modern hunter–gatherer sense. Although this idea is less specific about the nature of hominid activities than the home base hypothesis, the view that Plio–Pleistocene hominids transported resources to specific places for reasons other than social ones has important implications concerning the development of home bases and the pace of hominid behavioral evolution.

## The Home Base Hypothesis

Spurred by the finds from Olduvai, and more recently from Koobi Fora, Kenya, archeologists have become intrigued more and more with the reasons behind the evolution of humans. If, in fact, archeological sites provide direct traces of hominid activities, it is possible that the study of excavated remains will help in identifying "the patterns of natural selection that transformed these protohumans into humans" (Isaac, 1978). In this endeavor, the home base interpretation of the oldest sites is the most influential idea derived from archeological evidence about the evolution of human behavior.

Glynn Isaac, in particular, pointed out that the origins of certain fundamental differences between humans and nonhuman primates may be explored by using the archeological record (Isaac, 1976, 1978, 1984). Figure 1.1 lists some of these distinguishing features. Because diet and food acquisition are

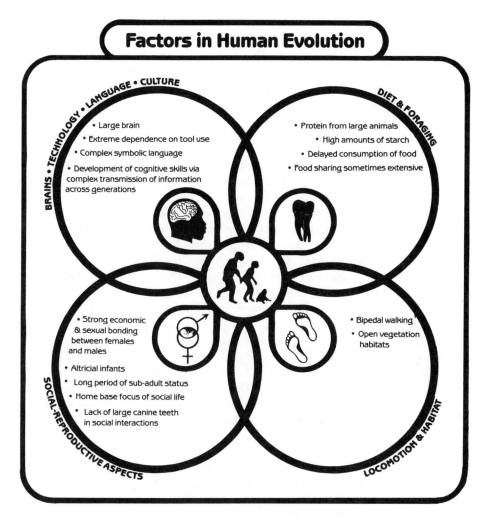

**FIGURE 1.1.** The distinguishing features of human evolution may be considered as an interaction among four systems: locomotion and habitat; social–reproductive aspects; brains–technology–language–culture system; and diet and foraging.

vital aspects of an animal's ecological niche and, therefore, evolutionary history, feeding activity is a salient point of comparison. The feeding behavior of modern humans tends to differ from that of nonhuman primates in two major ways. First, a relatively large percentage of the diet of many humans is composed of meat, especially from large mammals. Second, the eating of animal and plant foods is often delayed considerably after the food is obtained.

It is often carried back to a home base, which serves as the spatial focus for food exchange, eating, and social activity.

Furthermore, in contrast with other primates, tools are required to process many foods and for other tasks carried out at the home base or while foraging. Another notable difference is that human offspring have a longer period of maturation. Both male and female parents—bonded socially by economics, emotion, and offspring—often play important roles in nurturing their children. Spoken language, that is, symbolically coded information used as a conventional form of communication, acts as a crucial medium of learning and social intercourse. Once again, the home base serves as a spatial focus where family members meet, offspring are nurtured, and the most intensive social contacts with other individuals of the group occur.

The home base interpretation of archeological sites 2 million years old implies that, by that time, these distinctive characteristics had already started to evolve in concert. Traditionally, archeologists have drawn similarities between the materials excavated from Paleolithic sites and the debris discarded by modern hunter–gatherers at their campsites (Isaac, 1983a). A somewhat idealized conception of the home base, derived in part from studies of tropical hunter–gatherers such as the !Kung San of Botswana (Lee, 1979; Lee and DeVore, 1976), has provided a model for interpreting the sites from Olduvai, Koobi Fora, and other Plio–Pleistocene archeological localities. According to this model, concentrations of artifacts and fossils from these sites are the relics of home bases—relatively safe locations where hominids ate, slept, and met members of their social group. The home bases of early hominids were places around which foraging and social life were organized. Food, represented by the remains of animals, was carried there and given to children and adults who remained at the camp or to returning foragers who had less success in finding food. When such a system of home base activity had developed, a premium was placed on cooperation, language, and socially accepted means of delayed reciprocity which characterize human societies today (Isaac, 1978).

The implications of the home base interpretation have been explored amply in popular literature. Since home bases are a fundamental feature of hunter–gatherer socioecology, the supposed existence of home bases 2 Ma implied long-term continuity in the behavior of early hominids and modern humans, at least until about 10,000 years ago (Lee and DeVore, 1968: 3). The hunter–gatherer way of life thus has deep roots in our evolutionary past. Writers such as Desmond Morris (1969), E. O. Wilson (1978), and Robert Ardrey (1961, 1976) have invoked variations on this interpretation to support the view that modern human behavior has been shaped by our evolutionary past. Ardrey, for example, based his ideas about human evolution on one aspect of the hunting–gathering adaptation, namely hunting. According to his view, the necessity among early hominids to hunt animals in order to survive, supported putatively by evidence of numerous animal bones brought by hominids to their sites, placed a premium on aggressive and violent tendencies still manifested by humans today. Other authors have looked to the same archeological evidence to counter Ardrey's "hunting hypothesis." According to Leakey and Lewin (1978), for example, broken animal bones are indeed abundant at the earliest archeological sites, but these sites represent campsites where food sharing and cooperation were the crucial elements of behavior; thus, it is these traits that were particularly important to the course of human evolution.

Evidently, interpretations of Plio–Pleistocene archeological sites have significantly influenced ideas about human evolution and are discussed when considering the extent to which evolutionary history has created a distinctive and universal human nature. Fundamental to these issues is the question whether the "home base" provides the best interpretation of Plio–Pleistocene archeological sites. The origins of home bases has become a major topic of paleoanthropological study (Isaac, 1983a; Potts, 1984b). Because it ties together many important aspects of behavior, the home base hypothesis is a valuable focus for inquiry into the activities of early hominids at Olduvai.

## The Method of Inquiry

Investigation of this hypothesis and, more generally, of hominid activities at Olduvai requires extensive detective work on the formation of the archeological sites. Before hominid activities can be assessed from study of archeological materials, a sequence of questions must be examined about the possible ways in which the sites were produced and the role of hominids in making them.

First, it is crucial to ask why sites, in fact, occur in the sediments at Olduvai. Are the artifacts present in unusually high concentrations, as might be expected at an important area of hominid activity? Or are they only thinly scattered, as artifacts discarded over an ancient land surface? Do the fossils represent the original death areas of animals, or were the bones transported away from carcasses to new locations? The answers to these questions may vary from site to site. If the excavated remains are found to be concentrated in dense clusters, which processes were responsible for their accumulation? Some of the possibilities are water action, as in a stream that may have dumped its contents in a specific area; porcupines, hyenas, or other animals that collect bones; and hominids. If hominids were at least partly responsible, did they hunt game or scavenge from carcasses to obtain animal bones? What aspects of the faunal community did hominids exploit, and where did they collect raw materials for making tools? Finally, does the collection of bones and artifacts at Olduvai indicate the presence of home base activities similar to those exhibited by hunter–gatherers at campsites?

One of the fundamental notions not only in studying such issues about archeological sites, but in all critical thinking, is that there is more than one

**TABLE 1.1.** Factors Responsible for the Production, Alteration, or Preservation of a Cluster of Bones and Artifacts[a]

A. Environmental factors
  1. Population density and spatial distribution of animals and carcasses
  2. Rate of dispersal and destruction of bones/carcasses on the landscape
    a. Activity of mammalian carnivores
    b. Activity of avian scavengers
    c. Effects of insects, bacteria, and weathering
  3. Accumulation of bones by animals, especially porcupines, hyenas, leopards
    a. Use of site as bone accumulation area
    b. Modification of bones, intensity of site use, reuse of site
  4. Sedimentary processes: Water flow or other sedimentary medium as an agent of bone or artifact accumulation.

B. Hominid behavior

  1. Accumulation and transport of resources from the environment
    a. Stone tools and raw material: Location of sources
    b. Animal tissues: Hunted versus scavenged, distance over which bones were transported to site
    c. Plant tissues: Gathered versus consumed during foraging (away from site)
  2. Intentional modification and use of materials
    a. Flaking and use of stone
    b. Damage to bone (e.g., breakage, cut marks)
  3. Discard or placement of objects (e.g., creation of secondary refuse areas, placement of manuports)
  4. Secondary modification by hominids (e.g., breakage and subsurface migration of materials due to trampling)
  5. Intensity of activity
    a. Duration of site use
    b. Reuse of site and its materials

C. Modification of refuse after initial deposition

  1. Decomposition of plant remains
  2. Damage to bones on surface of site by scavengers (hominid or nonhominid) or due to trampling
  3. Contribution and removal of bones by animals
  4. Weathering of transported bone and stone on the land surface (factors 2 and 4 produce differential destruction of bone beyond that caused by the initial bone collector [s])

D. Site during burial

  1. Disturbance of spatial arrangement of objects by depositional medium
  2. Input of objects by depositional medium
  3. Removal of objects by depositional medium

**TABLE 1.1** (*cont.*)

E. Diagenesis

    1. Mineral replacement leading to fossilization

    2. Breakage of fossil bone and stone by earth movements and sediment load

    3. Chemical weathering of objects

F. Excavation

    1. Preferential recovery of objects due to excavation methods (e.g., sampling, sieving)

    2. Accidental breakage or loss of objects

G. Archeological observation

    1. Classification of materials (e.g., recognition of species and skeletal elements)

    2. Criteria by which each of the foregoing factors can be assessed and its influence on site formation inferred

    3. Collection of data pertinent to criteria that are diagnostic of site formation processes

"The factors listed here potentially affect reconstructions of site formation in Bed I Olduvai. This list specifies the major processes or influences that contributed to, altered, and preserved the remains hominids may have left behind or that may have imitated the traces of hominid activity.

possible answer to any question. It is striking that only over the past dozen years or so has this idea of multiple hypotheses been explicit in the study of the earliest hominid sites (Isaac, 1983a, b). During that time, there has been direct and detailed inquiry into whether hominids, in fact, were responsible for the remains excavated from the oldest sites and whether clusters of artifacts and animal bones were indeed home bases.

Study of early hominid activities involves several levels of analysis. The first level of analysis concerns hypotheses about site taphonomy, or the processes by which fossil bones and associated stone artifacts were deposited, damaged, and buried. Table 1.1 outlines the many factors that may help to produce and to alter a cluster of bones and artifacts. Nonhominid effects on site formation must be considered because they are known to mask evidence of hominids and to create traces quite similar to those made by hominids. Therefore, processes like water flow or feeding by hyenas or other carnivorous mammals may tremendously influence our inferences about hominid activity and may even determine whether such inferences are possible to make.

The taphonomic level of analysis relies upon the existence of evidence that uniquely characterizes each of the possible processes of site formation. To distinguish between bones collected by hominids and natural accumulations of bones on the landscape, or to discern bone damage inflicted by hominids from that produced by carnivores, each of these processes must leave distinctive, identifiable traces. Numerous studies in modern habitats and ethnoarcheological and experimental research have helped to identify some of the characteristic effects of taphonomic processes on animal bones and stone artifacts, though considerably more work is needed (e.g., Behrensmeyer, 1975, 1978; Binford, 1978, 1981; Brain, 1967, 1981; Gifford, 1980; Hill, 1975, 1979a; Isaac, 1967; Potts and Shipman, 1981; Schiffer, 1976; Shipman, 1981; Voorhies, 1969; Yellen, 1977). These studies provide paleoanthropologists with the groundwork from which to untangle the potentially complex combination of hominid activities and environmental and geological events that occurred in the past.

Further, taphonomic analysis involves more than simply identifying the processes that contributed to the formation of sites. Its goal is to reconstruct what the original assemblages of bones and artifacts transported to a site or distributed over a landscape may have looked like and, if possible, to make inferences about the original faunal communities from which bones were sampled. By identifying the taphonomic factors that affected site formation, it may be possible to reconstruct the history of alterations and samplings undergone by an assemblage of bones or artifacts. Such reconstructions help in making inferences about the ancient habitats from which these materials were obtained.

If, from taphonomic study, hominids are found to have played a clear role in the formation of a site, a second level of analysis is possible. This concerns the specific activities of hominids. Evidence for different kinds of hominid activities is sought from the composition of the bone and artifact assemblages and from patterns of damage and spatial distribution of materials at the site. Within this level of investigation the degree and significance of eating meat, the way hominids acquired food (e.g., hunting or scavenging), the methods by which tools were made, and the attraction of carrying stone materials and animal bones to a site are among the most important questions.

When inferences about hominid activities are compared over a sample of sites, it may be possible to generalize about the hominid adaptations that existed at a particular time and place. Thus, comparisons among hominid activity areas in Bed I Olduvai yield a number of possible explanations about why early hominids produced sites. The home base hypothesis is one such explanation. Generalizations about early hominid activities, comprising a third level of analysis, can be tested by examining still larger samples of archeological sites.

A fourth, and final, level of inquiry in the study of early hominid behavior concerns the evolutionary significance of hominid activity patterns. For example, what, if anything, do conclusions about the activities of hominids at

Olduvai imply about the course of human evolution? Ideas on the origin and development of home bases and associated behaviors are explored at this point. This final level of analysis is the furthest removed from the materials and sediments excavated by archeologists and is based on a chain of inferences about taphonomy and hominids. Yet it may lead to some of the most significant contributions to the study of human evolution.

This outlines the way in which this study into hominid activities at Olduvai is to proceed. In order to probe the major questions about hominids at Olduvai we must pursue a sequence of ideas that starts with geologic and taphonomic evidence; poses plausible explanations, including ones other than hominid activity, to account for the sites of stone artifact and bone preservation; and leads, ultimately, to an evaluation of the home base hypothesis.

# 2

# The Sites of Bed I Olduvai Gorge

It is important to realize from the outset that the early hominids of Olduvai did not live in a gorge. The Olduvai Gorge, located on the Serengeti Plain of northern Tanzania, is a relatively recent phenomenon. It is a canyon carved by modern streams over the past 200,000 years. These streams have cut through a basin of sediments laid down by a lake now vanished and by the streams that once entered it. The modern streams, originating from Lakes Masek and Ndutu in the Serengeti and from the slopes of the volcano Lemagrut, have cut out a "Main Gorge" and a "Side Gorge" which intersect to form a "Y" shape (Figure 2.1). On route to a local depression in the land, known as Olbalbal, the seasonally flowing channel waters have eroded a narrow slice of geological history almost 2 million years old. This slice preserves the bones and stone artifacts of the hominids and animals that once lived near the ancient lake and streams in the Olduvai region.

The purpose of this chapter is to describe the geological history and the general characteristics of the sites in Bed I that are studied here. Extensive research has been done by a number of investigators on the fauna, stone artifacts, geology, and past climates of Olduvai. This chapter provides a synthesis of that research, drawing heavily upon the geological research by Hay (1976).

The ancient Olduvai basin originated 2 Ma by the uplift of volcanic highlands to the east and south. Beneath the lavas that underlie the sediments of Bed I is a basement suite of metamorphic rocks. These latter rocks—mostly granite gneisses and quartzites—outcrop as hills at Kelogi (gneiss) and Naibor Soit (quartzite) on the border of the Olduvai Gorge (Figure 2.1). Volcanos supplied both fine ash and water-washed pebbles, cobbles, and boulders to the Olduvai basin. Ngorongoro, located to the east of the Gorge, last erupted about 2 Ma, probably providing the lavas that separate the Olduvai Beds from the basement rocks. This volcano and the southern ones (Sadiman and Lemagrut) furnished several kinds of lavas, such as basalt, trachyte, and nephelinite, some of which were useful to early hominids for making tools. Lavas and consolidated ashes, or tuffs, from the volcanos that surround Olduvai interfinger with the basin sediments. Some of these volcanic strata show chemical characteristics that have enabled firm potassium–argon (K–Ar) dating (Curtis and Hay, 1972; Evernden and Curtis, 1965; Fitch, Hooker, and Miller, 1978; Hay, 1976; see Cerling and Hay, 1986). Fission-track dating and paleomagnetic correlations have provided results in agreement with findings from K–Ar

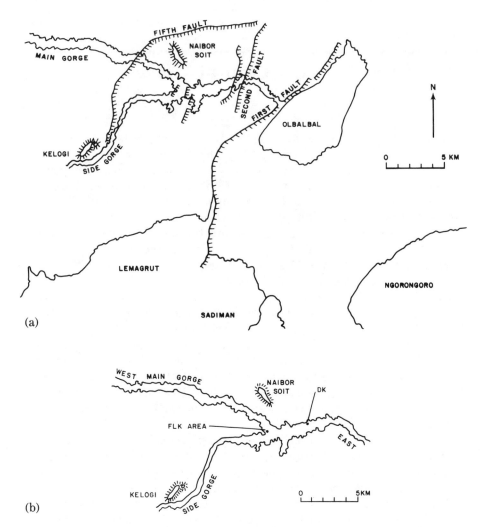

**FIGURE 2.1.** *(a)* Map of the Olduvai basin immediately surrounding the Gorge.
Based on Hay (1976). *(b)* Map of Olduvai Gorge with excavation
localities DK and the FLK complex noted.

methods (Fleischer, Price, Walker, and Leakey, 1965; Gromme and Hay, 1967,
1971).

According to Richard Hay (1976), who has carried out extensive geological
studies at Olduvai, the sequence of strata in the Gorge consists of seven major
geologic beds. The lavas that lie beneath the sediments of Bed I are dated
about 1.90 Ma. The deposits of Beds I and II, 1.87–1.20 Ma, reflect a period
of variation in the size of the ancient lake due to changes in the shape of the

basin (tectonic activity) and to climatic shifts. By the end of Bed II, the lake had disappeared entirely. Beds III and IV, representing the last 400,000 years of the Lower Pleistocene, are composed of deposits from streams that flowed westward, in nearly the opposite direction to that of the streams at Olduvai today. Tectonic uplift and depression continued to modify the Pleistocene drainage patterns of the Olduvai region. From about 600,000 to 15,000 years ago, the Masek, Ndutu, and Naisuisui Beds were deposited; during this period, the sediments of earlier times began to be eroded by streams heading toward Olbalbal.

Bed I, which forms the earliest sediments at Olduvai, spans a period of more than 50,000 years, probably closer to a period of 150,000 years (Figure 2.2). Near the base of the fossil and archeological sequence, a volcanic unit (Tuff IB) has yielded dates of 1.84 ± 0.3 Ma. Since about the first three-quarters of the worldwide event of magnetic polarity known as the Olduvai event, dated approximately 1.90–1.65 Ma, is recorded within Bed I, it is likely that the top of Bed I is about 1.70 million years old (Hay, 1976; Curtis and Hay, 1972).

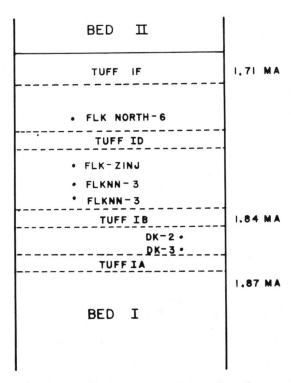

**FIGURE 2.2.** Stratigraphic sequences of volcanic tuffs and excavated levels in Bed I.

Excavations in this lowest geologic unit have been confined to two main areas: locality DK and the FLK complex (see Figure 2.1b). This investigation into the activities of early hominids at Olduvai focuses on six levels excavated in Bed I. In stratigraphic order from top to bottom these levels are:

FLK North Level 6[1]
FLK "Zinj" (Level 22)
FLKNN Level 2
FLKNN Level 3
DK Level 2
DK Level 3

As shown in Figure 2.1b, the DK locality occurs on the north bank of the eastern Main Gorge. DK–2 and 3, which are considered in detail in this book, are overlain by volcanic Tuff IB (Figure 2.2). These levels are dated between 1.84 and 1.87 Ma. The FLK complex consists of three erosion gullies where the Main Gorge and Side Gorge join. FLKNN is the northernmost locality in the complex. Level 3 at FLKNN is an ancient land surface that rests on top of Tuff IB. Level 2, immediately above, contained the only cluster of animal bones in Bed I that was not associated with stone artifacts. The horizon above Level 2 is equivalent with the "Zinj" level (Level 22) at locality FLK, the southernmost excavation in the complex. The "Zinj" level preserved by far the densest concentration of archeological materials from any level excavated in Bed I. Between this locality and FLKNN is FLK North. Six archeological levels were excavated at FLK North. The lowest layer, Level 6, lies about 1.5 m below Tuff IF, which marks the top of Bed I. Less than 180 m separate the two most distant excavations in this complex—FLK and FLKNN.[2]

## Ancient Environments

Geologic studies of ancient environments have helped greatly in reconstructing the past climates of Bed I and the taphonomic history of these sites. Based on geological research, Hay (1976) has defined the major environments of sedimentation and the geographic relationships among them. Figure 2.3

---

[1]Hereafter, these levels will read as follows, in order: FLK North–6; FLK "Zinj"; FLKNN–2; FLKNN–3; DK–2; DK–3.

[2]A comment on terminology: As noted in Chapter 1, *level* refers to a particular stratigraphic unit. Each level represents a distinct event of deposition. *Locality* refers to an excavated area of Olduvai Gorge. A locality (e.g., FLKNN) may involve more than one level. The term *site* is used in this book to refer to an excavated portion of a level in which stone artifacts and fauna were found. A site thus defines the unit of archeological/paleontological analysis. The remains at a site may or may not have been deposited by hominids. A site is designated by referring to a particular locality and stratigraphic level (e.g., FLKNN–3).

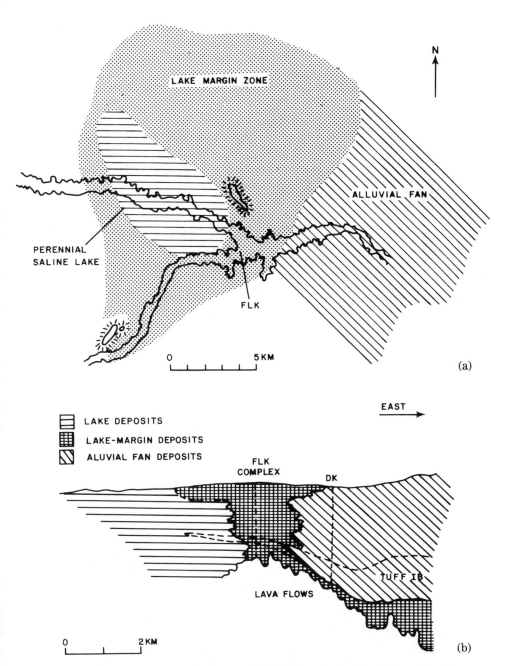

**FIGURE 2.3.** *(a)* Map of reconstructed lithofacies (and related depositional environments) for Bed I above Tuff IB. The FLK locality is noted. Based on Hay (1976). *(b)* Bed I lithofacies reconstructed (in section) by Hay (1976: 41) along the north wall of the Main Gorge. Locations of locality DK and the FLK complex are noted. DK Levels 1–3 are below Tuff IB. The FLK, FLKNN, and FLK North levels examined in this study are above Tuff IB.

illustrates the diverse types of sediment and their spatial relationships (lith-ofacies). All of the sites discussed in the present study are found in the eastern lake margin zone. Below Tuff IB, this lake margin zone was more extensive than later on when the rest of Bed I was deposited. Before Tuff IB was deposited, the lake margin, or area over which lake waters occasionally ex-panded, extended well to the east (a zone at least 5.4 km wide) and encom-passed the sediments at locality DK and beyond. Beneath Tuff IB, no zone of alluvial sediments has been observed east of the lake sediments. Tuff IB was laid down during a major eruptive phase of the volcano Olmoti around 1.84 Ma. The volcanic matter became part of an alluvial fan, spreading west-ward and constricting the area of periodic lake expansion to about 2 km wide. Afterward, the lake, lake margin, and alluvial zones fluctuated within the overall spatial pattern set by the eruption of Tuff IB. Due to fluctuations, these sedimentary environments can be observed to interfinger in the deposits of the Gorge today (Figure 2.3b). Toward the top of Bed I, between the deposition of Tuffs ID and IF, a period of lake regression occurred. During this time, the lake was smallest, on the average, than at any other period of Bed I. During the deposition of Bed I, the lake's diameter fluctuated between about 7 and 25 km. These fluctuations were controlled by climate and the balance between water inflow and evaporation. Sedimentary and geochemical evidence indicates that the perennial lake was shallow, saline, and alkaline, though fresher water generally inundated the western lake margin terrain (Hay, 1976: 41–53).

The high salinity and frequent fluctuations of the lake suggest that a semi-arid climate prevailed in the Olduvai region during Bed I times, though it was generally wetter than occurs at Olduvai today (about 566 mm of rainfall per year) (Hay, 1976; Cerling, Hay, and O'Neil, 1977; Cerling and Hay 1986).[3] The history of lake level fluctuations and geochemical indicators of climate and lake salinity suggest that a general drying trend occurred throughout the Bed I period.

[3]Cerling and Hay (1986) offer estimates of both rainfall and temperature based on oxygen and carbon isotope values from paleosol carbonates and certain as-sumptions concerning, for instance, the type of vegetation. Olduvai today has an average yearly temperature of 22°C and, as noted before, rainfall of 566 mm. Values for oxygen isotopes in Bed I suggest, under certain assumptions, a mean annual temperature of about 13–16°C. Carbon isotope values imply a similar range (12–15°C), if C3 grasses made up the entire vegetation. Alternatively, a flora dominated by C3 shrubs and trees, which implies an average rainfall greater than 800 mm per year, could also account for the carbon isotope data regardless of temperature. Soil carbonates are uncommon in Bed I Olduvai, which is also the case in modern environments with an annual rainfall greater than 750 mm. Cerling and Hay conclude that most of Bed I is characterized by conditions moister than today (more than 800 mm per annum) and cooler temperatures (by perhaps 7°C). It would appear that these isotopic data do not fully account for the arid period represented toward the top of Bed I, indicated by other geochemical, faunal, and floral evidence.

Pollen analysis provides further evidence for climatic shifts (Bonnefille and Riollet, 1980; Bonnefille, Lobreau, and Riollet, 1982). Four samples of sediment collected by Bonnefille contained enough grains of fossilized pollen for climatic analysis. One sample was obtained from Tuff IB, one from between Tuffs IB and ID, and 2 samples just below Tuff IF. By calculating the percentage of highland forest pollen in each sample, it is possible to draw a rough curve indicating the amount of regional rainfall over time. A relatively high amount of forest pollen in the sample from Tuff IB indicates a more humid environment than occurs today at Olduvai (Figure 2.4). This particular pollen spectrum reflects a mean annual rainfall of approximately 1000 mm. A slight

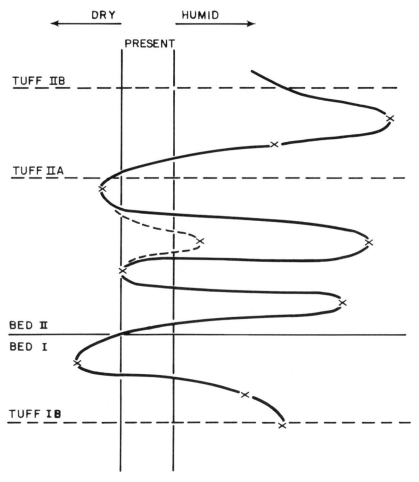

**FIGURE 2.4.** Rainfall curve based on the percentage of highland forest pollen for Beds I and II. Data points are indicated by "x." Based on Bonnefille and Riollet (1980) and Bonnefille *et al.* (1982).

decrease in rainfall is indicated by the sample above this. The samples from the top of Bed I, on the other hand, contained very little highland forest pollen, which suggests a mean annual rainfall on the order of 350 mm. This very arid environment supported small herbaceous plants and a more saline lake than during earlier times (Bonnefille and Riollet, 1980).

An overall change from humid to quite arid conditions is also suggested by faunal evidence. Fossilized urocyclid slugs, indicating a relatively moist habitat, were found below Tuff ID and were most common near the base of Bed I (Hay, 1976). The remains of rodents have also been found from excavated levels at FLK, FLK North, and FLKNN (Jaeger, 1976). The relative proportions of rodent taxa at FLK and FLKNN point to the presence of a perennial lake and lakeside bush vegetation. Murid rodents, which live in more moist and shady habitats than occur at Olduvai today, are especially abundant in Middle Bed I at these two localities. Several murid genera that live in the Serengeti region today are preserved in Bed I. Their presence suggests a variety of specific habitats: high grasslands on the border of swamps; riverine gallery forests; high, open savanna; *Acacia*-lined river channels through savanna; and bush–thicket–forest areas where arboreal species could live (Jaeger, 1976). Incidently, the presence of lake margin swamps in Bed I is also indicated by fossilized root channels of papyrus and other shore grasses (Hay, 1976). In the upper levels at FLK North, certain rodent species signal the existence of more arid conditions, especially the widespread occurrence of dry savanna. Rodents that live in riverine forest and dense thickets are not represented near the top of Bed I at FLK North.

The insectivores and birds provide similar indications about the climatic history of Bed I Olduvai. Elephant shrews *(Elephantulus)* and hedgehogs *(Erinaceus)* are rare at FLKNN and FLK but reach greatest abundance in the low to middle layers at FLK North, higher up in Bed I. A decline in rainfall is suggested by the increase in both of these insectivore genera toward the top of Bed I (Butler and Greenwood 1973, 1976). Moreover, diverse species of birds that inhabit aquatic, marshy, and wooded environments have been identified among the fossilized avian remains (Matthiesen, 1982). They include such forms as grebes, cormorants, pelicans, ducks, gulls, terns, and wading birds such as flamingos, herons, and storks. Flamingos indicate the proximity of brackish water. In accord with other climatic evidence, acquatic birds are most common in the lower half of Bed I (the levels at DK, FLKNN, and FLK), whereas land birds are most common just under Tuff IF at FLK North (information from P. Brodkorb reported by Hay, 1976).

As indicators of habitat, large mammals usually are not so sensitive as microfauna. Nonetheless, the large mammals of Bed I also suggest a diversity of habitats. This topic is investigated in Chapter 7. At that point, a close look at the fossil assemblages from Bed I will enable a reconstruction of the savanna communities of large mammals in which early hominids lived.

To summarize, the fauna, geology, and pollen evidence from Olduvai Bed

I document a "savanna-mosaic" habitat that contained areas of grassland, wooded grassland, woodland, and bushland (van Couvering, 1980). Waterside zones—including swamps, reedy bogs, and probably ribbons of riverine forest vegetation—were variable in extent, most widespread about 1.80 Ma, and highly limited in extent just before the last sediments of Bed I were deposited, 1.70 Ma.

## The Study Sites

Previous ideas about early hominid activities have focused upon stone artifacts and the bones of large mammals, the latter as possible refuse from the meals of hominids. Thus, to reassess widely held views about early hominids, especially those concerning home base activities, all of the artifacts and fossils of large mammals (>2 kg) from the sites of Bed I were studied in detail. In addition, some of the levels preserved the bones and teeth of crocodiles and shells of tortoises; these reptilian remains were also examined. The stratigraphy and sediments of each site were studied in detail in the field to supplement the geologic information provided by Leakey (1971) and Hay (1976).

From the fossilized bones, a variety of information was recorded: taxonomic identification (e.g., order, family, genus, species), skeletal part, indications of the animal's age (adult versus immature), size of the fossil fragments, bone surface condition, and types of bone breakage and surface damage (Potts, 1982). These types of data have helped to test ideas about the factors that could have affected the formation of the Olduvai sites. The uses of these data will become apparent as various questions about taphonomy and hominid behavior are considered in the following chapters.

Basic information about the excavations in Bed I is summarized in Table 2.1. Each of the six levels examined in Bed I contained numerous fossils of large mammals. In addition, the bones of small mammals (e.g., rodents and shrews), birds, snakes, lizards, amphibians, and fish were recovered by carefully sieving the sediments from these levels. It should be mentioned that taphonomic influences on small mammals and nonmammalian vertebrates have not been well studied; thus, the manner in which these small animal remains were deposited in each level is difficult to assess. Since all of the Bed I sites occurred in the lake margin zone, fragments of fish and the bones of water birds may have been incorporated in the sediments by the death of these animals nearby. Furthermore, it is known that the bones of small vertebrates are easily transported by slowly moving water (Dodson, 1973) and that burrowing animals may leave their remains behind when they die in the ground. The presence of birds and other small vertebrates in the Olduvai levels is still an important issue. In this study, data collection and taphonomic analysis were confined to large mammals (particularly animals larger than 10 kg).

**TABLE 2.1.** Information about the Sample of Excavated Sites from Bed I at Olduvai

| Level | Thickness of level (cm) | Estimated excavation area (m²) | Number of stone artifacts | Total weight of artifacts/ manuports (kg) | Total number of faunal specimens | Number of identified mammal[a] bone specimens | Number of crocodile and tortoise specimens | Number of unidentified mammal bone fragments | Minimum number of individuals (mammals) |
|---|---|---|---|---|---|---|---|---|---|
| FLK North–6 | 50 | 37 | 130 | 12.0 | 2258 | 740 | 2 | 1516 | 22 |
| FLK "Zinj" | 9 | 290 | 2647 | 72.4 | 40,172[c] | 614 | 68 | 15,247 | 36 |
| FLKNN–2 | 24 | 186 | 0 | 0 | 478 | 324 | 0 | 154[d] | 23 |
| FLKNN–3 | 9 | 209 | 72 | 13.8 | 2261 | 390 | 1578 | 293[d] | 34 |
| DK–2 | 68 | 345 | 1163[b] | 93.9[b] | 5422 | 832 | 3530 | 1000 | 41 |
| DK–3 | 9 | 345 | | | 2433 | 518 | 1067 | 848 | 36 |

[a]The term *mammal* refers to large mammals (>2 kg).

[b]The artifact samples from DK–2 and 3 are combined.

[c]The total number of faunal specimens from FLK "Zinj" includes approximately 24,243 specimens of microfauna, bird remains, and other unidentified mammal bone fragments.

[d]The number of unidentified mammal bone fragments from FLKNN–2 and 3 does not include approximately 33,000 fragments recovered from the combined sieving of both levels.

Although each bone assemblage had a large number of broken fragments that could not be identified to body part or taxon, many of these were pieces of long bone shaft that could be classified to a specific size class of mammal. The majority of the identified fossils from each site belonged to bovids, the family of gazelles and other antelopes. Each site also preserved the remains of equids (zebras and related "horses"), suids (pigs and warthogs), and carnivores (including the large cats, jackals, and hyenas and the small viverrids). Rhinoceros, elephant, giraffe, hippopotamus, and primates were present at some of the sites in Bed I.

Two species of hominids are known from these sites in Bed I. *Australopithecus boisei*, represented by the OH 5 cranium at FLK "Zinj," is characterized by a small cranial capacity (530 cc) relative to facial size. The cranium is robust with high crested markings for muscles involved in mastication. The molars and premolars provided a large occlusal area, spreading the force of chewing over a wide area. The morphology and microscopic wear on the teeth point to a vegetarian diet of some sort (Jolly, 1970; Walker, 1981). An immature mandible and fragments of a brain case (OH 7) from FLKNN–3 constitute the type specimens of *Homo habilis*. This hominid was more lightly built than the robust australopithecine and possessed a relatively larger cranial capacity. Several hominid postcranial bones come from the levels of Bed I. Studies of foot bones (OH 8) from FLKNN–3 and a tibia and fibula (OH 35) from FLK "Zinj" suggest that they differ from near contemporary specimens attributable to *Homo* from Koobi Fora, Kenya (Day, 1976; Wood, 1974). A hominid clavicle and hand bones from at least two individuals also were discovered in Level 3 at locality FLKNN (Day, 1976; Napier, 1962).

The number of stone artifacts at the five sites that contained stone tools varied considerably. The following observations were recorded for each artifact: the type of raw material from which it had been made, the type of flaking, size, and artifact type (Potts, 1982). All stone artifact assemblages from Bed I represent the Oldowan industrial complex, defined by the presence of core tools—such as choppers, discoids, scrapers, and polyhedrons (Leakey, 1971). These heavy-duty artifacts shaped by percussion flaking average about 10 cm in length and are most often made from waterworn cobbles of lava. Such flaked stones, however, make up a small minority of all artifacts from each excavated site. Debitage—the small slivers and fragments detached from core tools during flaking—accounts for the majority of the pieces in each stone artifact assemblage from Bed I. Small tools and flakes on the Oldowan levels are usually made from quartzite, whereas utilized pieces, which often show no signs of flaking, and manuports, which show no obvious signs of any utilization or flaking, are composed of a variety of raw materials. The detailed study of artifact types and characteristics of Oldowan tool assemblages has been carried out by Mary Leakey (1971). Figure 2.5 illustrates the major kinds of artifacts discovered in Bed I.

Because each site will be examined for clues about its formation and the

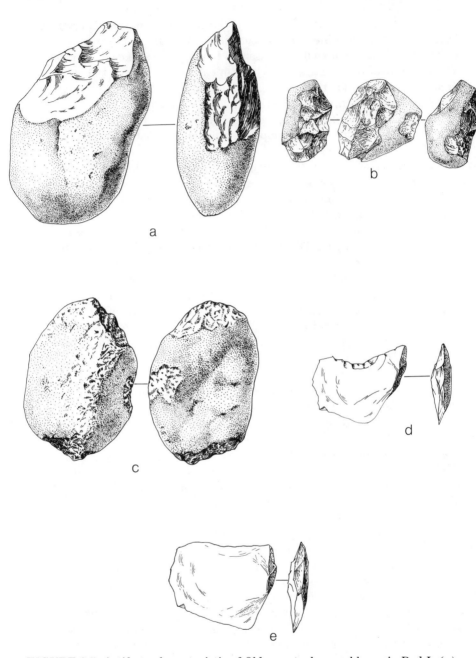

**FIGURE 2.5.** Artifacts characteristic of Oldowan tool assemblages in Bed I. *(a)* end chopper; *(b)* small polyhedron; *(c)* hammerstone; *(d)* utilized flake; and *(e) debitage* flake. Drawn by J. Perry after M. D. Leakey (1971).

possibility of hominid activity, it is important to know the unique features of geology, faunal composition, and lithic artifact composition for each site individually. A detailed account of the stratigraphy and excavation of each site can be found in other sources (Leakey, 1971; Potts, 1982).

## DK–2 and 3

The sediments from these levels were primarily lake margin silts. However, gravel and pebble-sized grains of volcanic and basement rock also occur throughout these sediments. Although these coarse grains are rare, their presence typifies the sediments under Tuff IB in an area 1.5 km to the west and east of locality DK. These particles are found dispersed through the sediments at this locality, though in a few places near DK the pebbles are aggregated in thin, lenticular beds (Hay, 1976: 46).

The top surface of DK–2 lies about 0.5 m under Tuff IB; it is about 68 cm thick. Under this layer is Level 3, which contained at its bottom a dense concentration of stone tools and bones on a paleosol, or ancient land surface. The land surface at the base of Level 3 was eroded prior to the deposition of the artifacts and bones. This surface contained several narrow, steep-sided channels 45–60 cm deep, strongly resembling game trails (Leakey, 1971: 23). Granules and pebbles were not preferentially associated with these gullies. Directly below Level 3, silts and clays occurred (Level 4) that filled depressions in the lava (vesicular basalt) underlying the Bed I sediments. The artifact and bone concentration in Level 3 also was found to lie partly on this underlying basalt in places where it poked through the silts of Level 4.

Although they occurred in the broad lake margin facies that existed prior to Tuff IB, the sites at DK may have been further from the perennial lake margin than the other sites of Bed I (see Figure 2.3). Yet the proximity of standing water is suggested by the presence of fossilized rhizomes resembling papyrus.

There is little evidence for a break in deposition above the base of Level 3. Stratification of the sediments could have been disrupted by the growth of roots or by burrowing animals, though no clear traces of these factors were found.

DK is unique among the Olduvai sites in the large number of crocodile specimens preserved. Over 85% of these were isolated teeth. Because teeth continually fall out and are replaced during a crocodile's lifetime, isolated teeth are abundant wherever crocodiles live. Such elements may have been deposited from the lake water during the burial of the sites at DK (Leakey, 1971: 249).

Two species of turtles and the tortoise *Geochelone* have been identified at DK. The former species are aquatic to semiaquatic in habitat, whereas the latter is a land dweller. The most common turtle species at DK, *Pelusios sinuatus*, shows a narrow range of variation in size compared with modern forms. Auffenberg (1981) suggests that this restricted size range may have resulted by selection from a more variable population, in accord with possible foraging practices by hominids.

All nine major taxa of large mammals were present in both Levels 2 and 3 at DK: bovids, suids, equids, carnivores, proboscideans, rhinos, hippos, giraffids, and primates. Within these major mammal groups, a greater number of taxa occurred in the DK faunal assemblages than at any other Bed I site—23 taxa of mammals from Level 3 and 25 from Level 2. This diversity is clearly related to the large number of specimens that could be classified taxonomically. Although each level at DK preserved a minimum number (MNI) of over 36 individuals of large mammals, no species was represented by a MNI of more than 4.

Excavation at DK was not confined to one continuous area (Figure 2.6). Three areas were involved, one trench 80 m and another 100 m away from the main excavation locus. In the main excavation a roughly circular configuration of loose basalt rocks was discovered at the base of Level 3. Most of the excavation trenches, including those separated from the main area, produced some basalt stones at this stratigraphic position, just above the basal lava. Except in the main excavation area, no circular or other obvious patterned arrangement was noted by Leakey (1971). These stones consist of the same vesicular basalt material as the underlying lava. In the main excavation

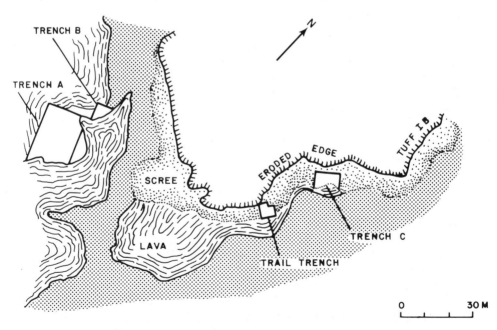

**FIGURE 2.6.** Map of excavation trenches at locality DK, Bed I. The levels below Tuff IB were excavated. Based on M. D. Leakey (1971).

area this basal lava juts up through the lower surface of Level 3 and, thus, occurs naturally at the base of this level. As Leakey observed, the proximity of the basalt and the main Level 3 horizon means that the rocks may have been detached by weathering rather than brought in by hominids or by other agents. Yet Leakey's view, adopted in many texts on early hominid archeology, is that this arrangement of stones reflects the activity of hominids, specifically the construction of a foundation for a shelter (Leakey, 1971: 24).

DK–3 is a classic "occupation site," known as a "living floor" in Leakey's terminology. Although the remains are considerably more dispersed in Level 2, it also contains "occupation site" debris. Both of these levels are examples of Isaac's "type C" sites, defined by the presence of numerous stone artifacts and bones from a variety of animals and originally believed to reflect the debris from hominid campsites (Isaac, 1971, 1978). The possible existence of traces of a hominid shelter would appear to support this interpretation.

Two other sites that have been interpreted as hominid "living floors" (i.e., especially thin layers of occupation debris) will be examined in the following chapters. These are FLK "Zinj" and FLKNN–3. The layers at these sites, like DK–3, were about as thick as the objects they contained, and both exhibited signs of having been old land surfaces—slightly weathered and marked by root casts.

## FLK "Zinj"

This site is notable because it is the largest, continuous exposure of a "living floor" area in Bed I. Actually, the excavation at the FLK locality traversed vertically about 12 m of sediment from numerous stratigraphic layers below Tuff IF. Other than the "Zinj" horizon, nine of these layers yielded stone artifacts or animal bones. But none of these approached the degree of concentration of remains found on the "Zinj" level. Two sedimentary features noted by Leakey (1971: 49) on the "Zinj" level were a small channel 35 cm deep and 53 cm wide and an oblong hollow 1.5 m long. These features were probably due to erosion or other natural causes; neither artifacts nor bones were associated preferentially with what would have been these relatively low-lying areas of the local land surface.

The FLK locality was situated in the lake margin zone, probably about 1 km from the border of the perennial lake. The remains of aquatic turtle *(Pelusios sinuatus)* and crocodile were scarce compared with their abundance at DK and FLKNN–3.

Most of the major taxonomic groups of large mammals were represented at FLK "Zinj," with the exception of proboscideans, rhinos, and hippos. A notable characteristic of FLK "Zinj" is the enormous quantity of small, mostly unidentifiable bone splinters. These number in the tens of thousands. Although unidentifiable bone fragments were recovered by sieving in each excavation trench of FLK "Zinj," they were concentrated especially in two of the ten trenches. A conservative estimate of 54% of the fragments were less than 1 cm in length. This smallest component of the bone assemblage, though, was not confined to any one part of the site. Moreover, some of the remains from the very dense cluster of fragmented bones in Trenches B and C were not fragmented at all; for example, 4 complete foot bones of *Equus* that articulated were found next to one another in this area of bone concentration.

Numerous artifacts, especially flakes and shattered chips, were found at FLK "Zinj." While most of this debitage was made from quartzite, 30% of the core tools from this site were of lava.

According to traditional comparisons made to campsites of hunter–gatherers, the primary area of fragmented bones at FLK "Zinj" gives the impression of an important area of hominid activity—in particular, a place where bones were smashed with stone tools and the fatty marrow obtained. This possibility will be examined in Chapter 5.

### FLKNN–3

The other "living floor" investigated in this study is FLKNN–3. The levels at FLKNN are younger in age than the DK levels but were formed before the FLK "Zinj" horizon. The silty clay of Level 3 varies in thickness due to the undulating surface of Tuff IB, which lay beneath it. FLKNN–3 was extensively marked by fossil roots, and fauna and artifacts were mostly confined to the top, weathered part of the clay. Like the FLK "Zinj" site, a distance of about 1 km probably separated FLKNN from the perennial lake border. The intermittent inundation of this locality by lake waters apparently encouraged the natural accumulation and burial of rodent remains and those of other microvertebrates, birds, and fish in these sediments, especially in the lower portion of Level 3 (Jaeger, 1976: 104).

In addition, Level 3 showed a notable concentration of turtle remains, including nearly complete and intact shells but very few internal skeletal parts. A minimum number of 17 turtles are represented by the material from this level. These remains are suggested by Leakey to reflect the foraging practices of hominids (1971: 250). The presence of shells that lack associated skeletal material is typical of turtles that have died on the land and have been eaten by a predator (W. Auffenberg, pers. comm.).

Antelopes, suids, equids, carnivores, and primates—including hominids—occurred in Level 3, but none of the very large mammals was present. As is typical of the excavated areas at Olduvai originally interpreted as "occupation sites," FLKNN–3 contained stone artifacts. But only a small accumulation was found. Interestingly, all of the tools/cores from this level were flaked from lava cobbles, yet most of the debitage is quartzite.

### FLK North–6

The youngest site examined in this study is FLK North–6, situated approximately 4.5 m above the level of the FLK "Zinj" site. Although this site also preserved stone artifacts and skeletal remains from a variety of large mammals, it has had a rather different interpretation in the paleoanthropological literature. An almost complete, fossilized skeleton of an elephant was found in FLK North–6, buried in a silty clay approximately 46 cm thick. Five trenches were dug into the hillside of FLK North, and six levels of artifacts and bone debris were encountered. Level 6 was reached in four of these trenches, but there were very few remains other than microfauna in two of them. Almost all of the large mammal fossils and the stone tools from Level 6 were discovered in a small area (37 m²) in the other two excavation trenches. Due to this spatial association of stone artifacts with the elephant skeleton, FLK North–6 has been referred to as a "butchery site" (Leakey, 1971; Isaac, 1971).

Like the other sites in Bed I, this particular one at FLK North lies in the zone of lake margin sediments. However, it was probably located a little further away from the perennial lake border than were the other sites in the FLK area. This interpretation stems from the fact that the size of the lake was smaller during the formation of the sites at FLK North than it was at any time previously.

The majority of the mammal specimens from Level 6 come from a single individual of the species *Elephas recki*. The large number of specimens results from the completeness of this elephant skeleton and extensive breakage of some of its bones. Minor earth movements occurred locally at FLK North. This factor was probably responsible for much of the breakage, as indicated by the presence of hundreds of fragments of elephant ribs and vertebrae that can be conjoined at clean surfaces where the fossilized bones were broken. Most of the major long bones of the elephant were found complete but crushed along their diaphyses. The elements of this skeleton that were *not* found during excavation were the tusks and 34 bones from the feet. All other bones from the carcass were present. The elephant was a very large individual, probably an adult; many of the epiphyses of the bones were unfused, but this commonly occurs in adult elephants today. In addition, a few pieces from at least one other elephant were found at FLK North–6. They include right and left distal epiphyses of the femur, two bones from the left forefoot, a few vertebrae, and several ribs.

Although considerable attention has been paid to the elephant carcass and to the "butchery site" interpretation, the set of mammal bones from this site closely resembles the fauna discovered at the other sites in Bed I. A diversity of antelope species was found. In terms of the MNI required to account for all the bones, the antelopes were the most abundant kind of animal at FLK North–6. As observed in other Bed I assemblages, suids were second most abundant. Excluding the fossilized breaks and bone splinters from the fragile elephant bones, most of the bone fragments that could not be identified in detail to taxon or body part came from relatively small or medium-sized ungulates, typical of all Bed I faunal assemblages. A small assemblage of 130 artifacts was found spatially associated with these skeletal remains.

## FLKNN–2

In contrast with the five sites mentioned so far, the final one studied from Bed I, FLKNN–2, contained no stone artifacts. This level was a silty tuff, 24 cm deep, extensively marked by root casts. Animal bones were found mainly in patches of clay near the base of this layer in the central portion of the excavation. The faunal collection was made up of bovids, suids, equids, and carnivores. No elephants, rhinos, hippos, giraffes, or primates were found. As is characteristic of all Bed I faunal assemblages, no one species dominated, a wide diversity of skeletal parts was preserved, and the bones were largely broken before fossilization. However, this site exhibited more complete bones than occurred at any other Olduvai site. No evidence of turtles or crocodiles was found; the absence of turtle remains is a particularly striking contrast to the collection of *Pelusios* from FLKNN–3, immediately underlying Level 2.

Leakey (1971: 43) feels that the accumulation of animal bones in this level cannot be attributed to hominids. Accordingly, FLKNN–2 affords an interesting comparison, especially regarding its mode of site formation, with the Bed I levels that contained both stone artifacts and animal bones.

### Other Comparisons

Taphonomic studies of several nonhominid accumulations of bones can be found in the paleontological literature. These studies provide crucial information about the features that characterize bone concentrations produced by agents other than hominids. In addition, information from two assemblages of bones in particular, one modern and the other ancient, will be examined in the following chapters to provide direct familiarity with nonhominid sites. First, an assemblage of modern bones collected by hyenas in Amboseli National Park, Kenya, was studied firsthand. This instance of bone accumulation by hyenas is especially important because the assemblage shows some obvious general similarities to the ancient bone assemblages from Olduvai (e.g., a high degree of bone fragmentation). This modern bone collection was obtained from a den used by spotted hyenas *(Crocuta crocuta)* at Amboseli. The den has been under observation for several years and has been described by Hill (1981, 1983, 1984). Spotted hyenas are the only agent known to collect bones at this den.

A second important source of comparative taphonomic information was obtained from a study by Shipman (1977, 1982) of the Miocene site at Fort Ternan, Kenya. The bones at this site evidently were accumulated by the movement of bones downslope to a low-lying area. Water action and the activities of animals may have been involved. Like the Amboseli hyena collection, the faunal assemblage from Fort Ternan provides salient points of comparison with the Olduvai bone collections. The comparison yields important evidence about the processes of bone accumulation in Bed I.

To summarize, the sites that will be examined in the following chapters include three areas previously viewed to be hominid "living floors"; a fourth hominid "occupation site" is represented by a thicker deposit of artifacts and bones; a fifth site preserved debris very similar to that of the "occupation sites" but also included an almost complete elephant skeleton; an accumulation of bones that had no stone artifacts associated with it completes the sample.

Inquiry into the role of hominids in making these sites and the behavior of the hominids that lived at Olduvai is possible due to meticulous excavations carried out by Leakey and detailed studies by her and other researchers on Olduvai fauna, geology, and climates. Sediments from each of the sites examined here, with the exception of portions of DK–2, were sieved using very fine mesh screens (approx. 1 mm). Thus, even the smallest stone flakes and fragments of mammal bones were recovered during excavation. Leakey's excavations provide the kind of detailed information needed to assess the taphonomy of these sites. Data from geological and paleoenvironmental studies also furnish valuable information that bears on questions concerning site formation and hominid behavior. In the following chapters, we will see how this evidence and the data from the fauna and stone artifacts help in investigating the nature and significance of hominid activities at the Olduvai sites.

# Part II

Formation of the Olduvai Sites

# 3

# Concentrations of Bones and Artifacts

Archeologists typically have assumed that the remains they excavate in a given place occur in a tight cluster that results from hominid activity. The home base hypothesis, for example, depends on this idea. According to the home base interpretation, aggregates of stone artifacts and animal bones represent campsites that formed when hominids carried stone tools and animal bones to well-defined areas where food was consumed and social activities were focused. As a result of these activities, stone and bone refuse tended to accumulate in tight concentrations, signaling the occurrence of ancient base camps.

To investigate how the sites of Bed I Olduvai were formed, we will first examine the assumption that the remains at each site were anomalous concentrations. It is necessary to see whether the degree and type of concentration of faunal remains could have resulted simply from the aggregation and death of the animals themselves. The degree of spatial clustering of stone artifacts must also be scrutinized to test whether it exceeded that which occurred as part of the general scatter of artifacts dropped on the landscape over time by hominids. If the concentrations of debris at the Olduvai sites were not especially dense, for example, then only the processes of natural animal death and occasional discard of artifacts by hominids need to be considered as factors responsible for site formation. Yet if the fauna and artifacts were highly clustered, then certain processes of animal bone and stone artifact transport and accumulation would have been involved.

## Clustering of Bones on Landscapes

One view, advanced recently by Binford (1981), is that many of the sites from Olduvai Beds I and II represent places where animals died and were exploited by carnivores and, ultimately, by scavenging hominids. Binford has questioned the assumption that animal bones at the Olduvai sites were concentrated beyond that expected at the death sites of animals. It is true that the biomass of African savannas is very high. Thus, there is considerable potential for large accumulations of bones to result just from the cumulative death of animals over time in an area (Binford, 1981: 15–16). Binford examined the skeletal part composition of the Olduvai faunal assemblages. Based on a multivariate comparison with models of bone assemblages produced by carnivores in dens and predation areas, he concluded that several of the Olduvai sites were areas where many animals had died or were places in the immediate vicinity of such death sites. This interpretation is given for FLK "Zinj," DK–3, and DK–2 (Binford, 1981: 273, 281).

Normal, attritional mortality of animals leading to the gradual deposition of bones on the landscape and catastrophic events or periods during which many animals die at once are indeed important processes leading to the accumulation of bones in African savannas. As we will see, certain features of the land, such as commonly used water holes or shade trees, can play an important role in concentrating animal carcasses. However, the problem about anomalous bone clusters at Olduvai requires us to consider the entire process of animal death, skeletal disarticulation, and bone dispersal that is known to occur in African habitats. The distinguishing features of animal death sites need to be defined, and information about these features, including spatial densities of bones on landscapes, must then be compared with information about bone assemblages from ancient sites.

Since ancient land surfaces have not been extensively excavated at Olduvai or at any other Plio–Pleistocene locality, questions about the relative concentration of remains in the excavated levels are difficult to answer directly. Nonetheless, studies of animal carcasses and bone distributions in modern African habitats have identified the major features of bone accumulations that result at or near animal death sites. Moreover, this research has been carried out in a variety of high biomass habitats, some of which are comparable with the ancient environments at Olduvai. Finally, there is valuable evidence about the distribution of artifacts and bones in the sediments at Olduvai and at other prehistoric localities. This evidence indicates that the remains from the sites of Bed I at Olduvai were indeed highly concentrated and, thus, one or more agents of transport were primarily responsible for the formation of these sites.

Observations in modern savannas have defined the following characteristics of death sites, landscape assemblages, and bone accumulations formed without significant transport by animals or other environmental processes (e.g., water flow) (Behrensmeyer, 1983; Behrensmeyer and Boaz, 1980; Coe, 1980; Hill, 1975, 1979b; Shipman, 1975). First, under conditions of normal animal turnover (attritional mortality) a very low degree of bone concentration results on a landscape. Second, relatively little mixing of the bones from different animals occurs at death sites or over the landscape, even when predators and scavengers have dispersed bones far away from carcasses. Third, the taxonomic and ecologic diversity of animals represented around death sites tends to be low. Fourth, vertebrae and other axial skeletal parts tend to remain near the death site, whereas limb bones tend to be removed. Finally, in an event or period of catastrophic mortality, such as results from a drought or a flood, there may be large concentrations of carcasses, but these events leave diagnostic geologic evidence.

The faunal assemblages from the Olduvai sites show none of the features that typify animal death sites or landscape assemblages of bones. Each of these characteristics is discussed in the following sections.

## Degree of Bone Concentration

As animals die, their bones disarticulate and are scattered over the landscape if they are not consumed or otherwise destroyed. Therefore, bones begin in clusters (skeletons) and then may be dispersed by the activities of carnivores and carrion feeders, kicking, downslope movement, wind, and water (Hill, 1975, 1979a; Toots, 1965a). The clustering of bones on a land surface, thus, depends initially on the rate and spatial clumping of deaths and, later, on the rate and distance of bone dispersal. Based on a study of land surface bones in three East African game reserves by Hill (1980a), the disarticulation and scattering of mammal bones is generally rapid in modern savanna mosaic habitats. The skeletal elements of mammals, regardless of size, are usually disjoined and highly scattered after a year, or sometimes in a matter of weeks (Hill, 1975). Hence, there is little chance for bones to become densely concentrated on landscapes, given typical mortality rates. Bones of very large mammals (e.g., elephant, rhinoceros, and giraffe), due to their size and the protection of massive soft tissues, would seem most likely to remain aggregated at the site of death. Yet the dispersal potential of such bones is also very high, given that the bones of such large animal carcasses may be spread over a kilometer or more (Behrensmeyer and Boaz, 1980; Hill, 1975). In general, on African landscapes, as skeletal disarticulation proceeds, so does scattering of the bones (Hill, 1979b).

Animal bones from each of the Olduvai sites were more densely concentrated than are bones on modern East African landscapes. Data regarding the spatial patterns of bones in modern savanna habitats help to demonstrate this point. Behrensmeyer has calculated the densities of landscape bones for six habitat types in the Amboseli Basin, Kenya, an area having an overall geomorphological and tectonic setting similar to that reconstructed for Bed I Olduvai (Behrensmeyer, 1983; Behrensmeyer and Boaz, 1980; Behrensmeyer, Western, and Boaz, 1979). All specimens for which body part and taxon could be identified were counted over an area of 8.75 km$^2$. This area included swamp, dense woodland, open woodland, plains, lake bed, and bush habitats—a sample that spans the range of habitats in East African savannas. Table 3.1 shows the average frequency of bone specimens for each of these habitats at Amboseli. The bone assemblages at Amboseli were accumulated over a period of attritional animal turnover during which bones were scattered and destroyed. Yet the figures on bone frequency represent maximum landscape densities for each habitat because sampling areas were chosen for their relatively high abundance of surface bones.

In comparison, Table 3.2 gives estimates of bone frequency for the sites in Bed I Olduvai. The densities of identified mammal bones on the Olduvai

**TABLE 3.1.** Land Surface Bone Densities for Six Habitats, Amboseli, Kenya[a]

| Habitat | Area sampled (km²) | Number of specimens | Estimated maximum bones/100 m² |
|---|---|---|---|
| Swamp | .98 | 6082 | .62 |
| Dense wood | .73 | 1989 | .27 |
| Open wood | 1.44 | 2691 | .19 |
| Plains | 1.60 | 4666 | .29 |
| Lake bed | 2.66 | 3244 | .12 |
| Bush | 1.34 | 1396 | .10 |
| Total | 8.75 | 20,068 | .23 |

[a]Data from Behrensmeyer and Boaz (1980: 74).

levels range from 51 to 3788 times greater than the highest average density at Amboseli (swamp habitat: approximately 0.6 bones per 100 m²).

It is important to examine not only average bone frequencies in modern habitats, but also the variation in bone clustering within each habitat. In fact, considerable variation occurs within each of the Amboseli habitats (Behrensmeyer, 1983). The swamp area shows the widest variation. In a sample of 44 bone collection units, each 1500 m² in size, over 50% contain fewer than 4 bones per unit (0.27 bones per 100 m²). However, two collection areas contain over 100 bones each; the highest concentration is about 11 bones per 100 m². Even compared with this maximum concentration of bones on the landscape, the Olduvai sites still possess spatial densities 3–214 times greater. Thus, the Olduvai sites appear to preserve unusually dense concentrations of bones compared with assemblages produced under conditions of mortality deemed representative of modern, high biomass habitats.

### Carcass Mixing

Studies of carcasses on modern landscapes also show that the mixing of bones from different individuals tends to be quite low (Hill, 1975, 1979b; Behrensmeyer, 1983). For example, an average of just one individual, and a maximum of three individuals, were found within the 1500 m² units of bone collection on the Amboseli landscape.

In contrast, the minimum number of large mammal individuals calculated in this study to derive from the thin paleosol levels from Olduvai ranged from 34 to 36, found in areas far smaller than those sampled at Amboseli. As indicated by Leakey's excavation plans, the bones from different carcasses show an extremely high degree of spatial mixing at these sites (Leakey, 1971). Bones lying next to one another were seldom from the same individual or even the same species. Based on this evidence, the Olduvai bone assemblages again appear to be accumulations produced mainly by processes that carried bones away from many carcasses to specific areas of concentration.

**TABLE 3.2.** Densities of Bones (Identified to Taxon) on Bed I Levels[a]

| Site | Estimated volume of sediment excavated (m³) | Depth of deposit (m) | Density of specimens (bones/m³) | Estimated areal density (bones/100 m²)[b] | Density of MNE (bones/m³) | Estimated areal density of MNE (bones/100 m²)[b] |
|---|---|---|---|---|---|---|
| FLK North-6[c] | 18.5 | .50 | 19.1 | 171 | 11.0 | 99 |
| FLK "Zinj" | 26.1 | .09 | 23.5 | 2349 | 13.9 | 1391 |
| FLKNN-2 | 44.6 | .24 | 9.8 | 65 | 4.8 | 43 |
| FLKNN-3 | 18.8 | .09 | 20.7 | 2073 | 12.9 | 1292 |
| DK-2 | 234.7 | .68 | 3.5 | 32 | 1.8 | 16 |
| DK-3[d] | 31.1 | .09 | 16.7 | 1665 | 8.7 | 875 |

[a]Densities based on both the number of specimens and the minimum number of elements (MNE) are provided. Areal densities are given per 100 m² to compare to figures from Amboseli.

[b]Areal density is based on each surface assemblage representing 9 cm when buried. This figure seems reasonable given that some of the bones themselves are this thick and given that the thin paleosols at FLK and FLKNN–3 are about 9 cm thick, on the average. So, for example, at DK–2, a 68 cm depth of deposit signifies 7.6 "surfaces" which are 9 cm thick. The average areal density is calculated by dividing up the number of bones among these "surfaces" and then dividing by the estimated area of excavation (see Appendixes). This method for obtaining an average surface density is applied to the relatively thick levels from DK–2, FLKNN–2, and FLK North–6.

[c]Without specimens from the *Elephas recki* carcass.

[d]Only the paleosol at the base of Level 3.

**TABLE 3.3.** Degree of Bone Articulation at Olduvai Based on Minimum Number of Elements

| Site | Number of articulated bones | Percentage articulation[a] | Average articulated unit size[a] |
|---|---|---|---|
| FLK North–6 | 12 | 3.3 | 2.0 |
| FLK "Zinj" | 2 | 0.7 | 2.0 |
| FLKNN–2 | 3 | 1.5 | 3.0 |
| FLKNN–3 | 7 | 2.9 | 2.3 |
| DK–2 | 0 | 0 | — |
| DK–3 | 0 | 0 | — |

[a]Based on Hill (1975: 127). See note, p. 42.

The number of articulated bones offers another way to look at carcass mixing. Hill (1975: 127) found that the percentage articulation and the average size of articulated units[1] were a good way to distinguish landscape assemblages and death sites from transported concentrations of bones. In two areas where predation by carnivores was especially focused (the delta pond and delta flats habitats of east Lake Turkana), the percentage articulation was 32.5 and 48.9, respectively, and the mean articulated unit size was 10.9 and 11.8, respectively. The degree of bone articulation at each of the Olduvai sites is extremely low compared to these predation areas (Table 3.3). In Hill's study the lowest degree of bone articulation in any modern habitat was in the open grassland at Murchison Falls Park, Uganda.[2] The degree of articulation was only slightly higher than at any of the Olduvai sites, but in that modern habitat the degree of bone concentration was extremely low compared to Olduvai (less than 1 bone per 100 m$^2$; Hill, 1975: 106). Thus, based on a combination of bone articulation and spatial clustering, there is no confusion between the overall pattern of the Olduvai bone accumulations and that typically found on modern East African landscapes, including predation arenas.

## Taxonomic and Ecological Diversity

Studies of carcasses further suggest that animals that die in the same specific locality tend to be of the same species or at least occupants of the same type of habitat. For example, multiple kills by predators—either as a massive predation event (Kruuk, 1972: 195) or over a period of time at an ambush site or watering hole (Schaller, 1967; Behrensmeyer, pers. comm.)—usually

[1]Percentage articulation = [(number of articulated bones) × 100]/ total number of bones
average articulated unit size = number of articulated bones/ number of articulated units
[2]Murchison Falls grassland: Percentage articulation = 7.3%; average articulated unit size = 3.5 (Hill, 1975: 128).

involve one preferred species of animal. The reasons for this are that many individuals in a single herd can become victims in a single predation event, or a predator may have a favored area of predation because a particular species repeatedly occurs there. Thus, bone accumulations at multiple kill sites often show low taxonomic diversity relative to the number of prey individuals or a collection of animals that at least occupied the same kind of habitat.

The Olduvai faunal assemblages show high taxonomic and ecologic diversity and, therefore, go against the suggested pattern of multiple kill sites. On the average, over 16 taxa of large mammals occur in each faunal assemblage from Olduvai (range: 10–25 taxa, based on Table 7.1). The most frequent species at each site, again on the average, is represented by a minimum number of about 6 individuals out of a total of over 32 individuals. Certainly no one species predominates in any of these bone assemblages. Furthermore, bones from woodland species and open plains species are known to occur in the same faunal assemblage (e.g., *Cercocebus* monkeys and the zebra *Equus oldoway-ensis* at DK Level 2). Or, as another example, animals known to be dependent on water and those that were not sometimes occur at the same site (e.g., *Hippopotamus* and *Oryx* at FLK "Zinj"). These are not combinations of species that were likely to die by predation or other causes in areas the size of the excavated sites in Bed I. This line of evidence, thus, also suggests that some biological or physical agents helped to concentrate these bones in places away from the original death sites of the animals.

*Presence of Axial Parts of the Skeleton*

The kinds of skeletal elements preserved in the Olduvai assemblages further indicate that postmortem transport and clustering of bones occurred rather than processes that usually operate on carcasses at death sites. Hill (1975, 1979a,b) has documented standard sequences of skeletal disarticulation in African ungulates. In general, limb elements are disjoined and dispersed from a carcass before axial elements (vertebrae, ribs, and pelvis); the latter tend to stay articulated longer and to remain at the death site. This same overall pattern in which axial elements remain at the death site has also been observed for predator kills and for a wide range of animals on savanna landscapes (Hill and Behrensmeyer 1984; Kruuk, 1972: 126; Shipman and Phillips-Conroy, 1977).

In contrast, all of the Bed I sites are typified by a disproportionately small frequency of axial elements relative to limb bones (Table 3.4). It is true that the spongy bone composition of vertebrae and ribs makes these parts more susceptible to destruction than are most limb bones. However, in well-documented cases of extreme bone destruction acting on complete carcasses, axial bones still outnumber limb bones (Binford and Bertram, 1977; Brain, 1969b; Potts, 1983). This is not the case at Olduvai, which suggests that the number of axial elements relative to limb bones in the original bone accu-

**TABLE 3.4.** Percentage Frequency of Axial Bones Relative to Limb Bones (Except Phalanges and Sesamoids) at Olduvai Based on the MNE

| Site | (MNE axial bones/ total MNE) × 100 |
|------|------------------------------------|
| FLK North–6 | 29.9[a] |
| FLK "Zinj" | 31.1 |
| FLKNN–2 | 11.4 |
| FLKNN–3 | 37.0 |
| DK–2 | 17.4 |
| DK–3 | 12.7 |
| Living bovids | 61.8 |

[a]Excluding elephant bones; with elephant, this percentage equals 45.8.

mulations were considerably less than expected at death sites. Once again, this inference implies that the Olduvai sites were neither typical death sites nor landscape assemblages.

*Indications of Catastrophic Mortality*

Events that lead to the death of many animals in one spot or over a region may result in higher than average densities of faunal remains. In particular, high mortality rates associated with drought or mass drowning produce larger concentrations of carcasses than occur in attritional death assemblages. Carcasses aggregated by mass drowning, such as during the wildebeest migrations of East Africa (Talbot and Talbot, 1963), provide such a large amount of carrion that many carcasses are not disturbed by scavengers (Coe, 1980). Subsequent burial of such an assemblage can be expected to preserve articulated or partly articulated skeletons. As we have seen, an extremely low number of articulated elements occurs at each Olduvai site, and this distinguishes the Olduvai faunal assemblages from accumulations resulting from mass drowning. In addition, catastrophic drowning (especially in the case of ungulate migrations) tends to produce an assemblage showing poor carcass mixing (since this is a function of bone disarticulation) and low species diversity. As noted earlier, these patterns do not characterize the six sites from Olduvai investigated here.

During drought conditions many individuals of different species may die within a short time, often aggregated around major water sources. However, geologic signs of drought, such as mudcracks, caliche, or evaporites associated with the fossils (Shipman, 1975), are not evident in Bed I. As noted earlier, fossil pollen and other evidence about the paleoenvironment indicate that the faunal assemblages at Olduvai were produced during a wide range of climatic conditions, from humid to arid. Finally, the high mortality rate caused by drought would tend to produce more carcasses than can be processed by scavengers; thus, drought assemblages often manifest many articulated or partly articulated skeletons (Coe, 1980; Shipman, 1975). Again, this indicator of a drought-produced faunal concentration also is not exhibited at the sites of Olduvai Bed I.

## Other Factors Affecting Bone Concentrations

It is important to note that none of these five suggested criteria is sufficient by itself for distinguishing transported clusters of bones from all types of death site or landscape assemblages. In fact, accumulations of bones at particular spots on the landscape may mimic certain features of transported assemblages but not *all* such features, as far as I am aware. For example, water holes where large African predators ambush prey may manifest large accumulations of bones compared to the rest of the landscape. Such concentrations of bones may be quite localized and exhibit multiple species (Haynes, 1983). Large, seasonal pans in the Kalahari, Botswana, are spots where San hunters repeatedly trap, kill, and process game animals attracted and constrained in their movements by water. In these cases, faunal remains accumulate in association with artifacts, pits, and stone rings that typify San hunting blinds (Brooks and Yellen, 1987). Some African hunters, in fact, may remove much of the axial skeleton, leaving behind certain segments of the limb skeleton at the kill and butchery site (J. O'Connell, pers. comm.; Yellen, 1977a). Finally, in Amboseli Park, Kenya, Behrensmeyer (pers. comm.) has observed bone concentrations around trees which are made by lions, leopards, and cheetah dragging whole carcasses or parts of kills into the shade.

In each of these examples, fixed natural resources (water, trees) govern the reuse of particular areas, and it is this reutilization of space that makes the resulting sites a potentially obvious part of the fossil record (Binford, 1982; Brooks and Yellen, 1987). However, in each case the resulting death sites or landscape accumulations of bone do not resemble the Olduvai bone concentrations in significant ways. First, while shade trees provide a context for greater degrees of bone concentration, species diversity, and carcass mixing than occurs on landscapes generally, the situation studied at Amboseli evidently does not provide nearly the degree of bone concentration or diversity of large mammals seen at least in those assemblages from thin, paleosol horizons at Olduvai. In addition, one apparent reason why bones accumulate under shade trees at Amboseli is that some carnivores bring entire kills to the trees; hence, these shade tree concentrations also take on the character of typical death sites, with an emphasis on axial elements (Behrensmeyer, pers. comm.). Bone concentrations from the water hole predation areas reported by Haynes mimic the Olduvai sites perhaps in the degree of clustering and in exhibiting variable degrees of bone weathering. However, bone scatters from individual animals can be discerned, and elements that are articulated or in anatomical order apparently are not rare (Haynes, 1983). Thus, as in the predation areas studied by Hill (1975), these death sites are signaled by the degree of carcass mixing or the degree of association among parts of the same carcass. Finally, the Kalahari pan margins exhibit mainly attritional assemblages of bones (e.g., teeth, horn cores), since meat bones (such as the limb bones that characterize the Olduvai assemblages) are carried away by people; in addition, the diversity of species and body sizes of animals evidently does not match that from any of the Bed I Olduvai sites (A. Brooks, pers. comm.).

It is clear that not all cases of untransported bone assemblages (death sites) or landscape palimpsests are typified by a low degree of spatial clustering of bones or, for example, by a low species diversity. Likewise, the absence of any one of these characteristics does not necessarily mean that bones were transported and collected at a site by physical or behavioral agents. Rather, it is the application of all five suggested criteria together that strongly suggests the transported nature of the Olduvai bone assemblages.

This does not mean that the Olduvai faunal assemblages reflect only transport of bones away from carcasses. The carcass, and undoubted death site, of an *Elephas recki* at FLK North–6 is associated with plentiful, disarticulated remains of other fauna; the death of the elephant at this site is evidenced by the fact that the only articulated bones at North–6 are elephant and that the spatial distribution of the skeletal elements are in partial anatomical order. Further, the site with the next highest number of articulated remains, FLKNN–3, contains a pair of articulated vertebrae and articulated tarsal bones from the medium-sized bovid *Kobus sigmoidalis*. These and other bones of perhaps the same skeleton suggest that this bovid died at or near to this site. Based on all criteria noted in this section, the other bones concentrated at FLKNN–3 were transported away from the original death sites to this delimited location.

In brief, from these various lines of evidence, the Olduvai faunal assemblages studied here represent neither the original death sites of many animals nor an accumulation produced over time by the dispersal of bones over a land surface. Instead, it appears that some physical or behavioral factors were responsible for the transport and accumulation of bones in well-defined areas at Olduvai. These factors were the *primary* ones responsible for the formation of these particular bone assemblages in Bed I.


## Clustering of Artifacts on Landscapes

A similar concern arises about the spatial clustering of stone artifacts at the five artifact-bearing sites in Bed I. Again, observations in the modern Amboseli basin suggest that some specific means of artifact collection was involved in the formation of the Olduvai sites. Throughout the Amboseli area, Late Stone Age (LSA) artifacts from the Holocene are visible on the ground (Foley, 1981). Their occurrence results from the ongoing depletion of the current landscape down to the level of an LSA land surface. Comparing this relatively recent situation with that at Olduvai, the average spatial density of stone artifacts at Amboseli is 8.5 to 228 times *lower* than that from any of the Olduvai sites (Table 3.5). Even the peak areal concentration at Amboseli— about 10 artifacts per 100 m² (Foley, pers. commun.)—is well below the degree of artifact concentration at the Olduvai sites. This is the case even though LSA human population densities and rates of artifact production may well have been higher than those during the Plio–Pleistocene at Olduvai.

Excavations at Olduvai provide a final and more direct line of evidence that the bone and artifact assemblages from the sites examined here were especially dense clusters within the ancient lake margin zone. Although several, successive levels of bone and artifact concentration were found at the FLK North and FLKNN localities, such clusters did not necessarily typify the lake margin zone. A larger sample of stratigraphic levels from the Bed I lake margin facies was excavated at FLK. This excavation sampled almost all of Bed I above Tuff IB. Out of the 21 horizons encountered, the majority (12) preserved no fossils or artifacts, although the sediments (clay, silt, and tuff) were very similar to those in Bed I which did contain sizable bone and artifact assemblages. These sterile horizons included some that were equivalent to the archeological levels at FLK North, less than 100 m away. Another seven levels contained only a very few artifacts (3 levels with none, 1 level with the highest frequency of 10) and a few animal bones. These bones were usually from only one animal. In one case where a few species were represented, elements such as teeth, which typically lie around the landscape for a long time, were a dominant part of the assemblage. Only two horizons— FLK–13 (61 cm thick) and 15 (30 cm thick)—contained a variety of animal

**TABLE 3.5.** Densities of Stone Artifacts at the Olduvai Sites[a]

| Site | Estimated volume of sediment excavated (m³) | Density (artifacts/m³) | Depth of deposit (m) | Estimated areal density (artifacts/100 m²)[b] |
|---|---|---|---|---|
| FLK North–6 | 18.5 | 7.0 | .50 | 63 |
| FLK "Zinj" | 26.1 | 101.4 | .09 | 913 |
| FLKNN–3 | 18.8 | 3.8 | .09 | 34 |
| DK[c] | 265.6 | 4.3 | .77 | 39 |

[a]Both volume and areal densities are based on estimates of the area of excavation from each level.

[b]Areal density is based on each surface assemblage representing 9 cm when buried. For example, at DK, a 77 cm depth of deposit signifies 8.6 "surfaces" which are 9 cm thick. The *average* areal density is calculated by dividing the number of artifacts from a level by the number of "surfaces" within that level, and then dividing by the estimated area of excavation.

[c]1142 artifacts in DK–2 (68 cm) and –3 (confined mostly to the lower 9 cm).

bones. These bones were concentrated at about the same degree, or slightly lower than that which was found in DK–2, which shows the lowest degree of bone concentration of any level examined in detail here. Artifacts also occur in these two FLK horizons but at a very low frequency, conceivably a typical landscape density of about 1 per 100 m². On the basis of this vertical sampling of the FLK strata, the lake margin zone in Bed I apparently was typified by low degrees of bone and artifact concentration, in their characteristics not unlike the more recent landscape assemblages discussed in this section. In comparison with the Bed I lake margin in general, it appears that other processes or variables affecting artifact concentration operated at the sites examined here.

Based on all criteria by which we can presently judge the concentration of remains at Olduvai, the bones and artifacts within each level show a tight spatial clustering. The information presented here indicates that processes of bone and artifact movement and concentration played a primary role in the formation of the Olduvai sites. These processes, whether geological or behavioral, served to transport materials to specific locations within the ancient lake margin zone at Olduvai. This means, however, that further questions arise about what taphonomic processes of bone and artifact accumulation acted at Olduvai. Furthermore, over what periods of time were bones and artifacts introduced to these sites? This question is taken up in the next section because, as we will see in the following chapters, the period of bone accumulation, in particular, bears significantly on ideas about site formation and the role of hominids at these sites.

## Duration of Bone Accumulation

The length of time represented by the Olduvai sites is just as important to investigate as the spatial patterning of the remains. How much time is represented by each accumulation of bones and artifacts? A time scale of a single season during a year versus one of 100 years would have considerably different implications about the ways in which processes of accumulation acted at each site. Accordingly, this information affects ideas about the factors responsible for accumulating the bones and artifacts.

Patterns of bone weathering provide one line of evidence about the period of site formation. Over time, the surfaces of bones crack and peel in response to daily fluctuations in temperature, moisture, and sunlight. The rate at which these changes in bone surface occur is known within broad limits. This information allows one to estimate the length of time bones lying on the landscape have been exposed to the elements. By observing the weathering features on surfaces of fossil bones it is possible to estimate the length of time over which bones accumulated at each site in Bed I Olduvai. This method for calibrating the period of bone accumulation is based on Behrensmeyer's study of modern bones in East African habitats (Behrensmeyer, 1978; Potts, 1986).

Unfortunately, no method has yet been devised to calculate the length of time over which stone artifacts have accumulated at a site. The artifacts from the sites of Bed I do vary in surface condition. Most pieces look very fresh on their broken (flaked) surfaces, whereas a few specimens from each site show exfoliated and crumbly surfaces. Presumably, a lava stone (the raw material that provides the most obvious signs of weathering condition) could be exposed to the elements for tens or hundreds of years before disintegration. However, the surface condition of stone artifacts from Olduvai could reflect several processes of decomposition—including daily fluctuations in temperature and humidity, burial and possibly transport by water, and soil conditions. Therefore, for the present, only the weathering rates of bones can help in understanding the length of time over which remains were accumulated at each site in Bed I.

The degree of bone decomposition that results from exposure to the air has been described as a series of six stages. Stage 0 refers to a fresh bone surface that shows no evidence of cracking or other signs of decay. A bone in Stage 5 shows the most extensive weathering possible before complete disintegration (Behrensmeyer, 1978). In East African habitats, as shown by Behrensmeyer's studies of swamp, woodland, bush, and plains habitats at Amboseli, bones exposed on the land surface seldom last longer than 15 years. Stage 5 weathering may be reached as quickly as 6 years from the time of death of the animal. Based on these rates, therefore, it is unlikely that bones will be found that have been exposed more than 6–15 years before burial. Bones may well have been deposited on a single surface for longer than 15 years, but the evidence will probably not be preserved.

There is considerable variation in the weathering rate of bones from a single carcass. Despite this variation, some generalizations about bone weathering rates in East African habitats are possible to make:

1. Bones in Stages 0, 1, or 2 usually have been exposed for 3 years or less.
2. Carcasses with any bones in weathering Stage 3 are about 4 years old or older.
3. Carcasses with any bones in Stage 4 are 6 years old or older (Behrensmeyer, 1978; pers. comm.).

The types of cracking, exfoliation, and splintering of bone that reflect climatic weathering are readily observed on the faunal remains from Bed I Olduvai. These weathering characteristics are distinguishable from surface modifications and aspects of decomposition (e.g., rounding, friability, and scoring of bone) that best emulate the effects of other taphonomic agents. These agents include sediment particle abrasion, carnivore digestive juices, plant roots, soil chemistry, and fossilization processes. Thus, evidence of subaerial weathering could be linked directly to Behrensmeyer's stages of weathering (Potts, 1986).

A number of factors are likely to affect the weathering patterns observed in any accumulation of transported bones. Since subaerial weathering ceases after the bones in a concentration are covered by sediment, variation in the weathering stages could reflect (1) differences in bone weathering rates, (2) differences in when bones in the assemblage were buried, (3) variation in the original weathering stages of bones transported to the accumulation site, or (4) differences in when fresh bones were introduced to the site. Only the latter factor relates specifically to the period of time of bone accumulation at a site.

Studies of bone collecting habits of animals help to evaluate these factors and to define the assumptions underlying the analysis of weathering patterns. In general, animals that collect bones to obtain edible soft tissue carry bones in a fresh state to the site of accumulation. This is certainly true of bones possessing meat, since weathering begins only with exposure of bone surfaces to the air. Moreover, this generalization is supported by studies of animal carcasses on modern landscapes. For example, carcasses monitored in the Serengeti (northern Tanzania) had a "resource life" ranging from several hours to no more than 11 days, after which hyenas and other carnivores generally did not visit the carcass or remove remains (Blumenschine, 1986). Bones exposed for that long after death and, generally, elements exposed for much longer periods (several months to a year) are in fresh condition (Stage 0). Thus, bones potentially attractive to most bone collectors (because some valued resource, such as edible marrow or meat, is provided) almost always will be in an unweathered condition. The bones collected by porcupines are one notable exception. Porcupines gnaw upon dry bones and, thus, may collect elements varying in their weathering characteristics. Besides porcupines, processes of bone accumulation which sample the environment irrespective of the resource potential of bones may be expected to transport specimens in virtually any weathering condition. Fluvial processes are undoubtedly the clearest example; assemblages with a strong contribution of bones carried by water action are indeed likely to be influenced most strongly by factor (3) mentioned above.

In addition, small skeletal elements and small fragments of bone tend to retain a fresh condition longer and tend to be buried more quickly than other specimens because of their size. These observations reflect the effects of factors (1) and (2). To include such small specimens in an analysis of weathering results in a biased distribution of weathering stages toward Stage 0, and, possibly, an inaccurate inference that almost all bones were deposited over a very short time and buried quickly. Such elements are best to exclude from the final analysis of bone weathering at Olduvai or elsewhere (Potts, 1986).

Instead, the most reliable set of specimens for analyzing differential weathering consists of major long bone pieces possessing at least a partial diaphysis and an articular end. This is so for several reasons. First, the shafts of major long bones provide a consistent bone surface on which processes of subaerial weathering act; hence, analysis of this restricted set of elements is likely to minimize the possible effect of differential weathering rates. Second, major long bone specimens also furnish a consistent surface for observing weathering characteristics. Besides the fact that weathering stages are well formulated for long bone diaphyses, observations of weathering are comparative; by restricting observations to a particular type of compact bone surface, the attribution of specimens to weathering stage is facilitated. Third, analysis of only this set of elements greatly delimits the size range of specimens classified to weathering stage. This aids further to control for differential burial of specimens, which is related to differences in the size of specimens, and (as noted above) to control for possible variations in weathering rate. Finally, this restricted size range of bones involves relatively large specimens, which at Olduvai are about the same thickness as each of the three thin levels (paleosols) in Bed I. Thus, in the case of DK-3, FLKNN-3, and FLK "Zinj," the potential influence of varied burial times on weathering patterns of the bones is again reduced.

As suggested above, differential burial of bones will depend on variations in the size of bones (small bones buried before large specimens, as a general tendency). Burial may also vary spatially within a site. That is, due to local topography, for example, certain areas of a site may be buried more quickly than other parts. Thus, a positive correlation between weathering stage and position of bones is expected if this spatial aspect of differential burial was in effect. Examination of site plans to see how the weathering stages of bones vary with their location over the site should help to assess this possibility.

Given these sets of controls on the factors which influence bone weathering, the time span represented by an accumulation of bones may be inferred from the distribution of weathering stages. To illustrate how bone weathering patterns serve to estimate periods of bone accumulation, Figure 3.1 provides the frequency of each weathering stage for identified long bones with shafts from the hyena den at Amboseli. Variation in weathering from Stage 0–4 indicates that bones were accumulated in the hyena den over several years; in fact, hyenas were observed to use this den for at least 10 years prior to collection of the bones for study. Therefore, this distribution of weathering stages is an example of an attritional, possibly gradual, accumulation of bones rather than one major, short-term pulse of bone transport by hyenas to the den. This assumes that bone weathering takes place at the den, that is, that hyenas collect bones containing meat or marrow; thus, the bones are in fresh condition.

With this example in mind, weathering data for the identified long bones from Olduvai are given in Table 3.6. Each faunal assemblage from Bed I shows a spread of bones from fresh (Stage 0) to weathered (Stage 3). Highly weathered bones occur at two sites, FLKNN–2 and 3, but fossils in Stage 5 are extremely rare. Moreover, a search of the site excavation plans for bones classified to weathering stage shows that microlevel variation in vegetation cover, soil conditions or differential burial, which would be expected to vary

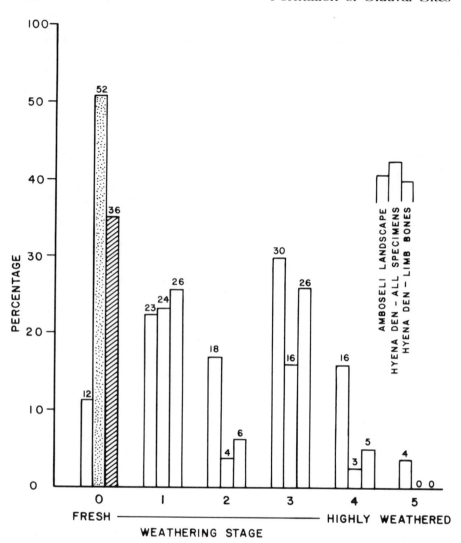

**FIGURE 3.1.** Percentages of different weathering stages for carcasses ($N = 52$)
from the Amboseli landscape, all identified specimens ($N = 422$)
from the modern spotted hyena den, and all major limb bone specimens ($N = 220$) from the hyena den. All three samples represent
attritional accumulations. Amboseli landscape data from Behrensmeyer (1978). Corrected from Potts (1986).

**TABLE 3.6.** Frequencies of Long Bones (with Diaphyses) in Each Weathering Stage

| | Stage | | | | | | | |
| | Fresh | Slightly weathered | | Weathered | Highly weathered | | | |
| Site | 0 | 1 | 2 | 3 | 4 | 5 | Total |
|---|---|---|---|---|---|---|---|
| FLK North–6" | 13 + 3 | 18 + 2 | 2 + 2 | 15 | 0 | 0 | 48 |
| | (27) | (38) | (4) | (31) | | | (100) |
| FLK "Zinj" | 66 | 43 | 22 | 18 | 0 | ?1 | 150 |
| | (44) | (29) | (15) | (12) | | (1) | (100) |
| FLKNN–2 | 9 | 27 | 12 | 23 | 2 | 1 | 74 |
| | (12) | (36) | (16) | (31) | (3) | (1) | (100) |
| FLKNN–3 | 11 | 9 | 6 | 7 | 1 | 0 | 34 |
| | (32) | (26) | (18) | (21) | (3) | | (100) |
| DK–2 | 17 | 20 | 16 | 45 | 0 | 0 | 98 |
| | (17) | (20) | (16) | (46) | | | (100) |
| DK–3 | 29 | 24 | 17 | 15 | 0 | 0 | 85 |
| | (34) | (28) | (20) | (18) | | | (100) |

"The numbers after the "plus" sign refer to long bones from the *Elephas recki* carcass. Percentages and the total for FLK North–6 do not include the *E. recki* bones. Row percentage for each site is shown in parentheses.

regularly in space, does not explain the differences in bone weathering at each site (Potts, 1982, 1986). Thus, variation in bone weathering within each site at Olduvai is believed to reflect the length of time bones were exposed on the ground.

Given the range of weathering rates defined by Behrensmeyer for modern bones, the data in Table 3.6 indicate that the remains collected at the Olduvai sites were from animals that had died over at least a 4-year period and at least a 6-year period for FLKNN–2 and 3. These estimates are based on the fastest rates of weathering. If *average* rates of weathering are assumed, all of the Olduvai faunal assemblages signify at least a 5- to 10-year period of time. Such a time span would apply to sites that were buried land surfaces (DK–3, FLKNN–3, and FLK "Zinj"). But, as illustrated in Figure 3.2, this 5- to 10-year interval represents a minimum estimate for bone assemblages from thicker deposits (DK–2, FLKNN–2, and FLK North–6).

Although this analysis seeks to control for the variety of factors which influence bone weathering patterns, Bunn and Kroll (1986) dispute the findings with the assertion that different weathering stages result only from the dif-

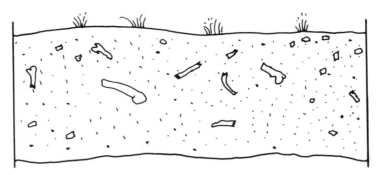

FIGURE 3.2. Animal bones accumulated on a stable land surface *(top)* contrasted with bones accumulated in a thicker deposit *(bottom)*. In the latter case, bones higher in the deposit were introduced later (and started to weather later) than bones in lower levels. Thus, the period of time over which the bone assemblage was introduced to this site is greater than that estimated by weathering.

ferential burial of bones. They claim that variation in weathering stages at the Olduvai sites does not reflect the time period of bone accumulation or the time span over which animals whose bones were transported to these sites had died. As we noted previously, if all of the bones in an assemblage had been introduced to a site over a brief period of, for example, several months, different weathering stages might reflect the cessation of weathering at different times by burial. However, the bones (and artifacts) excavated from DK-3, FLKNN-3, and FLK "Zinj" occurred as layers within thin, paleosol horizons about as thick as the objects themselves (Leakey, 1971; R. Hay, pers. comm.; pers. obs.). Therefore, at these sites the larger pieces of long bone shaft, to which this analysis has been confined, were unlikely to have been buried at widely different times. Rather, small bone fragments are likely to be buried quickly compared with the large bone pieces, even in the thin paleosols. By including all bone specimens in the analysis of weathering, the effects of differential burial of bones will be expressed. By not taking this precaution in mind, a very rapid rate of accumulation of bones at each of the Olduvai sites on the order of a few months might be concluded (Bunn, 1982; Kroll and Isaac, 1984; Bunn, pers. comm.).[1] As also was just noted, differential burial of bones is expected to show some spatial patterning across a site, that is, certain areas within a site are likely to be buried before others. However, no spatial patterning to weathering stages can be detected within sites found in the thin paleosols (Potts, 1986). Finally, the thicker, lake margin-type deposits of DK–2, FLKNN–2, and FLK North–6 would have been deposited over a period considerably longer than a single year or even several years based on Hay's (1976) study of sedimentation in Bed I. Despite the fact that differential burial must have played a role in the preservation of remains at these sites, the depth of the sediments makes it all the more unlikely that the bone concentrations at these sites were deposited within a single, brief time frame (within a year or a single annual season). The claim that site formation at Olduvai was extremely rapid, as traditionally assumed, thus is not feasible for either the thin paleosols or the thicker levels. An exception to this interpretation would apply if processes of bone accumulation were involved, such as water action or porcupines, which had collected bones that varied in their weathering stages at the time of transport.

Consequently, we can entertain three ways to explain the results of this analysis. First, it is possible that bones were introduced to each site continuously over a period of at least 5–10 years. A second possibility is that several pulses of bone accumulation occurred in each level, each pulse separated by

---

[1]Although they present no analysis of bone weathering at the Olduvai sites, Bunn (1982) and Bunn and Kroll (1986) state that since most bones exhibit Stages 0–2, the bones were exposed for a period of 2 years or less, and that much more rapid rates of accumulation on the order of a few months are not incompatible with these data.

an interval when no bones were contributed to the site. In these two cases, weathering patterns allow us to make a minimum estimate for the periods of site formation at Olduvai. Alternatively, a third means of site formation may have involved a single period of rapid accumulation of bones in different weathering stages, that is, bones that had already been exposed over a period of several years.

Each of these explanations still leaves wide open questions about how the fauna and artifacts became associated and about the means of their accumulation. Interpretations that stress that hominids had foraged for and collected animal bones at home bases imply that the artifacts and bones were associated as a result of hominid activities. However, the possibility exists that these two sets of remains were accumulated at the sites at different times—the stone artifacts by hominids and the bones by other animals. In that case, the association would not reflect hominid behavior. Further, an accumulation of these remains at each site primarily by water action would also imply a fortuitous association. These possibilities will be examined in the next two chapters.

# 4

# Physical Agents of Concentration

## The Water Transport Hypothesis

This chapter will consider whether the Olduvai bones and artifacts were concentrated by processes other than the activities of hominids or other bone-collecting animals. In this first section, the evidence for water flow at Olduvai will be examined. The second section will compare the Olduvai sites with a special instance of nonhominid bone accumulation—the case at Fort Ternan, Kenya.

All of the sites in Olduvai Bed I were buried by sediments introduced by water. Energetic water flow, such as stream or river activity, is known to produce accumulations of fossil bones and also aggregations of stone artifacts (e.g., Isaac, 1977; Voorhies, 1969). Thus, it is possible that water transport was primarily responsible for the concentration of artifacts and bones at the Olduvai sites.

Several kinds of information help to test the hypothesis that water action removed remains from, or contributed remains to, an archeological site (Figure 4.1). The sites of Bed I Olduvai show a mixture of clues concerning water transport; but, in general, they do not show the combination of sedimentary, faunal, and stone tool evidence that is diagnostic of accumulation by water action.

The first line of evidence regarding water flow is sedimentology. Both coarse-grain (coarse sand to cobbles in size) and fine-grain sediments (clay and silt) can be transported by high energy environments. For example, rapid flood waters often produce poor sorting of sediments according to grain size. A less energetic medium of deposition, however, can carry and ultimately deposit only fine-grain sediments, such as occur in lakes. All of the sites in Olduvai Bed I occur in predominantly fine-grain sediments: silts and clays.

Level 2 at FLKNN is a fine-grain tuff containing clay. Level 6 at FLK North, FLK "Zinj," and FLKNN–3 are all clays containing some silt. The local tuff that buried the top of the "Zinj" horizon at FLK was an ash deposited in quiet water: It shows uniform thickness and grades upward from coarse to fine (as do air-borne tuffs that were deposited in the quiet waters in the middle of the ancient lake). Rootmarks in the tuff, and possibly other forms of bioturbation (e.g., burrowing, trampling), appear to have been the only possible source of disturbance to this volcanic layer that sealed the "Zinj" level at FLK. In some contrast, this same tuff at the FLKNN locality (less

1. Sedimentology

2. Paleogeography

3. Small stone artifacts

4. Preferred orientations of bones

5. Transport abrasion on objects

6. Bone hydraulic transport groups

**FIGURE 4.1.** Six indicators of hydraulic transport of archeological remains.

than 150 m away) appears slightly disturbed by water reworking; it varies in thickness from 18–35 cm and is sandy, the result of winnowing of finer material (R. Hay, pers. comm.).[1] Thus, on geological grounds, while the FLK "Zinj" site was buried under very low energy conditions, more energetic water action occurred close by.

All levels at locality DK are primarily sandy and silty clays. In contrast with other Bed I sites, however, DK is characterized by large numbers of gravel- to pebble-sized particles (2–64 mm) made of feldspar, quartzite, and lava. These are dispersed throughout otherwise fine-grain levels which together are 1.3 m thick. Field records indicate the discovery of hundreds of such small stones during excavation. They are not confined to the excavated locality but are characteristic of the deposits below Tuff IB over at least 200m on the north side of the Gorge. All of these clasts are rounded, but not usually spherical.

Hay (1976: 45, 48) has suggested that these pebbles may have arrived at the site by sheetwash across the landscape, such as might occur over a gentle downslope due to heavy rain. Pebbles of pink feldspar and of Engelosin phonolite indicate an input from the north because stones of this composition are distinctive of the northern part of the Olduvai basin (R. Hay, pers. comm.). Yet the feldspar possibly came from a now buried source much nearer to the site (M.D. Leakey, pers. comm.). Sources of quartzite pebbles in the basin were probably located to the west and north of the DK locality, in the vicinity of Naibor Soit, where a scree of slightly more angular pebbles covers the slopes today. Rounded lava pebbles of welded tuff, basalts, trachyandesite, nephelinite, and vesicular basalt also occur throughout the DK sediments below Tuff IB; these stones suggest input from the volcanic sources to the east and south. Before the deposition of Tuff IB, streams from the eastern volcanic highlands carried lava pebbles toward the lake margin facies (Hay,

[1]At FLKNN this local tuff covered excavated Level 1, which was not included in this study.

1976: 48). Yet there are no stream channel features evident in the exposed lake margin facies near DK or any other locality in Bed I. The lack of illite clay from the micaceous basement rocks of the Olduvai basin in the sediments at DK (Hay, pers. comm.) suggests that the pebbles were moved *not* by clay flow but, more probably, by water that lacked a significant clay sediment load.

The presence of these pebbles in the DK sediments is probably more significant than has been noted in previous interpretations of the excavations at DK. Locality DK may have been a relatively low-lying area fed by occasional water washes from several directions. The place itself, however, evidently occurred in the typically nonenergetic lake margin area, where pebbles transported by more energetic mediums were dropped. Therefore, bones and artifacts already at the site before water activity occurred would not have been transported away; rather, pebbles and other bones and artifacts would have been added to the preexisting accumulation by water action. The fact that coarse-grain material existed in the Olduvai basin during the span of Bed I indicates that fine-grain sediments at other Bed I sites truly reflect low-energy environments, rather than simply the availability of only fine-grain sediments to energetic flows of water.

Overall, therefore, sedimentology strongly indicates that energetic, rapid water was not responsible for accumulating the remains excavated in Bed I. Rather, all of the sites occur in sediments that represent quiet depositional environments, with the addition of one or more energetic pulses at DK carrying pebbles and possibly other material from several areas.

However, it is important to look also for other lines of evidence concerning hydraulic activity. A second source of information about water action is the paleogeography of Olduvai, based on Hay's reconstructions from extensive geological and geochemical research. All Bed I sites occur in the lake margin facies, where lake waters periodically rose and retreated. Ancient stream channels are not visible in the vicinity of the sites or in any part of the lake margin facies exposed today in the Gorge. Such channels are isolated to an alluvial fan facies to the east (above Tuff IB), in which streams flowed to the west–northwest (Hay, 1976: 50). The alluvial facies, as exposed in the Gorge, is 1 to 2 km from the Bed I sites (see Figure 2.3). Thus, stream action can be largely discounted as a major factor in the accumulation of stone artifacts and bones. The sites occur in contexts where water action was dissipated over broad areas, that is, not confined to channels. In addition, nowhere in the eastern lake margin facies are beach environments known. Finally, velocities of lake water rise or sheetwash would not be so high as those ordinarily associated with stream channel flow (Chow, 1959).

One point of interest regarding site DK is its location—almost 3 km further east than the other Bed I sites studied here. Based on sedimentary evidence, the eastern margin of the perennial lake was no further east during the deposition of DK–2 and 3 than during later Bed I times (see Figure 2.3b). Moreover, detailed geological sections (Hay, 1976) show that below Tuff IB the sediments at FLKNN–3 km closer to the lake basin center—exhibit clear features of exposure to air; they are root-marked and are neither thicker nor more massive than the deposits at DK. During the period represented by DK–2 and 3, therefore, locality FLKNN evidently was not inundated by lake water. This suggests that the lake expansions that covered and helped to bury the remains at DK were relatively extensive. Such lake level changes would have been greater than were needed to inundate the FLK complex of sites, since the latter apparently were closer to the perennial lake border.

Because it is somewhat independent of the excavated archeological remains, geological evidence is the most important basis on which to judge the effect of water flow on bones and artifacts. Nonetheless, the bones and artifacts can be treated as sedimentary particles themselves and, thus, can provide information about water transport.

The presence of small stone artifacts has been suggested to be an indicator of site disturbance by water action (Harris, 1978; Isaac, 1967). The propensity of particles to be moved and deposited by water depends on particle size. The size of artifacts at a site may indicate whether water flow was energetic enough to lift small objects from the substrate and to transport them away from the larger ones.

In each of the five artifact-bearing levels at Olduvai, the percentage of debitage (small, sharp fragments that resulted from percussion flaking) is high. However, the proportion of debitage in these artifact assemblages does not differ greatly from that found in stream channel assemblages from other early archeological sites.[2] All of the Olduvai sites preserved artifacts under 2 cm in length, but only at FLK "Zinj" do such small artifacts appear in great abundance compared with that found in stream channel assemblages.[3] The size of artifacts found at the Olduvai sites thus does not distinguish well between definite stream channel and lower energy lake margin contexts.

The preferential orientation of bones is yet another possible sign of hydraulic activity. It is known from flume studies that bones tend to align both parallel and perpendicular to the direction of water flow. Water depth, the initial orientation of bones, and their sizes and shapes influence which preferred orientation a bone will take (Hanson, 1980; Hill, 1975; Toots, 1965b; Voorhies, 1969). A. Hill and A. Walker (pers. comm.) have noted that such a criss-cross orientation pattern of bones is evident on the site plan of FLK "Zinj" (Leakey, 1971: Fig. 24). The preferred orientations are close to a north–

---

[2]Debitage makes up 73–93% of the artifact assemblages from the Olduvai sites. Yet at Koobi Fora, Kenya, channel sites exhibit 57–97% debitage (Harris, 1978: 223). Thus, percentage of debitage by itself is probably not a good indicator of site disturbance by water flow.

[3]About 38% of the stone artifact assemblage from the "Zinj" site is less than 2 cm in length. The other Bed I artifact collections range from 5 to 17%; however, 12.5% of an artifact assemblage from a channel conglomerate in Olduvai Bed II is in this size range (Potts, 1982).

south/east–west pattern and are shown by long bones and pieces of long bone shaft on every major section of the plan. A similar pattern is visible on the site plan of FLKNN–3. Again, bones with definite long axes tend to align in a north–south/east–west pattern.

Systematic error in drawing the bones on the site plans apparently did not occur (M.D. Leakey, pers. comm.). In that case, few explanations other than the effect of water flow seem plausible. For the late Middle Pleistocene cave site at Lazaret, France, it has been suggested that preferred bone orientations may have occurred through foot traffic and kicking (de Lumley, 1969a). At Lazaret three preferred orientations appear when long bone shafts over 10 cm are plotted within the area interpreted to be an ancient shelter. Two of these orientations, comprising 54% of the bone sample, fall into a criss-cross pattern; one of these latter orientations is aligned with the long axis of the shelter. Rib shafts at Lazaret (de Lumley, 1969a: Fig. 32) also show a preferred alignment with the length of the proposed shelter. While sediments that may have been washed in through fissures occur in the cave, the site is generally thought to have been undisturbed by water flow. The idea that preferential bone orientations can reflect foot traffic requires experimental testing. But for the present this suggestion means that preferred orientations may sometimes be produced under conditions other than hydraulic effects. Experiments have shown that significant movement of objects does not necessarily occur when water flow acts to reorient objects (Isaac, 1967). Yet it is not known whether flows that reorient large bones can also serve to winnow much smaller, easily transported objects. If this is the case, the various pieces of evidence from FLK "Zinj" about water flow conditions are contradictory.

The orientations of fossilized bones from a small excavation at Olduvai contemporaneous with the DK levels has been studied by Hill (1975). Two, or possibly three, peaks in azimuth were found; all of these peaks were north–south. Since the heavier ends of crocodile teeth in this assemblage generally pointed southward, this probably was the direction from which water flowed. This information supports the idea that water flow affected locality DK, as inferred from geological evidence.

A fifth indicator of water action is the presence of abrasion on objects incurred during their movement by water. Energetic water flow can cause grains of sediment to abrade bones and artifacts carried by the flow. Transport in streams, for instance, tends to abrade, or round off, the projecting parts of bones (e.g., muscle markings and articular ends). Edges and the raised borders between flake scars on artifacts may also be abraded. Furthermore, rounding is usually evident over the entire specimen rather than confined to just a small portion. This occurs because the entire bone or artifact generally is subject to abrasive sedimentary particles during its movement in water.

The bones and artifacts from Bed I mostly show no rounding. Rather, the edges of objects usually are as well-defined as on modern, untransported bones. However, some specimens do show rounding, which in many cases matches well the wear characteristic of hydraulic transport. Of all Bed I artifact assemblages studied, the one recovered from DK–2 and 3 manifests the greatest number of abraded pieces (see Figure 4.2).

Abrasion on bones is somewhat harder to assess. The cortical surfaces of bones from Olduvai exhibit two kinds of deterioration other than that of climatic weathering. One type involves rounding off of edges, while the other involves a rounded and porous appearance to articular surfaces especially, possibly from chemical destruction of bone. Both kinds of surface wear are found on a few mammalian bones from all sites.

Some of the small-sized bone fragments from FLK "Zinj" show the rounding off of sharp, broken edges characteristic of water transport; yet others of similar size are very fresh and unabraded (Figure 4.3). In particular, the bovid remains at FLKNN–3 were noted to show abrasion on broken edges and loss of some morphological detail; again, this was sometimes accompanied by the peculiar worn, porous appearance on the cortical surfaces of some, but not all, of these specimens.

Table 4.1 provides the percentages of mammalian specimens from each level showing obvious surface wear, including those with both articular and nonarticular surface rounding. If such bone surface wear were linked solely to hydraulic transport, then these data rather strongly contradict other lines of evidence for water effects at the Olduvai sites. For example, the DK levels,

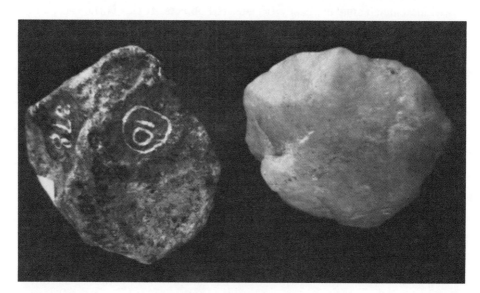

**FIGURE 4.2.** One lava artifact *(left)* and one quartzite artifact *(right)*, both classified as discoids, from site DK. Both show rounding of edges and facets, similar to the results of transport abrasion.

(a)

(b)

**FIGURE 4.3.** *(a)* Two long bone shaft fragments from FLK "Zinj," cutting B, strip 12′–16′. *Left:* Specimen shows extreme rounding of edges. *Right:* Specimen is in fresh condition, showing sharp, unabraded edges. *(b)* Two bovid unciforms from site FLK "Zinj": Specimen on left shows smooth articular surface and fresh edges. Specimen on right shows surface deterioration and extreme rounding of surface details. Size is poorly correlated with deterioration.

**TABLE 4.1.** Number of Abraded Bones from the Six Olduvai Sites and from the Amboseli Hyena Den

| | DK-3 (N = 550) | DK-2 (N = 472) | FLKNN-3 (N = 398) | FLKNN-2 (N = 320) | FLK "Zinj" (N = 1220) | FLK North-6 (N = 652) | Amboseli Hyena Assemblage (N = 394) |
|---|---|---|---|---|---|---|---|
| Percentage of specimens with obvious abrasion | 11 | 13 | 20 | 26 | 15 | 17 | 6 |
| Percentage of specimens with abrasion as primary surface condition on articular and nonarticular surfaces | 6 | 5 | 11 | 11 | 4 | 3 | 4 |

which on sedimentological grounds show the most water disturbance of all Bed I levels, here yield the lowest percentages of mammalian bones with major rounding. In addition, the well-rootmarked, clay paleosol at FLKNN–3 bears the highest percentage of bones showing rounding on both articular and nonarticular areas.

With other factors equal, *small* bone elements should be most easily picked up and moved by water. Only at FLKNN–2 and 3 and at FLK North–6 is the mean length of abraded specimens considerably less than the mean for *all* specimens from each level. At FLK "Zinj," the mean length is only 5 mm different from the mean for all specimens; while such bones at DK–2 tend to be *larger* than all other specimens from the same level. Every level shows several large and heavy bones with surface abrasion—over 10 cm long and sometimes from elephants and other very large animals. The chances are minimal that these latter specimens were moved by water under the most energetic flow conditions conceivable, on geological grounds, at these sites.

It is important to note that several processes may mimic transport abrasion. Plant roots and soil chemistry may dissolve some fine details of bone morphology and, thus, produce rounding. Further, bones and bone fragments that have been attacked by hyenas at the Amboseli den occasionally showed both types of surface deterioration noted on Olduvai specimens, often without any other obvious signs of tooth damage (Table 4.1, last column). These non-hydraulic factors, then, mimic transport abrasion to some presently undocumented degree. Thus, it is unwise to associate all bone surface abrasion with hydraulic transport. Nonetheless, the presence of surface rounding suggests that a small set of bones experienced different taphonomic effects from that of other bones at each Olduvai site; water transport probably affected some of the elements in this subset.

A final observation that provides information about hydraulic effects is the sorting of skeletal elements based on their susceptibility to water movement. Flume experiments have shown that under controlled conditions some skeletal elements are likely to be transported more easily than others. For instance, pioneering studies by Voorhies (1969) showed that the sternum, sacrum, ribs, and vertebrae of coyote and sheep are often lifted from substrates earlier and carried for longer distances than are the mandible and cranium. Complete skeletal elements are conveniently grouped into three categories: "lag," "intermediate," and "highly transportable." Water flow tends to produce a spatial sorting of elements according to these categories. A set of bones that has not been affected by water transport tends to consist of a wide range of elements from all three transport groups. In contrast, an assemblage influenced highly by water action should exhibit, ideally, a fairly narrow diversity of elements according to transport group. The accumulation may consist of bones from any of the three groups but with a clear predominance of bones belonging to only one group. For instance, it may consist of only easily transported bones or perhaps only the lag elements left behind.

TABLE 4.2. Voorhies' Bone Transport Groups Based on Characteristic Susceptibility to Hydraulic Movement (15 Trials Each on Disarticulated
Sheep and Coyote Bones)[a,b]

| Group I (highly transportable) | Group II (intermediate) | Group III (lag) |
|---|---|---|
| Ribs | Femur | Skull |
| Vertebrae | Tibia | Mandible |
| Sacrum | Humerus | |
| Sternum | Metapodials | |
| | Pelvis | |
| | Radius | |
| - - - - - - - - - - - - - - | - - - - - - - - - - - - - - | - - - - - - - - |
| Scapula | Scapula | Ramus |
| Phalanges | Ramus | |
| Ulna | Phalanges | |
| | Ulna | |

[a]From Voorhies (1969:69). [b]Elements below the dotted line are intermediate
between the two groups in which they appear.

In addition, because of their small size, microfaunal remains are more likely
to be transported away from an accumulation of bones than are those of large
animals.

The transport groups constructed by Voorhies for sheep and coyote bones
are presented in Table 4.2. Table 4.3 furnishes analogous experimental data
for human bones (Boaz and Behrensmeyer, 1976).[4]

Bone density and size (weight) are major factors invoked to explain experimental flume results. Dense and heavy bones tend to belong to the lag
category, whereas small, light bones travel most easily. Based on density
and weight measurements, predictions have been made about which bones
of large mammals are most easily transported (Behrensmeyer, 1975: 490).
Phalanges, sesamoids, podials, vertebrae, and ribs share this characteristic
for all six mammalian taxa analyzed in that study (Ovis, reduncines, suids,
alcelaphines, Equus, and Hippopotamus).

[4]The agreement between these two data sets is not great, which partly indicates
taxonomic variation in the transport tendencies of particular skeletal elements.
The major overlaps between these experimental results are: (1) mandibles are
placed in the "lag" category; (2) the tibia and the radius (proximal ends only for
human bones) occur in the "intermediate" group; and (3) some vertebrae and
the sacrum fall into the "highly transportable" group. One major inconsistency
is that bones with high surface area to volume ratios (e.g., ribs, sacra, and scapulae)
occur in Voorhies' Group I but in Boaz and Behrensmeyer's Group III. Some of
these differences may be due to experimental conditions: (1) a fine sand substrate
in Voorhies' experiments versus a coarse sand substrate used by Boaz and Behrensmeyer; (2) different gradients of the stream table; and (3) the human bones
were placed into the flume current whereas the coyote and sheep bones apparently
were placed on the flume bed before water was introduced.

**TABLE 4.3.** Human Bone Hydraulic Transport Groups[a]

| High transport group | Lag: negligible movement | Lag: no movement |
|---|---|---|
| Talus | Mandible with teeth | Hemimandible |
| Proximal ulna | Vertebra T1 | Mandible without teeth |
| Metatarsal I and IV | Proximal tibia | Molar |
| Vertebra T12 | Proximal radius | Incisor |
| Proximal humerus | | Cranial vault pieces |
| Acetabulum | | Patella |
| Calcaneum | | Proximal radius |
| Cuboid | | Distal radius |
| Sacrum | | Rib |
| Cranium | | Atlas |
| | | Proximal femur |
| | | Scapular fragment |
| | | Clavicle |

[a]Based on Boaz and Behrensmeyer (1976:56).

However, the transport and accumulation of bones by water is a very complex phenomenon. Hydraulic movement and deposition of a bone are influenced by its shape, breakage, and orientation relative to the flow; and irregularities of the substrate, including vegetation, may deter the movement of bones that are otherwise easily transportable (Behrensmeyer, 1975; Chow, 1959; Hanson, 1980; Shipman, Johnson, and Stahl, 1981a). Thus, an excavated assemblage of bones will not necessarily present a straightforward picture of the hydrodynamic history of the assemblage.

Nonetheless, with these cautions in mind, the skeletal elements present at the Olduvai sites provide some further clues about the effects of water on the bone remains. Each site in Bed I has numerous elements from each hydraulic transport group, based on a combination of Voorhies' and Behrensmeyer's predictions. The elements vary greatly in original density, weight, shape, and breakage characteristics. Tables in the Appendix show which skeletal elements are preserved from small, medium, and large bovids at each site.[5] The most easily transported elements—phalanges, podials, sesamoids, ribs, and vertebrae—are present along with lag elements such as mandibles and isolated teeth. Long bones, which are well represented in the Olduvai assemblages, fall into the "intermediate" transport category. The Bed I faunal assemblages, therefore, are not sorted according to bone transport group.

At first glance, the scarcity of certain skeletal elements seems to suggest a slight prevalence of lag elements in each assemblage. It is tempting to attribute the relative paucity of vertebrae, ribs, and sacra to the ease with

[5]See Appendix Tables A-4, A-13, B-4, C-4, D-4, and E-4.

which such bones are transported by water. However, other easily transported bones are plentiful in these assemblages. Phalanges, podials, and sesamoids comprise about 35–40% of the elements in living ungulates. All of the Olduvai sites preserve considerable numbers of these bones, either above or slightly below the 35% mark (Table 4.4). DK–2 and 3 show the highest proportions of small, easily transported elements of bovids. These data suggest very strongly that these accumulations are not lag assemblages. The scarcity of vertebrae and other axial remains appears to result from factors other than winnowing by water action. As discussed in the previous chapter, high frequencies of limb bones relative to axial elements typifies processes of transport by animals of bones away from death sites.

Besides this evidence, microfaunal remains occur on all Bed I levels. Experiments on the water transport of mouse, toad, and frog bones indicate that small microfaunal bones are easily moved by even slow water velocities (6–35 cm/sec) (Dodson, 1973). The presence of microfauna in each Olduvai level further suggests that the bone remains of large mammals are not lag assemblages. Instead, if water transport did have an effect, the bones of microfauna more likely were introduced to the site during the deposition of sediments, as Leakey (1971: 250) proposes for FLKNN–3.

In summary, the preceding analyses indicate that the bone and artifact assemblages from Olduvai Bed I are not primarily hydraulic accumulations. Sedimentology, paleogeographic context, and bone transport groups suggest this conclusion most strongly. Other criteria provide mixed results and provide some indication that water action was a taphonomic factor in the formation of each site. High energy flood conditions were not involved nor, apparently,

**TABLE 4.4.** Percentage Frequency of Small, Easily Transported Limb Bones (Phalanges, Podials, and Sesamoids) Relative to the Total MNE (in parentheses) for Bovids and Nonbovid Mammalian Taxa

| Site | Bovids (%) | Nonbovid taxa (%) | Total (%) |
|---|---|---|---|
| FLK North–6 | 43.5 (168) | 25.2 (195) | 33.6 |
| FLK "Zinj" | 32.1 (302) | 15.8 (57) | 29.5 |
| FLKNN–2 | 13.1 (107) | 59.6 (99) | 35.4 |
| FLKNN–3 | 24.7 (154) | 35.7 (56) | 27.6 |
| DK–2 | 44.7 (329) | 34.4 (90) | 42.5 |
| DK–3 | 39.3 (196) | 25.7 (74) | 35.6 |

were long-duration, low-energy conditions of water flow, which would have produced well-sorted bone assemblages. Probably, the excavated assemblages reflect quiet water flow acting for a short period of time, having the potential to move some objects within the original accumulation at each site, and, rarely, to introduce others to it. The presence of sand- and pebble-size sedimentary particles at locality DK implies that some small- to medium-sized bones could also have been introduced to the sites at this locality; however, the bones of medium-sized to very large-sized ungulates probably were concentrated at the DK sites prior to water flow. Sheetwash of rain over the landscape which drained into a low-lying area appears to be indicated by the accumulation of pebbles from many different directions at DK. The bones of small animals could have accompanied the pebbles.

We have also seen that not all criteria believed to give evidence of water transport are necessarily reliable. For instance, the abrasion of bones and artifacts potentially offers the best archeological evidence for water transport at Olduvai. Yet, in general, interpretation of surface rounding is not clear. To take an example outside of Olduvai: The fact that 26% of the bones in a sample from the Fort Ternan site show moderate to extreme abrasion, otherwise manifesting little sign of water flow (Shipman, 1977), indicates how poorly this potentially valuable line of evidence is understood.

## Nonhominid Accumulation: The Case of Fort Ternan

Many fossil bone accumulations are known for which hominid activity can be largely dismissed as a possible cause due to the time and place represented by such accumulations. For instance, bone assemblages from the Tertiary of North America could not have been produced by hominids since humans are not known in the New World before the Upper Pleistocene. Published accounts of North American bone quarries indicate that fluvial or other situations involving water flow were responsible in many cases for concentrating the faunal remains.

Bone concentrations from some East African sites dated to the Miocene represent a different situation in that energetic water activity evidently was not involved. Assemblages ranging from small pockets of bones to large, dense accumulations have been discovered in fine-grain sediments associated with Miocene volcanic deposits in the rift valley region. Excavations at Fort Ternan, Kenya, a Middle Miocene locality, have yielded one of the largest accumulations with an areal density comparable with those at the Olduvai sites. Furthermore, the assemblages recovered from Fort Ternan show a wide variety of taxa, a full range of skeletal elements, and high degrees of bone breakage. Therefore, the faunal assemblage from this site exhibits the major characteristics found in the bone aggregations from Olduvai.

The current consensus is that hominids did not yet exist 14 Ma, the age of the Fort Ternan site; thus, hominids were not responsible for collecting the bones at Fort Ternan. The hominoid *Kenyapithecus*, which is found at this site, generally is not considered to have been a bone collector. Moreover, the high representation of large-bodied mammals among the broken bones at Fort Ternan suggests that a primate the size of *Kenyapithecus* did not contribute to the overall patterning of this bone assemblage. Finally, from previous taphonomic study by Pat Shipman, there are no clear signs that water transport was the primary means of bone accumulation at the site. Hence, the Fort Ternan site affords an intriguing challenge to the interpretation of the sites at Olduvai. If a large bone concentration can occur without water transport, does Fort Ternan serve as a reasonable analog *that did not involve hominids* for the process of bone accumulation at Olduvai?

The Fort Ternan remains have been extensively studied from a taphonomic viewpoint (Shipman, 1977, 1982; Shipman *et al.*, 1981b). The fine-grain sediments and the lack of skeletal element sorting and preferred orientations suggest that high-energy hydraulic transport was not a major agent of bone accumulation. A combination of other processes are thought to be responsible for bone transport to the Fort Ternan site: downslope movement of bones, short distance water wash of the bones to a low-lying area, and the activities of carnivores (Shipman, 1977). Fort Ternan appears to represent a savanna–forest ecotone. Both open-country savanna species and forest-dwelling animals are preserved at the site. The potential for drawing such diverse species together via downslope movement or water washes would have depended upon regional physiography and the proximity of forest and savanna.

The bone concentrations from Fort Ternan and the levels of Olduvai Bed I are alike in a number of ways. Yet these similarities, as explored later, partly reflect generally similar ecological settings. The assemblages from Olduvai and Fort Ternan differ mainly in details of skeletal element representation, differences that suggest somewhat distinctive modes of bone accumulation. The major points of comparison are presented in the remainder of this chapter. Unless otherwise noted, the Fort Ternan data come from Shipman's study of the fauna excavated in 1974 and of the Leakey collection excavated during the 1960s (Shipman, 1977).

A wide variety of species were identified in the Fort Ternan assemblage, a pattern that also applies to the Olduvai levels and to many faunal assemblages from early archeological sites. The taxonomic diversity of Fort Ternan bovids and carnivores is characteristic of a savanna community; other aspects of taxa variation suggest affinities with woodland–bushland communities (Andrews, Lord, and Evans, 1979). Similarly, the fauna from Bed I Olduvai represents a largely savanna ecosystem, including some woodland–bushland elements.

However, per number of specimens, the Fort Ternan collections show a higher taxonomic diversity than occurs in any Bed I faunal assemblage (Figure 4.4). The relatively high diversity at Fort Ternan may be partly a matter of

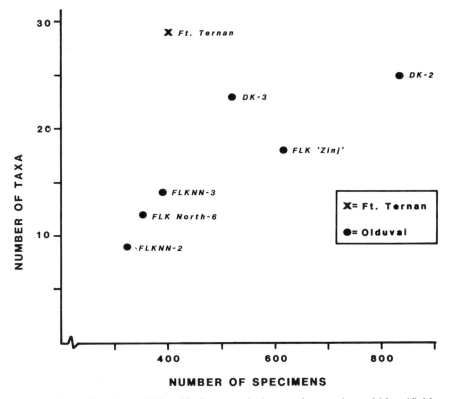

**FIGURE 4.4.** Number of identified taxa relative to the number of identifiable specimens at Fort Ternan (1974 collection) and the Olduvai sites.

sampling savanna and forest taxa at the ecotone site. Patterns of skeletal element preservation (discussed later) also help to account for the large number of taxa per number of specimens. For example, the Fort Ternan assemblage shows an abundance of gnathic–cranial remains, which are assigned more easily to taxon than are postcranial remains. In addition, at Fort Ternan a low number of specimens are preserved per MNI; thus, relatively more individuals and more taxa are represented for a given sample size of specimens than occurs at Olduvai.

Bovids are the most frequent among specimens identified to taxon: 60% in the 1974 faunal collection and 75% in a sample from the Leakey excavations. Relative to other taxa, these frequencies of bovids fit well within the range of bovid representation at the six Bed I sites (see Tables 7.2–7.6). The relative abundance of other mammalian taxa also compares well with that observed in Olduvai faunal assemblages (Table 4.5). The only major disparity is provided by the suids, which are much more abundant in the Olduvai site faunas. A further similarity concerns the faunal body sizes from the two sites. Very

**TABLE 4.5.** Relative Abundance of Mammal Taxa at Fort Ternan (1974 and Leakey collections combined) (in Percentage)[a]

| Taxon | % Specimens ($N = 1626$) | % MNI ($N = 268$) |
|-------|--------------------------|-------------------|
| Bovids | 70 | 69 |
| Carnivores | 5.5 | 7 |
| Giraffids | 7 | 9 |
| Rhinos | 5 | 4 |
| Proboscideans | 8.5 | 3 |
| Primates | 2 | 5 |
| Suids | 0.6 | 1 |
| Tragulids | 1.6 | 2 |

[a]Data from Shipman (1977).

small (microfauna) to very large mammals are represented at Fort Ternan and on the Olduvai Bed I levels. Medium-sized animals dominate both sets of fauna (Table 4.6).

Therefore, the bone accumulations at Olduvai and Fort Ternan underwent taphonomic processes that produced similar relative taxonomic and body size frequencies. These similarities must at least partly reflect the availability of taxa of similar body sizes and roughly similar relative abundances (i.e., similar environments).

Furthermore, there are several similarities between Olduvai and Fort Ternan in postcranial bone representation. In the Leakey excavation at Fort Ternan, the proportions of bovid axial and long bone specimens fall within the range of observed frequencies for those elements at Olduvai. Axials comprise 30% of all bovid postcranials at Fort Ternan; the corresponding frequencies at Olduvai range from 10 (DK–3) to 41% (FLKNN–3). Table 4.7 documents the similarity in the proportions of bovid long bones between Fort Ternan and FLK "Zinj" at Olduvai. These similarities, however, must be viewed against one major skeletal element difference between Olduvai and

**TABLE 4.6.** Percentage Abundance of Mammal Size Classes Represented by Bones Identified to Taxon, Fort Ternan[a]

| Size class | 1974 collection ($N = 398$) | Leakey collection ($N = 3314$) |
|------------|------------------------------|----------------------------------|
| Very small (5 lb.) | 11.8 | 4.1 |
| Small (5–150 lb.) | 3.8 | 2.7 |
| Medium (150–1000 lb.) | 74.4 | 87.1 |
| Large (1000 lb.) | 10.2 | 6.1 |

[a]Data from Shipman (1977).

**TABLE 4.7.** Frequency of Bovid Long Bones from Fort Ternan (Leakey collection) and FLK "Zinj" Olduvai

| Site | Humerus | Radius | Ulna | Femur | Tibia | Metapodials |
|------|---------|--------|------|-------|-------|-------------|
| Fort Ternan | | | | | | |
| ($N = 423$) | 92(22%) | 57(13%) | 31(7%) | 70(16%) | 47(11%) | 126(30%) |
| FLK "Zinj" | | | | | | |
| ($N = 146$) | 25(17%) | 23(16%) | 13(9%) | 16(11%) | 22(15%) | 147(32%) |

$x^2 = 5.54$; df $= 5$; $0.3 < p < 0.5$.

Fort Ternan—the relative contribution of teeth and of other cranial remains to the collections. The representation of such specimens at Fort Ternan is quite high (Table 4.8). In the 1974 collection, bovid postcranial bones are so scarce ($N = 33$) relative to cranial pieces that statistical comparison of their relative proportions to those from Olduvai is meaningless.

An additional parallel between Fort Ternan and Olduvai concerns the presence of small bone fragments. Over half of the bone assemblages from Fort Ternan consist of indeterminate pieces, those which could not be identified to taxon or to specific skeletal element. This is true for each of the large mammal assemblages from Bed I Olduvai, as it is for many archeological bone assemblages. However, out of 938 fragments from Fort Ternan assigned to skeletal part but unidentifiable to taxon, only 10% were classified as long bone pieces—considerably below the corresponding 30–50% representation of miscellaneous long bone fragments at the Olduvai sites.

The bone accumulation from Fort Ternan is enormous compared with that from any one Olduvai level. Some individual species are represented by hundreds of specimens and by a minimum number of over 50 individuals. However, this assemblage, relative to every Olduvai level, exhibits an extremely low number of specimens (E) per MNI (Table 4.9). The majority of macromammalian taxa at Fort Ternan is represented by fewer than 5 specimens per MNI. The average for all such taxa is 6.1, as is the average for bovids. This pattern contrasts greatly with that at Olduvai. None of the Bed I levels shows fewer than 14 specimens per MNI for all mammalian macrofauna. The average bovid representation for all six sites is 22.2 specimens per MNI (11.1 in the lowest ratio, which occurs at FLKNN–2); 8.0 is the corresponding ratio for nonbovid taxa. When examined taxon by taxon, almost all taxa at every Bed I site show E/MNI ratios above the Fort Ternan average. Only giraffids consistently fall below, and rhinos are also low compared with this taxon at Fort Ternan. The fairly consistent, and large overall, difference in E/MNI ratio suggests that the accumulation of skeletal remains at Fort Ternan was more piecemeal—possibly bone by bone or as part of small articulated units—compared with the accumulation of bones at the Olduvai sites. The kinds of skeletal elements preserved support this idea.

TABLE 4.8. Percentage Frequency of Tooth, Gnathic, and Other Cranial Remains Relative to Identified Specimens within Major Taxa: Fort Ternan and Olduvai Bed I[a]

| Taxon | Fort Ternan | | DK–3 | DK–2 | FLKNN–3 | FLKNN–2 | FLK "Zinj" | FLK North–6 |
|---|---|---|---|---|---|---|---|---|
| | 1974 collection | Leakey collection | | | | | | |
| Bovid | 83 | 50 | 36 | 40 | 29 | 28 | 31 | 29 |
| Nonbovid | 79 | 62 | 68 | 70 | 44 | 39 | 50 | 16[b] |
| Total | 81 | 55 | 46 | 48 | 35 | 33 | 34 | 21[b] |

[a]Fort Ternan data from Shipman (1977).
[b]Includes *Elephas recki* specimens. Without them, nonbovid taxa = 73% and total = 40%.

74

**TABLE 4.9.** Ratio of the Number of Specimens to Minimum Number of individuals (E/MNI) for Various Mammal Taxa: Fort Ternan (1974 and Leakey Assemblages Combined) and Olduvai Bed I[a]

| Taxon | Fort Ternan | DK-3 | DK-2 | FLKNN-3 | FLKNN-2 | FLK "Zinj" | FLK North-6 |
|---|---|---|---|---|---|---|---|
| Bovids (all) | 6.1 | 19.8 | 31.7 | 19.4 | 11.1 | 25.1 | 26.2 |
| Small | — | 11.0 | 17.7 | 8.5 | 7.0 | 22.3 | 27.7 |
| Medium | — | 12.6 | 15.3 | 28.4 | 15.9 | 23.7 | 18.4 |
| Large | — | 8.4 | 15.0 | 6.0 | 5.2 | 9.0 | 5.0 |
| Equids | — | 11.0 | 5.7 | 10.0 | 6.0 | 7.0 | 1.0 |
| Suids | 3.0 | 13.0 | 18.8 | 7.0 | 29.0 | 6.6 | 17.8 |
| Carnivores | 4.8 | 5.5 | 5.5 | 7.7 | 5.0 | 11.5 | 5.0 |
| Giraffids | 4.4 | 4.0 | 3.0 | — | — | 2.0 | 3.0 |
| Rhinos | 8.1 | 6.0 | 7.0 | — | — | — | 5.0 |
| Hippos | — | 10.0 | 12.0 | — | — | — | 1.0 |
| Proboscideans | 19.9 | 7.5 | 5.5 | — | — | — | 193.5 |
| Primates | 2.7 | 5.0 | 12.5 | 13.0[b] | — | 8.0 | — |
| Tagulids | 5.4 | — | — | — | — | — | — |
| All taxa | 7.1 | 14.0 | 20.3 | 13.3 | 14.1 | 17.7 | 33.6[c] |

[a]Fort Ternan data from Shipman (1977).
[b]8.0 for nonhominid primates only.
[c]17.6 without *Elephas recki* carcass remains.

Every taxon at Fort Ternan is represented predominantly by gnathic and other cranial remains (see Table 4.8). These elements, especially isolated teeth, usually can be accommodated into a small MNE (mandibles, maxillae, or complete crania). Many, if not most, of the Fort Ternan individuals may be accounted for by a minimum number of a single mandible or cranium. The ratio of MNE per MNI shows that this is *not* the case for the Olduvai Bed I assemblages (Table 4.10). This ratio ranges from 7.6 to 17.3 for bovids across the Bed I sites. Nonbovid taxa possess substantially fewer bones per individual (mean ratio equals 4.3). The low ratios for giraffids and proboscideans may well be due to the large size of these animals. Carnivores on the Olduvai sites tend to be either small species or juveniles of larger species (e.g., *Crocuta* and *Leo*). The bones of such animals tend to undergo a high degree of preferential destruction. Thus, the Olduvai carnivores also typically show MNE/MNI ratios less than 4.0 (though they usually show E/MNI ratios well above the Fort Ternan carnivores). Suids and equids (medium-sized animals) have ratios above 5.0, the largest for nonbovid taxa. Excluding hominid remains, primates show a lower ratio than 5 (i.e., 3.8).

Furthermore, small limb elements (phalanges, carpals, tarsals) are well represented in the Olduvai faunal assemblages (Table 4.11). Although such small bones are most likely to be winnowed from an assemblage by hydraulic activity, their relative abundance at Olduvai (based on the MNE for each skeletal element) is almost as great as occurs in living skeletons (e.g., about 34% in living bovids) (Table 4.12).

The frequency of these elements suggests that articulated limb units containing these small bones were transported. In line with this hypothesis, among bovid size classes, large bovids show the lowest ratio of specimens per MNI on all Olduvai levels and the lowest ratio of MNE/MNI at five out of the six sites. The size of articulated units is a limitation on any agent of bone transport; larger animals would tend to be transported in smaller units. Moreover, the relative number of small limb bones in the Amboseli hyena assemblage falls well within the range expressed in each Olduvai assemblage (Tables 4.11 and 4.12). Hyenas do return articulated limbs to this den (A. Hill, pers. comm.).

In contrast, Fort Ternan should be expected to have relatively fewer phalanges, podials, and sesamoids, if such bones were not introduced to the site as part of articulated units. (The assumption here is that when small limb bones are introduced as part of articulated units, they tend to occur in abundance—i.e., the tightly packed set at the end of the limb.) This expectation is met. In the 1974 collection, only 3.7% of the specimens ($N = 346$ specimens identified to taxon and body part) were small limb bones; only 6 (2.9%) out of 205 bovid specimens were small bones (Table 4.11). This 1974 excavation was done with utmost attention to bone recovery and included careful sieving; thus, the low abundance of these small bones probably is not a matter of

**TABLE 4.10.** Ratio of Minimum Number of Bones to Minimum Number of Individuals (MNE/MNI) for Various Mammal Taxa at Olduvai

| Taxon | DK–3 | DK–2 | FLKNN–3 | FLKNN–2 | FLK "Zinj" | FLK North–6 | Mean |
|---|---|---|---|---|---|---|---|
| Bovids (all) | 10.9 | 17.3 | 11.8 | 7.6 | 15.1 | 16.8 | 13.5 |
| Small | 8.2 | 12.2 | 6.2 | 5.0 | 17.0 | 21.3 | — |
| Medium | 6.0 | 7.5 | 16.3 | 10.1 | 12.4 | 12.0 | — |
| Large | 5.4 | 11.5 | 5.5 | 4.7 | 7.0 | 3.0 | 5.5 |
| Equids | 7.5 | 4.0 | 9.0 | 6.0 | 5.6 | 1.0 | 5.5 |
| Suids | 4.2 | 3.7 | 4.0 | 15.6 | 3.4 | 4.8 | 5.9 |
| Carnivores | 3.0 | 2.5 | 3.4 | 3.0 | 5.0 | 3.5 | 3.4 |
| Giraffids | 2.6 | 2.6 | — | — | — | 3.0 | 2.3 |
| Rhinos | 2.5 | 5.0 | — | — | — | 5.0 | 4.1 |
| Hippos | 4.5 | 6.0 | — | — | — | 1.0 | 3.8 |
| Proboscideans | 3.0 | 2.0 | — | — | — | 79.5 | 2.5[a] |
| Primates | 4.0 | 7.2 | 11.0[b] | — | 1.3 | — | 5.9 |
| All taxa | 7.4 | 10.2 | 7.1 | 9.0 | 10.1 | 10.2[a] | |

[a]Excludes *Elephas recki* remains.
[b]Includes hominid remains. Without them, ratio = 3.0.

**TABLE 4.11.** Percentage Representation of Small Limb Bones (Phalanges, Podials, and Sesamoids) Relative to All Identified Specimens: Bed I Olduvai, Amboseli Hyena Den, Fort Terran

| Taxon | DK-3 | DK-2 | FLKNN-3 | FLKNN-2 | FLK "Zinj" | FLK North-6 | Amboseli | Fort Terran | |
|---|---|---|---|---|---|---|---|---|---|
| | | | | | | | | 1974 collection | Leakey collection |
| Bovid | 22 | 24 | 15 | 9 | 19 | 28 | 15 | 3 | 14 |
| Nonbovid taxa | 12 | 13 | 30[a] | 35 | 9 | 10[b] | 22 | 5 | 8 |
| Total | 19 | 21 | 20[a] | 23 | 18 | 16[b] | 17 | 4 | 13 |

[a]Includes hominid remains. Without them, nonbovid taxa = 19% and total = 16%.
[b]Includes *Elephas recki* carcass. Without elephant bones, nonbovid taxa = 3%.

78

**TABLE 4.12.** Percentage Representation of Small Limb Bones (Phalanges and Podials) Based on MNE for Bovid and Nonbovid Taxa: Bed I Olduvai and Amboseli Hyena Den

| Taxon | DK–3 | DK–2 | FLKNN–3 | FLKNN–2 | FLK "Zinj" | FLK North–6 | Amboseli |
|---|---|---|---|---|---|---|---|
| Bovids | 23 | 35 | 21 | 10 | 25 | 36 | 25 |
| Nonbovid taxa | 24 | 39 | 44[a] | 47 | 15 | 21[b] | 23 |
| Total | 24 | 34 | 29[a] | 28 | 24 | 28[b] | 25 |

[a]Includes hominid remains. Without them, nonbovid taxa = 31% and total = 23%.
[b]Includes *Elephas recki* remains. Without them, nonbovid taxa = 8% and total = 34%.

recovery bias. The Leakey collection produced a considerably higher percentage of small bones (13% over all taxa), but still lower than was manifested
at each Olduvai site or in the Amboseli hyena den (Table 4.11).[6]

The Fort Ternan assemblage, like those from Olduvai, shows considerable
variation in bone weathering stages in line with attritional processes of death,
disarticulation, and bone accumulation. However, the set of differences between the two sites mentioned previously points toward an important distinction between the bone accumulation processes at the Fort Ternan and
Bed I sites. The Olduvai assemblages show signs of accumulation over time
by processes operating on articulated carcasses, whereas the Fort Ternan
bone concentration possibly occurred only after a prolonged period of skeletal
disarticulation. The latter interpretation accords with explanations of either
water transport (Hanson, 1980: 175–176) or of some behavioral agent that
operates on isolated bones or small bone units (e.g., porcupines). For Olduvai,
however, the idea of mass mortality can be largely rejected (see Chapter 3),
and we have seen that water transport cannot have been the primary cause
of aggregation at any of these sites. Instead, based on the variety of criteria
assessed so far, the bone accumulations at Olduvai largely point to the activity
of behavioral agents, such as carnivores and hominids, which collect bones
and meat from hunted or scavenged prey animals.

[6]Klein and Cruz-Uribe (1984: 71–75) suggest that podials are relatively abundant
in assemblages that have been fragmented and partially destroyed by postdepositional agents, such as trampling. Isolated teeth are also expected to be abundant in such assemblages. Relative to Fort Ternan, however, the Olduvai assemblages exhibit *high* numbers of podials and *low* numbers of isolated teeth, while
the degree of bone fragmentation in the two sets of assemblages is about the
same. These points indicate that podial representation in the comparison between
Olduvai and Fort Ternan reflects factors other than postdepositional attrition.

# 5

# Behavioral Agents of Bone Accumulation

## Introduction

A variety of mammals and birds collect bones, either as a result of foraging or waste elimination of consumed bone. Microfaunal remains are especially susceptible to scatological concentration (Mellett, 1974). Scats of carnivores and raptorial birds, *in situ* death of burrowing animals, and water action may have been major sources of microfauna recovered from Bed I Olduvai. Since small vertebrates from these levels have not undergone taphonomic analysis, none of these processes of accumulation is necessarily discounted here. The scats of owls, hominids, or small mammalian carnivores (e.g., genets) have been suggested as causes for the accumulation of microfauna at one site (FLK North level 1/2) which was not part of this study (Andrews, 1983; Leakey, 1971: 253).

The bones of larger fauna also may be accumulated by animals. In particular, porcupines, hyenas, and leopards are known in Africa to transport bones to particular places. Meat on the bones is often consumed or, in some cases, the bones themselves are eaten or gnawed by these species. Each of these possible agents of bone collection at Olduvai will be considered in turn.

## Porcupines

Porcupines drag bones and other objects to their lairs. They tend to collect dry bones and evidently show no interest in fresh bones with meat on them. The frequent presence of incisal gnawing on bones, which porcupines practice to grind their incisors to a managable size, is the primary sign that an assemblage was collected by this animal (Brain, 1981: 139–140). In a porcupine bone collection reported by Hendey and Singer (1965), 60% of the bones showed incisal gnaw marks, while 61% of the bones were gnawed in the Nossob porcupine lair sample examined by Brain (1980). Brain (1981: 117) further reports that in eight bone accumulations attributed to porcupines a range of 22–100% of the bones had the very broad, shallow grooves typical of porcupine gnawing. Since a sizable proportion of the bones porcupines collect bear incisal gnawing, this activity is believed to be the major function of porcupine bone collecting. In the late Pleistocene assemblage at Swartklip, Klein (1975: 285) takes the extremely rare occurrence of porcupine gnawing to mean that the bones were not collected by porcupines.

The same conclusion would apply to the sites in Bed I Olduvai, since incisal gnawing (recognizable by eye) is very rare—less than 1% of the specimens.[1] Its occurrence at FLK "Zinj," and rare examples of incisal gnawing at other sites, do suggest that *Hystrix* was a minor source of bone modification and, very possibly, of bone removal at the Bed I sites. Interestingly, bones belonging to *Hystrix* have been identified from every Bed I site investigated here (Leakey, 1971: 292). Nonetheless, it appears highly unlikely that porcupines introduced more than an insignificant fraction of the bones and bone fragments to these accumulations.

## Leopards

Leopards are well known for carrying their kills into trees or other places hidden from or inaccesible to other animals. Accumulations in caves that have been ascribed partly to leopards have been reported; but these occur in situations where other taphonomic agents (particularly porcupines) helped in collecting the bones (Brain, 1981; Bunn, 1982; Simons, 1966). Brain (1969c, 1981) holds that leopards were one source of the large bone accumulations in the Swartkrans cave. Thus, in general, leopards may be potentially important bone accumulators in and around caves. However, sizable bone accumulations by leopards have not been reported in open-air settings, like those at Olduvai.

Furthermore, leopard prey consists almost entirely of small to very small ungulates (Brain, 1969c, 1981; Kingdon, 1977; Kruuk and Turner, 1967). This size range of prey reflects well the feeding strategy leopards employ—carrying whole carcasses away from the death site (Lamprecht, 1978). According to figures from the Serengeti over an 8-year study, medium-size game[2] represent less than 10% of the animals consumed by leopards (Kruuk and Turner, 1967). In contrast, granting preservation biases against small animals, medium-size animals comprise a clear majority of the individuals at every Olduvai site. More striking is the fact that large bovids, and other large to very large-size taxa, are usually as frequent as small prey (see Chapter 7). Overall, the faunal body sizes from the Olduvai accumulations are inconsistent with the body size and prey sizes of leopards.

## Hyenas

There used to be debates as to the role of hyenas in accumulating bones. Dart (1956, 1957) and Hughes (1954) argued that hyenas, and carnivores in general, do not accumulate bones. Numerous observations of hyena bone-

---

[1]In a sample of fossil bones examined under the scanning electron microscope for tooth marks and cut marks (discussed later in this chapter), six (8%) exhibited incisal gnawing. The bones bearing these marks, though, were a set of proximal ribs of *Equus oldowayensis* found at FLK "Zinj." The frequency of incisal gnawing is lower than this overall in the Bed I faunal assemblages.

[2]Size class C (72–320 kg). See Table 5.1.

**TABLE 5.1.** Definition of Body Size Classes of Macromammals, with Reference to Modern Species

| Class | Description | Average size range |
|---|---|---|
| A | Very small | 2–10 kg (e.g., duikers, dik-dik) |
| B | Small | 10–72 kg (e.g., *Gazella, Antidorcas, Aepyceros*) |
| C | Medium | 72–320 kg (includes Burchell's zebra) |
| D | Large | 320–820 kg (includes Grevy's zebra) |
| E | Very large | >820 kg (e.g., giraffe, hippo, rhino, and elephant; includes no living bovids) |

collecting behavior at dens found in various locales[3] demonstrate that hyenas do indeed accumulate substantial numbers of animal bones in certain situations. Spotted, striped, and brown hyenas were responsible for the den accumulations studied in these localities. Yet not all hyenas collect bones at their dens. This variance may be due to the fact that weaned juveniles forage with the adults in some hyena groups (Kruuk, 1972) but are provisioned with food at the den by adults in other groups (Hill, 1978, 1980b; Skinner, Davis, and Ilani, 1980). Bone accumulations observed at hyena dens are sizable, often 100 bones or more.

Hyenas are capable of inflicting extensive damage to bones, including elements from small to very large animals (Richardson, 1980). Bones from the Olduvai sites are generally broken, which suggests that hyenas were the most likely of all carnivores to have accumulated and/or modified these bone assemblages. In addition, remains of *Crocuta* (the spotted hyena) have been recovered from the DK, FLK, and FLK North localities in Bed I (Leakey, 1971: 292). Thus, at least one species of hyena lived in the vicinity of the sites during their formation.

In fact, the best evidence for carnivore activity at Olduvai comes from a study of bone damage. Scoring of bone by carnivore teeth and by the stone tools of hominids has been identified on specimens from the Olduvai sites. Study of these types of bone damage offers some initial clues about the interaction between two possible agents of bone accumulation at Olduvai—carnivores and hominids.

## Tooth Marks and Cut Marks

During study of the faunal remains from Olduvai, numerous fossils were noted to show scratches, grooves, and other damages on their surfaces. One possibility was that these damages represent cut marks made by stone ar-

[3]Examples include the Serengeti (Kruuk, 1972: 244; Sutcliffe, 1970), the southern Kalahari (Mills and Mills, 1977), the Transvaal (Bearder, 1977), Israel (Skinner et al., 1980), Amboseli (Hill, 1978, 1980b, 1984), Nairobi (Bunn 1983b), and Olorgesailie (Shipman, pers. comm.).

tifacts during butchery. Convincing evidence that these bone surface marks were produced by stone tool edges would support the presumed behavioral/causal association generally drawn between the stone artifacts and at least some of the faunal remains concentrated at the Olduvai sites. Observation of these surface marks using scanning electron microscopy (SEM) shows that some of them are indeed stone cut marks, though other types of marks, including carnivore tooth marks, also occur (Potts and Shipman, 1981).

Cut marks on animal bones have been documented previously from paleo-Indian sites (e.g., Frison, 1971, 1974; Guilday, Parmalee, and Tanner, 1962; Parmalee, 1965). A study by Guilday *et al.* (1962) defined criteria for recognizing butchery marks. In their study, only linear marks that appeared repeatedly on a number of specimens in exactly the same anatomical location were believed to be caused by human tools during meat processing. Cut marks were noted to be straight scratches, often in a parallel set of two or more. Dirt in these scratches distinguished such marks from excavation/preparation damage. These researchers described metal knife cuts as "fine and deeply incised with a V-shaped cross-section," while stone implements left a coarser, slightly more U-shaped cross-section. Yet, they added, this "U *vs.* V cross-section, and the fine *vs.* coarse scoring on bone, should not be taken too seriously on any one individual specimen." Furthermore, actual butchery was thought to be involved only if the locations of the marks made sense anatomically, that is, were positioned in areas of muscle attachment or of ligaments that directly connected bones bearing meat (Guilday *et al.*, 1962).

Multiple grooves, sometimes parallel to one another, occur on Olduvai bones. More frequently, scratches on bones were not parallel and, most often, were observed to occur singly, isolated from other such marks. The problem in identifying the causes of any of these marks is that grooves can be made on bone surfaces by a variety of processes. As Guilday *et al.* point out, metal excavation and preparation tools leave scratches. Surface scratches on Olduvai fossils often had only tiny amounts of dirt in them. Yet some of the most mineralized fossils from Olduvai displayed scratches, quite impossible to replicate with an excavation pick, without much matrix inside. Thus, this criterion for recognizing excavation/preparation damage was difficult to apply in these cases.

Of special interest is the fact that carnivore teeth produce surface damages ranging from fine scratches to broad gouging. Numerous bone fragments from the modern hyena den at Amboseli show surface scratches, including fine, shallow ones which strikingly resemble marks found on specimens from the densest patch of bone fragments at the FLK "Zinj" site. These fine, shallow scratches from the Amboseli hyena collection also closely resemble shallow experimental cut marks on fresh bone. In addition, Sutcliffe (1970) has documented sets of parallel grooves made on bone surfaces by hyenas. Thus, there is potential for misidentifying carnivore marks as stone cut marks.

These causes of bone surface damage, in addition to marks produced by rodent gnawing, root etching, abrasion by wind- and waterborne sedimentary particles, and beak marks of birds have been studied using SEM (Potts and Shipman, 1981; Shipman, 1981). Marks made by these processes on modern bones were compared with experimental cut marks made by freshly flaked stone tools. As a result, morphological criteria were defined by which cut marks of various kinds could be distinguished from similar marks produced in other ways. The preparation of epoxy replicas of modern and fossil bone surfaces for SEM examination was that developed by Walker (Rose, 1983; Walker, 1981; Walker, Hoeck, and Perez, 1978). Both the modern and the fossil bone surface replicas were examined under 20–50 × magnification.

Cut marks made when using a stone edge in different orientations and motions relative to the bone surface possess different microscopic characteristics. In general, cut marks are grooves with regular sides and show either V-shaped cross-sections or fine striations. Slicing and scraping actions with a stone edge on bone produce numerous, fine, parallel striations. These striations are confined to each major groove produced by slicing (when the edge is drawn along the direction of its long axis). On the other hand, scraping

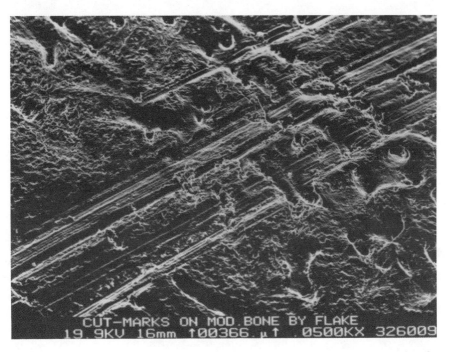

**FIGURE 5.1.** SEM micrograph of a slicing mark on a modern bone during butchery. A basalt flake was used. Since the flake was held at an oblique angle to the bone surface, the mark shows some of the characteristics of a scraping mark, namely the striations cover a broad area.

**FIGURE 5.2.** SEM micrograph of a fresh, sharp basalt flake edge (at the line of
light/dark contrast). Note the deviations along the edge, which may
produce the fine striations from slicing and scraping actions.

(drawing the edge across the bone perpedicular to the edge's long axis) leaves
the striations spread across an area of bone rather than confined to a major
groove. During use of a stone tool, a combination of these two actions is
common and produces a mixture of the two microscopic characteristics (Figure
5.1). As seen in Figure 5.2, the edge of even an extremely sharp, thin stone
flake is not perfectly straight. Probably each side to side deviation or irreg-
ularity along the edge produces its own microscopic track when the edge is
drawn across a bone. Multiple, microscopic striations are produced within
and around each groove detected by eye. Despite the fine depth of field possible with the SEM, scraping marks and very fine slicing marks generally
showed no cross-sectional shapes discernable at the standard magnifications
of up to 50 times. As experiments by Walker and Long (1977) showed, a wide
variety of cross-sections (rounded, V-shaped, and either wide or narrow at
the top) may occur during slicing actions with stone tools. In contrast, chopping
marks, produced by striking the bone surface with an edge at a roughly perpendicular angle, exhibit V-shaped cross-sections with bone often crushed
inward on the sides or at the bottom of the groove. Chopping marks usually
are broader at the top than slicing marks (because the stone edge penetrates
further into the bone) and show no fine, parallel striations (Figure 5.3).

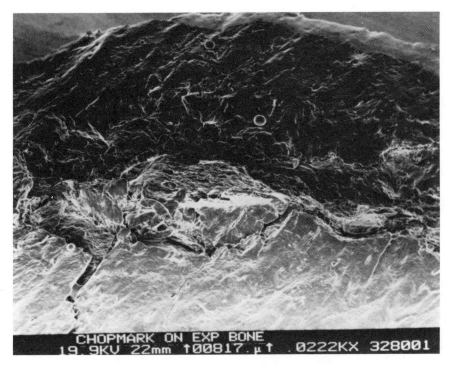

**FIGURE 5.3.** SEM micrograph of a stone chopping mark on a modern bone. Bone pieces have been crushed into the lower side of the V-shaped groove.

In our original study Potts and Shipman (1981: 577) concluded that none of the other processes that mimic cut marks at a macroscopic level produce the same microscopic characteristics as do slicing, scraping, or chopping with a stone edge. Since then, scratches on Miocene fossils from fluvial settings in Pakistan and experimental trampling of bones in sands have demonstrated that damage produced by animal trampling may mimic cut marks at a microscopic level (Behrensmeyer, Gordon, and Yanagi, 1986). Not only does trampling in sands and gravels mimic the microscopic *effects* of stone tool use, but it also replicates the process—the interaction between a stone edge and bone. This research and others (Andrews and Cook, 1985; Fiorillo, 1984; Oliver, 1984) mean that the sediments in which bones are found become highly important in recognizing cut marks. Although rounded pebbles occur at locality DK, the sites of Bed I Olduvai are characterized by homogeneous, fine-grain silts. Angular particles of sand or grit do not appear to be a factor in damaging the surfaces of bones at these sites. Behrensmeyer *et al.* (1986) also comment that cut marks illustrated in the original SEM study of Olduvai (Potts, 1982; Potts and Shipman, 1981) were not replicated during trampling experiments.

Marks produced by carnivore teeth on fresh bone and by metal tools on

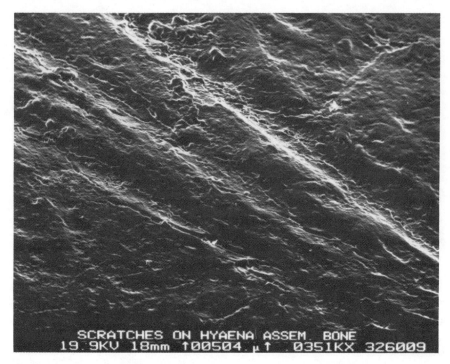

SCRATCHES ON HYAENA ASSEM BONE
19 9KV 18mm ↑00504 μ↑ 0351KX 326009

**FIGURE 5.4.** SEM micrograph of three grooves caused by carnivore teeth on a
modern bone from the Amboseli hyena den. Fine striations are
absent.

fossils possess microscopic characteristics that differ from stone tool cut marks.
These features proved particularly significant for interpreting scratches on
bones from Olduvai. Tooth scratches made by carnivores show round or flat
bases and lack the fine, parallel, microscopic striations of slicing and scraping
marks (Figure 5.4). Metal excavation or preparation tools leave grooves with
irregular edges, and bridges of fossil bone often connect the opposite sides
of each groove; they typically are not V-shaped in cross-section and do not
show fine striations (Figure 5.5). All of these patterns mentioned so far were
observed in the control set of bones in which the causes of damage are known
(Potts and Shipman, 1981; Shipman, 1981).

During this study of the Olduvai fauna, a sample of 76 fossil bone surfaces
from sites in Beds I and II were examined using SEM. This sample was
chosen to represent the range of surface damage types as seen by eye, as
well as to cover a wide range of skeletal parts and taxa. From this sample,
86 marks were classified according to their microscopic traits; some bone surfaces showed more than one type of mark. Table 5.2 gives the frequency of
specimens with each type of mark. Of these marks, 28% more closely resemble

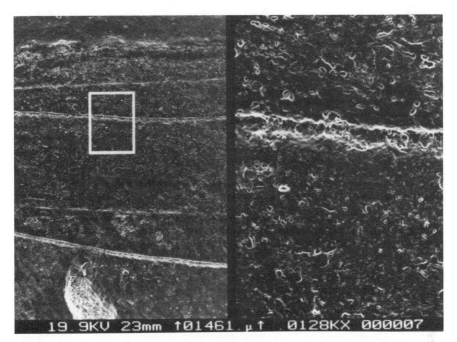

**FIGURE 5.5.** *Left:* SEM micrograph of a set of fine preparator's scratches made with metal tools on a fossil bone. *Right:* A close-up of the region enclosed by the white rectangle. Note the groove's irregular sides and bridges of bone joining the sides of the groove together in some areas. No fine striations are visible.

cut marks of various kinds than damage caused by any other process investigated so far (Figure 5.6).

All six sites studied from Bed I contained bones with cut marks and grooves most closely matched by tooth scratches and gnawing made by carnivores and rodents. The 48 tooth-marked bones included six proximal ribs of *Equus oldowayensis* bearing the broad, parallel grooves of rodent gnawing. Almost all of the remaining marks bear a closer similarity to carnivore tooth scratches. At a macroscopic level, these latter grooves do not resemble human gnawing of bone as described, for example, by Brain (1969a) and Binford (1981: 147–148). Instead, the tooth scratches were produced either (1) by strong impact from a ridge of enamel, such as in the action of a carnivore carnassial tooth, or (2) by a relatively sharp cusp drawn with considerable force over the bone surface without other teeth or cusps leaving a mark on the surface (since these marks often appear in isolation). The action of the protruding cusps of carnivore teeth fits this latter pattern, while the morphology of hominid teeth is incongruent with such marks. Significantly, slicing and chopping marks were present on at least one specimen from FLKNN–2, the level without

**TABLE 5.2.** Frequencies and Locations of Different Types of Marks on Fossils from Beds I and II, Olduvai Gorge"

| Type of mark | Number of specimen | Locations | Taxa | Sites |
|---|---|---|---|---|
| Slicing | 14 | Metatarsal shaft (2), radius shaft (2), limbshaft fragment (2), humerus shaft, metacarpal shaft, proximal ulna, distal metacarpal, rib shaft, tibial crest, proximal radius | *Elephas recki, Kobus sigmoidalis, Equus oldowayensis,* giraffid indet., small bovid indet., large bovid indet., bovid indet., medium–large mammal indet. | DK–2 and 3, FLKNN–2 and 3, FLK "Zinj," FLKN–6, MNK Main |
| Scraping | 5 | Scapula blade, humerus shaft, radius shaft, metatarsal shaft, limb shaft fragment | *Kobus sigmoidalis, Equus oldowayensis,* giraffid indet., med. mammal indet., large mammal indet. | DK–3, FLK "Zinj," MNK Main |
| Chopping | 5 | Metacarpal shaft (2), metapodial shaft, proximal phalanx shaft, limb shaft fragment | *Parmularius altidens, Equus oldowayensis,* bovid indet., mammal indet. | DK–2 and 3, FLKNN–2, MNK Main |
| Tooth/gnawing | 48 | Limb shaft fragment (12), proximal rib (6), humerus shaft (4), rib shaft (3), femur shaft (3), tibial crest (2), metacarpal shaft (2), proximal metacarpal (2), scapula glenoid, proximal ulna, radius shaft, radioulna shaft, mandibular corpus, hyoid, parietal vault, proximal femur, acetabulum, distal tibia, fibula shaft, metatarsal shaft, cuneiform, indet. fragment | *Kobus sigmoidalis, Megalotragus kattwinkeli, Elephas recki, Deinotherium* sp;; *Equus oldowayensis, Cercocebus, Homo habilis,* Tragelaphini indet., Reduncini indet., Antilopini indet., medium–large bovid indet., medium mammal indet., large mammal indet., very large mammal indet., mammal indet., indet. | DK–2 and 3, FLKNN–2 and 3, FLK "Zinj," FLKN–6, FLKN Deino. level, MNK Main, TK Upper Floor |

"Seventy-six surfaces were examined. Ten of these surfaces possessed marks classified into two different types of marks. Number in parentheses after skeletal location signifies the number of times different specimens showed a particular type of mark in that location. From Potts and Shipman (1981).

stone artifacts. Therefore, association with stone tools is not a prerequisite for the occurrence of bones with cut marks (also shown by Bunn 1981: 576). In addition, surface marks on several bones from the elephant carcass at FLK North–6 were examined. Shipman (in press) and Bunn (1982) have confirmed the presence of tool slicing marks on metapodials and ribs of this elephant.

Evidence for cut-marked bones at the Olduvai sites makes it highly unlikely that the spatial associations between these bones and artifacts are entirely accidental. On the other hand, in this small sample of bones studied by SEM, carnivore tooth marks outnumber stone tool cut marks, and in Shipman's continued studies (1986a, 1986b) they are about as numerous as cut marks. Hyenas were the main source of the modern analogues for carnivore tooth damage. The great similarity between many of the Olduvai bone surface marks and the modern hyena marks is further reason to consider this potential bone collector as a taphonomic agent at Olduvai. The abundance of such tooth marks in samples of surface-modified bones[4] indicates that hyenas and possibly other carnivores may have affected significantly the ancient faunal patterns at the Olduvai sites.

Tooth scratches on bone surfaces are not the only basis for this idea. Bones found in or around known dens of spotted hyenas in Kenya show a number of bone breakage patterns that relate to specific ways these hyenas treat bones. Figures 5.7–5.11 illustrate the most notable damage patterns: holes in the articular ends of long bones, especially through the proximal articular ends of antelope metacarpals and metatarsals; circular or oval pits into areas of cancellous bone; gnaw marks that are typified by a scraped, dissolved, and often sinuous appearance; abrasion confined to the articular surfaces of long bones, which apparently comes from sucking on the epiphyseal ends; and bone flakes, wider than they are long, with artifact-like platforms and gently curving bulbs of force. My impression from examining at least some of the bones associated with several hyena dens is that under varying circumstances, possibly linked with the diverse habits of hyenas themselves, bones in different dens show idiosyncratic damage patterns. Hence, not all bone accumulations made by hyenas will show even these very notable damages found in the den assemblages I examined.

Nevertheless, in all of the Bed I levels these same special damage patterns occur, although they are rare. Figures 5.12–5.15 provide some examples. Figure 5.13 compares the damage found on a modern bovid metacarpal with strikingly similar damage on a bovid metacarpal from DK–2. FLK "Zinj" (Figure 5.15) and sieved material from FLKNN–2 and FLKNN–3 furnished bone flakes that match those from the modern hyena den at Amboseli in shape and metric characteristics. The flakes from the Olduvai levels often possessed

---

[4]Of the surface-modified bones studied by Shipman (1987) and Potts and Shipman (1981), 42–56% were so tooth-marked.

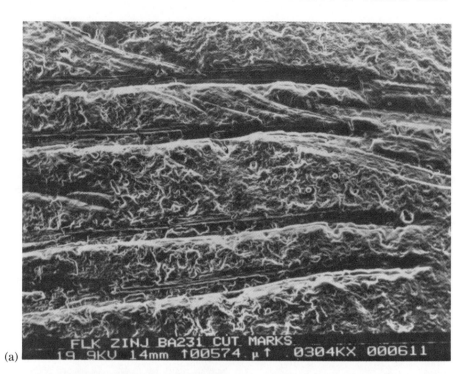

(a)

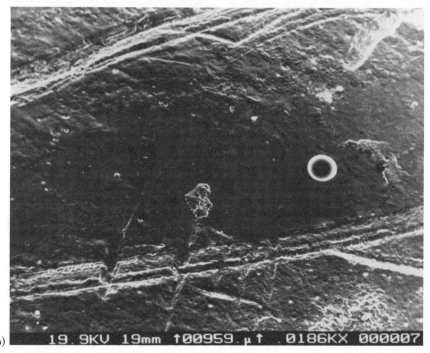

(b)

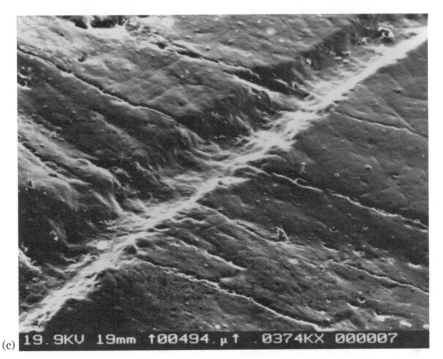

(c) 19.9KV 19mm ↑00494.µ↑ .0374KX 000007

**FIGURE 5.6.** *(a)* SEM micrograph of a set of slicing and scraping marks on a specimen from FLK "Zinj." *(b)* SEM micrograph of two slicing marks (going across the photo) with overlying carnivore tooth marks that intersect the slicing marks at an angle. This specimen is from FLK "Zinj." The tooth marks interrupt the sides of the slicing mark grooves and the fine striations within them. *(c)* SEM micrograph of a carnivore tooth mark on a specimen from DK.

cortical bone platforms combined with dorsal surfaces consisting partly of a broken surface of a long bone shaft and part of the marrow cavity. Thus, flake detachment, which occurred from the inside of the marrow cavity, was accomplished as portrayed in Figure 5.16. This same, specific flake pattern was observed in the Amboseli hyena den collection.

Although bone flakes, of course, can be made with a hammerstone (see p. 112), the similarity between this and other damage patterns noted on the Olduvai bones to those made specifically by hyenas suggests that a hyena-like carnivore was responsible for at least some of the modified bones at these sites. This evidence documents further observations made by Leakey (1971: 43, 50) of carnivore modifications to bones from the Bed I sites.

Furthermore, it is clear that carnivores damaged bones directly at the site. The presence of certain types of gnawing and breakage attributed to carnivores implies that the damage occurred at each site. That is, the degree

**FIGURE 5.7.** Damage by spotted hyenas: Proximal articular surface of a bovid metatarsal from the den at Amboseli. Holes produced in the proximal ends of metapodials are common in this hyena den bone assemblage.

**FIGURE 5.8.** Damage by spotted hyenas: Shallow, oval pit in the cancellous bone of a scapula found at a den in Masai Mara Reserve.

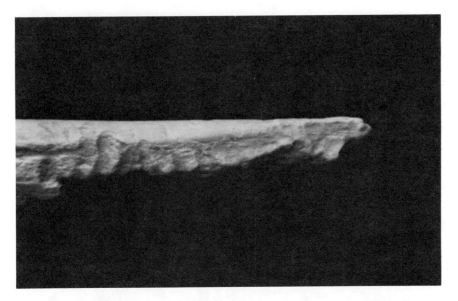

**FIGURE 5.9.** Damage by spotted hyenas: Gnawing marks and rounding of bone on a metacarpal shaft from the modern hyena den assemblage at Amboseli.

of modification is inconsistent with the idea that these particular bones were carried to these sites after modification by carnivores elsewhere. Hence, while there is evidence for hominid modification of bones at the artifact sites, we also have evidence for carnivore activity right at these same places.

Does this evidence mean that carnivores may have been the primary bone collector at the Olduvai sites?

In response to this question, there are two important points to consider. First, the actual number of identifiable carnivore tooth marks versus tool cut marks does not specify whether carnivores or hominids were more important in modifying bones brought to each site. All observable surface marks and the carnivore damage patterns described here make up a small fraction of the total damage inflicted on the bones at each site. Although progress is being made in the study of bone damage (Bonnichsen and Sorg, in press), the vast majority of bone modifications from Olduvai are fractures that currently cannot be ascribed safely to either hominids or carnivores. The percentage of specimens that exhibit tooth marks is difficult to calculate due to problems of discerning carnivore tooth damages, in all their wide variety, from other possible causes of modification to fossil bones. Modern carnivore assemblages do not present this problem: Since one is fairly confident that

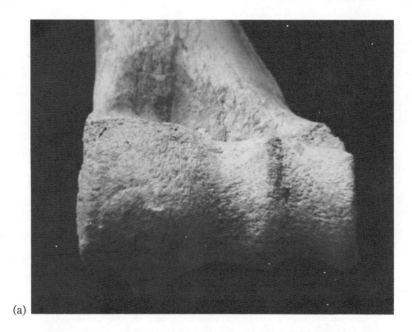

(a)

(b)

FIGURE 5.10. Damage by spotted hyenas: Surface deterioration and rounding observed on the articular surfaces of *(a)* a distal humerus and *(b)* a distal metacarpal from the Amboseli assemblage.

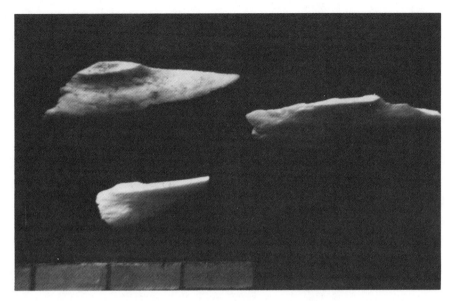

**FIGURE 5.11.** Damage by spotted hyenas: Three bone flakes from the Amboseli den. Each shows a cortex platform *(at top)* and gently curving bulb of force.

all modifications are due to carnivores, the vast majority of damages can be counted as tooth marks. In the Olduvai assemblages, definitely less than 25%, and probably less than 15%, of the bone specimens exhibit damage patterns that are apparently diagnostic of carnivores (as illustrated in this chapter, Haynes [1980a], Binford [1981], and other sources). However, since most of the bone modifications cannot be safely attributed to any specific cause, these percentages may underestimate the frequency of carnivore-gnawed bones to an unknown degree. Similarly, the number of bones with tool cut marks is bound to greatly underestimate the frequency of bones actually damaged by hominids.

A second point is that the causes of bone damage may not provide conclusive evidence as to the primary cause of bone accumulation (Potts, 1984a; see p. 143). Because carcasses undergo a series of modifications by hunters and scavengers, bones may bear the marks of several agents of damage. Yet the transport of bones away from death sites may occur at any time during the sequence of visits by animals to carcasses. In other cases, scavengers may modify bones after they have become part of an accumulation produced by other agents. Thus, evidence for bone damage by carnivores or hominids does

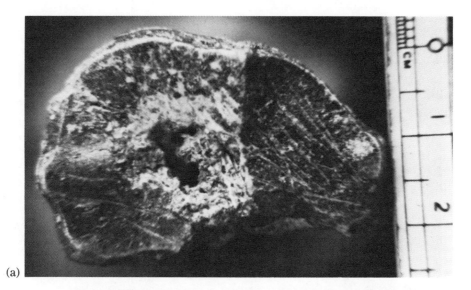

(a)

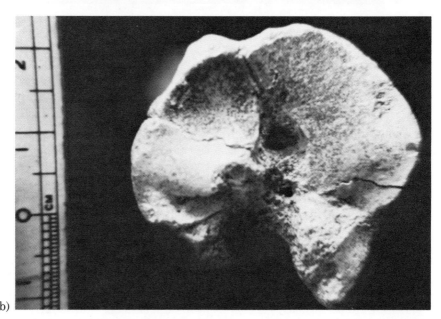

(b)

**FIGURE 5.12.** *(a)* Tragelaphine metacarpal from site FLKNN–2 showing a hole
and SEM-analyzed tooth scratches in the proximal articular surface. *(b)* Pits and irregular damage to proximal end of a reduncine
metatarsal from FLKNN–2. The pits are an enlargement of a natural indentation in the bone. These are also found in metapodials
from the Amboseli hyena den.

**FIGURE 5.13.** Holes into the marrow cavity through the proximal ends of *(left)* a bovid metacarpal from DK–2 and *(right)* a bovid metacarpal from the Amboseli hyena den.

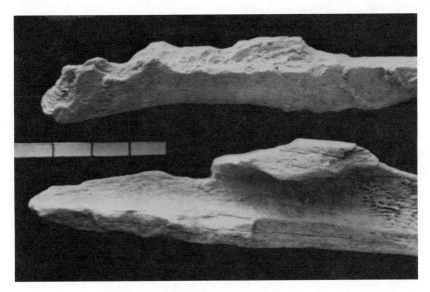

**FIGURE 5.14.** *Top:* From FLKNN–2, the border of a left innominate showing sinuous, rounded appearance typical of hyena-gnawed bones. *Bottom:* From the modern hyena den at Amboseli, a long bone shaft showing sinuous, rounded appearance.

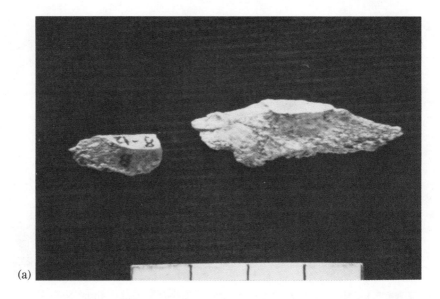

(a)

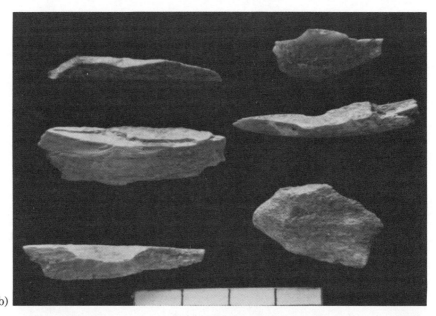

(b)

**FIGURE 5.15.** From FLK "Zinj": *(a)* two bone flakes with cortical platforms and
gently curving bulbs of force, and *(b)* a variety of bone flakes with
platforms and bulbs. Several of these show the special pattern
that results from broken diaphysis flaking, also seen in the Amboseli hyena den. The scale is in centimeters.

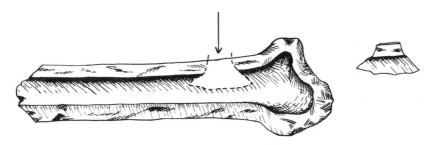

FIGURE 5.16. Diagram of special flake pattern found at FLK, FLKNN–2/3, and the Amboseli hyena den. *(Left)* Force is applied to the cortex of a broken limb bone shaft, adjacent to the broken surface. *(Right)* Dorsal surface of the resulting flake: The platform is cortex; the dorsal surface consists of the original broken diaphysis surface *(at top)* and the curving marrow cavity surface *(at bottom)*.

not imply that either one was primarily responsible for the transport and concentration of bones at Olduvai. Instead, we need to rely on other skeletal and contextual data to assess the relative contributions of carnivores and hominids as agents of bone concentration.

## Carnivore Activity at Olduvai

Based on modifications to the fossil bones, hyenas (or a carnivore comparable in the way it damaged bones) must be considered as an agent of bone accumulation at ancient Olduvai. A variety of criteria have been suggested by previous researchers for distinguishing carnivore bone collections from those produced by hominids. These suggestions have come from studies of modern hyena lairs and alleged ancient ones and also from observations of damage inflicted by various living carnivores on carcasses. Table 5.3 lists various points of evidence that, according to a number of sources, indicate whether carnivores were primarily responsible for the concentration of bones in ancient settings. Klein (1975, 1980) was among the first to give explicit criteria for judging the role of hyenas in accumulating bones; his criteria are incorporated in this list.

The usefulness of each criterion in Table 5.3 needs to be assessed, as it is clear that researchers disagree about the power of some of these criteria to distinguish hyena/carnivore accumulations from other types of bone concen-

**TABLE 5.3.** Possible Indicators of Bone Accumulation by Carnivores, Especially Hyenas

| Indicators |
| --- |
| 1. Lack of associated artifacts |
| 2. Size of mammals represented |
| 3. Representation of carnivore remains |
| 4. Sedimentary evidence of burrows or other aspects of den structure |
| 5. Pattern of skeletal element representation |
| 6. Cranial bone representation in large bovids |
| 7. Frequency of complete bones |
| 8. Patterns of bone damage: |
|    a. Fracture patterns of long bone shafts |
|    b. Bone flaking |
|    c. Degree of bone fragmentation |
|    d. Epiphysis-first destruction of long bones |
|    e. Differential preservation of epiphyses and elements |
|    f. Relative timing of carnivore and hominid damage |

trations. The modern hyena den at Amboseli, Kenya, provides a useful source of data to examine many of the criteria in the list. In addition, this latter assemblage shows several characteristics that are strikingly similar to some classic features of archeological sites. Thus, it is appropriate to describe this modern hyena assemblage at this point.

*Amboseli Spotted Hyena Den*

The bone assemblage from the Amboseli den was accumulated by spotted hyenas *(Crocuta crocuta)*. It consists of 1694 specimens systematically collected from the den in 1975 and 1977 by Hill (1981, 1983, 1984). As described by Hill, the bones were left by hyenas in a natural, open-air depression (about 20 m long and 4 m wide) which was cut into the dry lake flats at Amboseli. The den has several entrances situated on the border of this depression, leading off from the central area of bone accumulation. Specimens of large mammals (> 2 kg) make up most of this assemblage (99%); 38% of these specimens were identified taxonomically to at least family level. The others were non-identified fragments and include 686 pieces of limb bone shaft (66% of the unidentified fragments). Based on bone weathering stages (p. 51) and observations of the den, hyenas had accumulated this large number of bones over at least a 10-year period. This faunal assemblage falls well within the range of sample sizes, degree of spatial concentration, and degree of bone fragmentation exhibited by the sites of Bed I Olduvai.

Mammals in size-class C (Table 5.1), especially wildebeest and Burchell's zebra, dominate this assemblage by far (Table 5.4). Mammals in size-class B

**TABLE 5.4.** Percentage Frequency of Mammal Taxa in the Amboseli Hyena Den[a]

| Taxon | Size class (Table 5.1) | E (N = 640) | MNE (N = 435) | MNSU (N = 140) | MNI (N = 52) |
|---|---|---|---|---|---|
| Bovids: | | | | | |
| *Gazella thomsoni* | B | 3% | 4% | 5% | 8% |
| *Gazella granti* | B | 6 | 7 | 11 | 10 |
| *Tragelaphus scriptus* | B | 0.3 | 0.5 | 0.7 | 2 |
| Sheep/goat | B | 0.2 | 0.2 | 0.7 | 2 |
| *Connochaetes taurinus* | C | 48 | 53 | 40 | 33 |
| *Bos taurus* | D | 3 | 3 | 5 | 6 |
| *Syncerus caffer* | D | 0.2 | 0.2 | 0.7 | 2 |
| Indeterminate | — | 16 | 1 | — | — |
| Equids: | | | | | |
| *Equus burchelli* | C | 21 | 27 | 26 | 23 |
| *Equus asinus* | C | 0.8 | 0.9 | 3 | 4 |
| Suid: | | | | | |
| *Phacochoerus aethiopius* | B | 0.2 | 0.2 | 0.7 | 2 |
| Carnivores: | | | | | |
| *Panthera leo* | C | 0.2 | 0.2 | 0.7 | 2 |
| *Panthera pardus* | B/C | 0.3 | 0.5 | 1 | 2 |
| *Felis caracal* | B | 0.6 | 0.7 | 2 | 2 |
| *Canis mesomelas* | B | 0.3 | 0.5 | 0.7 | 2 |
| *Crocuta crocuta* | B/C | 0.3 | 0.5 | 1 | 2 |

[a]Four methods of estimating taxonomic abundance are provided: Number of specimens (E), minimum number of elements (MNE), skeletal units (MNSU), and individuals (MNI). See Chapter 7 for explanation of these methods.

**TABLE 5.5.** The MNE from the Limb and Axial Regions for Major Mammal Taxa in the Amboseli Hyena Den[a]

| Taxon | Forelimb | Hindlimb | Total limb | Axial |
|---|---|---|---|---|
| All bovids | 119 | 92 | 237 | 39 |
| Small | 16 | 16 | 35 | 11 |
| Medium | 93 | 72 | 190 | 27 |
| Large | 8 | 2 | 11 | 0 |
| Equids | 41 | 44 | 103 | 15 |
| Suids | 0 | 1 | 1 | 0 |
| Carnivores | 2 | 2 | 4 | 3 |
| Totals | 162 | 139 | 345 | 57 |

[a]"Total limb" includes forelimb, hindlimb, and bones not specified to either limb.

are relatively rare (e.g., only 10% of the ungulate specimens, but 24% of the MNI for ungulates). Size-class D is even more rare (3% of specimens, 8% of MNI), and animals from classes A and E are largely absent.[5] Bird specimens, including ostrich, do occur but make up only 0.9% of the assemblage. The representation of carnivores is also low. Although they comprise 10% of the MNI, only 1.7% of the number of specimens and 2.4% of the MNE are of carnivores. Suids show a similar pattern of representation. An extremely low number of specimens (or MNE) per MNI for carnivores and suids suggests that the collection or treatment of these taxa at the den differed from that of bovids and equids.[6]

Table 5.5 shows the number of forelimb, hindlimb, and axial bones preserved at the den for each major mammal taxon. The dominance of limb bones over axials is clear, as expected in an assemblage of bones transported away from death sites. Limb bones (MNE = 345) outnumber axial elements (MNE = 57) by over 6 to 1. This contrasts greatly with the ratio in living ungulates, in which axial bones are at least 50% more numerous than limb bones.

A high number of complete, undamaged specimens also occurs in the hyena den assemblage. Out of 640 specimens identified to taxon, 27% are complete. Podials and phalanges contribute greatly to this high frequency of whole bones: 83% of 75 carpals and tarsals, and 76% of 38 phalanges are complete. Over 9% of the identified sample consists of complete major long bones; out of 180 metacarpal and metatarsal specimens identified to family level, 22% are whole. Observations of hyenas and other carnivores in the wild indicate that podials and phalanges are either consumed completely or left undamaged (Richardson, 1980: 113). In addition, the metapodials of ungulates are thick-walled and strongly constructed; thus, they are fairly resistant to fracture (Voorhies, 1969: 20). Yet the fact that ungulate metapodials bear little meat or marrow,

[5]Two specimens of springhare *(Pedetes)* were present (size-class A).

[6]E/MNI for bovids = 47.3; equids = 9.9; carnivores = 2.2; suids = 1.0.

and so are not so valuable nutritionally as other long bones, may best explain why metapodials occur complete more often than other major limb bones.

To evaluate whether carnivores contributed importantly to the process of bone concentration at Olduvai each aspect listed in Table 5.3 will be considered. As this is done, it is pertinent to compare the features of the Amboseli hyena accumulation with criteria proposed by other investigators to be diagnostic of carnivore bone accumulations.

*Artifact Associations*

The first point in this list is the absence of artifacts directly associated with bones. Both Klein (1975) and Brain (1981) use this criterion as one of several to infer the relative role of carnivores versus hominids in producing fossil bone accumulations. However, others have pointed out that artifact–bone associations, including those at Olduvai, may be spurious (e.g., Binford, 1981). It is clear that the causes of associations need to be tested and, as we have seen, stone tool cut marks and carnivore tooth marks both occur on the bones from Olduvai. With regard to the issue of artifact–bone associations, FLKNN–2 is especially important to examine. This site contained no stone artifacts. With no such artifacts to bias the interpretation, the remains from FLKNN–2 help to test whether faunal material alone can be used to discern processes of bone accumulation. Accordingly, evidence from bones and their geologic context needs to be examined.[7]

*Size of Mammals*

Hyenas kill and scavenge ungulates of medium size (class C) most frequently (Kruuk, 1972; Pienaar, 1969). This is seen particularly in bone accumulations made by spotted hyenas, whereas brown and striped hyenas sometimes concentrate the bones of small prey animals (Mills and Mills, 1978; Skinner, Davis, and Ilani, 1980). The assemblage from the spotted hyena den at Amboseli is made up mostly of medium-sized ungulates. Medium-sized individuals constitute 61% of the minimum number of antelopes in the Swartklip assemblage studied by Klein, a figure that is consistent with a hyena origin for that assemblage (Klein, 1975). However, the majority of large mammals living in savanna habitats are medium-sized ungulates. Therefore, any accumulation

[7]After the original study of these six Olduvai sites was completed (Potts, 1982), the author had the opportunity to analyze another fossil bone concentration excavated in upper Bed I which lacked associated artifacts. This site, previously undescribed, is called "Long K." It is situated in fine-grain silts in the lake margin facies and occurs about halfway between DK and the FLK site complex. The bone assemblage from Long K exhibits a number of important similarities to that from FLKNN–2. In this analysis of processes of carnivore bone accumulation, comments about Long K will be made where applicable. Description and full analysis of this site is in preparation.

**TABLE 5.6.** Percentage Frequency of Bovid Size Classes According to the MNI and the E for the Olduvai Sites and the Amboseli Hyena Den

| Site | Small (%) | | Medium (%) | | Large (%) | | Total (N) | |
|------|-----|-----|-----|-----|-----|-----|-----|-----|
|      | MNI | E   | MNI | E   | MNI | E   | MNI | E   |
| Amboseli den | 34 | 17 | 53 | 78 | 13 | 5 | 32 | 389 |
| FLK North–6 | 30 | 38 | 50 | 58 | 20 | 4 | 10 | 216 |
| FLK "Zinj" | 35 | 35 | 50 | 59 | 15 | 6 | 20 | 449 |
| FLKNN–2 | 7 | 5 | 50 | 75 | 43 | 20 | 14 | 154 |
| FLKNN–3 | 22 | 14 | 67 | 81 | 11 | 5 | 18 | 245 |
| DK–2 | 21 | 23 | 58 | 57 | 21 | 20 | 19 | 306 |
| DK–3 | 24 | 18 | 41 | 57 | 35 | 25 | 17 | 240 |
| Long K | 43 | 43 | 53 | 56 | 3 | 1 | 30 | 396 |

of bones of macromammals, regardless of cause, can be expected to show a frequency of 50% or more for mammals in size-class C. Nonetheless, it is useful to note whether the Olduvai assemblages are consistent with this fact.

Indeed, all of the sites from Bed I Olduvai show a prevalance of medium-sized ungulates. The frequencies of different taxa, examined in detail in Chapter 7, document this point. Table 5.6 provides body size frequencies for bovids from the six Olduvai sites and from the Amboseli hyena den. At Olduvai, medium-sized bovids do not fall below 50% of MNI or of the number of specimens at any site except DK–3. Only one assemblage (FLKNN–3) shows an MNI above 60% for medium-sized bovids, such as occurs at Swartklip. However, over 70% of the bovid specimens from two sites—FLKNN–2 and FLKNN–3—are assigned to this size class, a feature that is also found in the Amboseli hyena assemblage. Overall, though, bovid size frequencies do not distinguish clearly among these assemblages which might be attributable to carnivores or another specific bone collector. Obviously, "consistency indicators" cannot be expected to discriminate between carnivore and hominid modes of bone concentration.

## Carnivore Representation

In general, the relative frequencies of various species is a poor indicator of the causes of death and accumulation of faunal remains (Brain, 1980: 123; Shipman and Phillips-Conroy, 1977). This is due to the fact that prey preferences of carnivores, including hyenas, may vary greatly over time and from region to region (Curio, 1976; Kruuk, 1972). Yet one feature believed to characterize the bone accumulations of carnivores is a relatively high representation of carnivore remains (Brain, 1981; Klein, 1975). In Klein's study of Swartklip, carnivores accounted for 22% of the MNI for ungulates and carnivores combined (MNI = 205). In contrast, late Pleistocene archeological sites in South Africa show less than 13% carnivores (Klein, 1980). A very high percentage of small carnivores (20–40%) has been observed in the dens of brown and striped hyenas.[8] The accumulation at Swartklip also may have been produced by brown hyenas (Klein, 1975).

However, Sutcliffe (1970) has reported that carnivore remains are not common in the dens of spotted hyenas living today in the Serengeti. In fact, the data from Amboseli indicate that this may generally be the case for the bone accumulations of spotted hyenas (Table 5.4). In this assemblage, carnivores make up only about 2% of the specimens and the MNE. Carnivores account for 12.5% of the MNI, but this is still within the range of carnivore frequencies in assemblages believed to be of human origin in southern Africa and below that thought to be diagnostic of carnivore accumulations.[9] In addition, no carnivores are reported out of 66 identified mammal specimens collected from a spotted hyena den in the Namib Desert (Henschel, Tilson, and von Blottnitz, 1979). Consequently, the frequency of carnivores is not necessarily a good indicator of bone concentration by spotted hyenas.

The faunal assemblages from Olduvai exhibit a wide range of carnivore frequencies. FLKNN–2, the site that lacked artifacts, has the lowest representation of carnivores—approximately 1.5% of the specimens, which compares well with the carnivore frequency in the modern Amboseli den, but only 4% of the total MNI for mammals. Carnivores represent between 5 and 21% of MNI in the Olduvai faunas associated with stone artifacts. These frequencies span the known range of carnivore representation in both hyena- and human-produced bone assemblages (see Figures 7.2–7.6).

*Sedimentary Evidence*

Burrows are a typical feature of dens used by hyenas. At the site of Swartklip, bones were found in "pockets" of sediment, which suggested to Klein (1975) that the bones had been accumulated in burrows.

The bones recovered from the Olduvai sites did not occur in clusters similar to bones accumulated in the burrows of a den. Clear microstratigraphic evidence for a den structure (e.g., one or more filled-in burrows) is lacking for all Bed I sites. However, Leakey (1971: 43) remarks that the sediments of FLKNN–2 consisted of two parts—a fine-grain tuff and a clay. The clay occurred in patches at the base and central portions of the level, and it was in

[8]In eight dens of brown hyenas in the Kalahari, carnivores made up an average of 39% of the macromammal specimens (Mills and Mills, 1978). Carnivores comprised 23% of the MNI in dens of striped hyenas in Israel (Skinner *et al.*, 1980).

[9]As noted previously, carnivores make up less than 13% of late Pleistocene bone assemblages attributed to humans (Klein, 1980). In Brain's (1981) study, 13% carnivores is the highest figure for bone accumulations attributed to humans; the average is 7.3%. Based on MNI, these percentages reflect the number of carnivores divided by the total number of large mammals (not carnivore–ungulate ratios, as defined by Brain).

these clay patches where the fossils mainly were found. The significance of this pattern, which was not observed in any other level, is unclear. The clustering of bones may signify their occurrence in collapsed burrows; but clear stratigraphic evidence for such burrows at the excavated site does not occur now nor did it occur, apparently, during excavation. The bones collected from the Amboseli hyena lair come from the loose silts lying in a surface depression on the plains. The sediment immediately outside this depressed den area, where bones are relatively scarce, consists of a hard caliche. It is speculative that this dual sedimentary pattern is a valid analog for the context of fossils at FLKNN–2.

### Skeletal Representation

Sutcliffe (1970) has suggested that bovid metapodials and distal humeri are relatively numerous in assemblages accumulated by spotted hyenas. Hill (1983) also has noted this pattern in the Amboseli hyena assemblage. Furthermore, as shown in Table 5.7, radioulnae are also frequent in this modern den assemblage. Altogether, metapodials, radioulnae, and distal humeri comprise almost 40% of the MNE for bovids in this spotted hyena den.

Table 5.7 also shows the frequencies of these skeletal elements at the Olduvai sites. The artifact sites are consistent in having combined frequencies of metapodials, radioulnae, and distal humeri of 26% or lower. The nonartifact sites of FLKNN–2, Long K, and the Amboseli den have combined frequencies of 27% or higher. Only at FLKNN–2 are the frequencies of these three elements consistently high. In fact, with a combined frequency of 50% of all elements, FLKNN–2 exhibits a greater relative abundance of these elements than in the Amboseli den. This is also true when the bovid data are broken down by size class. In these aspects of assemblage composition, therefore, FLKNN–2 differs from the other Olduvai sites. Not only does it align more closely with the den assemblage at Amboseli than do the artifact sites, it also

**TABLE 5.7.** Percentage Frequency of Bovid Metacarpals and Metatarsals, Radius/Ulnae, and Distal Humeri in the Assemblages at Amboseli and Olduvai, Based on Total MNE

| Site | Total MNE | % Metapodials | % Radius/ulna | % Distal humerus |
|------|-----------|---------------|---------------|------------------|
| Amboseli den | 296 | 15 | 15 | 8 |
| FLK North–6 | 168 | 5 | 8 | 4 |
| FLK "Zinj" | 303 | 11 | 9 | 6 |
| FLKNN–2 | 107 | 19 | 18 | 12 |
| FLKNN–3 | 155 | 7 | 7 | 2 |
| DK–2 | 329 | 8 | 8 | 5 |
| DK–3 | 197 | 15 | 4 | 6 |
| Long K | 288 | 10 | 9 | 8 |

shows the suggested pattern of skeletal parts for hyena accumulations as well as, or better than, the modern spotted hyena assemblage at Amboseli. Bone assemblages from the artifact sites do form a continuum: FLKNN–3, for example, shows the lowest frequencies for these three skeletal parts (16% combined), while DK–3 (25%) and FLK "Zinj" (26%) exhibit the highest percentages.

Furthermore, FLKNN–2 shows a pattern of skeletal region representation that differs from what occurs at the artifact sites in Bed I—namely, a clear prevalence of forelimb bones over hindlimb elements across all bovid size classes (see Figure 8.1).[10] Some bovid size classes represented at the artifact sites do show a forelimb dominance, but never to the extent observed for small, medium, and large bovids at FLKNN–2. In Chapter 8, we will take a look at the significance of this pattern of preservation at FLKNN–2 and the other Olduvai sites. In that chapter, it is pointed out that the predominance of forelimb elements in a transported bone accumulation may relate to the relative timing of access to carcasses by bone collectors. For the moment, it is notable that there is an obvious difference in skeletal region representation between FLKNN–2 and the artifact sites, and that it may indicate a difference in the process of acquiring bones from ungulates in the environment. At the Amboseli den, there is a slight dominance of forelimb over hindlimb elements, evident in medium and large bovids.

## Cranial Representation in Large Bovids

In Pleistocene archeological bone concentrations studied by Klein (1975), the larger the species, the better it is represented in an assemblage by cranial pieces than by postcranial parts. At Swartklip, Klein noticed that the reverse was true: Large bovids were better represented by postcranial bones, whereas cranial pieces were more common for smaller bovids. Klein views this pattern as a reasonable carnivore strategy: The limbs of large animals are more portable than skulls to carnivore collectors.

The Amboseli hyena accumulation does not exhibit this pattern very strongly. The representation of cranial bones[11] for small, medium, and large bovids in this assemblage is 13, 5, and 21%, respectively. Thus, cranial remains are, in fact, best represented for large bovids, although cranial bones are more abundant in small bovids than in medium-sized species.

The faunal assemblage from FLKNN–2 shows an intriguing pattern, one which follows Klein's prediction for a hyena accumulation but which exhibits the opposite trends of cranial bone representation to that observed in the Amboseli example. Although this Olduvai bone assemblage bears the highest

[10]In the bone accumulation from Long K, the other nonartifact site known in Bed I, forelimb bones also are more abundant than hindlimb elements for all bovid sizes.

[11]MNE for cranial bones divided by MNE for cranial plus postcranial elements.

relative frequency of large bovid individuals in Bed I (Table 5.6), not a single cranial piece of large bovid is present. However, over 14% of the MNE for medium-sized bovids are cranial. No small bovid cranial pieces exist at this site; but this is not inconsistent with hyena activity because spotted hyenas are known to crush and consume small skulls (Richardson, 1980). At least one cranial bone of large bovids occurs in each of the artifact-associated assemblages from Olduvai. DK–2 and FLKNN–3 show dramatic decreases in the percentage of large bovid cranial bones relative to smaller bovids, like the pattern at FLKNN–2. However, interpreting the pattern of cranial bone representation at FLKNN–2 is complicated by the fact that this pattern (0, 14, 0 for bovid size classes B, C, and D, respectively) greatly differs from that noted previously for the modern hyena den, even though it may be consistent with Klein's proposal for hyena accumulations. These conflicting points of evidence and interpretation suggest that cranial bone representation in large bovids is not always a reliable criterion and is not diagnostic of bone accumulations made by all species of hyenas.

*Frequency of Complete Bones*

To my knowledge, the relative representation of complete, or unbroken, bones has not previously been used as an indicator of hyena activity. As shown in Table 5.8, at least 15% of the identified specimens from each Olduvai site are unbroken, whereas the frequency of complete bones for the Amboseli hyena den is 27%. With almost 25% of its specimens complete, FLKNN–2 is closest to the hyena den in this regard. When only long bones are considered, the Amboseli hyena assemblage is even less similar to the Olduvai sites in its high percentage of complete specimens. FLKNN–2 again is closest to the

**TABLE 5.8.** Frequencies of Complete Specimens and Long Bones at Amboseli and Olduvai[a]

| Site | E | Complete specimens (%) | Complete long bones (%) | MNE | Complete long bones (%) |
|------|-----|------|------|-----|------|
| Amboseli den | 640 | 27.2 | 9.4 | 203 | 29.6 |
| FLK North–6[b] | 383 | 20.6 | 2.6 | 49 | 20.4 |
| FLK "Zinj" | 614 | 17.6 | 1.6 | 104 | 9.6 |
| FLKNN–2 | 324 | 24.7 | 5.2 | 75 | 22.6 |
| FLKNN–3 | 390 | 15.6 | 0.8 | 40 | 7.5 |
| DK–2 | 832 | 20.3 | 1.8 | 121 | 12.4 |
| DK–3 | 518 | 17.8 | 2.5 | 89 | 14.6 |

[a]E is the number specimens of mammals identified to family level. MNE is the minimum number of elements for major limb bones. The frequency of complete long bones is calculated based on E and MNE.
[b]Excludes elephant remains.

modern hyena concentration on this comparison. Relative to the number of specimens identified to family level, FLKNN–2 exhibits an intermediate percentage of complete long bones between that of the Amboseli den and the five stone artifact sites. As noted earlier, complete metapodials are particularly abundant in the spotted hyena assemblage. Among the Olduvai sites, this feature is again best portrayed at FLKNN–2.[12]

Interpreting the abundance of complete bones is complicated by the fact that agents other than carnivore or hominid activities may cause bones to break. Trampling and weathering are two such factors. Bones deposited on relatively stable land surfaces may be exposed to these processes more so than bones deposited during higher rates of sedimentation. In fact, two out of the three Olduvai assemblages that come from thin paleosols (FLK "Zinj" and FLKNN–3) exhibit the lowest percentages of complete bones. This suggests that the percentages of complete specimens in Table 5.8 mirror post-depositional factors in addition to the actions of bone collectors.

*Summary.* Overall, the fossil bone concentration at FLKNN–2 corresponds more closely than do the other Olduvai assemblages to characteristics of bone collections made by carnivores, especially spotted hyenas. Certain aspects of skeletal element representation and the abundance of complete bones are the points of greatest similarity between FLKNN–2 and the spotted hyena den from Amboseli, though there are also differences. The frequency of carnivores at FLKNN–2 appears not to conflict with the comparatively low representation of carnivores in the spotted hyena den studied here. On other lines of evidence, this one Olduvai assemblage matches well with criteria suggested by Klein to identify prehistoric hyena accumulations. Most of these similarities must be treated as only circumstantial evidence for the cause of bone accumulation at FLKNN–2; none of the criteria in isolation from the others is an adequate indicator of hyena activity.

Other osteological evidence, concerning bone breakage and destruction, has been proposed as a means for distinguishing carnivore bone accumulations from human ones (Table 5.3). Some of these putative taphonomic markers are controversial, especially as they have been applied to late Pleistocene bone assemblages in North America. It is useful to discuss briefly these possible ways of discerning hominid from carnivore activity.

### Patterns of Bone Damage

*Long Bone Fracture Patterns.* Predators appear to impose distinctive damage patterns on the bones of their prey (e.g., Brain, 1981; Dodson and Wexler, 1979; Haynes, 1980a; Richardson, 1980; Shipman, 1981). Since stone

---

[12]At the Amboseli den, 58% of MNE for metapodials are complete. At FLKNN–2 the figure is 31%. The average for the artifact sites is 16% (range: 11% at FLKNN–3 to 25% at FLK North–6). In the Long K assemblage 32% of the metacarpals and metatarsals are complete.

tools used by hominids provide a means for breaking bones that differs from carnivore teeth, it is likely that hominids leave unique breakage patterns as well.

Fractures that curve obliquely down the shafts of long bones have received particular attention in this regard. Such spiral fractures have been produced repeatedly during experimental breakage of long bone shafts using stone tools (Bonnichsen, 1973, 1978, 1979; Sadek-Kooros, 1972). Accordingly, spiral fractures originating on long bones near midshaft have been suggested to typify human stone tool damage of fresh bones. More recently, this idea has come under strong criticism (e.g., Binford, 1981). Spiral fractures can no longer be considered a diagnostic sign of hominid activity.

Table 5.9 summarizes observations by various researchers concerning the breakage of long bones under various conditions, often experimentally controlled. It is clear that spiral breaks are produced not only by twisting the ends of a fresh long bone after percussion but also simply by percussive force itself. Furthermore, spiral fractures can be caused by agents other than stone tools, including weathering and premortem bone breakage. Moreover, spirally fractured long bones are abundant at Miocene and Pliocene fossil sites in North America, which indicates that such fractures are not reliable indicators of hominid activity (Myers, Voorhies, and Corner, 1980). Long bones may be broken in a spiral pattern due to carnivore gnawing, and trampling by herd animals can break bison-sized long bones (Haynes, 1980a).

In addition, evidence from the Olduvai bones does not suggest that spiral fractures were the dominant pattern of breakage of long bone shafts. Classic spiral fractures, showing smooth break surfaces curving obliquely along the diaphysis, were very seldom observed on the identified long bone specimens in Bed I. Although curved breaks present on the fragments of limb bone shafts could well be segments of spiral fractures (Figure 5.17), such breaks are only as common at Olduvai as are straight or planar breaks which, various experimenters claim, reflect the breakage of weathered bones.

Furthermore, both stone tool cut marks and carnivore tooth marks are known to be associated with long bones broken in a spiral manner. The sample of bones examined by SEM illustrates further the role of both carnivores and hominids in breaking the shafts of long bones at the Olduvai sites. Sixteen diaphysis fragments were part of the sample examined microscopically. Only 3 of these had grooves that best matched stone tool cut marks, while 12 marks most closely resembled carnivore tooth scratches. This finding does little to refute the possibility that carnivores were responsible for breaking long bone shafts and for the spiral fracture segments observed on the fragments at each site.

*Bone Flaking.*       Patterns of bone flaking have been suggested by Bunn (1981, 1982) to distinguish carnivore from hominid bone damage. Experimental percussion of limb shafts with a hammerstone produces broad bone flakes and broad, arcuate indentations along the line of bone flaking.[13] In contrast, small notches along some broken limb shafts occur among bones modified by hyenas. Bone flakes produced by N. Toth and the author during several sessions of experimental bone percussion with a hammerstone support Bunn's description of bone flaking produced by a stone hammer. These flakes ($N = 14$) were purposefully produced by striking along the broken edge of cow limb bone shafts. Although a broad range of flake sizes were produced, they were all broader than long ("side-struck" in stone-flaking terminology). In addition, the flake platforms tended to be broad relative to platform thickness, thus providing broad, shallow indentations into the bone "core."

However, it was surprising to find flakes that fall well within the metrical and overall shape range of these hammerstone flakes in the Amboseli hyena assemblage (see Figure 5.11). These hyena-produced flakes were on the average $2.7\times$ as broad as they were long (compared with $3.0\times$ for the experimental flakes made by hammerstone) and had platform breadths that fall within the 4–17 mm range shown by the tool-produced flakes. As noted earlier (Figure 5.15), bone flakes from Olduvai (especially at FLK "Zinj" and FLKNN–2/3 indet.) that show clear platforms and bulbs are very similar to the hyena flakes, much as they are to experimentally produced flakes made by hammerstone. Moreover, small, biting indentations along broken limb shafts occurred rarely in the Amboseli hyena assemblage; no flakes that had a shape derived from such indentations were observed.

Brain (1981: 141–142) further states that it is difficult to distinguish bone flakes and points of impact made by hyenas from those made by humans. He provides photographs that show a great degree of similarity (at the points of tooth and stone tool impact) between long bones broken by hyenas and humans. Moreover, although Binford (1981: 157, 163) claims that stone impact scars on bones broken for marrow are "quite distinctive," he carefully portrays these scars as small, crescent-shaped notches—the kind of indentation Bunn's study concludes is diagnostic of *carnivore* damage. The inconsistency or overlap between these proposed diagnostic traits strongly suggest that bone flakes and indentations on broken limb bone shafts from the Bed I sites presently provide little evidence for hominid versus carnivore activities. Noting carnivore modifications on bones from FLK "Zinj," Bunn (1981: 576) also sees a difficulty in making a clear interpretation of bone breakage patterns at this site.

It is clear that several processes (e.g., carnivore teeth, stone tool use, and trampling) may break bones by dynamic loading in a highly confined area.

---

[13]"Flaking" here refers to conchoidal fracture. The term "flake" means a fragment that possesses the same features as a stone flake (e.g., indications of a platform or bulb of force). This usage differs from Brain's (1981) use of the term "flake," which is any splinter or fragment of long bone diaphysis that preserves less than half the circumference of the shaft.

**TABLE 5.9.** Summary of Observations on Spiral Fracture and Other Long Bone Breakage Patterns[a]

| Conditions | Results | Reference |
|---|---|---|
| 1. Strike small metapodial shaft with hammer and twist | 1. Spiral fracture | 1. Sadek-Kooros (1966, 1972, 1975) |
| 2. Strike small metapodial shaft with hammer, no twisting | 2. Oblique or transverse fractures (depends on position of blows) | 2. Sadek-Kooros (1966, 1972, 1975) |
| 3. Random blows with hammer on small metapodial | 3. Irregular fracture, breaks do not conform to specific shape categories | 3. Sadek-Kooros (1966, 1972, 1975) |
| 4. Strike midshaft, either shaft or ends of bone rest on anvil | 4. Spiral fracture starts at midshaft, stops before reaching epiphyses; conchoidal fracture and splintering at load point | 4. Bonnichsen (1973:14, 24) |
| 5. Chewing of bones by large carnivores | 5. Spiral fracture starts at end of bone | 5. Bonnichsen (1973:14); Clark (1977; 28) |
| 6. High-velocity impact on shafts of large bones, no twisting | 6. Conchoidal fracture, short flakes removed along shaft axis | 6. Bonnichsen (1978:108) |
| 7. Bone hit against stationary anvil | 7. Oblique or transverse fractures | 7. Biberson and Aguirre (1965: 174, App. B) |
| 8. Strike metapodial midshaft (on anvil) with hammer | 8. Transverse breaks unlike long spirals produced by Sadek-Kooros | 8. N. Russell (pers. comm.) |
| 9. Bones broken by hammer by !Kung San | 9. Formal breakage type categories not related to bone tool production | 9. Yellen (1977a) |
| 10. Strike proximal surface of metatarsal | 10. Split lengthwise | 10. Noe-Nygaard (1977:230) |

114

| | | |
|---|---|---|
| 11. Fracture before dehydration | 11. Smooth, curvilinear fracture edges | 11. Biddick and Tomenchuk (1975:243–244) |
| 12. Fracture after development of weathering cracks | 12. Jagged-edge, or stepped, fracture | 12. Biddick and Tomenchuk (1975:243–244) |
| 13. Fracture after development of weathering cracks | 13. Sharp break transverse to long axis; no conchoidal, spiral fracture | 13. Frison, Walker, Webb, and Zeimans (1978:388) |
| 14. Strike dry long bone | 14. Only longitudinal breaks; does not flake as well as fresh bone | 14. Frison (1974:31); Clark (1977:33) |
| 15. Strike dry cow humerus | 15. Some spiral fractures, beveled break surface; diamond-shaped fragments show segments of spiral fractures; no special flakes with bulbs and platforms | 15. Personal observation |
| 16. Weathered humeri/tibiae on East African landscape | 16. Smooth diagonal (spiral) fractures, oriented at low angle to long axis | 16. Hill (1980a:141) |
| 17. Carnivore fracture of dry, weathered bones | 17. Spiral and linear fractures | 17. Haynes (1980a:349) |
| 18. Carnivore fracture of fresh bones | 18. Sometimes spiral fracture; no linear breaks | 18. Haynes (1980a:349) |
| 19. Trampling of slightly weathered bones (inferred) | 19. Some spiral fractures and flake scars | 19. Myers *et al.* (1980) |

[a]The first column denotes the conditions of each observation. The second column describes the bone breakage result. Reference to the observer is given in the third column.

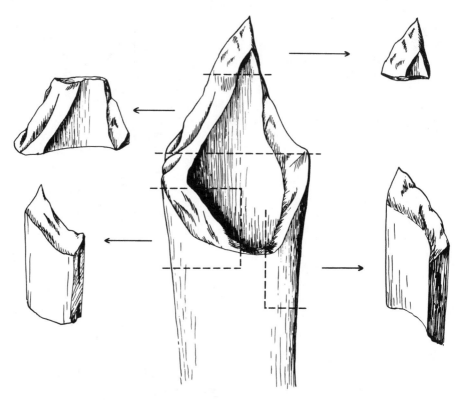

**FIGURE 5.17.** Diagrams of some bone diaphysis fragments that show characteristic segments of long bone spiral fractures.

Breakage traits such as spiral fractures, bone flakes, and broad impact points are useful in defining hominid activity only if they can distinguish among these several processes. Observations mentioned previously concerning bone damage of known origin indicate that there is a great deal of overlap in the bone fracture attributes produced by carnivores and stone tools. This overlap results undoubtedly from the similar mechanical characteristics of the skeletal elements broken in each situation (e.g., collagen fiber orientation, stress strength, bone freshness). Much more detailed observations of different breakage processes and how they interact with inherent properties of bone are required before damage attributes furnish essential distinctions between taphonomic agents (Hill, 1980a; Shipman, 1981).

*Bone Fragmentation.*    Breakage of bones into small pieces on archeological sites is often taken to indicate the presence of human food refuse produced by the extraction of marrow (Cleveland, Flenniken, Huelsbeck, Mierendorf, Samuels, and Hassan, 1976; Leechman, 1951; Vehik, 1977). This link between comminuted bone and marrow processing has been documented in ethnographic contexts, for example, among the San (Yellen, 1977a), Hottentots (Brain, 1967), and Cree (Bonnichsen, 1973). Thus, long bones, in particular, that have been fragmented into small pieces might be construed to signal human activity. In addition, it has been claimed that an abundance of long bone fragments less than 5 cm long indicates human food refuse (Brain, 1969b). But this idea has been retracted. Brain (1980) has pointed out that bone fragmentation by humans is variable, and that its degree and the size of fragments produced may be affected by trampling. According to Klein (1977, 1980), a high amount of bone fragmentation may reflect intense human activity and slow sedimentation rates because these two factors permit trampling and other kinds of destruction unrelated to subsistence to act on bones before burial.

It appears that carnivore tooth marks are relatively abundant on the bones from Bed I Olduvai, suggesting that carnivores were a factor involved in fragmenting bone. Table 5.10 gives the percentages of mammal bones that could not be assigned to taxon due to their fragmentary nature. The relative frequency of bone fragments is quite variable. FLK "Zinj" yielded huge numbers of such fragments, concentrated especially in two excavation trenches (Leakey, 1971: Figure 24). Interestingly, the majority of bones chosen for SEM inspection came from this concentration, and they showed a higher proportion of carnivore tooth marks than occurred on all other bones studied

**TABLE 5.10.** The Percentage of Probable Mammalian Fossils that Were Indeterminate to More Specific Taxon due to Fragmentation[a]

| Level | Percentage indeterminate |
|---|---|
| FLK North–6 (N = 2240) | 67 |
| FLK "Zinj" (N ~ 15,861) | 96 |
| FLKNN–2[b] (N = 470) | 31 |
| FLKNN–3[b] (N = 514) | 24 |
| DK–2 (N ~ 1832) | 55 |
| DK–3 (N = 1015) | 49 |

[a]Sample sizes include mammal indeterminate fragments and specimens assigned to mammal taxon to at least the family level.

[b]Almost all of the macromammal specimens from the sieving of FLKNN–2 and 3 combined (due to mixing of levels) were indeterminate fragments. So the percentages for each of these levels is probably considerably higher.

from Bed I. Carnivore tooth scratches also were more numerous than tool cut marks in the sample from FLK "Zinj."

The bone assemblage from the Amboseli hyena den confirms that a high degree of bone fragmentation can occur in a carnivore accumulation. Of 1694 specimens picked up from the den, 62% were pieces that could not be identified taxonomically to family, and 66% of these pieces were fragments of limb bone shaft. These frequencies correspond well to the range of bone fragmentation observed in the assemblages of Bed I Olduvai. Furthermore, 14% of a random sample of such fragments from the modern hyena collection are of the small, comminuted size ($\leq 20$ mm) often associated with marrow processing by humans.

If weathering was an important factor in the fragmentation of bones at Olduvai, it is expected that specimens in higher stages of weathering would be the least likely to remain complete and undamaged. Table 5.11 shows that this does not appear to be the case for long bones. Those elements that manifest higher weathering stages are not necessarily more likely to be broken. In some cases, the opposite occurs (DK–2, FLKNN–2, and FLK "Zinj"). This trend would seem to reflect an interaction between bone deposition rates, sedimentation (burial) rates, the period of bone exposure, and specific processes of bone damage. On the other hand, complete (unbroken) bones are rare overall in assemblages that occur in stable paleosols (FLK "Zinj", FLKNN–3, and DK–3) (see Table 5.8). This relationship between stable land surfaces and breakage suggests that relatively slow burial offered a greater chance for bone breakage to occur. Trampling and weathering, together, would have played a role in this process.

In brief, then, due to poor discrimination between hominids and carnivores regarding fragmentation of bone and due to the action of other processes of bone breakage (e.g., trampling), the presence and degree of bone fragmentation offer little distinction between hominids and carnivores as collectors of the bones at Olduvai.

*Differential Preservation of Epiphyses.*     Ethnographic observations by Brain (1967, 1969a, 1981) document what are now classic patterns of differential bone preservation that result from feeding on bones by people and their dogs. Epiphyses from the opposite ends of long bones do not survive equally well under these two considerable sources of bone attrition. The survival of epiphyses follows a predictable pattern correlated with the specific gravity or compactness of the bone (proportion of soft cancellous bone) and with the fusion time of the epiphyses. "Elbow" joints (distal humerus and proximal radius) preserve better than their respective opposite ends. Proximal femora and distal tibiae are disproportionately preserved over their opposite ends; and proximal metapodials are destroyed less often than the distal ends. Various researchers (e.g., Klein, 1980) have applied these predictions to faunal assemblages in order to show their susceptibility to attritional agents, including humans, carnivores, rodents, and trampling. Yellen (1977: 315) also

**TABLE 5.11.** Frequency (*N*) of Specimens of Mammal Long Bones Identified to Family in Each Surface Weathering Stage and the Percentage that are Complete or Nearly Complete (Proximal End, Distal End, and Shaft Represented): Bed I Olduvai and Amboseli Hyena Den

| Weathering stage | DK-3 | | DK-2 | | FLKNN-3 | | FLKNN-2 | | FLK "Zinj" | | FLK North-6 | | Amboseli | |
|---|---|---|---|---|---|---|---|---|---|---|---|---|---|---|
| | N | Percentage | N | Percentage | N | Percentage | N | Percentage | N | Percentage | N | Percentage | N | Percentage |
| 0 | 29 | 14 | 17 | 0 | 11 | 9 | 9 | 11 | 66 | 2 | 13 | 23 | 59 | 15 |
| 1 | 24 | 25 | 20 | 15 | 9 | 0 | 27 | 15 | 43 | 9 | 18 | 11 | 45 | 33 |
| 2 | 17 | 18 | 16 | 12 | 6 | 0 | 12 | 33 | 22 | 9 | 2 | 0 | 9 | 11 |
| 3 | 15 | 20 | 45 | 20 | 7 | 14 | 23 | 43 | 18 | 22 | 15 | 33 | 46 | 30 |
| 4 | — | — | — | — | 1 | 0 | 2 | 50 | — | — | — | — | 8 | 25 |
| 5 | — | — | — | — | — | — | 1 | 0 | ?1 | 100 | — | — | — | — |

has observed similar patterns of bone preservation in an ethnographic situation involving human and carnivore activity. Quantitative information from Nunamiut Eskimo faunal assemblages produced by humans and dogs (Binford and Bertram, 1977) substantiate most of the observations made by Brain regarding epiphysis preservation. These data indicate that Brain's predictions for humerus, radius, tibia, and metacarpal epiphyses are very well met; but the proximal ends of femora and metatarsals do not consistently outlast their distal ends. Brain's data (1967) show that the opposite ends of femora and metapodials are indeed least discrepant in their abundance under destructive influences. Hence, it appears that the relative frequency of femur and metapodial (especially metatarsal) epiphyses are not so reliable indicators of attritional processes as are the ends of other long bones.

Table 5.12 summarizes information about the preservation of long bone epiphyses in bovids.[14] All six Olduvai sites exhibit some of the predicted features of an assemblage that has undergone considerable attrition. As expected, femora show little or no evidence of a proximal–distal end disproportion. Three of the assemblages correspond only partially to the predicted patterns of survival. DK–3 and FLK North–6 meet the expected pattern of epiphysis preservation for the humerus and radius but not for the tibia (or metapodials). FLKNN–3 does not match the predictions for the usually highly indicative humerus. This partial lack of correspondence to the expected pattern of preservation means either:

1. These three assemblages were open to less attrition than the ethnographic assemblages studied by Brain and by Binford and Bertram. The ethnographic assemblages underwent intensive human modification and feeding on the remains by dogs. Interestingly, the special hyena damage patterns discussed earlier (p. 91) are rarest on these three Olduvai levels.

2. On these particular levels, hominids and carnivores, although acting as important attritional agents, did not use tissues inside the bones to the extent that humans and dogs did in the modern ethnographic cases. In the latter situations, bone damage primarily resulted from extensive processing and use of bone tissue by people and dogs. A different pattern of differential epihysis destruction from that in the ethnographic cases may have been produced at Olduvai if hominid and carnivore activity did not focus so intensively on bone tissue destruction but on soft tissues. Whether such a distinctive use strategy actually accounts for the epiphysis survival pattern evident in these three Olduvai assemblages is unknown.

In contrast, at FLK "Zinj," the level with extensive bone fragmentation, the predicted pattern of epiphysis representation occurs in all long bones (except the femur). DK–2 shows the same pattern, except for the less reliable

---

[14]The appendixes provide information broken down by bovid body size classes.

**TABLE 5.12.** Minimum Number of Epiphyseal Ends for Bovid Long Bones: Olduvai Bed I and Amboseli Hyena Den

| Element | | DK–3 | DK–2 | FLKNN–3 | FLKNN–2 | FLK "Zinj" | FLK North–6 | Amboseli |
|---|---|---|---|---|---|---|---|---|
| Humerus | Proximal | 3 (+)[a] | 2 (+) | 3 (–) | 1 (+) | 6 (+) | 2 (+) | 1 (+) |
| | distal | 11 | 17 | 3 | 13 | 19 | 6 | 21 |
| Radius/ | Proximal | 8 (+) | 24 (+) | 11 (+) | 18 (+) | 26 (+) | 12 (+) | 32 (+) |
| ulna | distal | 3 | 12 | 2 | 4 | 3 | 7 | 15 |
| Tibia | Proximal | 8 (–)[b] | 4 (+) | 1 (+) | 2 (+) | 7 (+) | 4 (?) | 9 (+) |
| | distal | 8 | 22 | 4 | 6 | 11 | 5 | 14 |
| Metapodial | Proximal | 20 (–) | 23 (–) | 8 (–) | 20 (+) | 30 (+) | 6 (–) | 41 (+) |
| | distal | 25 | 29 | 10 | 15 | 19 | 8 | 36 |
| Femur | Proximal | 4 | 3 | 1 | 1 | 8 | 1 | 3 |
| | distal | 8 | 4 | 0 | 3 | 6 | 4 | 3 |

[a] ( + ) Agrees with predicted preservation bias.
[b] ( − ) Contrasts with predicted preservation bias.

metapodials. Finally, FLKNN–2 also shows the predicted pattern as clearly as occurs at FLK "Zinj." Both of these sites are quite similar to the modern hyena collection from Amboseli in the relative representation of epiphyseal ends (Table 5.12). Therefore, the bones from these two Olduvai sites, and to some extent from DK–2, provide evidence of long bone attrition that is consistent with either human plus carnivore (e.g., dog) modification or only carnivore (hyena) activity by itself.

Brain's work in Hottentot villages suggested that skeletal element representation, in general, follows predictable tendencies based on inherent durability of different bones. Binford and Bertram (1977) further suggest that the pattern of bone survivorship depends greatly on the age structure of the population of carcasses introduced to a site. They argue that without knowing the ages of the animals, it is difficult to predict what the preservation tendencies of different elements will be. The importance of age results from the fact that bone compactness varies with age. This complicating factor also makes sense given Brain's conclusion that the age of epiphysis fusion correlates highly with differential preservation of epiphyses.

The precision of carcass age determination demanded by Binford and Bertram's analysis (i.e., in terms of months after birth) is not possible from the Olduvai faunal remains. Moreover, any predictions of bone survivorship from an inferred carcass age structure would be circular, since the original age structure had already been subjected to the alterations of differential bone preservation. Therefore, a precise set of expectations about skeletal element preservation for a set of bones under attritional influences cannot be made. The Olduvai faunal assemblages (see data in appendixes) do follow some generally expected tendencies of preservation, for example, low number of vertebrae and ribs, which undergo rapid destruction. But the relative abundance of many skeletal elements is difficult to divorce from disproportions in the original frequency of elements introduced to the sites. Furthermore, a comparison of skeletal element representation in the Amboseli den, the surrounding plains habitat, and the Hottentot/dog assemblage studied by Brain reveals overall similarities. Thus, skeletal element data are not adequate to distinguish among the diverse attritional agents that acted upon the assemblages (Behrensmeyer and Boaz, 1980: 90).

In short, these various considerations about differential bone preservation at Olduvai indicate that significant attrition occurred to the bone assemblages, but the patterns of attrition cannot rule out those associated with carnivores or with humans and carnivores combined. Evidence for significant attritional processes suggests a possible reason for the scarcity of bones in weathering stages 4 and 5. Although carnivores probably were not attracted to extremely weathered bones, activities such as trampling and kicking could have acted to completely disintegrate bones made fragile by very high degrees of weathering.

**TABLE 5.13.** Percentage of Ungulate Long Bone Specimens (Possessing at Least One Articular End and Part of the Diaphysis) Which Are "Isolated Ends" Versus More Complete Diaphyses[a]

| Site | Number of long bones specimens | Isolated articular ends in percentage |
|---|---|---|
| Amboseli den | 98 | 37 |
| FLK North–6 | 32 | 62 |
| FLK "Zinj" | 97 | 82 |
| FLKNN–2 | 43 | 33 |
| FLKNN–3 | 33 | 73 |
| DK–2 | 95 | 59 |
| DK–3 | 73 | 73 |
| Long K | 109 | 48 |

[a]Modified from Potts, 1984a.

*Epiphysis-First Destruction of Long Bones.*     Another line of evidence believed to distinguish carnivore from hominid bone modification concerns the destruction of limb bone epiphyses and shafts. It is generally assumed that when carnivores break or gnaw upon long bones, they tend to attack the epiphyseal ends first. This pattern of long bone destruction makes anatomical sense since compact bone is thinnest in epiphyseal areas and nutritious spongy bone is closest to the surface. Carnivore-gnawed assemblages, thus, may possess a high proportion of long bone ends where the opposite epiphysis is gone but much of the shaft is left intact. Carnivores are known also to destroy both ends of a long bone. Consequently, the cylindrical diaphysis is either left intact or, sometimes, it is broken into splinters. In contrast, humans using stone tools tend to break long bones at the shaft leaving the epiphyses largely intact. As a result, assemblages of limb bones cracked by humans for marrow are characterized by articular ends with one-third or less of the shaft attached (Binford, 1981; Bonnichsen, 1973, 1979).

Table 5.13 gives the proportion of such isolated ends from the Bed I sites and the Amboseli hyena den. At all of the Olduvai *artifact* sites, isolated ends are relatively abundant. They make up no less than 59% of the total number of long bone specimens (possessing at least one epiphysis and a portion of shaft). In contrast, the Amboseli den and the two nonartifact sites in Bed I exhibit fewer isolated ends, less than 50% of specimens. The type of pieces typically produced by carnivore gnawing alone comprise 67 and 52% of the specimens at FLKNN–2 and Long K, respectively.

The latter two sites also manifest high proportions of cylinders (relative to either the total number of long bone specimens or MNI). As indicated in Table 5.14, these data again suggest that limb bone damage at FLKNN–2

**TABLE 5.14.** Frequencies of Long Bone Cylinders[a]

| Site | Number of cylinders | Number of long bone specimens[b] | MNI | Index A | Index B |
|------|------|------|------|------|------|
| FLK North–6 | 6 | 127 | 22 | 4.7 | 27.3 |
| FLK "Zinj" | 12 | 894 | 36 | 1.3 | 33.3 |
| FLKNN–2 | 17 | 119 | 23 | 14.3 | 73.9 |
| FLKNN–3 | 18 | 159 | 34 | 11.3 | 52.9 |
| DK–2 | 8 | 145 | 41 | 5.5 | 19.5 |
| DK–3 | 11 | 426 | 36 | 2.6 | 30.6 |
| Long K | 27 | 267 | 48 | 10.1 | 56.0 |
| Amboseli den | 17 | 1020 | 52 | 1.6 | 32.7 |

[a]Index A equals the percentage represented by cylinders of long bone specimens sampled from each site. Index B equals (the number of cylinders) × 100/MNI.

[b]Based on taxonomically identified material and all nonidentified fragments from each site, except FLK "Zinj." A sample of 1363 nonidentified pieces out of approximately 15,250 macromammal fragments were examined from "Zinj." Figures also do not include "FLKNN–2/3 level indeterminate."

and Long K was often inflicted just by carnivores alone.[15] With the exception of FLKNN–3, the lower relative abundance of cylinders at the other sites corresponds with the evidence (Table 5.13) for a greater degree of shaft damage typical of human activity.

However, at the artifact sites cylinders do occur, and not all of the long bone specimens represent isolated ends that typically result from tool fracture of shafts. Indeed, all of the sites show a dual pattern of damage to major limb bones, some sites more strongly than others. For example, FLKNN–2 is found to have a very high percentage of epiphyses that are *undamaged* (Table 5.15). This might seem to contradict the evidence regarding carnivore activity at this site (relatively high number of cylinders and few isolated ends of long bones). The latter indicates that epiphysis-first gnawing of unbroken long bones prevailed at this site. Yet those epiphyses that survived tended not to be damaged at all. When it occurred, damage to epiphyses at FLKNN–2 tended to result in total destruction. This is a pattern that might be expected where carnivores take time to gnaw the ends of bones in an intensive way. Yet the high numbers of undamaged epiphyses and complete bones at this

[15]Carnivores, though, do not always leave cylinders intact but may gnaw on long bone shafts until they break. This intensive type of diaphysis fragmentation is seen in the Amboseli hyena assemblage, as indicated by the low cylinder indexes in Table 5.14. Thus, a low proportion of cylinders, by itself, does not necessarily mean that carnivore activity was absent. However, a high frequency of cylinders, especially when coupled with low numbers of isolated articular ends, is considered here to be a clear indication of carnivore activity.

**TABLE 5.15.** Damage (Exposure of Cancellous Bone) to Articular Ends of Major Long Bones

| Site | Number of epiphyses | Percentage undamaged | Percentage damaged |
|------|---------------------|----------------------|--------------------|
| Amboseli den | 300 | 59 | 41 |
| FLK North–6 | 69 | 67 | 33 |
| FLK "Zinj" | 139 | 60 | 40 |
| FLKNN–2 | 104 | 71 | 29 |
| FLKNN–3 | 52 | 54 | 46 |
| DK–2 | 159 | 65 | 35 |
| DK–3 | 103 | 63 | 37 |
| Long K | 131 | 59 | 41 |

nonartifact site indicate that such attack upon long bones did not always occur.[16]

FLKNN–3 provides another example of a dual pattern of damage to long bones. The high frequency of cylinders at FLKNN–3 is particularly striking compared with the low cylinder indexes at the other artifact sites. The data on isolated long bone ends suggest that bones at this site were often broken through the diaphysis. Yet, clearly, not all bones were processed in this way. Carnivores appear to have created cylinders through epiphysis-first gnawing such that the proportion of cylinders converges upon that at FLKNN–2. This is intriguing given that FLKNN–3 exhibits the clearest differences of all the artifact sites from FLKNN–2 in features of limb bone representation and frequencies of complete bones (Tables 5.7 and 5.8). These two features link together the Amboseli hyena den, FLKNN–2, and Long K in a strong manner. FLKNN–3 differs from these three assemblages to a greater degree than any other artifact site on the basis of these measures. Nonetheless, relatively high proportions of cylinders suggest that carnivores at least occasionally had access to complete limb bones at this site. At the other artifact sites, we see

[16]The Amboseli hyena den also exhibits a high proportion of complete limb bones and a percentage of isolated ends of long bones which is very similar to FLKNN–2 (Table 5.13). However, limb bone damage at Amboseli reflects a combination of extensive and intensive destruction not evident at FLKNN–2. In the modern den, 41% of epiphysis specimens were damaged. That is, a considerably greater proportion of epiphysis pieces were damaged (but still survived) in the modern den. This percentage is higher than at any Olduvai site except for FLKNN–3 (Table 5.15). Furthermore, cylinders are very rare in the Amboseli den compared to the Olduvai sites (Index A = 1.6; Index B = 32.7; see Table 5.14). This corresponds with intensive shattering of limb bone shafts by hyenas at the den, an activity that they carry out at one particular location within the den area (Hill, 1983).

a combination of the kind of diaphysis destruction that typifies human activity along with partial gnawing of bone ends.

Another way to look at limb bone damage is to identify specimens that bear clear signs of carnivore tooth marks and see which parts were destroyed. Eighteen such specimens were identified from the artifact sites during the SEM study of bone surface damage: 28% of these long bones possessed both epiphyses, and 44% still had one epiphysis. This tentatively shows (1) that access to marrow tissues was not always accomplished by carnivores attracted to the bones, and (2) epiphysis marrow was not always the only, or major, attraction these bones held for carnivores.

Overall, the data on long bone damage do not discriminate absolutely among the faunal assemblages from Bed I Olduvai and those produced by carnivores, especially hyenas. FLKNN–2 (and Long K, based on preliminary analysis) exhibit certain characteristics expected of assemblages modified solely by carnivores. The other sites resemble or differ from the assemblage made by spotted hyenas at Amboseli depending on which characteristic is examined. Damage to diaphyses played a larger taphonomic role at these artifact sites than at the nonartifact sites in Bed I. Paralleling this trend, however, are patterns of damage that were probably inflicted by carnivores. These patterns of bone modification mimic in certain ways modification of bones accumulated by carnivores. Thus, at FLK "Zinj" and DK–2, the preservation of limb bone epiphyses is biased in ways expected in a carnivore accumulation. At FLKNN–3, diaphysis cylinders are relatively abundant. None of the artifact sites, however, appears to show a combination of features that strongly indicates accumulation of bones by carnivores, despite good evidence that carnivores helped to modify the bones at these sites.

*Relative Timing of Carnivore and Hominid Damage.*        Clearly, each of the Bed I faunal assemblages shows evidence for hominid and carnivore modification. Many of the criteria discussed previously do little to link primarily one of these agents to the patterns of faunal representation and bone damage at these sites. However, bone weathering stages potentially offer a rough, relative time calibration for judging the priority of bones introduced by animals to the site and, thus, may suggest the priority of different agents of bone damage. Carnivores are mainly attracted to bones as food sources; thus, as expected, study of wild carnivores indicates that they typically do not bother with bones more than 6 months old (Richardson, 1980). If it is assumed that carnivores and hominids left their traces mainly on fresh bones, then the weathering stages associated with cut-marked and carnivore-damaged bones should indicate roughly the temporal priority of these agents at each site. Given variation in the weathering rates of bones, this indication of temporal priority will not be exact. Nonetheless, on the average, damages associated with higher weathering stages will have happened earlier than damages seen on less weathered bones, because the former bones were presumably exposed and introduced to the site at an earlier time. In turn, this information may provide some insight into whether one agent was the initial source of bone accumulation.

Table 5.16 presents this information in detail for each Olduvai site. Since bones with only the clearest indications of weathering (e.g., long bone shafts, ribs, vertebrae) and with only the most certain signs of hominid and carnivore damage were used in this analysis, the sample of bones for each site is small. Stone cut marks, most of which were identified with the aid of SEM, were used to define hominid-modified specimens. Carnivore-modified bones were ones bearing carnivore tooth marks identified during the SEM study and other damages (e.g., holes in articular ends, canine punctures) strikingly like those observed on hyena-damaged bones. To summarize:

**DK–3:** Nine cut-marked bones show weathering Stages 0–2; carnivore damage ($N = 6$) occurs on bones with Stages 0–1 or 2.

**DK–2:** Hominid-modified bones ($N = 9$) show weathering Stages 0, 1, and 3; carnivore damage ($N = 9$) spans this same set of stages, 0–3.

**FLKNN–3:** Two hominid slice marks occur on bones showing Stages 1 and 2; five carnivore-damaged bones occur: four show weathering Stage 0, one shows weathering Stage 3.

**FLKNN–2:** One cut-marked bone was observed that shows either weathering Stage 0 or 1. Eleven specimens with carnivore damage range from Stage 0 to Stage 4 (mostly Stage 1 or above).

**FLK "Zinj":** The clearest examples ($N = 7$) of hominid cut marks observed via SEM possess weathering Stages 0–2. More than nineteen carnivore-damaged specimens span this same range. Both hominid- and carnivore-modified bones are mostly Stage 0.

**FLK North–6:** Only one clear cut mark appears, and that is on a bone with Stage 0/1. Six carnivore damages are associated with weathering Stages 0–2, but mostly Stage 0.

At the five artifact sites, there appears to be no clear priority of hominid or carnivore agents of bone damage, as reflected in these small samples of specimens. Rather, hominids and carnivores seem to have inflicted tell-tale damage on the bones over about the same period of time, as though over a succession of occupations or visits at each site. The information adduced from this exercise does not correspond to the traditional concept of archeological sites as areas of hominid occupation, first and foremost, followed by abandonment when carnivores and other agents gained access to refuse left by hominids. This evidence, however, does not refute the possibility that such a standard sequence of occupation and abandonment may have occurred more than once, if not often, over a period of several years. Only at FLKNN–2 is there clear priority—that of carnivore modification—although just one hominid-damaged bone is known with any confidence from this site.

A number of indications of carnivore activity, some of which attempt to distinguish it from hominid activity, have been discussed in this section. Some

**TABLE 5.16.** The Weathering Stage (in Parentheses) Attributed to Bones with Stone Tool Cut Marks and with Carnivore Damages from the Six Olduvai Sites[a]

| DK-3 | DK-2 | FLKNN-3 | FLKNN-2 | FLK | FLK North-6 |
|---|---|---|---|---|---|
| **Hominid-modified specimens** | | | | | |
| Bovid metapodial (0) | Bovid tibia (0) | Mammal radius (1) | Equus metacarpal (0/1) | Bovid radioulna (0) | Elephas proximal phalanx (0/1) |
| Mammal limb shaft (0) | Bovid humerus (0) | Mammal rib (2) | | Bovid humerus (0) | |
| Equus metacarpal (1) | Bovid phalanx (0/1) | | | 2 Mammal limb shafts (0) | |
| Equus humerus (1) | Bovid metacarpal (0/1) | | | Mammal fragments (0) | |
| Bovid limb shaft (1) | Bovid tibia (1) | | | Bovid tibia (0/1) | |
| 2 Mammal limb shafts (1) | Bovid ulna (3) | | | Bovid metatarsal (2) | |
| Mammal limb shaft (2) | | | | | |
| **Carnivore-modified specimens** | | | | | |
| 2 limb shafts (0) | Cercocebus femur (0) | Mammal rib (0) | Mammal limb shaft (0) | Equid rib (0) | Carnivore ulna (0) |
| Equus metacarpal (0) | Bovid metacarpal (1) | Bovid vertebra (0) | Bovid humerus (1) | Bovid metacarpal (0) | Elephas vertebra (0) |
| Mammal vertebra (0) | Bovid radius (1) | Bovid scapula (0) | Bovid metacarpal (1) | 7 Mammal limb shafts (0) | Elephas limb shaft (0) |
| Bovid humerus (1) | Bovid metacarpal (2) | Hominid parietal (0) | Mammal limb shaft (1) | Bovid hyoid (0) | Mammal rib (0) |
| Suid humerus (1/2) | Bovid tibia (3) | Bovid metacarpal (3) | Equus radioulna (1/2) | Bovid rib (0) | Bovid femur (1) |
| | 2 Bovid metatarsals (3) | | Mammal femur (2) | Bovid scapula (0) | Bovid tibia (2) |
| | Bovid metacarpal (3) | | Shaft fragment (2) | Mammal vertebra (0) | |
| | Bovid humerus (3) | | Bovid humerus (2/3) | 2 Bovid metatarsals (0) | |
| | | | Bovid metacarpal (3) | Bovid metacarpal (1) | |
| | | | Bovid metatarsal (4) | Mammal limb shaft (1) | |
| | | | | Bovid metatarsal (2) | |
| | | | | Bovid tibia (2) | |

[a]Most small distal limb bones are not included.

aspects of bone representation and damage at the Olduvai sites can be accounted for by hyenas, as suggested by comparisons with the Amboseli den or with criteria proposed by other researchers concerning hyena activity. This is especially true for FLKNN–2. The latter assemblage differs from the other Olduvai bone accumulations on a number of details, while maintaining an overall similarity to them. The ways the FLKNN–2 assemblage differs from the artifact-associated assemblages all tend to converge on patterns most obvious in the spotted hyena bone collection at Amboseli. The balance of evidence appears to favor the idea that the FLKNN–2 assemblage was produced primarily by hyenas. Based on bone weathering, the apparent priority of carnivore damage to this set of bones makes this hypothesis the most attractive for now.[17]

The one known cut-marked bone at FLKNN–2 is intriguing. The specimen is an unbroken equid metacarpal that bears a clear set of slicing marks and a chopping mark on the distal end. This bone is part of an associated set of nine forelimb bones that formed an articulated unit carried to the site. A carnivore tooth mark is evident on the proximal end of the radioulna in this set. A carnivore bone collector may have scavenged this bone after the hominid cut marks had been made (Potts, 1982; Potts and Shipman, 1981). A plea for plausibility does not make this suggestion correct. The point, though, is that the presence of a cut-marked bone at FLKNN–2 does not contradict the balance of evidence that the bone accumulation at FLKNN–2 was produced to a large extent by a carnivore bone collector. Chapter 8 will explore in greater detail questions about the use of bones and animal tissues and the sequence of carcass utilization by carnivores and hominids at Olduvai.

## The Role of Hominids

We have explored a wide variety of features that have been suggested to characterize bone concentrations made by carnivores, particularly hyenas. Some of these features consistently distinguish carnivore assemblages from other types of bone accumulation. Other features (e.g., certain body sizes) are not special to carnivore assemblages. Still others (e.g., high percentage of carnivore remains) simply are not seen in all accumulations produced by carnivores.

In contrast with this wide variety of suggested criteria, very few diagnostic signs of hominid activity have been proposed. Archeologists have long assumed

[17]The bone assemblage from Long K is similar to that from FLKNN–2 in ways that also suggest a carnivore origin for this accumulation. The bones of Long K exhibit plentiful carnivore gnawing; no cut marks were found despite intensive search; no clear artifacts occur at the site; complete metapodials, distal humeri, and radioulnae are very abundant; the number of shaft cylinders is relatively large and the number of "isolated" articular ends is low.

that the presence of artifacts alone means that materials associated with artifacts also resulted from human activity. As is evident in this study, this
assumption can no longer be considered safe in light of the awareness developed over the past 15 years about taphonomic biases and multiple agents
of site formation. If we concentrate specifically on behavioral modes of accumulation, there are only two lines of evidence that I would consider to be
clear and consistent indicators of hominid activity at Plio–Pleistocene sites.
Stone tools obviously represent one diagnostic sign that hominids were present. Second, certain patterns of bone damage—namely, tool cut marks and
long bone breakage that is focused on diaphyses over epiphyses—also appear
to be valid indicators of hominid activity. These criteria must be weighed
against the evidence for carnivore activity and other factors of site formation.

The matter of bone modification was treated in the previous sections of
this chapter which dealt with carnivores. Cut marks made by stone tools
show that hominids processed animal bones at sites where stone tools were
also left. Moreover, long bone shafts were broken at the expense of epiphyses
to a greater extent at the artifact sites than at FLKNN–2 or Long K. It is
certain that bone processing at sites with artifacts involved hominids, not
exclusively carnivores. Since most of the cut marks on these bones are slicing
marks, it is also clear that hominid activity was not focused just on breaking
long bone shafts for marrow.

The two nonartifact sites in Bed I vary in certain ways from sites where
artifacts occurred; these variations converge on features generally seen in
bone concentrations made exclusively by a carnivore bone collector. Therefore,
either a different *primary* mode of bone transport and concentration is represented at the artifact sites (i.e., hominids as opposed to carnivores) or, at
the very least, hominids contributed to these sites more (and carnivores less)
than they did at FLKNN–2 or Long K. In the formation of the latter sites,
hominids appear to have contributed very slightly, if at all.

Do the stone tools add further evidence about the accumulation of bones
at the artifact sites? Transport and concentration of stone artifacts indeed
represent the "other half" of site formation at these particular sites. To ignore
this fact would provide an incomplete view of site formation. While the simple
presence of artifacts is not deemed sufficient evidence to link all or most
faunal assemblage patterns to hominid activity, we have seen that the use
of tools by hominids did involve at least some of the animal bones. Furthermore, the process of artifact accumulation at these delimited spots paralleled
the behavioral transport of bones to these same places. That is, the process
of artifact transport comprised part of the context of animal bone transport.
The artifact sites yielded assemblages of stone ranging from a few kilograms
to over 70 kg in total weight, and they include a diversity of raw materials
(see Table 8.6). For the most part, this amount and diversity of stone material
must have been transported and concentrated at these sites by hominids,
since neither an animal agent nor water flow played an important role in

moving them. Stones were carried from sources located in different parts of the Olduvai basin, in some cases several kilometers from the sites.

This process of stone transport to sites strongly conflicts with the idea that carnivores were the primary agent of bone transport to the artifact sites. Utilization of bones by bone collecting carnivores, especially hyenas, tends to leave little in the way of edible or otherwise usable soft tissue. Hypothetically, it is difficult to imagine what attractive resources could have been found by hominids in patches of bones that were disarticulated, cleaned of meat and ligaments, and mostly broken—as occurs in accumulations made by modern carnivore bone collectors away from death sites. If carnivores, in fact, initiated the accumulation of bones at each site and continued to be the primary collectors of bones, it implies that hominids brought stone on multiple occasions from diverse sources (including apparently unmodified manuports) to specific places where they could use sparse, if any, resources on bones previously collected and utilized by carnivores. This idea could well make sense if the Olduvai artifact sites were kill sites where hominids gained access to carcasses previously exploited by carnivores, as suggested by Binford (1981). However, the evidence discussed in Chapter 3 shows convincingly that this was not the case. The fundamental taphonomic inference about the Olduvai sites is that they were not death site accumulations. Rather, they predominantly represent concentrations of bones transported to specific, delimited spots on the landscape.

These two indicators of hominid activity—bone damage and the *process* of artifact transport to sites—imply that hominids played an important role in the accumulation of bones at these sites. Indeed, these inferences strongly suggest that hominids played a more important role than carnivores in concentrating the bone remains found at the artifact sites and, thus, represent the *primary* agent of transport for artifacts and bones to these sites. This conclusion in no way ignores or lessens the obvious impact carnivores made to site formation as agents of bone damage, in particular. Nor does it imply that hominids were responsible for all bones transported to the artifact sites.

# 6

# Conclusions on Olduvai Taphonomy

In the preceding chapters, I have established the roles of the various agents responsible for producing a sample of sites from Olduvai. To do this, it has been necessary to discuss the ways by which the effects of each taphonomic process can be recognized in the faunal remains, artifacts, and their geologic contexts. The sites of Bed I Olduvai were examined for evidence of water action, animal and hominid activities, and other processes such as the death and disarticulation of animals. This section briefly summarizes the results.

First, the clustering of bones within each Olduvai level was found not only to exceed that created by repeated mortality of animals, but also to differ on several other grounds from the death sites of African ungulates. The Olduvai sites do not meet any of five criteria that characterize the death areas of animals resulting from either attritional or catastrophic mortality. The elephant skeleton at FLK North–6 represents the remains of an animal that had died at the site. However, the bone accumulations at the other sites, and the remainder of the FLK North–6 bone assemblage, mostly exhibit the signs of a different process: the transport and concentration of bones away from death sites. Limb elements are very numerous and axial parts scarce, even when the potential for biased destruction of axial bones is taken into account. This is one indication of the process of bone clustering and suggests that the transport of limb bones to the sites was especially important. Based on bone weathering features and broad estimates of weathering rate, it appears that bones were accumulated at each site over at least a 5- to 10-year period.

Second, the stone artifacts are also clustered to an unusual degree. Five of the six sites display a greater concentration of stone artifacts than is preserved on later Stone Age land surfaces. Furthermore, comparison of the six sites with other levels excavated in Bed I indicates that the faunal remains and stone artifacts at each site were accumulated in unusually high concentrations relative to the lake margin area, in general, at ancient Olduvai.

Third, water flow was not the primary means of bone and artifact accumulation at any of the Olduvai sites. This inference is based upon the following clues: fine-grain sediments, a lake margin location of the sites with no stream channel facies close by, and the lack of sorting of bones according to their water transport tendencies. All of the Olduvai sites, however, were buried by lake waters and show evidence of varying degrees of water flow effects. The presence of numerous, waterworn pebbles and some artifacts with abraded surfaces suggests that water flow had an impact at locality DK. Some of the remains at DK–2 and DK–3 were probably contributed via water flow from several directions, which was possible if the DK locality was a local low spot in the sedimentary basin.

Overall, the taphonomic analyses in Chapter 4 indicate that biological factors—carnivores, hominids, or some other animal—rather than physical–geological agents primarily were responsible for transporting bones to the Olduvai sites. The possibility that hominids played a primary role depends on whether significant taphonomic differences exist between the Olduvai bone concentrations (considered case-by-case) and documented examples of non-hominid bone accumulations. The Fort Ternan fossil site, the spotted hyena den assemblage from Amboseli, and diverse reports of other bone accumulations and damage patterns produced by carnivores and other animals were used for this comparison.

The Miocene site of Fort Ternan, Kenya, illustrates that transported, dense concentrations of faunal remains can be created by processes other than hominid activities. Important differences do exist between Fort Ternan and the Olduvai sites in patterns of skeletal element representation which reflect how bones were accumulated. Specifically, at Fort Ternan there is a very high frequency of cranial parts, low number of specimens per MNI, and low percentage of small, distal limb elements compared to Olduvai. These details of skeletal part occurrence suggest that the collection of bones at Fort Ternan was relatively piecemeal—a bone at a time or in small articulated units. Because of their potential taphonomic significance, these differences are believed to outweigh the notable overall similarities between the two sites in the representation of taxa, body sizes, and some skeletal elements. However, the latter similarities are equally intriguing because they offer a rather obvious message: A dense accumulation of broken bones from numerous mammal species does not certify hominid activity. This type of bone assemblage, even when it occurs in Pleistocene sediments that contain hominid traces, must undergo detailed, comparative taphonomic analysis before behavior is inferred from faunal data. This is now a well-established principle in archeological faunal analysis.

For Olduvai, we may confine our attention mainly to behavioral hypotheses of bone transport. The simple juxtaposition of stone artifacts and bones, though, does not immediately eliminate the possibility of a fortuitous association. Nor does it eliminate the possibility that hominid activity at each site was minimal. Cut marks made by tools have been documented on bones from each of the sites in Bed I, and this means that the fauna–tool associations are not completely fortuitous. Use of tools by hominids on at least some of the animal bones implies that the transport of stone artifacts and of animal bones was linked in some manner. This behavioral link between carried stones and animal bones is especially evident in that both kinds of remains were clustered in the same spatially delimited places (except at FLKNN–2 and Long K, where no artifacts occur). However, tooth marks and types of bone damage that best match those made by mammalian carnivores (canid to at least hyaenid in size) also occur on the bones from each of the Olduvai sites. Much of the damage by carnivores represents extensive fragmentation or destruction of bony parts. This strongly suggests that carnivore activity occurred directly at each site. It is imperative, therefore, to assess the relative contributions of hominids and carnivores to the faunal assemblages at Olduvai.

Table 5.3 lists patterns of bone damage and assemblage makeup that, according to various sources, are believed to characterize carnivores and accumulations produced by carnivore bone collectors. As we saw in Chapter 5, many of these proposed diagnostic and descriptive patterns do not occur in all bone assemblages made by carnivores today. The reason, in part, is that our current knowledge of carnivore bone accumulations and damage includes significant variation in the species observed (e.g., spotted hyenas versus wolves) and in observation conditions (e.g., bones fed to zoo animals versus bones recovered from natural dens and kill sites). Even within a species, bone damage and selection of parts for transport may vary with environmental factors (Haynes, 1980b; Hill, 1980a). Although there may be features in common to all carnivore bone accumulations, it is still unclear how well these features distinguish carnivore collections from bones collected and modified by hunter–gatherers.

Nonetheless, using these proposed characteristics in Table 5.3 as a guide (and the hyena assemblage from Amboseli, Kenya, as a test case), the Olduvai faunal collections form a continuum. Relative to the stone artifact sites, FLKNN–2 and Long K are at the end of the range of variation in several aspects of body part frequency and bone damage. Based on these variations that reflect both the modification *and* transport of animal bones, the bone collector(s) at FLKNN–2 and Long K probably differed from the primary collector(s) at the artifact sites. Except for the elephant skeleton at FLK North–6, there do not appear to be consistent variations that imply different primary agents of bone concentration among the artifact sites. Some of the distinctive features of the FLKNN–2 and Long K assemblages converge on patterns observed in modern hyena bone collections, especially that of spotted hyenas in Amboseli. Based strictly on osteological analysis, spotted hyenas (or a similar carnivore in the way it damaged and collected bones) appear to have played a greater role in creating these two sites than any of the artifact sites. The weathering patterns of bones showing tooth marks and cut marks also suggest the priority of carnivore damage to the bones at FLKNN–2; the absence of tool marks and abundance of gnaw marks indicate the same at Long K. No clear priority of hominid or carnivore modification is evident at the artifact sites.

Given the presence of cut marks, the stone artifacts become the strongest diagnostic sign of hominid activity at the latter sites. The mode of stone artifact transport and accumulation is part of the context of bone accumulation at these five sites. Artifact and bone transport to these delimited locations were parallel processes, which cut marks show were linked in some manner. The variety of raw materials, in some cases their quantity, and the presence of apparently unflaked and unused pieces of raw material (manuports) indicate that hominids transported stone over distances of at least 2–3 km to the same spots where bones also were transported. There is no modern parallel nor sound basis in foraging to think that hominids repeatedly carried stone tools and raw materials to open-air faunal concentrations of carnivores to extract something from bones previously selected, transported, and modified by those carnivores. Hominids, therefore, must have played a more important role and carnivores a less important role in transporting bones to the artifact sites. These sites, in general, contrast with the "primarily carnivore" mode of bone accumulation inferred for sites FLKNN–2 and Long K. These inferences permit us to treat the degree of hominid behavior as a variable to account for any consistent differences that occur between the artifact and nonartifact sites (i.e., differences that are not likely due to other taphonomic factors). As we will see, FLKNN–2 and Long K represent important points of comparison for the purpose of defining site patterns attributable uniquely to hominid activities.


## Discerning Hominid from Carnivore Contributions to Sites

The preceding summary ends by emphasizing the contextual evidence present at the site of a bone accumulation. That is, where hominids repeatedly transported stones to a specific point on the ancient landscape, the parallel processes of stone and bone transport to that site become necessary to explain. Cut marks mean that inferences about the agents of bone accumulation cannot ignore the artifact evidence for repeated visits by tool-carrying hominids to these sites. This contextual evidence, along with differences in the bone remains from the two inferred carnivore sites and the five artifact sites, identifies hominids as a more important agent than carnivores in the accumulation of bones at the artifact sites. This contextual approach complements a type of "residual approach" to discerning the relative contributions of hominids and carnivores to the Olduvai sites (cf. Binford, 1981: 246). The residual approach adopted here is outlined at the end of the previous section: The influence of hominids is a variable that can be studied by documenting the consistent differences between the artifact sites and sites made primarily by carnivores that were contemporaries of hominids. In this study, the latter is represented by only two sites, FLKNN–2 and Long K. Consistent differences in, for example, species and skeletal unit representation become attributable to hominid activity since that is the important variable of site formation that is missing or small in its effect at the latter two sites and consistently present and relatively large in its effect at the artifact sites.

### Bones: Binford's Approach to Residues

The residual approach to site formation has been well defined by Binford (1981), whose writings have stimulated many refinements in archeological inference and in thinking about past human behavior. Binford's ideas about residuals were presented in *Bones: Ancient Men and Modern Myths* as a prelude to his own analysis of Olduvai. A brief review of this work is necessary to point out problems inherent in the residual approach, in general, and how the present taphonomic study of Olduvai differs from Binford's.

First, differences between Binford's analysis and my own arise from differences in data base and the treatment of data. In some cases, the analyses in *Bones* are based on mistaken assumptions about the preliminary data base published by Leakey (1971). For instance, the category of "long bone shafts" in Leakey's initial faunal tally was assumed to be "cylinders" (tubular shafts of long bones with the articular ends missing). In fact, this assumption over-estimates the number of cylinders, since many of these pieces are actually shaft splinters. Long bone cylinders are diagnostic of the gnawing activities of carnivores. The actual number of such cylinders is significantly lower than is presented in the *Bones* analysis (Table 5.14). Consequently, the type and intensity of carnivore activity at these sites is somewhat diluted from that supposed by Binford. A more serious problem in handling these data is that the *Bones* analysis lumps together all body sizes of fauna, from small gazelles to elephants. This is inherent in the preliminary faunal data published by Leakey (1971). However, the analysis in *Bones* violates one of the principles of taphonomic study: control for the potentially large biases (sampling effects) related to body size. These initial drawbacks, of course, do not invalidate the fact that carnivores have had an impact on these assemblages. Nor do they invalidate one of the points of Binford's analysis, that the Olduvai sites are open to interpretations other than the home base hypothesis. However, such problems do influence his inferences about particular sites, which are not upheld according to the analyses here.

The major part of the *Bones* analysis is a multivariate comparison of skeletal element frequencies in 24 levels from Olduvai Beds I and II and four types of carnivore site: two models of kill sites (for large prey and small prey) and two models of den sites (again involving large and small prey). The latter are models for interpreting skeletal element representation at Olduvai. This analysis is the crux of Binford's residual approach. The basis of this approach is to identify the patterns of skeletal part frequency evident at the Olduvai sites that conform to patterns in the carnivore models; the aspects of assemblage composition from Olduvai that conform are thus attributed to carnivores. Since, according to Binford, we know the characteristics of bone assemblages produced by carnivores (and can generate models of them), we can factor out the carnivore contribution to the Olduvai sites; the remainder of the variation (the residual pattern of skeletal part representation) can then be attributed to hominids (or, technically, to any noncarnivore factors involved in site formation).

One of the most important objectives of the *Bones* analysis is to measure the roles of hominids and carnivores in site formation. However, I would contend that there are two sets of flaws in this analysis that make this goal of measurement still an unsolved challenge. The first involves the interpretation of particular sites from Olduvai and the second concerns a more serious flaw with the strict residual approach.

First, in the *Bones* analysis several points of agreement between the Olduvai sites and the carnivore models are imputed that are not correct. These points are fundamental to the interpretation of Olduvai site formation. The following list briefly summarizes the differences of interpretation about the Olduvai sites included in this study:

1. DK–3, DK–2, and FLK "Zinj" are interpreted in the *Bones* analysis to have been death/kill sites, since these three sites align best with the carnivore kill site models (Binford, 1981: 273, 275, 276, 281). The kill site models are developed from Hill's data regarding ungulates on African landscapes (Hill, 1975) and Binford's data on wolf kills. Thus, the kill site interpretation of these three faunal assemblages from Olduvai refers to either the death locations of animals or to the scattering of bones away from, but in the vicinity of, such locations. As we examined closely in Chapter 3, however, these three sites do not show any of the characteristics that typify kill sites or landscape assemblages. In fact, Hill's data, which formed an important part of this assessment, clearly illustrate the dissimilarities between these Olduvai sites and kill/landscape assemblages, based on skeletal parts and also the degree of bone concentration, carcass mixing, and species diversity. The analysis in *Bones* also attributes the FLK "Zinj" site to a large ungulate kill model, while the DK sites align with small animal kill sites. In fact, among the sites studied here, FLK "Zinj" exhibits the highest percentage of *small* bovids (Table 7.24) and preserves very few large, nonbovid ungulates. On the other hand, both of the DK levels possess high frequencies of medium and large bovids, hippos, giraffes, rhinoceros, and proboscideans compared with the other Bed I sites (62% of the total MNI at DK–3; 54% of the MNI at DK–2). In short, the attributions made by the multivariate analysis in *Bones* do not conform to the facts of faunal representation.

2. In the *Bones* analysis, two sites—FLKNN–2 and FLK North–6—were correlated with carnivore den assemblages (high Q-mode factor loadings). While this suggests that the bones at these sites were transported, Binford also judges these assemblages to signify "the death site of several large mammals together with background scatters of other (mainly bovid) remains" (1981: 272–273). In addition, these assemblages were judged not to have sustained much impact from agents of bone destruction. Besides FLKNN–2, FLK "Zinj" is another assemblage claimed to be relatively untouched by attrition. Yet

these two sites, in fact, show the clearest signs of differential attrition associated with carnivore gnawing, as shown by the disproportionate preservation of proximal and distal ends of limb bones (Table 5.12). The same pattern
of preservation is found in the spotted hyena den at Amboseli. "Zinj" also
manifests a huge number of small bone splinters (> 20,000 as a very conservative estimate) which also appear to come from heavy destructive agents,
not just weathering (see p. 118). I would agree that FLKNN–2 is like a carnivore den assemblage. However, the supposed similarities between this site
and FLK North–6 appear to be anomolous from a taphonomic standpoint.
Comparisons of skeletal representation and body size indicate important differences between these two sites. For instance, among the sites examined
here, FLK North–6 and FLKNN–2 differ more than any two assemblages
in preservation of elements such as metapodials and humeri (Table 5.7). Further, due to the elephant carcass at FLK North–6, the number of axial remains
is extremely high for any of the Bed I sites, whereas FLKNN–2 has extremely
few axial remains. FLK North–6 has the highest relative representation of
very large ungulates (53% of MNE); FLKNN–2 has the lowest (0%). Small
bovids are the best represented antelopes at FLK North–6 (64% of bovid
MNE), whereas FLKNN–2 is dominated by medium and large bovids (93%
of bovid MNE). The last two points illustrate the lack of comparability between
these two assemblages in animal body sizes, which affects comparisons of
differential preservation of body parts and of skeletal elements overall. It is
curious that the assemblage at FLK North–6 compares well in the factor
analysis with the transported, carnivore den models, since this is the site
with the clearest case among the Olduvai sites of an animal that had died at
the spot of excavation. The strong contribution of elephant vertebrae and
ribs even provide the skeletal element indicators of this. Presumably, due to
this elephant and the (apparently incorrect) claims about differential attrition
of skeletal parts, Binford overrides the similarity to the den models by con-
cluding that this site and evidently FLKNN–2 are palimpsests of death sites.
Again, the analyses of Chapter 3 make that conclusion untenable.

　· 3. FLKNN–3 is judged to be different from the other sites, an assemblage
of parts selected and taken away from animal kills that had already been
utilized by carnivores. This assessment is based on the relative scarcity of
axial and head parts (distal limb bones are also said to be poorly represented),
while appendicular parts such as distal humeri and scapulae are said to be
overrepresented. The former are parts likely to be left directly at a kill site,
while the latter are most likely to be scattered about an animal kill site. However, in fact, FLKNN–3 has the second highest percentage of axial parts
among the Bed I assemblages and the lowest frequency of distal humeri.
Scapulae are not especially well represented (e.g., MNE of 6 out of an MNI
of 18 bovids; only 1 out of an MNI of 16 nonbovids). Yet this contrasts with
13 bovid mandibles and 10 nonbovid mandibles, which suggests that skulls
are not poorly represented. Likewise, the representation of distal limb bones

is about the same as at the other artifact sites in Bed I. Binford's conclusions about FLKNN–3 are based on the following two characterizations: Its most common bones are those that yield only bone marrow as edible material (1981: 281), and hominids scavenged these marrow bones already disarticulated and took them to another location for consumption (1981: 275). First, the data on proximal versus distal long bones from FLKNN–3 (Table 8.3) contradict the notion that bones bearing only marrow are the most common. Second, the interpretation that the FLKNN–3 assemblage consists of elements carried to the site already disarticulated is surprising given that the bovid fauna (64% of the MNE) is dominated by most of a skeleton of *Kobus sigmoidalis*, which must have been introduced to the site in a mostly articulated state. This is the only site in Bed I with such an occurrence in the bovid fauna. Factor 5 in the *Bones* analysis seems to render this occurrence in part (1981: 277) but then leads to the self-contradictory interpretation (mistakenly ascribed to site FLK Level 15) that hominids were processing marrow bones at the places where they obtained them, not at places to which bones were transported (1981: 278).

To conclude, for every Olduvai site considered here, there appear to be interpretations presented in *Bones* that are unwarranted. In some cases, the overall interpretation of a site differs from that developed in this book; in other cases, some particular aspect of site taphonomy (e.g., degree of bone attrition) is just not perceived by the analytical methods used in *Bones* or is at odds with the more detailed data now available. I do not dispute that some of the conclusions drawn in *Bones* about Olduvai may have been warranted by the manipulations performed upon Leakey's preliminary data. Inferences may be sound but still shown to be inaccurate when a refined data base is then examined (e.g., Bunn and Kroll, 1986). However, for each of the sites studied here Binford's specific conclusions do not fit the data on skeletal element frequencies, especially when the data are considered by body size and taxa, nor do they hold up against the taphonomic inferences developed in the previous chapters. Indeed, the inference that carnivores and hominids were involved in the formation of these sites accords well with the taphonomic interpretations presented here. But the fact that specific site interpretations presented in *Bones* cannot be accepted is important since Binford's development of ideas about hominid scavenging and revisions concerning early hominid archeology (Binford, 1985) were initiated by his Olduvai analysis and have been sustained by the illusory view that the resulting interpretations were correct. The view presented in *Bones* that the Olduvai sites predominantly are palimpsests of death sites, or natural accumulations of bones on the landscape in areas of carnivore predation, does not apply to the sites investigated in this book. As we saw in Chapter 3, when compared with multiple criteria that distinguish kill sites and land surface scatters, the Olduvai sites all provide consistent evidence for transport and concentration of bones in specific spots on the landscape.

*Dealing with Assemblage Similarities in the Residual Approach*

A fundamental aspect of the residual approach developed in *Bones* is that the role of hominids in the formation of a site is restricted to whatever is not attributable to carnivores. Since all modern carnivores obtain access to animals primarily by hunting and prefer meat-bearing bones, a residual approach based on a carnivore activity model prohibits *a priori* the possibility that hominids also occasionally or frequently hunted, thus gaining access to meat-bearing bones. This is a serious problem inherent in the strict residual approach. It denies the possibility of overlap or general similarities between these two agents in the skeletal elements, species, body sizes of fauna, etc., that they utilized. It might be argued that this kind of similarity would imply that early hominids were behaving like carnivores and not like humans. But this is beside the point when it comes to understanding whether these hominids did hunt or eat meat in some manner.

In fact, it is clear that similarities do exist between bone assemblages produced by carnivores and modern humans (e.g., Binford, 1981: 237). It is difficult to find patterns of skeletal element representation applicable to the bone concentrations of all carnivore bone collectors in Africa today (essentially only hyenas and leopard). The high frequency of distal humeri and metapodials relative to other major limb bones appears to earmark some hyena assemblages, largely because these elements are left undamaged in those sites. This should not automatically imply, though, that distal humeri and metapodials in the assemblages of Bed I Olduvai be ascribed to carnivores and eliminated from the realm of hominid activity.[1] We have also seen that the "primarily carnivore" assemblage at FLKNN–2 and the artifact-associated assemblages overlap a great deal in skeletal elements, species, and body sizes of fauna. Do we then remove these similarities from consideration as possible effects of hominid activity at the artifact sites? I think the answer must be no. But what recourse is there if our goal, in fact, is to separate the effects of carnivores and hominids in order to define their relative contributions to the assemblages and to compare their behavioral contributions to the fossil record?

*Look at Bone Modifications.*     Two other approaches may be proposed. The first is to define the contributions of hominids, carnivores, water action, and remains left over from animal death sites (i.e., the agents that had major and minor inputs to the Olduvai sites) on the basis of characteristic patterns of bone damage. This might be termed the *bone modification approach*. It is based on the idea that the subset of faunal remains that exhibits carnivore

---

[1] In fact, this implication of the high frequency of metatarsals and metacarpals in hyena accumulations runs counter to the repeated suggestion in *Bones* that metapodials are residuals attributable to hominid activity (scavenging) because carnivores leave these elements behind at kill sites (Binford, 1981).

gnawing is attributable to carnivores, and that if 8% of the bones have cut marks and 3% have carnivore tooth marks, then this measures the relative contributions of these two agents to the bone assemblage in question. This method of analysis derives from studies of cut marks, which in practice have confined the discussion of hominid activities to those bones in an assemblage that bear tool cut marks (e.g., Bunn and Kroll, 1986). Unfortunately, this approach has tended to ignore carnivore tooth marks and other types of bone modification and what they imply about site taphonomy.

Nonetheless, the bone modification approach would seem to offer enormous potential for investigating relative contributions of different agents to archeological sites. So, for example, tool cut marks at the Olduvai artifact sites do occur on bones of species that are present at the "primarily carnivore" site at FLKNN–2; they do occur on skeletal elements that modern carnivores also tend to accumulate; and they are present on unbroken limb bones, even though a high proportion of unbroken limb bones characterizes some carnivore bone accumulations. In other words, the residual approach might ignore these bones in discussions of hominid activities because they are subsumed under "carnivore activity." But damage features show that hominids indeed were involved with these bones.

The existing drawbacks of this approach, however, are several. This approach depends on recognizing cut marks and other types of damage and on the occurrence of such marks on a sizable sample of bones in a faunal assemblage. Although all researchers investigating cut marks on Plio–Pleistocene bones agree that certain examples of surface modification on the Olduvai bones are indeed cut marks, it is less easy to find agreement about how many there are and the meaning of their anatomical location. Conservative but definite evidence for cut marks takes into account microscopic, macroscopic, and sedimentologic data together. However, the *quantification* of cut marks requires decisions about what to do in the more ambiguous cases. The fact that the latter exist, and that the bone modification approach to measuring the relative roles of different agents has not yet been successfully applied to Olduvai, is illustrated by discrepancies between Shipman (1986a) and Bunn and Kroll (1986) in their assessments of Olduvai cut marks (see Chapter 8). Even if we confine our attention to one proposed set of diagnostic modifications, the vast majority of bone damage features in the Olduvai assemblages and probably at other sites cannot be attributed to either stone tool or carnivore tooth, even though hominids and carnivores are clearly the two agents primarily responsible for the bone concentrations at Olduvai. This is partly the result of overlap in the damage to bones produced by these two agents. Moreover, carnivores do not leave diagnostic marks on all bones of a carcass from which they obtain meat. When people use stone tools to butcher an animal, an even lower percentage of the bones tends to bear cut marks, usually much lower than 20% (R. Meadow and E. Wilmsen, pers. comm.). Therefore, different agents of bone modification do not have the same probability of leaving traces, much less diagnostic traces, on the bones with which they come in contact. This undermines the objective of the bone modification approach.

A final problem is that identifying the cause of bone damage does not necessarily indicate how bones came to rest in a particular spot. For the Olduvai sites, we are interested in inferring primary and secondary processes of bone transport. The bone modification approach assumes that the agents of bone modification accurately portray the relative roles of those agents in *transporting* and accumulating faunal remains. However, it would seem that the causes of bone damage do not always yield a clear interpretation about the agents responsible for the concentration of bones. For example, numerous observations of African scavengers and predators show that they do attack animal bones without taking them away from where they were found (e.g., death sites, human garbage dumps). The evidence in the Olduvai assemblages for tool cut marks and carnivore tooth marks reflects evidence for damage; there seems to be no *a priori* reason to assume that the evidence for damage relates directly to the agent responsible for transporting a particular bone. The distinction between the means of bone damage and the means of bone transport and accumulation is an important one and requires independent sources of evidence for each before transport is simply equated with modification. This is perhaps the most serious difficulty that faces the bone modification approach to the sites of Bed I Olduvai.

*The Contextual Approach.*     The conclusions reached in Chapter 5 arise from an alternative line of inference, called the *contextual approach.* In the case of the Olduvai sites considered here, this approach is based on a sequence of inferences. First, we ascertained that each assemblage of bones represents mainly a behaviorally transported collection brought to specific, delimited spots on the landscape. That is, the possibilities are limited to accumulations such as those found in porcupine lairs, carnivore dens, and campsites, to name some examples. Death sites and other landscape assemblages, including palimpsests of partial carcasses adjacent to death sites, do not account for the combination of features evident in each of the Olduvai faunal concentrations.

Second, once behavioral transport to specific spots was determined, cut marks became the primary evidence that hominids handled and processed the bones. Likewise, carnivore gnaw marks, destruction of epiphyses, and other specific damage patterns signal that carnivores were involved with these bones directly at these sites. Yet bone modification by hominids and carnivores is evidence strictly for just that, and it does not necessarily inform us about the means of transport of a bone to a site. In other words, a mark made by a hominid tool could be taken off by a scavenging carnivore to its den and vice versa. In order to understand how the bones got to these sites, we have to consider other lines of evidence. Here, the parallel process of artifact concentration becomes a line of contextual evidence that cannot be ignored or isolated from the process of bone concentration.

The third part of this sequence of inferences, therefore, concerns the degree and nature of artifact accumulation. At the five artifact sites, tools and stone raw materials are concentrated at the same delimited locus as the bones, and these accumulations are well beyond that expected on a landscape over time through the casual discard of artifacts. In other words, these sites were specific foci to which hominids brought artifacts. The final point is that it remains doubtful at best, in the context of open-air savannas, that hominids repeatedly transported stone tools and raw materials to places of bone concentration that, if they were not primarily hominid areas of bone transport, served as dens, lairs, or other major foci of bone accumulation of carnivores.[2] Hominids, thus, are considered to have been primarily responsible for the accumulation of bones at the artifact sites. Although no clear burrows or similar evidence was noted at FLKNN–2, the evidence of bone damage and skeletal representation (and no evidence of repeated hominid visits to this site during its formation) suggests that carnivores played the primary role in concentrating bones there, and the same holds for Long K. By considering contextual clues, then, we are able to rank in importance the agents that introduced bones (and artifacts) to the sites at Olduvai. Hominids, carnivores, and hydraulic processes rank from primary to tertiary as the most important contributors to the formation of most of the artifact sites. Hydraulic factors were more important at DK than at any other locality in Bed I, while the death of the elephant played an added, important role at FLK North–6. Finally, the transport and modification of bones by carnivores were probably the dominant factors at FLKNN–2 and at Long K. Although identifying the *primary* collectors of bones and artifacts is a significant result of this analysis, the contextual approach also recognizes the importance of secondary agents, clearly evident at Olduvai, which might have brought bones and artifacts to sites. By acknowledging the impact of these secondary processes, we can identify those site patterns that can and cannot be expected to inform us about hominid behavior and ecology. Thus, for instance, taphonomic analyses suggest that water flow had a small role to play in Olduvai site formation, though somewhat greater at DK. But since water flow affects small bone fragments and microfauna very easily, data on these objects can be expected to provide ambiguous information about hominid activities. Large, dense objects such as manuports or large mammal bones are likely to offer a more reliable basis for testing ideas about the behavior of the bone and artifact collectors at these sites. Because each site was covered by lake waters, the accumulation

[2]Cave sites, such as those of the later Pleistocene of Europe, provide a different context. Because caves and rock shelters offered excellent shelter for hominids and for a wide range of carnivores and other animals, these sites were obvious foci for the accumulation of bones by a variety of agents. Even with the presence of artifacts, hominids probably were one of many, and not necessarily a significant species, using a cave site.

of aquatic animals (e.g., crocodiles, fish, and water birds) by hominids or carnivores cannot be considered unless further taphonomic studies of these animals prove otherwise.

Similarly, one of the strongest effects of carnivore modification, which occurs at each Olduvai site, is the destruction of long bone ends. Therefore, analyses that depend on, say, the frequency of tool cut marks on the ends of long bones will not necessarily yield precise results pertinent to hominid butchery or other activities, for we must expect that destruction of articular ends by carnivores had an effect. As a final example, prolonged periods of site formation are evident at Olduvai during which hominids and carnivores were active on multiple occasions. This implies that the spatial distribution of objects at each site has undergone much transformation, and spatial analysis cannot be expected to offer a simple rendering of the history of activities, much less a strict rendering of hominid activities.

Hence, faunal or skeletal patterns that are idiosyncratic (i.e., occur as a weak pattern at only one of the artifact sites) or the transport of *individual* bones cannot be ascribed to hominids given the potential impact of these other factors at the artifact sites. In fact, the contextual approach does not attribute specific subsets of bones to particular agents of accumulation. The reason is that reliable methods have yet to be formulated to identify, in most cases, the agents of transport for individual bones based simply on their presence (and damage characteristics) in a cluster of faunal remains.

Instead, according to contextual evidence, only the most general site patterns that are reliably related to the transport and accumulation of bones and artifacts can be expected to inform us about hominid activities. For the faunal remains, these patterns involve broad frequencies of species (taxonomic) and body parts represented at the artifact sites. Inferences drawn from contextual clues direct our subsequent analyses of hominid activities toward those bone remains and artifacts that are likely to preserve the effects of hominids (as the primary agent of transport) even in light of modifications produced by secondary agents acting at the artifact sites (e.g., carnivores).

In practice, all three approaches outlined here may be employed, for they inform us in different ways about the diverse aspects of site formation. The analyses in the following chapters will employ primarily a combination of the contextual and residual approaches. One of the advantages of the contextual approach is that it enables us to consider the similarities between hominids and carnivores as users of carcasses and as bone collectors. That is, overall similarities between FLKNN–2 and Long K, on the one hand, and the artifact sites, on the other, in the species and body parts observed are taken to represent similarities between carnivores and hominids as the main agents responsible for bones at these sites. However, such similarities must be treated as hypothetical and should be considered against the evidence for consistent differences between carnivores and the Olduvai artifact sites. Comparisons between these particular artifact and nonartifact sites enable us to see how faunal assemblages with a greater overall contribution by hominids differ from assemblages with a greater overall contribution by carnivores *within the context of the ancient environment at Olduvai*. Such a comparison permits us to extract residual patterns of faunal and skeletal composition in the "primarily hominid" assemblages that do not overlap with those in the "primarily carnivore" assemblages at Olduvai. Moreover, this can be done without reference to possibly inappropriate models based in the present. It is quite possible that modern and ancient savanna ecosystems in East Africa differed in significant ways. We know, for instance, that extinct carnivores like the running hyena *(Euryboas)* and the machairodonts lived in East Africa 2.0–1.5 Ma. The presence of these taxa may have meant that the competitive milieu among carnivores differed substantially from the present. In addition, the species of hunters and hunter/scavengers underwent considerable change during this period in East Africa (Walker, 1984). It is clear that the competitive milieu among carnivores can affect greatly the availability and selection of skeletal parts by bone collectors for transport to dens or elsewhere. Therefore, analogies to the present should be avoided in defining·the differences among early carnivore and hominid bone collectors at Olduvai. The FLKNN–2 and Long K bone assemblages are significant because they allow us at least two points of comparison within the ancient Olduvai environment itself to see how the artifact sites consistently differ from sites where primarily a carnivore had collected bones over a period of time. Unfortunately, there are not other fossil assemblages yet studied from Olduvai that are demonstrably similar to carnivore assemblages, for these would enhance the baseline against which primarily hominid assemblages of transported bones can be assessed.

The final chapters of this book will adopt this multiple approach to site interpretation at Olduvai. Relying on the distinction between "primarily hominid" and "primarily carnivore" assemblages, we will examine broad patterns of bone and artifact composition and data on bone modification in order to assess similarities between these two types of site. The residual approach, which contrasts these "primarily hominid" and "primarily carnivore" assemblages, will define those patterns at the artifact sites that do not overlap with what we know about carnivores at Olduvai based on the FLKNN–2 and Long K sites. These patterns, thus, will help to identify activities or ecological roles specific to the tool-using hominids at Olduvai.

In the remaining chapters, we will apply what we have found out about Olduvai site taphonomy to broader questions regarding hominid activities, paleoecology, and the home base hypothesis. The present chapter will conclude with a look at one site in particular—FLK North–6. This site has usually been interpreted as an elephant butchery site. It deserves special attention because this traditional view separates it from the other artifact sites, which have been referred to by previous researchers as occupation sites, campsites, or home bases.

## FLK North–6: Butchery Site?

Because of the association of stone artifacts with the skeleton of an elephant *(Elephas recki)*, FLK North–6 generally has been viewed as a butchery site (Clark, 1970; Isaac, 1971; Isaac and Crader, 1981; Leakey, 1971). This type of site, also called a "Type B" site, refers to the presence of a single, large, mammal skeleton and spatially associated stone tools (Isaac and Crader, 1981). The Type B site represented at FLK North–6 is often construed to be the place where an elephant had died by either "natural causes" or hominid hunting. After hominids had butchered the animal, the slightly disarticulated carcass and stone artifacts from this event were left behind; secondary scavengers could also then gain access to the carcass, further disturbing the spatial position of the bones and consuming parts of the carcass. Bones of other animals found at this site are said to be very few, probably representing a background assemblage of bones scattered over the landscape. Thus, a brief, isolated episode of butchery has been the dominant interpretation of this site, as is true of other Type B sites.

Based on Leakey's description (1971) and field notes, we noted in Chapter 2 that almost all of the elephant skeleton was found in excavation. There were 130 stone tools, consisting mainly of sharp flakes and manuports of quartzite and lava and a few modified cobbles (tools/cores). A claim has been made that the artifacts at this site were not spatially associated with the elephant remains but were "inversely correlated" with these remains; instead, the artifacts are said to be associated with the background scatter of nonelephant bones (Binford, 1981: 273, 280). It is clear from the excavation records that this assertion is incorrect: Level 6 in the FLK North excavation was uncovered in four trenches. In the two smaller trenches (labelled II and III), numerous remains of microvertebrates and larger birds and fish were discovered, but no artifacts, in an area just less than 5 m². On the other hand, all of the stone artifacts, all of the elephant bones, and over 95% of the other large mammal remains were confined to trenches IV and V, representing about 32 m². Besides this differential association of artifacts with large mammal bones, the fact that the stone artifacts are distributed mainly on the immediate periphery of the elephant carcass in trenches IV and V does not conflict with the idea that hominids butchered this animal (see Figure 6.1). Further, the total assemblage of nonelephant bones from this site represents an unusual concentration of bones and exhibits none of the diagnostic criteria for landscape assemblages, death sites, or palimpsests of death sites (Chapter 3). The degree of concentration of artifacts is also within the range of variation of the other Bed I sites we have examined here. The accumulation at FLK North–6 appears to represent an unusually dense concentration in a specific, delimited area. Thus, this site, like the others in Bed I Olduvai, represents the repeated transport of bones and artifacts to the same spot on the landscape. The spatial association

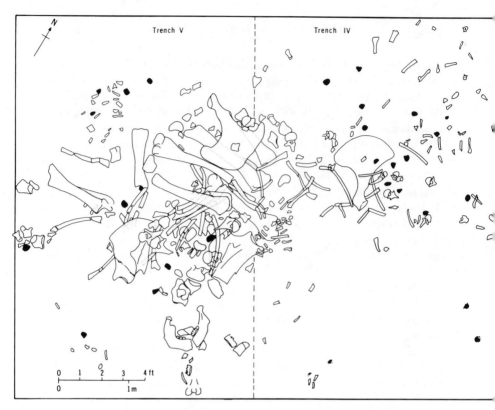

**FIGURE 6.1.** Site plan of FLK North–6, dominated by the partial skeleton of
an elephant. Bones are shown in outline, stone artifacts are shown
in black. Drawn from M. D. Leakey (1971).

between stone artifacts and animal bones, including the elephant remains,
appears to be undebatable, and the notion of "inverse correlation" cannot be
demonstrated.

Although there is little bony evidence for butchery on the main elephant
skeleton, a few linear grooves that appear to be cut marks were noted on
these remains (Bunn, 1982; Shipman, in press). This shows that hominids
were active at this elephant carcass. One of the very massive hip bones was
found to lie on top of a quartzite artifact. This could mean that the elephant
fell at the site after some artifacts already had been deposited. Although the
bones of the carcass were preserved in roughly anatomical position, the in-
nominates seem to have been displaced from a natural death position, which
according to Leakey (1971: 64) may have happened through the actions of
hominids or carnivores. The position of the innominate on top of the artifact
could have occurred after hominids had cut into the elephant carcass. Due to
postburial breakage and fragility of the elephant's bones, breakage patterns

that might relate to hominid butchery or the activities of other animals appear to be obliterated.

Although the bones of *Elephas recki* account for over half of the identified large mammal specimens, elephant remains represent only 9% (i.e., two) of the MNI from FLK North–6. Other than the main elephant carcass, the remainder of the faunal assemblage compares quite favorably to the faunal assemblages from the other artifact sites. As was noted for other sites in Bed I, the non-elephant faunal remains at FLK North–6 are more densely concentrated and represent a much larger number of species, individuals, and limb elements (versus axial remains) than expected for a death site area. Despite the fact that these remains occurred in a thick deposit (50 cm), they do not show the characteristics of a background assemblage of remains (Chapter 3). As we will also see in later chapters, FLK North–6 cannot be distinguished from the other artifact sites in the species, body size, and habitat diversity represented in the assemblage and in the relative representation of various taxa, of specific skeletal elements, and of skeletal regions.

In brief, the features that mark other Bed I faunal assemblages as behaviorally transported accumulations apply equally well to the nonelephant assemblage from FLK North–6. These remains demonstrate that FLK North–6 cannot have been simply a butchery site of an elephant. Rather, this site has had a more complex taphonomic history involving at least the *in situ* death of an elephant, transport of bones and artifacts by hominids, and contributions from carnivores (bone modification and possibly some bone transport also). Based on Bunn's assessment (1982) of the HAS site at Koobi Fora and analyses by Crader (1983), all of the purported butchery sites from the early Pleistocene had such complicated histories and, therefore, cannot represent isolated butchery sites. In other words, pure Type B sites do not seem to exist. Rather, at least some reported cases of butchery site may represent Type C sites (whatever they mean behaviorally) superimposed on a Type B site. In addition, use of the term "butchery site" or "processing site" to refer only to instances of isolated carcasses and stone tools may be too confining. It is clear from the preceding analyses that hominids processed parts of carcasses in contexts where a wide variety of animals are preserved. FLK North–6 was undoubtedly the death site of the elephant. But the butchery site interpretation has drawn attention away from the other fauna collected at this site. Consequently, attention has been drawn away from the overall similarity between this artifact site and the others in Bed I. To the extent that hominids can be considered to represent the primary agent of bone accumulation, no functionally distinctive pattern of hominid activity (e.g., "butchery" as opposed to "living floor") needs to be invoked for the nonelephant faunal accumulation at FLK North–6.

Unfortunately, the relationship between the death of the elephant and the collection of other bones at this particular locus is still unclear. One possibility is that the elephant died directly on the spot to which other bones and stone

artifacts had been transported and accumulated. This association would represent a rather surprising coincidence if the elephant had simply died there
without the direct action of hominids. Alternatively, the death of the elephant
may have preceded the accumulation of other faunal remains and stone artifacts at this site. As such, the elephant carcass may have provided an initial
focus of hominid activity; stone tools were used and left at the site, and other
animal remains were transported to the site later. One source of evidence
for the sequence of bone exposure—surface weathering—provides inconclusive
evidence concerning these ideas. The bovid and other non-elephant remains
span weathering Stages 0–4, with about equal numbers of long bones falling
into Stages 0, 1, and 3. The elephant remains are predominantly in fresh
condition (though many of these specimens have crumbly surfaces most probably due to postburial conditions). However, two leg bones exhibit weathering
Stage 2, and one rib is provisionally assigned to weathering Stage 3. The
latter extends the age of the carcass prior to site burial back nearly as far
as the nonelephant remains. A further factor is that the weathering of elephant
bones tends to occur more slowly that does that of smaller animals due to
the thick covering of soft tissues that remain on an elephant even after butchery or attack by scavengers. Although the pattern of weathering hints that
the elephant bones were exposed to the air after some of the nonelephant
bones had been exposed, a slower rate of elephant carcass decomposition
could well account for this pattern. The fact that the bones of the carcass
were found in roughly anatomical position and not scattered away from the
site of death suggests that most of the bones were held in place and possibly
protected by soft tissues for some time after death.

To conclude, FLK North–6 is a site with a taphonomic history that is perhaps more complicated than any of the other artifact sites by virtue of the
elephant carcass. This spot was the death site of the elephant, and hominids
did use stone tools on it, undoubtedly to take meat, fat, hide, or some other
external substance from the carcass. "Elephant butchery site," however, is
an oversimplified rendering of the formation of this site. The nonelephant
bone remains make FLK North–6 similar to the other artifact sites we have
examined here. The analyses of the next chapters will focus on aspects of
bone accumulation and artifact transport that are common to all of the artifact
sites.

# Part III

Hominid Behavior and Paleoecology

7

# Paleocommunities and Environments of Olduvai

## Introduction

An assemblage of fossil bones represents a sampling of one or more ancient habitats. The fossils may all come from a single animal community, tightly confined in space and time. Alternatively, species from several separate habitats and time periods may be aggregated at one site. The species of animals present in the fossil assemblages at Olduvai reflect the ways that the agents of bone accumulation sampled animal communities in the ancient Olduvai basin. Taphonomic study of the Olduvai sites makes it possible to analyze the paleoecological settings of the early hominids. By understanding the ways bones were aggregated at a site, we gain insight into how bones were transformed from living animals into fossil assemblages and then attempt to reverse the process: infer past communities of animals and their environments from fossil remains.

The presence of tool cut marks on bones from Olduvai suggests that hominids used and deposited stone artifacts during the same period when at least some of the animal bones were also brought to a site. By itself, this evidence means that the assemblages of animal bones associated with artifacts do inform us about the ecological *settings* that hominids inhabited. On the basis of contextual evidence, specifically the parallel processes of artifact and bone accumulation, I have suggested further that hominids were, in fact, mainly responsible for the accumulation of animal bones at the sites where artifacts were also densely concentrated. This interpretation further implies that the faunas from these sites provide information about both paleocommunities in which hominids participated and interactions with particular animal species.[1] (These interactions were not necessarily predator–prey relationships, a matter

[1] I use the term "paleocommunity" to connote preserved aspects of ancient communities typically averaged over time and space. For example, the diverse species of mammals represented in a single faunal assemblage from Olduvai may have derived from a time *range* and may have been transported to the site from a variety of habitats. This implies that some of the animals concentrated in the same faunal assemblage may never have seen one another or have been part of a single interacting web of species. Thus, the term "community" from the study of modern ecology is not necessarily appropriate. Inferences about a paleocommunity are often unable to disentangle seasonal or other short-term variations

*(continued)*

that Chapter 8 will explore.) In other words, data about, say, the relative abundances of specific taxonomic groups (e.g., equids, different tribes of bovids, carnivores) may offer evidence not only about the settings of hominids but also about how the tool-making hominids interacted with their environment, such as the percentages of different large mammals transported back to sites. In this sense, we can explore some ideas about the paleoecological roles (autecology) of early hominids who helped to create the sites investigated here.

However, the preceding chapters have also shown that site formation at Olduvai involved, to varying degrees, taphonomic processes other than hominids. As explained in Chapter 6, adequate methods have not yet been proposed to judge what percentages or particular sets of bones were contributed to a given site by different taphonomic agents. In the case of Olduvai, the key behavioral agents are carnivores and hominids, with contributions also from water flow and other mechanisms of dispersal of bones from carcasses. If we could assign a definite cause of damage to every modified bone found at a site, and if the cause of bone damage corresponded with the agent that brought the bone to that site, then the contributions of different processes of bone transport could be precisely specified. Yet that is not the current state of the art, as we discussed in the previous chapter. This implies that for the "primarily hominid" sites and the "primarily carnivore" sites only the most general patterns of faunal representation are likely to provide valid information about the paleoecology of hominids and carnivores. Only those activities of hominids and carnivores most closely tied to overall site production and to the accumulation of materials will be considered in the final chapters of this book, since these activities are the ones that the preceding taphonomic analyses allow us to evaluate most readily.

## Inferring Paleoecology from Faunal Assemblages

### Availability and Selectivity

The species represented in a behavioral accumulation of bones may furnish various kinds of information about past environments: general environmental settings (e.g., rainfall or aridity), specific habitats within an area (e.g., veg-

---

or to identify differences between contiguous habitats. Yet these types of heterogeneity are typically the focus of modern ecological studies. From the viewpoint of a paleoecologist working on mobile, large-bodied, and long-lived species (which these hominids probably were relative to most other mammals), such small-scale temporal and spatial variations in ecology, although undoubtedly crucial to the reproductive success of some individuals, represent low-level oscillations that probably do not capture the long-term changes or stability within a region (i.e., ecological history in the context of evolutionary time). Paleocommunity inferences may provide the broader scale patterns of species distributions, abundances, and interactions that partly define ecological history and influence the evolution of particular taxonomic groups.

etation zones), and the species with which the accumulation agent(s) interacted. The faunal assemblages from Olduvai, at the least, provide information
on which species were present in the ancient areas inhabited by hominids.
From this information, the relative abundance of different species or groups
of related species (taxa) can be considered, as can the importance of specific
kinds of habitats within the Olduvai basin. The latter type of inference, of
course, depends upon species that are sensitive indicators of general habitat
type or of specific ecological characteristics. Faunal assemblages also reflect
ways that agents of bone accumulation sampled the environment. Taking the
variety of taphonomic processes into account, the faunas at the Olduvai sites
were determined by those *particular* species with which hominids and carnivores interacted, the species that were sampled by lake waters (and for
DK, possibly sheetwash) that covered each site, and by species that had died
in the vicinity of each site during its formation.

In brief, then, the relative abundance of various taxa in a bone accumulation
reflects (1) the *availability* of the bones of each taxon in the environment,
and (2) preferential *selection* from available faunal material by the agents of
bone accumulation. A third factor also significantly influences taxonomic frequencies in bone assemblages: the preferential susceptibility of the bones of
different taxa to transport and destruction.

Relative availability of each taxon depends on population size, density,
and generation time for each species. Generally, small species have shorter
generation times and life spans than do larger fauna; thus, the former potentially contribute more individuals and carcasses per year within an environment than do large species. Since they require smaller areas in which
to sustain themselves, small animals also may occur in high population densities. Comparisons of taxonomic abundance among species grossly different
in body size will be biased by these factors. Comparing taxa of broadly similar
body size should help to control for some of these variables that produce
differences in taxonomic availability.

The culling of faunal material from the environment and its accumulation
at a site may sometimes produce a representative sample of species from the
environment. Carnivores, as predators and potential agents of bone accumulation, are sensitive to fluctuations in the availability of particular species.
However, the taxa that they exploit depend on the body sizes a particular
predator or scavenger is able to kill, dismember, and/or transport. Furthermore, predators/scavengers tend to use different habitats (patches) within
an area preferentially. Since species abundance typically varies with habitat,
taxonomic abundance within an assemblage may reflect the preferential use
of habitats rather than the relative availability of species throughout the environment overall.

The questions about availability versus selection of fauna indeed pertain
to hominids as collectors of faunal remains at archeological sites. For example,
Klein (1977: 21; 1980) considers fluctuations in species from Middle and Late
Stone Age sites to reflect either changing human hunting practices or variation

in species availability as part of overall change in the environment. Either explanation, or both of them, could apply. Yet it is quite difficult to decide this issue (i.e., to separate species availability from faunal sampling "preferences").

Finally, once bones are brought to an assemblage, the remains of different taxa may incur different amounts of destruction or removal. For example, cheetahs tend to destroy more of a baboon skeleton than an antelope skeleton. The reasons are that certain bones are stronger in an antelope than in a baboon and because a baboon skeleton has meaty parts that in an antelope are left untouched by carnivores (Brain, 1981: 26). Thus, in a count of skeletal elements or bone fragments, the abundance of baboons in a bone assemblage made by cheetahs would be greatly underestimated compared with the abundance of antelopes. In addition, data on sheep bones in Navajo settlements indicate that, averaged over the entire skeleton, only 12.5% of the bones survive the highly destructive effects of humans and dogs (Binford and Bertram, 1977). Under similar degrees of bone attrition, it is likely that species that were rare in some original accumulation would not be represented at all. Further, bones of small species and of juveniles of any body size tend to be destroyed more rapidly than the remains of large, adult animals (e.g., Behrensmeyer, Western, and Boaz, 1979). Given the same initial abundance in a bone collection, smaller species or ones represented by many juvenile individuals potentially undergo greater amounts of bone destruction than do big species. Comparison of taxa of roughly similar body sizes, again, may help somewhat to counter this size bias.

### Estimating Relative Abundance

The relative abundance of taxa is usually calculated by using either the *number of specimens* (E) or the MNI attributed to each taxon. Relative meat yields for different species, based on the weight of meat occurring on an average sized animal of each particular species, also have been estimated from archeological faunal assemblages. But this technique is useful only when all bones on a site were collected (by hominids) in the form of complete animals. Such an assumption is not appropriate for the analysis of Olduvai faunal assemblages, nor is it necessarily safe to apply to modern humans who use large portions of animal carcasses (Binford, 1978).

The use of MNI to quantify relative taxonomic frequencies in faunal assemblages has met much criticism (e.g., Grayson, 1978; Lyman, 1979; Payne, 1972). First, MNI overemphasizes the relative frequency of taxa represented by only a few specimens and, in turn, underestimates those taxa with many identified specimens. The sample sizes for different taxa need to be considered. One way to counter this sample size effect is to use other estimates of taxon frequency in combination with MNI. For example, the MNE represented by a taxon may signify a *maximum* estimate of the number of individuals, as though each bone came from a different individual. The E attributed to each taxon is another kind of maximum estimate (as though each identified fragment came from a different individual), unless destructive processes have completely removed traces of particular species. MNI and E often express the range of the possible number of individuals represented by the preserved and identified bones recovered from a site. Sample size effects on the MNI of different taxa will be picked up when taxa are compared according to the number of specimens.[2] If relative taxonomic frequencies are about the same when estimated by MNI, MNE, and E, then presumably the sample size biases of MNI would not apply.

Another problem with MNI, or with any other single estimate of taxa abundance, is that it does not consider the unit of skeletal transport. An animal bone collector may transport skeletal remains in any of a number of forms: as fragments, as complete bones, as articulated units, or as entire skeletons. Since the exact unit of bone transport is unknown, and would be useful to ascertain in itself, there is no intrinsic reason why MNI should give a more accurate estimate of the number of individual skeletons represented by the specimens on a site than one of the other estimates of taxonomic frequency. If hominids, for example, acquired and transported different taxa in different ways, MNI would greatly distort the relative numbers of carcasses of those taxa that hominids had encountered in their habitat. Acquisition of a carcass by predation means access to the entire carcass at once, whereas a scrounging type of scavenging may result in access to only small articulated units or individual bones. In addition, very large animals are likely to be transportable in smaller units than are small animals. Since the unit of bone transport may have varied according to taxon (or body size), a variety of methods for comparing taxonomic abundance must be used in order to assess the possible relative proportions of taxa. In this way, a range of estimates (and interpretations) of taxonomic representation can be considered for each assemblage.

In this study, I have used four different methods to estimate taxonomic frequencies:

### 1. Number of specimens identified to each taxon (E)

As noted previously, E estimates the maximum number of individuals represented by a set of bones and bone fragments. It is a valid indicator of relative taxonomic abundance either if equal numbers of identifiable bone fragments result from each carcass of each taxon, or if each specimen comes from a different carcass. These two assumptions (equal fragmentation/identifiability,

[2]Much as MNI is inadequate for comparing taxa frequencies, the number of specimens also misrepresents relative taxonomic abundance. Bone breakage, for instance, can lead to differences in the number of *identifiable* specimens per species (Noe-Nygaard, 1977). Hence, the number of specimens for each taxon, by itself, is an unsatisfactory way to assess relative abundance.

and each fragment signifies an individual) are deemed here to be rather unlikely.

### 2. Minimum number of elements (MNE)

As an estimate of the number of individual bones represented for each taxon, MNE would provide an accurate estimate of relative taxon frequency if the same number of bones were obtained from each carcass or if each bone were acquired from a different carcass. Again, this assumes that fragmentation of bones beyond recognition operated equally on all taxa.

### 3. Minimum number of skeletal units (MNSU)

This estimates the number of forelimbs, hindlimbs, axial skeletal units, and skulls that are needed to account for all specimens found at a site for each taxon. MNSU provides a more valid estimate (than any other method) of relative taxonomic abundance if articulated units representing less than whole carcasses were introduced to the site and if the same number of anatomical units, on the average, were introduced from each carcass. The value of this concept is discussed by Lyman (1979). Since skeletons typically disarticulate in forelimb, hindlimb, axial, and cranial units (Hill 1975; 1979b), MNSU is an estimate of taxon frequency that may closely correspond to the bone units accumulated by at least some behavioral agents of bone transport. Alternative units are discussed by Lyman (1979) and Binford (1981).

### 4. Minimum number of individuals (MNI)

This estimate would reflect the relative abundance of diverse taxa most accurately if, for each taxon, entire carcasses or the same portions of all carcasses were brought to the site. In cases where only small portions of each carcass were returned to a site, nonhomologous parts of two or more different carcasses would be counted as one individual. Moreover, since an MNI count of *one* could reflect anything from a single skeletal element to an entire carcass, differences among taxa in their handling (e.g., transport) and utilization by a bone collector can be greatly distorted by MNI. Therefore, the previous other estimates must be used with MNI before the proportionate availability of different taxa to the bone collector can be assessed.

Since different species, body sizes, or ecological circumstances may have elicited diverse means of bone procurement and transport, the four estimates of taxon frequency ideally should be *combined* in various ways. For example, MNI for small gazelle and MNSU for equids, which are larger in size, may provide the most appropriate comparison between these two taxa in terms of their relative abundance. To try *all* combinations of these estimates among the various taxa, of course, would make this type of faunal analysis enormously complicated. Instead, each taxon can be examined in turn by noting how its abundance relative to other taxa is affected when different taxon frequency estimates are employed. In this way, taxonomic frequencies that are particularly striking or anomalous when using one kind of estimate can be tested by substituting the alternative estimates.

## Abundances of Large Mammals at Olduvai

This background enables us to examine how taxa are represented in the faunal assemblages of Bed I Olduvai. The taxa, or groups of species, employed in this analysis are bovids (antelopes), equids (zebras), suids (pigs), carnivores, proboscideans (elephants and deinotheres), rhinoceros, hippopotamus, giraffids, and primates. Table 7.1 gives the MNI calculated in this study for each species of large mammal identified in the Olduvai assemblages.[3] Tables 7.2 through 7.6 furnish the proportions of taxa, using higher taxonomic categories, from each site, according to the four methods of estimating taxonomic abundance. Tables in the Appendix provide further information about relative taxonomic frequencies for each site.

To understand what these data mean regarding hominid ecology or habitats, it would be ideal to possess census data about the animals in the ancient Olduvai environments. Evidence concerning the way taxa were dispersed throughout various habitats during the accumulation of each faunal assemblage would also be very useful. Because such "paleo-census" information is unavailable, it is, as remarked earlier, at best difficult to tell whether the taxonomic proportions within these assemblages reflect general environmental circumstances or idiosyncratic preferences of the bone collector (in terms of specific habitat use, predation/scavenging strategies, or the units of bone transport).

Two avenues of analysis are open. First, taxonomic representation in a variety of modern environments can be used as a comparative baseline. Certain patterns of taxonomic representation and body size proportions appear to be good indicators of habitat or of specific ecological variables across a wide

---

[3]In this research, MNI is calculated based on specimens previously identified by specialists who have worked on particular taxa (e. g., for bovids, Gentry and Gentry, 1978) and on pieces originally labelled as unidentified fragments but which could be readily assigned to species or genus. Many of the unidentified fragments were pieces of long bone shaft that could be assigned to broad classes of mammal body size. Much more detailed comparisons, as shown by Bunn and Kroll (1986), can increase the number of small fragments assigned to skeletal part and, thus, increase MNI as well. There is no true MNI given that MNI partly reflects the intensity of comparisons between fossil fragments and modern osteological collections. Moreover, MNI is not an adequate measure of the true number of individual animals represented in a bone assemblage due to the reasons stated before. In this study, MNI establishes some *lower* limit estimate of the number of individuals as part of a range of estimates used to test specific ideas about relative taxonomic abundance. These MNIs are higher than estimates based on Leakey's preliminary analysis of the Olduvai faunas (Leakey, 1971) but not so high as possible if each of the tens of thousands of fragments from the Bed I sites were considered in utmost detail. This "imprecise" aspect of MNI is not believed to offer a problem to the analysis of taxonomic frequencies since the other three estimators of abundance provide higher and alternative kinds of estimates.

TABLE 7.1. Frequencies of Macromammal Taxa Based on the MNI Represented in Each Bed I Level

| | DK-3 | DK-2 | FLKNN-3 | FLKNN-2 | FLK "Zinj" | FLK North-6 | Long K |
|---|---|---|---|---|---|---|---|
| Bovids (13 taxa): | | | | | | | |
| *A. recki* | 4 | 4 | 4 | ?1 | 7 | 3 | 5 |
| Antilopini indet. | | | | | | | 8 |
| *T. s. maryanus* | 1 | 2 | | 1 | 2 | 1 | |
| Medium tragelaphini | 1 | | 1 | 1 | | | |
| Species smaller than *T. s. maryanus* | 1 | 1 | | | | | |
| Large tragelaphini | 1 | | | | | | |
| *K. sigmoidalis* | 1 | 2 | 10 | 6 | 4 | | |
| *P. altidens* | 3 | 4 | 1 | 1 | 4 | 3 | 15 |
| *Parmularius* sp. nov. | | | | | | | 1 |
| *Connochaetes* sp. | | | | | | | 1 |
| *M. kattwinkeli* | 2 | 2 | | | | | |
| Large alcelaphini | | | | 1 | 1 | 1 | |
| *S. acoelotus* | | | | | | | |
| Bovini indet. | 2 | 1 | | | 1 | | |
| *H. gigas* | | | | 2 | | | |
| *Oryx* sp. | | | | | | | |
| Medium hippotragini | | 2 | | | 1 | 1 | |
| Large hippotragini | 2 | | | | | | |
| Large bovid indet. | | | 2 | 1 | | | |
| Very large bovid indet. | | 1 | | | | 1 | |

160

| | C1 | C2 | C3 | C4 | C5 | C6 | C7 |
|---|---|---|---|---|---|---|---|
| **Suids (4 taxa):** | | | | | | | |
| Meso.-Kolpoch. limnetes | 3 | 3 | 1 | 4 | 1 | 4 | |
| Phacochoerus sp. | 1 | 1 | 1 | | | | 2 |
| Metridioch. andrewsi | 1 | 1 | 1 | | | | |
| Notochoerus sp. | | | 1 | | | | |
| Indet. | 1 | 1 | 1 | | 4 | | |
| **Equids (3 taxa):** | | | | | | | |
| E. oldowayensis | 2 | 2 | 4 | 1 | 1 | 4 | 4 |
| E. burchelli | | 1 | | 3 | 1 | | |
| Equus indet. | | 1 | | | | | |
| Hipparion sp. | | | 1 | | | 1 | 3 |
| **Rhino (2 taxa):** | | | | | | | |
| C. simum | 1 | 1 | | | | 1 | |
| Diceros sp. | 1 | 1 | | | | | |
| **Hippo (1 taxon):** | | | | | | | |
| H. gorgops | 1 | 1 | | | | 1 | |
| Hippo. indet. | 1 | | | | | 1 | |
| **Carnivores (10 taxa):** | | | | | | | |
| G. primitivus | | | 1 | 1 | 1 | | |
| G. debilis | | | | | 3 | | |
| Mungos minutus | | | | | 3 | | 3 |
| Canis africanus | | | | | | 2 | 3 |
| Canid indet. | 1 | | 1 | | | | |
| P. recki | | | | 1 | | | |
| C. mesomelas | | | 1 | | | 1 | |
| H. hyaena | | | | 1 | | | |
| C. crocuta | 1 | | | | | | 1 |
| Dinofelis sp. | | | | | | | |
| Felid indet. | | | | 1 | | | 2 |
| Carnivore indet. | 2 | 2 | 1 | | 1 | | |

(continued)

TABLE 7.1. (cont.)

| | | | | |
|---|---|---|---|---|
| Giraffid (3 taxa): | *G. jumae* | 1 | | |
| | *G. stillei* | 1 | | 1 |
| | *Giraffa* sp. | 1 | | |
| | *Sivatherium* sp. | 2 | | 2 |
| Proboscids (2 taxa): | *E. recki* | 1 | | |
| | Elephantid indet. | 1 | 1 | |
| | *D. bozasi* | 1 | | |
| Primates (6 taxa): | *Papio* sp. | 1 | | |
| | *Theropithecus* sp. | 1 | | |
| | *Cercocebus* sp. | 1 | 1 | |
| | Cercopithecid indet. | 1 | | 1 |
| | *Galago* sp. | 1 | | 1 |
| | *Australopithecus boisei* | | | 1 |
| | Hominid indet. | 2 | | 2 |

**TABLE 7.2.** Raw Frequencies and Percentages of Different Taxa from Bed I Levels Based on MNI[a]

| Level | Bovids | Suids | Equids | Carnivores | Proboscideans | Rhinos | Hippos | Giraffids | Primates | Total |
|---|---|---|---|---|---|---|---|---|---|---|
| FLK North-6 | 10 | 4 | 1 | 2 | 2 | 1 | 1 | 1 | 0 | 22 |
| | (45) | (18) | (5) | (9) | (9) | (5) | (5) | (5) | | (100) |
| FLK "Zinj" | 20 | 5 | 5 | 2 | 0 | 0 | 0 | 1 | 3 | 36 |
| | (56) | (14) | (14) | (6) | | | | (3) | (8) | (100) |
| FLKNN-2 | 14 | 5 | 3 | 1 | 0 | 0 | 0 | 0 | 0 | 23 |
| | (61) | (22) | (13) | (4) | | | | | | (100) |
| FLKNN-3 | 18 | 5 | 1 | 7 | 0 | 0 | 0 | 0 | 3 | 34 |
| | (53) | (15) | (3) | (21) | | | | | (9) | (100) |
| DK-2 | 19 | 6 | 3 | 2 | 2 | 1 | 1 | 3 | 4 | 41 |
| | (46) | (15) | (7) | (5) | (5) | (2) | (2) | (7) | (10) | (100) |
| DK-3 | 17 | 5 | 2 | 2 | 2 | 2 | 2 | 3 | 1 | 36 |
| | (48) | (14) | (5) | (5) | (5) | (5) | (5) | (8) | (3) | (100) |
| Long K | 30 | 2 | 7 | 9 | 0 | 0 | 0 | 0 | 0 | 48 |
| | (62) | (4) | (14) | (19) | | | | | | (100) |

[a]Numbers in parentheses are percentages.

**TABLE 7.3.** Raw Frequencies and Percentages of Different Taxa from Bed I Levels Based on MNSU[a]

| Level | Bovids | Suids | Equids | Carnivores | Proboscideans | Rhinos | Hippos | Giraffids | Primates | Total |
|---|---|---|---|---|---|---|---|---|---|---|
| FLK North-6 | 31 | 8 | 1 | 4 | 10 | 2 | 1 | 3 | 0 | 60 |
| | (51) | (13) | (1.6) | (6.6) | (16) | (3) | (1.6) | (5) | | (100) |
| FLK "Zinj" | 71 | 11 | 11 | 4 | 0 | 0 | 0 | 1 | 3 | 101 |
| | (70) | (11) | (11) | (4) | | | | (1) | (3) | (100) |
| FLKNN-2 | 37 | 13 | 5 | 2 | 0 | 0 | 0 | 0 | 0 | 57 |
| | (65) | (23) | (9) | (3.5) | | | | | | (100) |
| FLKNN-3 | 39 | 9 | 4 | 7 | 0 | 0 | 0 | 0 | 7 | 66 |
| | (59) | (14) | (6) | (11) | | | | | (11) | (100) |
| DK-2 | 64 | 10 | 6 | 3 | 4 | 4 | 4 | 5 | 9 | 109 |
| | (59) | (9) | (5.5) | (3) | (4) | (4) | (4) | (4.5) | (8) | (100) |
| DK-3 | 45 | 10 | 6 | 4 | 4 | 4 | 4 | 4 | 3 | 84 |
| | (54) | (12) | (7) | (5) | (5) | (5) | (5) | (5) | (4) | (100) |
| Long K | 97 | 2 | 16 | 14 | 0 | 0 | 0 | 0 | 0 | 129 |
| | (75) | (2) | (12) | (11) | | | | | | (100) |

[a]Numbers in parentheses are percentages.

**TABLE 7.4.** Raw Frequencies and Percentages of Different Taxa from Bed I Levels Based on MNE[a]

| Level | Bovids | Suids | Equids | Carnivores | Proboscideans | Rhinos | Hippos | Giraffids | Primates | Total |
|---|---|---|---|---|---|---|---|---|---|---|
| FLK North-6 | 168 | 19 | 1 | 7 | 159 | 5 | 1 | 3 | 0 | 362 |
|  | (46) | (5) | (0.2) | (2) | (44) | (1.3) | (0.2) | (0.8) |  | (100) |
| FLK "Zinj" | 303 | 17 | 28 | 10 | 0 | 0 | 0 | 1 | 4 | 362 |
|  | (83) | (5) | (8) | (3) |  |  |  | (0.3) | (1) | (100) |
| FLKNN-2 | 107 | 78 | 18 | 3 | 0 | 0 | 0 | 0 | 0 | 206 |
|  | (52) | (38) | (9) | (1.5) |  |  |  |  |  | (100) |
| FLKNN-3 | 155 | 20 | 9 | 26 | 0 | 0 | 0 | 0 | 33 | 243 |
|  | (64) | (8) | (4) | (11) |  |  |  |  | (14) | (100) |
| DK-2 | 329 | 22 | 12 | 5 | 4 | 5 | 6 | 7 | 28 | 418 |
|  | (79) | (5) | (3) | (1.2) | (1) | (1.2) | (1.4) | (2) | (7) | (100) |
| DK-3 | 197 | 23 | 15 | 6 | 6 | 5 | 9 | 8 | 4 | 273 |
|  | (72) | (8) | (6) | (2) | (2) | (2) | (3) | (3) | (1) | (100) |
| Long K | 288 | 2 | 42 | 23 | 0 | 0 | 0 | 0 | 0 | 355 |
|  | (81) | (0.5) | (12) | (6.5) |  |  |  |  |  | (100) |

[a]Numbers in parentheses are percentages.

**TABLE 7.5.** Raw Frequencies and Percentages of Different Taxa from Bed I Levels Based on E[a]

| Level | Bovids | Suids | Equids | Carnivores | Proboscideans | Rhinos | Hippos | Giraffids | Primates | Total |
|---|---|---|---|---|---|---|---|---|---|---|
| FLK North-6 | 262 | 71 | 1 | 10 | 387 | 5 | 1 | 3 | 0 | 740 |
| | (35) | (10) | (0.1) | (1.3) | (52) | (0.6) | (0.1) | (0.4) | | (100) |
| FLK "Zinj" | 510 | 33 | 35 | 23 | 0 | 0 | 0 | 2 | 11 | 614 |
| | (83) | (5) | (6) | (4) | | | | (0.3) | (2) | (100) |
| FLKNN-2 | 156 | 145 | 18 | 5 | 0 | 0 | 0 | 0 | 0 | 324 |
| | (48) | (45) | (5.5) | (1.5) | | | | | | (100) |
| FLKNN-3 | 252 | 35 | 10 | 54 | 0 | 0 | 0 | 0 | 39 | 390 |
| | (65) | (9) | (3) | (14) | | | | | (10) | (100) |
| DK-2 | 602 | 113 | 17 | 11 | 11 | 7 | 12 | 9 | 50 | 832 |
| | (72) | (14) | (2) | (1.3) | (1.3) | (0.8) | (1.4) | (1) | (6) | (100) |
| DK-3 | 356 | 65 | 22 | 11 | 15 | 12 | 20 | 12 | 5 | 518 |
| | (69) | (13) | (4) | (2) | (3) | (2) | (4) | (2) | (1) | (100) |
| Long K | 402 | 6 | 50 | 35 | 0 | 0 | 0 | 0 | 0 | 493 |
| | (82) | (1.2) | (10) | (7) | | | | | | (100) |

[a]Numbers in parentheses are percentages.

**TABLE 7.6.** Taxonomic Abundance Based on MNE for Very Large Animals, MNSU for Large and Medium-Sized Animals, and MNI for Small Animals and Carnivores[a]

| Level | Bovids | Suids | Equids | Carnivores | Proboscideans | Rhinos | Hippos | Giraffids | Primates | Total |
|---|---|---|---|---|---|---|---|---|---|---|
| FLK North-6 | 24 | 8 | 1 | 2 | 6[b] | 5 | 1 | 3 | 0 | 50 |
| | (48) | (16) | (2) | (4) | (12) | (10) | (2) | (6) | | (100) |
| FLK "Zinj" | 49 | 11 | 11 | 2 | 0 | 0 | 0 | 1 | 3 | 77 |
| | (64) | (14) | (14) | (3) | | | | (1) | (4) | (100) |
| FLKNN-2 | 35 | 13 | 5 | 1 | 0 | 0 | 0 | 0 | 0 | 54 |
| | (65) | (24) | (9) | (2) | | | | | | (100) |
| FLKNN-3 | 35 | 9 | 4 | 7 | 0 | 0 | 0 | 0 | 3 | 58 |
| | (60) | (16) | (7) | (12) | | | | | (5) | (100) |
| DK-2 | 55 | 10 | 6 | 2 | 4 | 5 | 6 | 8 | 4 | 100 |
| | (55) | (10) | (6) | (2) | (4) | (5) | (6) | (8) | (4) | (100) |
| DK-3 | 35 | 10 | 6 | 2 | 6 | 5 | 9 | 8 | 1 | 82 |
| | (43) | (12) | (7) | (2) | (7) | (6) | (11) | (10) | (1) | (100) |
| Long K | 97 | 2 | 16 | 9 | 0 | 0 | 0 | 0 | 0 | 124 |
| | (78) | (2) | (13) | (7) | | | | | | (100) |

[a]Numbers in parentheses are percentages.
[b]The elephant carcass is counted as 1 (MNI = 1), but the other elephant remains ($N$ = 5) are counted separately and estimated by MNE.

167

range of geographical areas today. The faunal data from Olduvai can be considered in the light of these patterns to judge how well particular ecological zones or habitats were represented at Olduvai during the formation of each site. Second, the ancient faunal assemblages can be compared with one another. This permits recognition of consistencies or of changes in taxonomic abundance. These intersite patterns of taxonomic representation, then, can be tested against paleoclimatic inferences from geology and pollen (Chapter 2) and against sensitive taxonomic indicators of habitat. This provides a basis from which to infer whether intersite taxonomic patterns reflect sampling of the overall environment or the specific behaviors/preferences of the bone collectors.

## Frequencies of Animals in Modern Savannas

Tables 7.7 through 7.15 contain recent census data on the abundance of taxa in 17 African game reserves. All of the areas are savanna–mosaic settings. They represent mostly open grassland to relatively "closed" bush–savanna environments. These census areas provide a wide range of alternative climatic, physiographic, and vegetation analogues to the Olduvai area during Bed I site formation.

Family or order taxonomic units, such as bovids, suids, or carnivores, are used rather than individual species because these higher taxa are less affected by idiosyncrasies in migrations from year to year or in census counts. The relative abundance of these higher taxa tends to be more consistent in the same types of environment than is the case for individual species. For example, in Nairobi National Park, the four most abundant species in the 1961 census were wildebeest, zebra, kongoni, and impala (ranked from highest to lowest). In contrast, 5 years later in the same type of environmental setting and during the same time of year, the rank abundance was kongoni, impala, Grant's gazelle, and zebra (Foster and Kearney, 1967). Although the abundance of particular species varied widely over time, the relative proportions of bovids (as

**TABLE 7.7.** Percentages of Some Mammal Taxa in the Serengeti Game Reserve, Tanzania

| Taxon | Frequency (Kruuk)[a] | Frequency (Schaller)[b] |
|---|---|---|
| Bovids | 72 | 82 |
| Zebra | 26 | 16 |
| Suid (warthog) | 1.5 | 2 |
| Giraffe | 0.7 | 1 |
| Total sample | 1,083,000 | 953,000 |

[a]From Kruuk (1972:83).
[b]From Schaller (1972:198–203).

**TABLE 7.8.** Percentages of Mammal Taxa in the Serengeti Game Reserve, Tanzania[a]

| Taxon | Living frequency | Estimated deaths per year[b] |
|---|---|---|
| Bovids | 87 | 91 |
| Zebra | 10.3 | 7 |
| Suid (warthog) | 1.5 | 1.5 |
| Giraffe | 0.7 | 0.4 |
| Elephant | 0.2 | .05 |
| Rhino | .04 | .02 |
| Hippo | 0.1 | .04 |
| Total sample | 2,336,200 | 344,685 |

[a]According to Houston (1979:264).
[b]"Estimated deaths per year" is based on estimated mortality rates in the Serengeti region.

a group) and equids, for example, remained quite stable. Furthermore, the grouping of species in the Olduvai assemblages into higher taxa furnishes larger sample sizes, which are better for judging the degree of similarity among sites. The modern data are presented using the same taxonomic groupings in order to facilitate comparison between ancient and recent taxonomic frequencies.

There is a consistent ranking of bovids, equids, and suids according to their relative abundance in recent African savannas. Bovids are always most abundant, followed by zebra (equids) and then suids. This ranking is constant despite habitat variations within savanna–mosaic type of environments. For example, the Serengeti is dominated by broad, treeless grasslands, while the

**TABLE 7.9.** Percentages of Some Mammal Taxa in Nairobi National Park According to Censuses Taken from 1961 to 1969[a]

| Taxon | 1961 | 1962 | 1963 | 1966 | 1967 | 1968, 1969 |
|---|---|---|---|---|---|---|
| Bovids | 74 | 80 | 79 | 76 | 80 | 83 |
| Zebra | 21 | 13 | 13 | 12 | 15 | 10 |
| Suid (warthog) | 4 | 5 | 6 | 4 | 3 | 4 |
| Carnivores | | | | 1 | | |
| Giraffe | 1.5 | 2 | 2 | 2 | 2 | 3 |
| Rhino | | | | .02 | | |
| Hippo | | | | 0.1 | | |
| Primates | | | | 5 | | |
| Total sample | 6283 | 3798 | 3831 | 4010 | 3807 | 3579 |

[a]Data from Foster and Kearney (1967), Foster and McLaughlin (1968), and Rudnai (1973:78).

**TABLE 7.10.** Percentages of Various Mammal Taxa in the Ngorongoro Crater Reserve, Tanzania, in 1964 Census[a]

| Taxon[b] | 1964 |
|---|---|
| Bovids | 77 |
| Zebra | 23 |
| Hippo | 0.1 |
| Rhino | 0.1 |
| Elephant | 0.1 |

[a]Data from Turner and Watson (1964).
[b]Total sample = 22,074.

Tarangire *Acacia* savanna is typified by relatively closed vegetation and little in the way of open plains. Different data sets from the Serengeti suggest that sizable variations occur in the relative proportions of bovids and equids. According to Kruuk's data (1972: 83), bovids are only 2.8 times as abundant as equids, whereas Schaller's data (1972: 198–203) indicate a 5:1 ratio between bovids and equids. Moreover, the more recent and larger census sample that Houston (1979: 264) uses suggests that bovids are 8 times more frequent than equids in the Serengeti area. Similar variations are encountered in studies in Nairobi Park, Kenya, where bovids range from 3.5 to 8.3 times the abundance of zebra in censuses taken in different years. Finally, in a sample of 10 closed-vegetation game reserves in West and Central Africa, where zebra do not live, bovids are again the dominant large mammal (Table 7.15). Suids are abundant in some of these areas; however, the modal abundance for suids in this sample is 5% and for bovids 93% of all large mammals.

To generalize, then, equids usually form between 10 and 25% of the main population of ungulates sampled in these African game reserves; they are from 3 to 8 times less frequent than bovids. Bovids consistently comprise 70% or more of this population. Suids seldom reach higher than 5%, or lower than 1.5%, of the large mammals sampled. Hence, they tend to occur at about one-tenth to one-half the frequency of equids, whereas bovids are typically 25 times as abundant as suids in regions where equids also exist (range: 13.2–60 times more frequent than suids). In the 9-year census data from Nairobi Park (an "open" environment, i.e., low percentage of bush and tree cover), bovids consistently form 80% of the fauna, zebra from 13–21% (but most often 13%), warthog 3–6%, and giraffe consistently 2% of the animals sampled.

The very large mammal species—elephant, rhino, hippo, and giraffe—tend to occur at a variable but consistently low frequency in these environments. No general pattern is evident in the relative proportions or ranking among these large taxa in modern savanna–mosaic areas. For example, elephants may manifest a much higher frequency than hippopotamus in one area (Table 7.14) but fall well below the abundance of hippos in another (Table 7.13). Each of these very large mammals usually represents less than 5% of the

**TABLE 7.11.** Percentages of Various Mammal Taxa in the Amboseli Basin, Kenya[a]

| Taxon | April 1969 | July 1969 | September 1969 | October 1969 | December 1969 | January 1970 | March 1970 | April 1970 | July 1970 |
|---|---|---|---|---|---|---|---|---|---|
| | | | | | Dates of census | | | | |
| Bovids[b] | 66 | 50 | 49 | 53 | 85 | 93 | 64 | 96 | 56 |
| Zebra | 27 | 45 | 39 | 34 | 8 | 3 | 28 | 2 | 39 |
| Elephant | 5 | 6 | 3 | 3 | 5 | 2 | 2 | 0.1 | 2 |
| Giraffe | 1.3 | 0.4 | 0.2 | 5 | 0.1 | 0.9 | 1 | 2 | 2 |
| Monkey | 1 | 4 | 9 | 6 | 1 | 0 | 4 | 0 | 1 |

[a]Data from Western (1973).
[b]Wild bovids only; cattle are excluded, although they make up 50% of the total bovid number of individuals and biomass in the basin.

TABLE 7.12. Percentages of Various Mammal Taxa in Tarangire Reserve.[a]

| Taxon | 1958 | 1961 |
|---|---|---|
| Bovids | 74 | 70 |
| Zebra | 19 | 18 |
| Suids (warthog) | 3 | 3 |
| Giraffe | 2 | 2 |
| Elephant | 0.7 | 5 |
| Rhino | 0.2 | 0.6 |
| "Other herbivores" | 0.6 | 0.2 |
| Lion | 0.5 | 0.3 |
| "Other carnivores" | 0.2 | 0.4 |
| Total sample | 2794 | 5083 |

[a]Data from Lamprey (1964).

total mammals sampled and typically falls below the frequency of suids in environments where this taxon occurs.

Primates also typically occur at a frequency below 5%, though in one monthly census at Amboseli (Table 7.11), bovids were only 5.4 times more abundant than monkeys.

Finally, data on the relative abundance of carnivores are not plentiful. However, censuses in various environments suggest that the maximum carnivore representation among macromammals is near 1%. In the two Tarangire counts, carnivores represent 0.7 and 0.8% of the sample. The carnivore frequency relative to ungulates in the 1966 Nairobi Park census was 1.1%. Bourliere (1965) estimates that lion to ungulate ratios in Virunga National Park (Zaire) is about 1:292. Schaller (1972: 460) reports census data obtained by Hendrichs for the Serengeti; carnivores constitute about 1.6% of the total large mammal population. Delany and Happold (1979: 324–327) gathered in-

TABLE 7.13. Percentages of Various Mammal Taxa from Census Data for a Short Grass Savanna Area (600 km²) South of Lake Edward[a]

| Taxon | 1958 | 1959 |
|---|---|---|
| Bovids[b] | 71 | 69 |
| Suids | 3 | 3 |
| Hippo[c] | 21 | 23 |
| Elephant | 5 | 5 |
| Total sample | 22,708 | 20,915 |

[a]Data from Bourliere (1965:203).

[b]Bovid count is underestimated since the small (and abundant) duiker was not included.

[c]Census was taken as part of a study of hippos; so hippo count may be more complete than for other taxa.

**TABLE 7.14.** Counts of Various Mammal Taxa in Garamba National Park (4800 km$^2$) during 1963[a]

| Taxon | Frequency |
|---|---|
| Elephant | 5694 |
| White rhino | 1202 |
| Hippo | 168 |
| Giraffe | 426 |
| Total sample | 7490 |

[a]Data from Bourliere (1965:204).

formation from various African habitats on carnivore and ungulate densities. Carnivores (lion, leopard, cheetah, spotted hyena, and wild dog) show an average density of 0.28 animals per km$^2$. In contrast, the density of ungulates in six savanna and savanna–woodland areas[4] is 29.05 animals per km$^2$. Typically, then, the areal densities of carnivores are about 1% that of noncarnivore macromammals. However, small, omnivorous carnivores, such as the mongoose *(Mungos)*, sometimes occur in considerably higher densities than do larger carnivores (Rood, 1975).

Tables 7.16–7.20 provide further information specifically on bovid representation in modern African savannas, namely the relative frequency of body size classes. (See Table 5.1 for body size classes.) In general, medium-sized bovids outnumber small antelopes. This relationship holds especially in relatively open environments, although one census from the Serengeti (reported by Houston, 1979) indicates small bovids to be somewhat more abundant than medium-sized species. In the more closed-vegetation situation at Tarangire (Table 7.20), however, small bovids clearly dominate; medium-sized antelopes fall below 20%. The most consistent pattern concerning bovid size in all of the game areas is that large bovids are rare. Large-sized antelopes are always fewer in number than small bovids; yet at Tarangire they rise to above 10% of the total number of bovids, which partly reflects the relative dearth of medium-sized forms in this natural game reserve.

*Large Mammals as Indicators of Specific Environments*

Certain taxa are sensitive to specific ecological and climatic conditions. Therefore, the presence of particular species or groups of species in a bone assemblage, recent or ancient, may help to infer environmental conditions. Table 7.21 provides some generalizations about large African mammals that readily reflect certain kinds of habitat or particular feeding strategies.

[4]The areas included were Albert National Park (short grass savanna), Garamba National Park (mixed savanna), Lake Nakuru National Park (woodland–grassland), Kafue (grassland), Fete Ole (Sahelian savanna), Rwenzori National Park (grassland savanna), and Comoe Valley (woodland savanna).

**TABLE 7.15.** Percentages of Large Mammal Taxa from Ten Game Reserves in West and Central Africa[a,b]

| Taxon[c] | Arli | Deux Bale | Po | Saint-Floris | Bouba Ndjida | Yankari | Fina | Pendjari | Comoe | Kainji |
|---|---|---|---|---|---|---|---|---|---|---|
| Bovids | 88 | 95 | 87 | 92 | 94 | 63 | 63 | 86 | 97 | 90 |
| Suids | 12 | 2 | 5 | P | 5 | 35 | 37 | 14 | 3 | 4 |
| Giraffids | 0 | 0 | 0 | 1 | P | 0 | 0 | 0 | 0 | 0 |
| Rhinoceros | 0 | 0 | 0 | 0 | .08 | 0 | 0 | 0 | 0 | 0 |
| Elephants | P[d] | 3 | 8 | 6 | .5 | 2 | P | P | .3 | 6 |

[a]Based on aerial and ground censuses summarized by Milligan et al. (1982).
[b]Range of rainfall in these areas is 900–1200 mm per year.
[c]No equids live in these reserves.
[d]P = Present.

**TABLE 7.16.** Percentage Representation of Bovid Size Classes in the Serengeti Game Reserve, Tanzania[a]

| Bovid size class | Frequency (Kruuk) | Frequency (Schaller) | Living frequency (Houston) | Mortality frequency (Houston) |
|---|---|---|---|---|
| Large (buffalo, eland) | 7 | 7 | 6.5 | 3 |
| Medium (wildebeest, Kongoni, topi, waterbuck)[b] | 53 | 59 | 39 | 30 |
| Small (Grant's, Thomson's gazelle, impala) | 40 | 33 | 54 | 67 |
| Total sample | 778,000 | 770,000 | 2,037,300 | 313,950 |

[a]Based on data from Kruuk (1972), Schaller (1972), and Houston (1979).
[b]Kruuk's data also include reedbuck in the medium-size class count.

In addition, Vrba (1980) has presented a rather convincing link between the frequencies of certain bovids and general environmental setting. Type A habitats are characterized by closed vegetation (a relatively high proportion of bush and tree cover) and concomitant high rainfall. In the sample ($N = 10$) of Type A environments Vrba presents, precipitation ranges from 600 to 1200 mm per year (mean = 860 mm). Type B habitats ($N = 6$) are open and drier, typified by broad grassland areas and a range of rainfall from 200–772 mm per annum (mean = 480 mm). As is evident from Table 7.21, certain taxonomic groups of bovid species (tribes) exhibit adaptations to specific ecological characteristics. For instance, the gazelles (Antilopini) are mainly grazers, while most tragelaphines (the tribe composed of bushbucks and kudus) are browsers. The wildebeest and hartebeest group (alcelaphines) are similar ecologically to the antilopines. The latter are small, cursorial antelopes, often adapted to conditions of water shortage in open habitats; alcelaphines are also cursorial and graze in open country (Dorst and Dandelot, 1970; Gentry, 1976; Gentry and Gentry, 1978). Vrba has documented a close relationship between habitat type and the percentage of antilopines plus alcelaphines (relative to all other bovids). In the Type A environments examined by Vrba, antilopines and alcelaphines account for less than 30% of all bovids (and, actually, antilopines are not present at all).[5] In all of these areas, some tribe other than the alcelaphines or antilopines comprises the dominant type of bovid. In contrast, in Type B environments alcelaphines or antilopines are the main bovid tribe. These two tribes together constitute over 60%—and usually over 70%—of all bovids in these open, dry areas. On the average, antilopines plus alcelaphines represent 10% of all bovids in Type A habitats and 75.5% of the bovids in Type B environments.

[5]Vrba (1980) does not include the impala *(Aepyceros)* in the Alcelaphini. The impala is a mixed browser–grazer seen in both closed bush vegetation and open grassland areas.

**TABLE 7.17.** Percentage Representation of Bovid Size Classes in Ngorongoro Crater Reserve, Tanzania[a]

| Bovid size class | Frequency |
| --- | --- |
| Large (eland) | 2 |
| Medium (wildebeest, kongoni, waterbuck) | 84 |
| Small (gazelles) | 14 |
| Total | 16,958 |

[a] Data from Turner and Watson (1964).

The antelopes killed or scavenged by various carnivores tend to reflect this connection between bovid tribe and habitat. In the Serengeti (Type B environment), data from Kruuk and Turner (1967) indicate that alcelaphines and antilopines comprise from 55 to 95% of the bovids killed by lion, leopard, cheetah, and the wild dog. In Schaller's (1972) Serengeti study, these tribes make up 87–98% of the bovids in the kills of these same predators and constituted 82% of the living bovid population in this area. In contrast, in Kruger National Park (South Africa)—a Type A habitat—alcelaphines and antilopines comprise only 1–31% of bovids killed by carnivores (lion, cheetah, leopard, wild dog, spotted hyena, and brown hyena); these two tribes account for 10% of the living bovids in Kruger Park (Pienaar, 1969). These patterns of carnivore

**TABLE 7.18.** Percentage Representation of Bovid Size Classes in Nairobi National Park from Various Years[a]

| Bovid size class | 1961 census | 1966 census |
| --- | --- | --- |
| Large (eland) | 1 | 2 |
| Medium (waterbuck, bushbuck, kongoni, wildebeest) | 68 | 49 |
| Small (Grant's, Thomson's gazelle, impala) | 31 | 49 |
| Total | 4631 | 2993 |
| | 1968–1969 census | |
| Large (eland, buffalo) | 2 | |
| Medium (waterbuck, bushbuck, kongoni, wildebeest, reedbuck)[b] | 61 | |
| Small (Grant's, Thomson's gazelle, impala) | 37 | |
| Total sample | 2957 | |

[a] Data from Foster and Kearney (1967) and Rudnai (1973:78).

[b] A relative decrease in medium-sized bovids is due entirely to a decrease in wildebeest; by 1969 the wildebeest population coming as far north as Nairobi Park had recovered.

**TABLE 7.19** Percentage Representation of Bovid Size Classes in Amboseli Basin[a]

| Bovid size class | Date of census | | | | | | | | |
|---|---|---|---|---|---|---|---|---|---|
| | April 1969 | July 1969 | September 1969 | October 1969 | December 1969 | January 1970 | March 1970 | April 1970 | July 1970 |
| Large (eland, buffalo) | 19 | 0.5 | 17 | 12 | 4 | 2 | 11 | 26 | 0.8 |
| Medium (wildebeest, kongoni, oryx) | 42 | 86 | 69 | 66 | 54 | 20 | 73 | 31 | 73 |
| Small (Grant's, Thomson's gazelle, impala) | 39 | 13 | 14 | 22 | 42 | 78 | 16 | 42 | 26 |
| Total sample | 5909 | 3684 | 3847 | 4653 | 2954 | 4135 | 6618 | 3833 | 6140 |

[a]Data from Western (1973).

**TABLE 7.20.** Percentage Representation of Bovid Size Classes from Census data
in Tarangire Reserve[a]

| Bovid size class | 1958 | 1961 |
|---|---|---|
| Large (eland, buffalo) | 12 | 15 |
| Medium (waterbuck, wildebeest, kongoni, lesser kudu) | 11 | 17 |
| Small (impala, Grant's gazelle) | 71 | 63 |
| Very small (dik-dik) | 6 | 6 |
| Total | 2063 | 3577 |

[a]Data from Lamprey (1964).

predation in Type A and B areas undoubtedly reflect opportunistic acquisition
of prey species based on their relative abundance.

Several other cases provide further tests of Vrba's link between bovid
tribe and environment. First, Amboseli is a dry, open environment with typically less than 400 mm rain per year; it is one Type B area not considered
by Vrba. There, alcelaphines and antilopines also predominated each monthly
count during the 1969–1970 census. They usually represented well above 60%
of all bovids; in one month their frequency did drop to a low of 56% (Western,
1973). Second, although it is described as an *Acacia* savanna–mosaic area,
the Tarangire reserve exhibits relatively closed vegetation. In this habitat,
antilopines and alcelaphines account for only 13% of the bovids (Lamprey,
1964). This figure compares well with the expected Type A habitat pattern.
Finally, in the sample of 10 Type A areas (900–1200 mm of rainfall per year)
summarized by Milligan, Ajayi, and Hall (1982), antilopines do not occur at
all and alcelaphines comprise an average of 20% of all bovids. Even in the
reserve with the highest percentage of alcelaphines (35.3% in Saint-Floris),
alcelaphines are not the dominant bovid tribe. In these Type A regions, either
reduncines or hippotragines constitute the prevalent type of antelope. These
further tests of Vrba's habitat-bovid tribe correspondence tend to support
that relationship and make it a useful baseline against which to analyze ancient
habitats at Olduvai.

## Paleoecology of Bed I Olduvai

*Antelopes and Paleoenvironments*

To this point, we have drawn several generalizations that link the frequencies of large mammal taxa to features of modern African savannas. How
does this background information help to decipher the paleoecology of the
Olduvai sites?

The bovids in each assemblage reflect the presence of a variety of habitats,

**TABLE 7.21.** African Savanna–Mosaic Mammals that Typify Certain Ecological Conditions and Diets[a]

| Grazer | Browser | Mixed feeder | Water dependent (1) | Water independent | Open vegetation | Dense/woody vegetation |
|---|---|---|---|---|---|---|
| Zebra (1) | Black rhino (1) | Impala (1) | Wildebeest | Impala (1) | Oryx (4) | *Hippotragus* (sable/roan antelope) (4) |
| Wildebeest (1) | Giraffe (1) | Grant's gazelle (1) | Zebra | Grant's gazelle (1) | Zebra | Tragelaphines[d] |
| Most alcelaphines (4) | Elephant (1) | Warthog (1) | Eland | Dik dik | Alcelaphines | |
| Thomson's gazelle (2) | Dik dik (1) | Eland (1) | Elephant | Oryx (4) | Antilopines | |
| Grant's gazelle (2) | Most tragela-phines (4)[c] | Lesser kudu (1) | Buffalo | | Reduncines[d] | |
| Most antilopines (4) | | Waterbuck (4) | Reduncines | | | |
| Oryx (2) | | | Rhino | | | |
| Eland (2) | | | Warthog | | | |
| Topi (2) | | | | | | |
| Kongoni (1)[b] | | | | | | |
| Buffalo (1) | | | | | | |
| White rhino (3) | | | | | | |
| Hippotragines (4) | | | | | | |
| Reduncines (4) | | | | | | |

[a]Numbers in parentheses refer to the following references:
(1) Lamprey 1963; (2) Watson, Graham, and Parker, 1969; (3) Foster, 1967; (4) Gentry and Gentry, 1978; Vrba, 1980; Dorst and Dandelot, 1970; Gentry, 1976.

[b]Buffalo are grazers but with preference for denser vegetation than, for example, zebra (plains habitat).

[c]*Tragelaphus* species (bushbuck and kudus) are generally browsers; *Taurotragus* (eland) browses sometimes but regularly feeds on grass (Dorst and Dandelot, 1970; Gentry, 1976; Gentry and Gentry, 1978; Vrba, 1980).

[d]Alcelaphines and antilopines typically occur in open grasslands, whereas reduncines (e.g., *Kobus*) occur in grassy marshlands—such as in both low- and high-lying parts of floodplains. Tragelaphines occupy denser thickets and scrub (Gentry and Gentry, 1978).

as we noted earlier on the basis of sediments, pollen, and microfauna (Chapter 2). The occurrence of antilopines and alcelaphines has suggested previously that dry, open bushland or tree savanna plains were the habitats best represented in Bed I faunal assemblages (Gentry and Gentry, 1978: 55). The main antilopine species recognized at the sites studied here is *Antidorcas recki*. This species was a slightly smaller antecedant to the living springbok, an arid country grazer associated with typical plains species like wildebeest and zebra (Gentry and Gentry, 1978; Klein, 1980). In general, alcelaphines are also well represented at the sites in Bed I. This suggests the availability of short grass in open country or at least clearings with good visibility. In addition, alcelaphines can tolerate more arid conditions than can reduncines.

Despite these basic inferences about the Olduvai habitat, the frequency of alcelaphines and antilopines relative to other bovids in Bed I does not consistently follow the pattern of open, dry Type B habitats. Although alcelaphines or antilopines comprise the dominant bovid tribe at most of the sites in Bed I, this is not the case at FLKNN–2 and 3. Table 7.22 presents data on the abundance of these two bovid tribes, based on MNI. FLK "Zinj" and FLK North–6 exhibit the highest frequency of alcelaphines and antilopines (60%) among the artifact sites. Only Long K, in upper Bed I, has a percentage greater than this, that is as great as that found in Type B environments today. Rather, most of the Bed I bovid assemblages exhibit a relative frequency of bovid tribes that is intermediate between Type B and Type A habitats. On the other hand, FLKNN–2 shows a clear Type A pattern, with only

**TABLE 7.22.** Abundance of Antilopines and Alcelaphines Relative to Other Bovid Tribes, Based on MNI, Bed I levels

| Level | Bovid MNI | MNI antilopines/ alcelaphines | Frequency antilopines plus alcelaphines (in percentage) |
|---|---|---|---|
| Long K | 30 | 13 Antilopines 15 Alcelaphines | 93 |
| FLK North–6 | 10 | 3 Antilopines 3 Alcelaphines | 60 |
| FLK "Zinj" | 20 | 7 Antilopines 5 Alcelaphines | 60 |
| FLKNN–2 | 14 | ?1 Antilopine 2 Alcelaphines | 21 |
| FLKNN–3 | 13 | 4 Antilopine 1 Alcelaphine | 38 |
| DK–2 | 19 | 4 Antilopines 6 Alcelaphines | 53 |
| DK–3 | 18 | 4 Antilopines 5 Alcelaphines | 50 |

a 21% representation of alcelaphines plus antilopines—and possibly a lack of antilopines.

Reduncines *(Kobus sigmoidalis)*, which graze in the vicinity of water or marshy areas, dominate both assemblages at FLKNN. Moreover, *Hippotragus*, which occupies fairly dense vegetation today, is recognized only at FLKNN–2. This further suggests that bovids that prefer relatively closed vegetation are best represented in this assemblage. Moisture-loving reduncines are present in every Bed I level, except FLK North–6 and Long K, where open and possibly dry country forms prevail. However, one taxon that typifes such environments—the equids—is most poorly represented at FLK North–6. The occurrence of *Oryx* at FLK "Zinj" further suggests that open, dry areas were sampled in the vicinity of FLK following a period of moist, closed vegetation habitats represented at the FLKNN sites. With the exception of Long K, tragelaphines occur in every Bed I assemblage, although not in great abundance. These species indicate the occurrence of browse in relatively well-vegetated, bush areas.

In general, variations in the percentage of alcelphines and antilopines relative to other antelopes follows the climatic changes that Bonnefille reconstructs from pollen evidence (Bonnefille and Riolett, 1980; Bonnefille *et al.*, 1982), that Hay (1976) infers from geology, and that are suggested by microfauna (see Chapter 2). During a moist phase between Tuff IB and ID, the two FLKNN assemblages exhibit the lowest relative percentage of these two bovids among the Bed I levels. Moreover, highs of 60 and 93% are reached at FLK North–6 and Long K, respectively. These trends in bovid representation and the correlation with other indicators of paleoclimate suggest that the relationship of bovid tribe to rainfall and vegetation applies as well to East African ecosystems 1.8 million years old as it does today. The fact that the figure of 60% at FLK North–6 signifies a low percentage in an apparently arid environment may be due to either (1) the small sample sizes of bovids considered, or (2) preferential transport by bone collectors of those bovids that lived in bush habitats that persisted under arid conditions.

Turning now to bovid body size (Table 7.23), medium-sized forms are prevalent, as is found today in savanna–mosaic habitats. Furthermore, most of the Olduvai assemblages show a higher proportion of large bovids than occurs in the modern savanna areas surveyed earlier. This may partly reflect more closed vegetation areas (as is the case at Tarangire Reserve). However, the fact that large bovids are usually represented at 15% or above, that they are more abundant than small bovids at two of the Olduvai sites, and that their abundance also seems to be at the expense of medium-sized antelopes, suggests that size-related effects of differential preservation have influenced the patterns of bovid size representation. This bias potentially has its greatest expression at FLKNN–2, the only assemblage with less than 20% small bovids (7%) and greater than 40% large bovids (43%). Moreover, the small samples of bovids in any one size class demand that any general conclusions drawn from the proportions of bovid size classes be taken with caution.

**TABLE 7.23.** Frequency of Bovid Body-Size Classes, Based on MNI, for Bed I levels[a]

| Bovid size class | DK-3 | DK-2 | FLKNN-3 | FLKNN-2 | FLK "Zinj" | FLK North-6 | Long K |
|---|---|---|---|---|---|---|---|
| Large | 6 | 4 | 2 | 6 | 3 | 2 | 1 |
| | (35) | (21) | (15) | (43) | (15) | (20) | (3) |
| Medium | 7 | 11 | 7 | 7 | 10 | 5 | 16 |
| | (41) | (58) | (54) | (50) | (50) | (50) | (53) |
| Small | 4 | 4 | 4 | 1 | 7 | 3 | 13 |
| | (24) | (21) | (31) | (7) | (35) | (30) | (43) |
| Total | 17 | 19 | 13 | 14 | 20 | 10 | 30 |

[a]Numbers in parentheses are percentages.

## Other Taxa and Paleoenvironments

When we look at animals other than bovids, a combination of browsers (e.g., elephant, giraffe, black rhino at DK) and open country grazers (e.g., zebra, white rhino) appear at sites DK–2, DK–3, and FLK North–6. *Equus oldowayensis* appears to be an ancestor of the present-day Grevy's zebra *(Equus grevyi)*, which tends to inhabit more arid areas away from water compared with Burchell's zebra. *Equus burchelli* did exist in East Africa during the period of Bed I deposition and, in fact, is recognized at Olduvai from the bottom of Bed I to the top of Bed II. However, only one bone (a proximal radius) at DK–2 is the extent of *E. burchelli* representation in the assemblages investigated here. The dominant equid is *E. oldowayensis*, which occurs at all sites. *Hipparion* is also present at two sites, DK–2 and FLK "Zinj." The presence of equids implies the presence of open grasslands throughout the period of Bed I. By its morphological similarity to Grevy's zebra, the Olduvai form also suggests that drier country existed some distance from the moist, bushy, lakeside habitats inferred from other elements in the Bed I faunas, including rodents.

Very large mammals (greater than 820 kg) do not occur in every Bed I level. However, elements of several very large species occur at DK–2 and 3 and at FLK North–6. Although rhinoceros is rare throughout Bed I, both *Diceros* (black rhino) and *Ceratotherium* (white rhino) are present at DK–3. The former is a browser, whereas the "square-lipped" rhino is usually a grazer. The presence of both forms suggests the occurrence of trees or bush associated with grasslands. Interestingly, *Hippopotamus*, an aquatic mammal, is preserved at DK and FLK North–6, but not in the levels of Middle Bed I. The two localities where it occurs represent extremes in the degree of rainfall or moisture in Bed I, based on pollen and geological evidence. A variety of giraffids, which are browsers, occur in low abundance in Bed I and are not present at the sites (FLKNN) formed during moist periods with relatively closed vegetation.

In the FLKNN and FLK "Zinj" assemblages, large- and medium-sized bovids dominate the mammalian macrofauna. It has been suggested that larger mammals should be indicative of higher levels of rainfall (and the increased environmental productivity and stability that follow) (Western, 1980: 51). The fauna from Bed I levels do not reflect such a correlation: Very large mammals are rarest on the sites formed during periods of greatest moisture. The greatest diversity of very large mammals occurs on sites formed during periods of both apparently high moisture (DK) and relative aridity (FLK North–6). The sample sizes for these very large-sized taxa are small. Hence, the ecological significance of this apparently anomalous sampling of such taxa at these sites is difficult to assess.

Suids are present at every site in Bed I. The species called *Mesochoerus limnetes* (White and Harris, 1977) or *Kolpochoerus limnetes* (Cooke and

Wilkinson, 1978) is particularly prevalent. The suids may represent herbivores (especially grazers) or omnivores, and the variety of forms known from Bed I do not specify any particular habitat.

Among the primates, the presence of *Galago* at DK-2 and FLK "Zinj" indicates that arboreal substrates were nearby. The monkey *Cercocebus* is an indicator of forested areas near water, whereas other monkeys *(Papio* and *Theropithecus)* suggest the presence of more open habitats.

Finally, the diversity of carnivores known from Bed I implies that the environments of this period at Olduvai were quite similar to savanna–mosaic settings in East Africa today. At the sites we are examining, a form identical to the modern silver-backed jackal *(Canis mesomelas)* occurs at FLK "Zinj," both spotted hyena (DK-3) and striped hyena (FLKNN-3) are present, as well as a variety of viverrids (genets and mongooses). Although fossil remains of lion, leopard, and cheetah are known from Bed I, felids are very rare at the sites investigated here, present with certainty only at FLKNN-3.

## Further Comparisons to Modern Savannas

Although the species of large mammals from Olduvai are characteristic of savanna–mosaic settings, several discrepancies arise when we compare further the faunas of Bed I Olduvai to modern savannas. As we examine the data, it is important to realize that in an assemblage where one taxon has a particularly high percentage abundance, this will be at the expense of one or more other taxa, which will exhibit a lower percentage since all taxa must total 100%.

### Abundance of Bovids, Suids, and Equids

First, the relationship among bovids, suids, and equids usually differs from that which occurs in modern savanna–mosaic areas. When any one of the four estimates of taxonomic frequencies is used (Tables 7.2–7.5), or some useful combination of estimates is employed (Table 7.6), bovids rarely reach 70% or more of the large mammal samples from Bed I. In fact, only when MNE or the number of specimens is examined do bovids reach above 70% in any of the artifact-associated assemblages (FLK "Zinj" and DK). Antelope frequencies below 50% are not uncommon. Furthermore, equids rarely reach over 10% of the large mammals in these assemblages (typically 10–25% in modern savannas). More striking is the fact that at DK-3, FLKNN-3, and FLK North-6, equid frequencies are low even compared to bovid frequencies. That is, despite the relatively low bovid percentages, they are still 9 (or more) times as abundant as equids in these levels. When MNE or the number of specimens is considered, FLK "Zinj" and DK-2 also show this same low equid abundance relative to bovids. Only at FLKNN-2 and Long K, regardless of the taxonomic estimate used, do equids show an abundance relative to the total macrofauna and/or to bovids which matches the standards for modern savannas.

Suids, on the other hand, show high relative frequencies in all assemblages, with the exception of Long K. According to most methods of estimation, suids represent more than 5% of all large mammals and are consistently *more* abundant than equids. In relation to modern savannas, the suids at Olduvai are also high in abundance when compared specifically to bovids. Bovids are calculated to be 10 times more abundant than suids only when based on MNE, and this ratio holds for just two of the Olduvai sites (FLK "Zinj" and DK–2). This ratio of bovids to suids is still low compared to most modern savannas. Suids from the Lower Pleistocene were generally larger than suids today. Yet this greater size and possible durability of their bones do not mean that suids should be preserved preferentially over the larger equids or most bovids. Long K is the only assemblage in which the relationships among bovids, equids, and suids fall in the range of relative abundance known in modern savannas.

### Elephants, Hippos, Rhinos, and Giraffids

Very large mammals tend to be quite rare in the Bed I bone assemblages. MNI does tend to inflate the relative percentages of these rare taxa, but MNE and the number of specimens generally estimate the percentage representation of giraffids, hippos, rhinos, and proboscideans to be less than 5% and often 1–3%. Therefore, these taxa are represented in frequencies as low as in modern savannas. The exception is FLK North–6, where the *Elephas recki* skeleton was found. Because of this skeleton, E, MNE, and MNSU all overestimate the actual number of elephants represented. A minimum number of two elephants is present at this site, but even that represents 9% of all MNI in the assemblage. While the skeleton very likely means that one elephant died right at the site, the additional elephant material suggests a fairly high degree of transport of remains from one or more elephants.

Table 7.6 shows the relative abundance of taxa when different estimates are used to account for the ability to transport taxa of different body sizes. Theoretically, body size is an important influence on the ability of a bone collector to drag or carry a whole or partial carcass. Small animal carcasses are more likely to be carried intact than large mammals. Thus, if we think in terms of transport trips and the number of individual animals exploited, an MNI of 1 for small species may be equivalent to an MNSU of 1 for larger species. Very large mammals may be introduced to a site a bone at a time; thus, their representation relative to smaller taxa may be best reflected by MNE. When taxonomic abundance is calculated based on these hypothetical differences in transport potential, not only proboscideans at FLK North–6 maintain a high relative percentage, but rhinos, hippos, and giraffids also manifest fairly high frequencies. The DK assemblages exhibit a similar phenomenon (Table 7.6). Given that these assemblages also display a greater abundance of large bovids relative to smaller bovids than at other sites (except FLKNN–2), the effects of differential preservation are likely to account for the unusually high percentages of these very large mammals.

## Primates

Primates show a generally low abundance in Bed I. In Table 7.6, for instance, primates comprise 5% of the macromammals or lower. Other estimates of taxonomic abundance give a higher faunal percentage for primates at DK–2 and especially at FLKNN–3. At the latter site, hominid material dominates the primate fauna. However, even at these two sites the proportion of primates to bovids is not inordinately high compared to some instances in modern savannas (p. 172).

## Carnivores

Finally, carnivores are represented at a low absolute level in the Olduvai faunal assemblages. A low carnivore frequency (and biomass) relative to herbivores is expected given their positions in the food chain. As we noted for modern savannas, carnivores represent about 1% of all large mammals. For temperate and tropical areas together, the standing crop percentage for carnivores appears to vary more widely (1–4.5% according to Bakker [1972: 82]). The percentage of fossil carnivore remains in Miocene assemblages from Pakistan and Greece is 1% or less, relative to all macromammals found (J. Barry, M. Raza, N. Solounias, pers. comm.). Given this rather consistently low frequency of carnivores in modern and ancient environments, the relative percentages of carnivores in the Olduvai assemblages are actually slightly high. Particularly striking is FLKNN–3. In this assemblage, the MNI for carnivores reaches 21%, and the lowest estimate is 11% of the macrofauna (provided by MNE and MNSU). At other sites, the carnivore frequency is consistently greater than 1% and averages about 3%, based on all methods of estimating taxonomic frequency. Table 7.6 uses MNI to calculate carnivore frequencies and compares those frequencies with other taxa that are estimated using MNE and MNSU. This serves to minimize the contribution of carnivores to the total macrofauna. Yet carnivore percentages are still 2% or greater.

The carnivores from these particular sites in Bed I range in size from small to medium (e.g., hyena) with respect to all mammals (Table 5.1). Remains of animals of this size tend to be destroyed more easily than those of larger mammals. Thus, differential preservation biases due to size would tend to work against carnivores relative to equids, bovids (on the average), and larger mammals also represented at these sites. If only taxa of similar (small to medium) body size were considered—thus, controlling for preservation effects and to some extent for longevity and turnover—carnivores become even more highly represented at each Olduvai site compared with their abundance in modern savannas. Moreover, juvenile individuals, which tend to be preferentially destroyed, represent more than half of the carnivores preserved at the Olduvai sites. This demonstrates further that carnivores show an unexpectedly high occurrence that runs counter to the usual biases of preservation.

Before turning to the ecological significance of these faunal patterns, we can note two other intriguing features about the large mammal assemblages of Bed I Olduvai: species diversity and consistency in the abundance of higher taxa.

## Species Diversity

One of the most striking characteristics of the Bed I faunal assemblages is the diversity of species. Many taxa are represented by only a few specimens or MNE and sometimes by only a single MNSU. In possibly only one case (*Kobus sigmoidalis* at FLKNN–3) does a species significantly dominate the fauna.[6] Rarely is any one species represented by an MNI greater than 5. Narrow selection of mammalian species was not a characteristic of these Bed I bone accumulations.

Presumably this same conclusion would apply to the bone collectors primarily responsible for the accumulation of bones at each site. Table 7.24 provides an index useful for comparing taxonomic diversity among the sites. The index for each site is very high, confirming the highly diverse character of these faunal assemblages. This suggests a rather unspecialized approach to the transport of animal species to each site. Interestingly, the degree of species diversity does not appear to be affected by arid (e.g., FLK North–6) versus moist conditions (e.g., FLKNN–2 and 3). Overall, a slightly wider diversity of species appears to be preserved at the sites with stone artifacts than at FLKNN–2 and Long K. However, this may be largely an effect of sample sizes of identifiable specimens, given that assemblages with more faunal remains are likely to contain more species.[7] In any event, it would appear that hominids (as, conditionally, the most important cause of bone concentration at the artifact sites) were not specialists in the species or body sizes of carcasses they exploited. The faunal diversity from the artifact sites also implies that hominids transported bones of species that probably lived in more than one habitat or vegetation zone (at least open, grassy plains and a more densely vegetated zone).

---

[6]*K. sigmoidalis* accounts for 29% of the MNI for all large mammals from this site.

[7]FLKNN–2, Long K, and FLKNN–3 have the smallest sample sizes of identified specimens and have the lowest diversity indexes. Long K, though, has the highest number of MNI. Thus, its lower diversity index may indeed imply a less varied recruitment of taxa into the assemblage at this site.

**TABLE 7.24.** A Measure of Taxonomic Diversity (Simpson's $D$)[a] in the Faunal Assemblages from Bed I[b]

| Site | D |
|------|---|
| FLK North–6 | 0.87 |
| FLK "Zinj" | 0.91 |
| FLKNN–2 | 0.86 |
| FLKNN–3 | 0.86 |
| DK–2 | 0.95 |
| DK–3 | 0.95 |
| Long K | 0.84 |

[a]Simpson's $D = 1 - \Sigma (P_i)^2$, $P_i$ = relative abundance of the $i$th species measured from 0 to 1.0.

[b]Computation based on MNI for each species (Table 7.1).

In theoretical terms, a generalized use of resources in an environment is a response to a spatially heterogeneous, or mosaic, distribution of resources. Such an environment poses a "problem" in terms of how much time an individual spends within, and traveling between, each resource patch. The more general (less specialized) is the use of food items (or other resources), the higher the density of those resources. Thus, traveling time between resources, or patches, is decreased (Curio, 1976: 70, 72; Pianka, 1983; Schoener, 1971). Generalization not only tends to lower the cost of resource search, but also will decrease the transport time and distance to a fixed point on the landscape. For example, the !Kung San expand their diets with "less desired" food items when these items are closer to campsites than are highly desired foods (Lee, 1979: 175). In addition, the use of diverse resources may act as a buffer against temporal variation of resources (e.g., scarcity) (Gould, 1980: 110–111; Winterhalder, 1980). A low expectation (or a high search time) in finding a food item or other resource often requires generalization (Pianka, 1983: 279). This point does not imply that large mammals and their carcasses were rare in the ancient Olduvai environment. Other factors, such as the presence of competitors, may have the same effect as a low abundance of resources, that is, they tend to increase the range of resources used (MacArthur and Pianka, 1966; Schoener, 1971).

### Consistency in the Abundance of Taxa

Despite detailed differences between the faunal assemblages, the sites of Bed I show an interesting overall consistency in taxonomic abundance. Figures 7.1 and 7.2 depict this consistency, which primarily reflects standard relative and absolute frequencies of the three most abundant taxa: bovids, suids, and equids. The other taxa, when present, occur at a consistently low level.

How consistent is the relative abundance of Bed I taxa compared with taxonomic fluctuations in modern savannas? Table 7.11 provides monthly

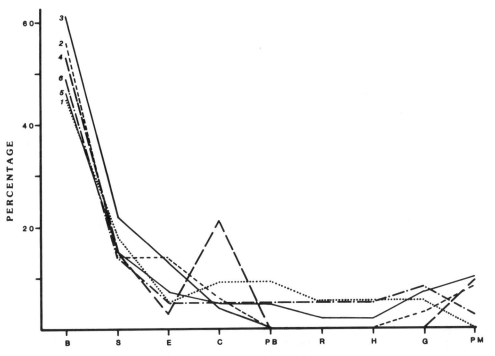

**FIGURE 7.1.** Percentage representation of taxa according to MNI for six sites in Bed I (Long K not included), based on Table 7.2. Taxa: *B* = bovids, *S* = suids, *E* = equids, *C* = carnivores, *PB* = proboscideans, *R* = rhinos, *H* = hippos, *G* = giraffids, *PM* = primates. Sites: 1 = FLK North–6, 2 = FLK "Zinj," 3 = FLKNN–2, 4 = FLKNN–3, 5 = DK–2, 6 = DK–3.

census data from Amboseli over a 16-month period; this information reflects seasonal fluctuations in taxa frequencies. Bovids fluctuated widely during the 1969–1970 study, varying from around 55% during several months to around 90% during other periods. Equids represented between 2 and 45% of the fauna reported by Western (1973). Elephants, giraffes, and monkeys occur at lower frequencies but show variations comparable to these same taxa in the Olduvai assemblages.

A statistic known as Kendall's coefficient of concordance helps to compare the faunas from the five artifact sites to five monthly censuses from Amboseli (October 1969–April 1970). This statistic compares the ranking of taxa according to their abundance.[8] The Amboseli censuses were obtained in a con-

[8]Kendall's coefficient *(W)* is a function of the degree of variance in rank and is used when judging concordance among more than two sets of ranks (Siegel, 1956). Here, *W* reflects the consistency in the ranking of taxa over the five Amboseli censuses and over the five Olduvai assemblages.

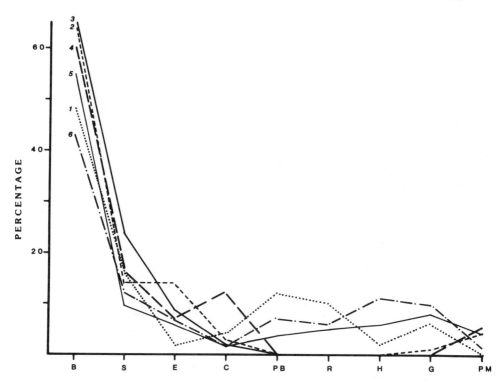

**FIGURE 7.2.** Percentage representation of taxa for six Bed I levels (Long K not
included), using mixed taxonomic estimates based on Table 7.6.
Taxa and sites designated in same way as in Figure 7.1.

sistent manner (Western, 1973). The available Amboseli data concern two
taxa (bovids and equids) that are generally the two most frequent taxa in
the environment, and three other taxa (elephant, giraffe, and monkey) that
occur at low frequencies. The Olduvai taxa chosen for comparison were bovids
and suids (which are the most abundant) and equids, giraffids, and proboscideans (which occur at low frequencies). While the taxa compared are broadly
very similar, they are not identical. Thus, consistency in taxonomic abundance
for Amboseli and Olduvai are compared in only a general sense. Further, the
5 Amboseli months considered represent taxonomic variations over less than
a year, and they do not combine the 2 months (July 1969 and April 1970) that
show, among the available data, the widest disparity in the ranking of taxonomic frequencies. The five Olduvai levels, in contrast, span a period of
50,000–150,000 years, during which climatic factors such as the degree of
aridity appear to have changed significantly (see Chapter 2).

Surprisingly, the Kendall's coefficient for Olduvai is higher (0.794) than
that for Amboseli (0.744), indicating a slightly higher concordance (less var-

iance) in the ranking of taxa for Olduvai than for Amboseli. Whether or not the difference between these two coefficients is considered to be meaningful, it is striking, nonetheless, that the fluctuation among the Olduvai assemblages in taxonomic frequency ranking is certainly no more than occurred in less than a year at Amboseli. One might expect taxonomic variance over many thousands of years, and under a variety of climatic conditions, to be greater than occurs between seasons within a single ecological setting. The five Olduvai accumulations analyzed here (the artifact sites) do not express such greater variance.[9]

One factor that clearly contributed to the consistency in taxonomic abundance was the effect of time-averaging. For example, the census data from Tarangire Reserve (Table 7.12) show considerable similarities in relative taxonomic frequencies between the 2 years 1958 and 1961. However, these yearly censuses were averages; variance within each taxa during the year was very high. In 1961, monthly counts for equids (zebra) range from 0 to 40% of the total mammal macrofauna; elephants from 0 to 18%. Among taxa with generally low abundance, suids (warthog) ranged from 1 to 7% of the fauna, and giraffe from 0.08 to 6%, in different monthly counts during that year. Yet by averaging over each year, the animal counts show quite constant proportions of taxa.

The Olduvai bone assemblages appear to be time-averaged not only over a year, but over at least several years (see Chapter 3). Thus, seasonal and yearly fluctuations in the availability of species and in the transport of their bones to sites are masked. Given that calibration of bone weathering is not refined to a monthly or seasonal scale, information about short-term temporal variations in the taxa introduced to the Olduvai sites is unavailable.

Other factors also could potentially contribute to the highly consistent recruitment of taxa into these faunal assemblages. For one, the bone collector could have developed a narrowly defined prey/carcass search image; as a result, bones would have been culled from particular taxa regardless of seasonal and yearly variations in availability. However, the diversity of taxa and body sizes represented by the bones in the Olduvai accumulations belies this possibility. Alternatively, bones may have been introduced to sites only during specific ecological conditions, during which particular animals became available in rather consistent proportions. In this sense, site formation at Olduvai may have been a response to only certain, narrow, ecological situations. Again, the evidence does not support this idea. The fact that site formation seems to have occurred during periods when climatic conditions varied from moist

[9]When the faunal assemblage from FLKNN–2 is included in this calculation, the concordance coefficient for Olduvai rises (0.809). This results from the fact that the FLKNN–2 assemblage shows taxonomic frequencies that are broadly similar to the other Bed I sites. However, the concordance value for Amboseli rises even more by including any other month's census; hence, the discrepancy between Olduvai and Amboseli becomes less.

(rainfall around 1000 mm per year) to arid (about 350 mm per year) suggests that bone accumulation was not elicited by a narrow set of environmental conditions. More specific, ecological limiting factors are at best difficult to consider. Finally, consistency in the abundance of taxa could have resulted from the preferred use of specific habitats by the bone collectors. The transport of species from such consistently used habitats might not have fully mirrored general environmental shifts. However, we have already seen that a range of habitats are represented by the faunas from each site. In addition, some of the variations between sites do seem to reflect general climatic conditions (e.g., the high percentage of alcelaphine and antilopine bovids at FLK North–6).

In conclusion, then, the consistency in taxonomic frequencies shown by the Olduvai assemblages relative to Amboseli seems primarily due to time-averaging effects. Thinking in terms of paleocommunities (see Footnote 1, p. 153), and taking into account the entire period of formation of each site, it thus appears that the bone collectors at the artifact sites exhibited a highly stable type of interaction with taxa in the Olduvai basin over a period of at least 100,000 years.

*Summary: Were the Olduvai Environments Essentially Modern Savannas?*

Comparison between the taxonomic frequencies of Bed I and modern savannas indicates a general similarity. The species of large mammals represented in Bed I undoubtedly signify a savanna–mosaic situation, but did this type of habitat necessarily have the exact same taxonomic characteristics as do modern savannas? Differential preservation can account for some of the discrepancies, but not others. For example, bovid frequencies (based on MNI and MNSU) are consistently lower than 70%, whereas bovid frequencies in modern savannas seldom fall below this level.[10] In contrast to modern savannas, equids tend to be rarer than suids in the Bed I assemblages and are present at a lower frequency compared to bovids than is the rule today.[11] The robusticity of bones of *Equus oldowayensis* suggests that preservation biases cannot account for these patterns. Carnivores are the flip side of this situation. In the Bed I assemblages, carnivores tend to be small in size relative to the other mammal taxa, yet they occur at slightly higher frequencies overall (and with respect to particular taxa) than is expected from modern data and fossil assemblages elsewhere.

To assess how similar the habitats of Bed I Olduvai were to modern savannas, we must take into account not only data about the large mammals but also the wide range of information about geology, fossil pollen, and mi-

[10]Bovids at Olduvai, however, more often make up about 70% of the fauna when E and MNE estimates are employed.
[11]The one exception to this is at Long K.

crofauna known from Bed I (Chapter 2). This kind of paleoenvironmental evidence helps to determine whether the abundance patterns of large mammals accurately reflect environmental settings or the specific activities ("preferences") of the two major bone collectors at Olduvai—hominids and carnivores.

These various lines of data combined tend to support the view of Gentry and Gentry (1978) based on the bovids alone. Certain bovids and other species (e.g., *Equus oldowayensis*) imply that open bushland and tree savanna were present throughout Bed I times. Furthermore, the proportion of alcelaphines and antilopines implies that the collection and transport of bones to sites mirrored climatic changes in a way that is consistent with variation in modern savannas, that is, from moist, closed vegetation savannas (Type A) to dry, open grasslands (Type B). The distribution of body sizes among the large mammals overall, and within bovids, in particular, also corresponds to what we see in modern savannas, though the latter show a wide range of variation in body size patterns. As we have noted in Chapter 2, the levels at DK and FLKNN (the oldest horizons in Bed I) represent a period of moist savanna. Fossil pollen, microfauna, geochemistry, and the bovids from FLKNN suggest an environment with about 1000 mm of rainfall per year, closed-canopy vegetation, and probably isolated patches of grassland and marsh (see also Kappelman, 1984). Although pollen and microfauna samples are not known from DK, the relatively common occurrence of urocyclid slugs and the isotopic chemistry of carbonate nodules below Tuff IB also indicates a moist habitat with rainfall of at least 800 mm per annum (Cerling and Hay, 1986; Hay, 1976). The FLK "Zinj" site appears to represent an environmental shift toward more open vegetation and probably drier climate. A mixture of grassland, *Acacia* woodland, and possibly patches of gallery forest may be inferred for the period of formation of this site. FLK North–6 and Long K represent the most arid period of Bed I—in fact, drier than Olduvai today, based on pollen evidence. This suggests that the vegetation should have been mostly open grassland, though moist areas may still have existed close to the lake, as implied by rodent genera indicative of marshes.

Although these inferences strongly support the idea that the climate, vegetation, and animal species of Olduvai were well within the range of East African savannas today, certain anomalies in large mammal representation still require some explanation.

For example, the high relative abundance of suids is hard to account for by environmental factors. Plio–Pleistocene suids were very diverse compared to modern pigs, and they simply may have comprised a larger proportion of the macrofauna at Olduvai than in modern savannas. There is an alternative explanation. In a sample of 10 Type A environments in western and central Africa (Milligan, Ajayi, and Hall, 1982), 4 show an unusually high proportion of suids overall and especially in relation to bovids (bovids only 1.1–6.7 times more numerous than suids). In addition, in Southwest Africa the abundance of warthog increases as rainfall (and primary production) increases (Thackeray,

1980). Thus, variation in modern savannas suggests that there are conditions under which suids become more abundant relative to other large mammals; those conditions obtain in closed vegetation, moist, Type A environments. However, this explanation does not account for the consistently high abundance of suids at the Olduvai sites, especially at two sites (FLK North–6 and FLK "Zinj"), which represent drier, more open environments.

The persistent, low abundance of equids and the relatively high representation of carnivores at the Olduvai sites are also anomalous when examined in the light of mammal frequencies in modern savannas and the other lines of environmental evidence from Bed I Olduvai. One alternative is that these unresolved discrepancies may provide clues about "selectivity," that is, the ecology of the bone collectors at Olduvai. Based on taphonomic analysis, we previously defined two types of bone assemblage that now afford an important comparison: the "primarily carnivore" assemblages at FLKNN–2 and Long K and the "primarily hominid" assemblages associated with stone artifacts. Although the Olduvai assemblages are by no means pure indicators of hominid versus carnivore activity, differences between these nonartifact and artifact assemblages should reflect to some extent the different degree of carnivore and hominid contributions to these sites. One way that FLKNN–2 and Long K do differ from the other bone assemblages is in the relative frequency of equids. At these sites, which appear to have a greater input from bone collecting carnivores, possibly hyenas, the ratios of equids to bovids and of equids to the total macrofauna are within the range of modern savannas.[12] The ratios from the artifact sites are all lower.[13] The evidence presented by these two "primarily carnivore" assemblages suggests that the abundance of equids in the environments of Bed I Olduvai was not necessarily outside the range of modern savannas. Since the low proportion of equids at other sites does not seem to be explained by, for instance, a lack of grassland or other environmental factors, it appears that the difference in equid abundance between the nonartifact and artifact sites reflects the bone transport habits and/or foraging patterns of hominids, given that hominids are the principal variable operating at the artifact sites and a missing influence at FLKNN–2 and Long K. This inference gains strength from the fact that the FLKNN–2 assemblage derives from a period of closed vegetation, that equids are not similarly abundant at the FLKNN–3 artifact site, and that equids are very scarce at the artifact site (FLK North–6) formed during a period of evidently the most extensive open grasslands.

In addition, faunal and geological evidence from Bed II also hints that the frequency of equids on Olduvai sites reflected hominid habitat use and bone

[12]All four methods of estimating taxonomic abundance support this point for Long K, and three out of the four support it for FLKNN–2 (Tables 7.2–7.5).
[13]FLK "Zinj" is a possible exception. Two of the four methods of estimating relative abundance show a low abundance of equids relative to bovids and all macrofauna, and two exhibit an abundance within the range seen in modern savannas.

transport rather than equid abundance in the environment at large. Equids comprise a substantial proportion of the archeological faunas for the first time at Olduvai in the middle part of Bed II (Leakey, 1971: 257). This period also marks the first time that artifact sites are known outside of the lake margin facies (Hay, 1976). Major contraction of the lake margin area during Middle Bed II times was a likely stimulus to this new distribution of archeological sites. One result of this shrinking of the lake margin zone was that the source of quartzite, an important material for making tools, apparently became located outside of the lake margin also for the first time in the history of the Olduvai basin (Hay, 1976: 101–104). Thus, to acquire at least this one stone material, hominids ventured on to the alluvial flood plains further from the lake. These lines of evidence, in turn, imply that hominids began to use habitats beyond the lake margin zone more frequently than during the period of Bed I. The concomitant rise in *Equus oldowayensis* at the archeological sites conforms well to the idea that hominids frequented areas that were most likely the drier plains habitats of that species. Accordingly, the low proportion of equids at the artifact sites of Bed I would correspond to a lesser degree of utilization or transport of bones from such habitats.[14]

Despite differences in the abundance of equids, faunas from the nonartifact and artifact sites of Bed I tend to be quite similar in taxonomic representation. Again, suids appear to be unusually "overabundant" in all assemblages except at Long K. This suggests that hominids and carnivores at times operated on similar constraints or strategies of foraging and bone collection when it came to suids. However, the relative abundance of suids at Long K, which falls in line with modern savannas, means that the bovid to suid ratio cannot be shown to have been lower in the Olduvai region, especially during the drier period of upper Bed I, than in savannas today. If this ratio were the same as in modern savannas, the high abundance of suids at other sites would also reflect the selection of species for transport to sites (and perhaps the preferred sampling of bush habitats) rather than the makeup of the faunal community at large. Thus, the proportions of suids, equids, and bovids at the Olduvai sites do not necessarily reflect differences between modern and ancient savannas at Olduvai.

We have also noted that all of the sites exhibit a high percentage of carnivores, though frequencies vary considerably. One of the lowest proportions of carnivores is recorded at FLKNN–2, whereas a very high abundance occurs

[14]Engelosin is a distinctive source of phonolite lava used for making tools to a small degree in Bed II and for many implements in Beds III/IV. No artifacts made of Engelosin phonolite are known from Bed I. Engelosin is situated 9–11 km north of the sites of Bed I and was never located within the lake margin facies. Hay (1976: 184) notes that Bed I hominids ranged 8–10 km to obtain gneiss at the Kelogi outcrop within the lake margin zone, but they apparently did not transport pieces a similar distance from Engelosin. This supports the idea that the toolmakers of Bed I preferentially used the lake margin over the alluvial plains, and that fauna transported to the Bed I sites should reflect this ranging pattern (e.g., low frequency of plains-living equids).

in the FLKNN–3 assemblage. We saw from the evidence of bone damage (Chapter 5) that the Olduvai assemblages, particularly those associated with stone tools, were subject to both hominid and carnivore modification. As we will now examine, the attraction of carnivores to these sites must have created a milieu that accounts for the high relative abundance of carnivores in the faunal assemblages. The study of paleocommunities thus leads us to compare further hominids and carnivores as bone collectors and foragers.

## Ecological Overlap among Carcass Users

Based on the faunas from FLKNN–2 and Long K, on the one hand, and the artifact assemblages, on the other, it is evident that hominids and carnivores overlapped in the species they exploited and transported to fixed points on the landscape. Yet even if we just look at the bone evidence from the artifact sites, there is ample illustration of ecological overlap between carnivores and tool-making hominids. Both hominid and carnivore damages are present on the bones from each site. The occurrence of both sources of damage, sometimes on the same bones and (rarely) overlapping one another on the same specimens (Potts and Shipman, 1981; Shipman, 1986a), suggests that hominids and carnivores were attracted not only to a common set of species but also, occasionally, to the same kinds of bones and even to the same places on the landscape. Does this mean that hominids and carnivores were in competition with one another at Olduvai?

The ways carnivores consume animal carcasses and respond to other species of carnivores in African environments today furnish some insights into this question. A wide range of field observers agree that the protection of carcass or meat resources by living carnivores from other species is an important aspect of carnivore behavior. Different species adopt distinct strategies (individual and social) for coping with carnivore competitors (Kingdon, 1977: 375; Lamprecht, 1978). For example, lions often fend off competitors while guarding a carcass; leopards, hyenas, and lions are known to cache parts of carcasses; cheetahs and hyenas tend to utilize a carcass very rapidly and incompletely, ingesting quickly as much meat as possible before competitors arrive.

The degree of competition for carcasses and meat among carnivore species is generally evaluated by the frequency of direct encounters and predations among these species. The evidence for such encounters and kills is extensive (Kingdon, 1977). Lions appropriate kills made by cheetah, hyenas, humans; other potentially significant competitors such as vultures and jackals, which venture close to a feeding lion, are sometimes attacked and killed. Lions are also known to chase and kill leopards (especially the young) (Kingdon, 1977: 310, 390). Although they seldom consume any carnivores they kill (Curio, 1976: 19–20), lions, nevertheless, may tear up these carcasses (Kruuk, 1975:

48). Leopards are known to kill cheetah (Kingdon, 1977: 310) as well as wild dogs and young hyenas (the latter for food). Estes (1967) observed one leopard to kill 11 jackals in 3 weeks. Wild dogs and hyenas are frequent scavengers on leopard kills (Turnbull-Kemp 1967). Leopard-feeding ecology may vary depending on the presence of other large cats in the vicinity (Kingdon, 1977: 310). Vultures, jackals, and especially hyenas are known to be major direct competitors for prey that wild dogs have killed. In addition, hyenas, leopards, and lions are potential predators of wild dogs (Estes and Goddard, 1967). Hyenas compete directly with conspecifics and other carnivores not only for particular carcasses but also for preferred portions of carcasses (Kruuk, 1975). Occasionally, a pack of hyenas has been observed to kill a lion in areas of frequent scavenging between these two species (Kingdon, 1977: 389). Kruuk (1975: 48) reports that a major cause of adult hyena mortality in Ngorongoro is due to fights with lions over kills. The predator apparently most affected by carnivore competition is the cheetah. Cheetahs lose a high percentage of their kills to other carnivores (Schaller, 1970), and predation, especially on juveniles, is considered to be an important cause of cheetah mortality and a key limiting factor on population size (Eaton, 1974: 39). Finally, the high proportion of carnivore remains in some hyena dens (Brain, 1980, 1981; Klein, 1975; Mills and Mills, 1977) is considered to reflect a high degree of interaction among hyenas and other carnivores.

Clearly, competition among African savanna carnivores has significant influence on their behaviors. This competition obviously is somewhat indirect, involving the exploitation of similar resources, but it also takes a direct form—interference competition and predation. The need to protect hunted prey from scavengers may lead to such direct interaction, but carnivore–carnivore predation sometimes occurs outside of carcass-protection situations.

The frequencies of carnivores in Olduvai faunal assemblages suggest a low-level selective sampling of carnivores from the general environment. Besides the interactions among carnivores, no other factor is known to create such differential sampling. Thus, carnivore abundance at the sites of Bed I would appear to reflect some degree of interaction among potential competitors (various carnivores and possibly hominids) for carcasses/bones at, or in the vicinity of, these sites.

Several ideas emerge from this interpretation. Based on the numerous reported observations of carnivore–carnivore predation, Kingdon (1977: 360) suggests that carcass-protection behavior is elicited mainly by the sight of small carnivores, which may lead to predation upon these animals. The carnivore remains from the Olduvai sites derive chiefly from small adults or juveniles. The level with the highest percentage of carnivores is FLKNN–3. A minimum number of seven different individuals is present, representing five different species. Three of the individuals are juveniles; three of the adults represent small carnivore species (canid size or smaller). Furthermore, for all of the sites combined the ratio of adult to juvenile to "unknown" (in terms of MNI) is 17:6:2. Of the 17 adults[15], 10 are small canid size or smaller (the others are ascribed to *Crocuta crocuta*, *Dinofelis*, the large canid *Canis africanus*, and an indeterminate felid). Despite the fact that the most notable carnivore bone damage patterns are typical of a hyena-sized animal, and that many of the SEM-determined tooth marks closely resemble hyena tooth marks in overall appearance, the kinds of carnivore remains represented in these assemblages are more in line with small animals typically selected for predation. Whether predation can be attributed to hominids or occurred among the carnivores is unknown.

If, as behavioral studies suggest, carnivore predation on other carnivores reflects the degree of competition, FLKNN–3 would represent a relative high point in competition among the animals attracted to carcass resources. Interestingly, the highest representation of hominid remains on any Olduvai level also occurs at FLKNN–3, including three bones with clear carnivore damage. The OH 8 hominid talus and calcaneus bear small carnivore puncture marks; the OH 7 parietal shows several, discrete, wide carnivore gnaw marks, probably from a large carnivore. These findings may signify the most direct expression of hominid–carnivore competition in Bed I at Olduvai.

## Opportunism as an Alternative Perspective to Competition

The viewpoint that we have inspected here so far is that promulgated by competition theory, which has been pervasive in the thinking of ecologists. However, another view of foraging and species coexistence has been presented in the ecological literature. According to this second perspective, animals that utilize the same species or kinds of food are able to coexist without competition because they are not so tethered to fine scale variations in food supply. Instead, they tend to take advantage of noncompetitive feeding opportunities as they arise. In some cases, this may be permitted by a "superabundance" of resources that renders competition unnecessary. Coexisting animals with similar diets also may use resources in different parts of the habitat or at different times, thus circumventing direct or indirect competition (Wiens, 1976, 1983).

Although this alternative perspective on foraging has largely developed out of studies of herbivorous birds and other animals, some evidence from field studies of carnivores supports it. While interactions do occur, carnivorous mammals and birds generally avoid competition by taking advantage of carcasses as opportunities arise. Thus, lions usually control a kill that they have made, whereas hyenas, jackals, and vultures gain access to the leftovers in sequence. This kind of scavenging sequence has been observed widely, and the feeding characteristics (e.g., anatomical, social) of carnivorous animals often conform to the opportunities specific animals typically face in consuming a portion of a carcass. By feeding at different times and on portions of carcasses

[15]Eight are from the Long K assemblage alone.

that require distinctive methods of access or chewing, carnivores tend to avoid competition.

The Olduvai sites provide strong suggestions of indirect competition and some potential for interaction among hominids and carnivores. Yet whether we emphasize competition theory or the opportunistic use of these sites by carnivores and hominids, it is the avoidance of competition with carnivores that is key to understanding the creation of the Olduvai artifact sites. Both perspectives on species coexistence imply that animals adopt ways of searching for and handling resources that obviate competition, though not necessarily eliminating it. Whether competition or opportunism is the stimulating factor behind these means of avoiding ecological overlap is of no special consequence here. In the case of Olduvai, the transport and use of carcasses would have associated hominids with potential predators. The avoidance of predation is likely to have been necessary for the long-term persistence of these activities by hominids at Olduvai. This idea is not based on a simple application of competition theory or the competitive exclusion principle. Rather, predator avoidance itself becomes the issue—as implied by evidence from the Olduvai artifact sites that hominids handled animal tissues and overlapped with carnivores in the use of these faunal remains and of particular spatial locations.

Theoretically, the intensity of competition and the chances for reducing predation are related to the amount of overlap in the types of resources used and in the time and space use of those resources (Pianka, 1983). Several means of reducing competition and predation may have been available to hominids. Three possible ways are considered here:

1. The use of different carcass resources from those utilized by carnivores
2. Extensive utilization and/or destruction of carcass resources otherwise attractive to carnivores
3. Only brief stays at sites where hominids accumulated animal tissues (i.e., avoidance of time/space overlap in the use of tissues)

## Use of Different Resources

While both hominids and carnivores sought carcasses, they may have utilized slightly different products from animal remains. Several resources are conceivably useful from carcasses: meat, marrow, fat, ligaments, tendons, hide, bones, etc. It has been suggested that the anatomical locations of hominid and carnivore damage would shed some light on which carcass portions were utilized by each agent (Potts and Shipman, 1981). Table 7.25 gives the data Shipman and I originally provided on the locations of stone tool cut marks and carnivore tooth marks identified by using the scanning electron microscope. Identified elements were divided into meat-bearing bones (major limb bones and axial elements) versus nonmeat bones (phalanges, podials, and metapodials). Based on this very small sample, a preferential occurrence of tooth

**TABLE 7.25.** Frequency of Stone Cut Marks and Tooth Marks on Meat-Bearing and Nonmeat-Bearing Bones[a]

| Bone | Cut mark | Tooth mark |
|------|----------|------------|
| Meat-bearing | 10 | 27 |
| Nonmeat bearing | 10 | 7 |

$X^2 = 5.04$, $df = 1$, $0.02 < p < 0.05$.
[a]After Potts and Shipman (1981).

marks on meat-bearing bones is evident, whereas cut marks occur equally on both types of bone.

Although one problem with this original analysis is that the sample size is so small, Shipman's (1986b) further study of this matter is based on nearly 2700 bone specimens from Bed I Olduvai, and it confirms the initial findings. A more difficult problem is that carnivores and hominids can obtain meat from bones without leaving any diagnostic trace. Thus, cut-mark and tooth-mark locations may not be demonstrative of the proportion of time spent on, or of resources obtained from, different skeletal areas. At present, these data are still only suggestive that carnivores focused on meat tissue and on meat-bearing bones much more exclusively than did hominids. Further studies of this issue have been carried out by Shipman (1986a, 1986b) and Bunn (Bunn and Kroll, 1986), but the results are contradictory (see Chapter 8).

Nevertheless, the appearance of stone cut marks in both nonmeat and meat-bearing areas is interesting in its own regard. Two cases of damage found on bones that join to form a single limb illustrate different approaches that hominids and carnivores had to processing a carcass. One of these cases occurs at FLKNN–2, a concentration attributed primarily to carnivores. Twelve bones from this site are derived from a single equid forelimb (humerus through middle phalanx). Clear gnawing by a carnivore, very similar to that inflicted by hyenas, and two distinct hominid tool marks are present on these bones. The cut marks, one due to chopping and the other due to slicing actions, are restricted to the distal end of an unbroken metacarpal. On the other hand, carnivore gnawing is found at the shoulder and elbow joints (proximal and distal humerus and the ulna olecranon). The other example of this phenomenon, at DK–2, involves slicing and chopping tool marks that were noted on the metacarpal and proximal phalanx from an associated set of forelimb bones of the bovid *Parmularius altidens*. These were the only cut marks present on this set of bones, and they left both the metacarpal and phalanx unbroken. Other than the bone itself, tendons and ligaments are the main tissues available in these distal limb areas, which contain little meat. However, the occurrence of cut marks on nonmeat bones, of course, may be part of meat-procuring activities (e.g., hide and meat stripping, skeletal disarticulation). Moreover, the occurrence of cut marks in meat-bearing areas does suggest that hominids handled meaty tissues. The implications of this will be taken up in Chapter 8. The point here is that although the anatomical distributions of carnivore tooth and hominid tool marks may have differed in some respects, this type of evidence is inconclusive as to whether hominids actually differed from carnivores in the carcass resources they utilized. Moreover, differences between the artifact and nonartifact sites in the processing of long bone shafts and epiphyses (see pp. 118, 231) suggest that both hominids and carnivores utilized marrow by processing bones in their distinctive ways ("diaphysis-first" versus "epiphysis-first").

## Destruction or Removal of Carcass Parts

There is a second way by which hominids could have reduced or perhaps circumvented competition with carnivores. Extensive utilization, destruction, or removal of consumable animal tissues by hominids, presumably, would have lessened the chances that carnivores would be attracted to the places used by hominids.

According to many ethnographic reports, hunter–gatherers and villagers at their living sites tend not to overlook any edible parts of a carcass before they abandon the remains (Binford and Bertram, 1977; Brain, 1967, 1969a, 1981; Cleveland et al., 1976; Lyon, 1970; Yellen, 1977). Long bones are fragmented almost without exception, as are other marrow bones. Bone grease often is extracted by boiling bones or bone fragments in water. In the case of the Kalahari San, fragmentation and maximum use of nutritious material on and inside the bones evidently serves to minimize carnivore attraction to campsites. The remains are abandoned to scavenging hyenas and smaller wild carnivores, which abound in the northern Kalahari. These animals appear to consume podials and other small limb bones, since no marrow-rich bones are left after humans abandon the sites (Yellen, 1977). The Hottentots, Eskimo, and Navajo also practice high degrees of bone destruction through extensive utilization of meat and marrow. The broken bone remains also are left to carnivores, but in these cases the carnivores are domesticated dogs.[16] These carnivores also consume small podials and phalanges and destroy the few remaining marrow-rich pieces. The absence or very rare presence of complete, unaltered bones or bone portions on such modern human sites attests to the intensity of bone utilization for nutrition by humans and domesticated carnivores.

Turning to Bed I Olduvai, the patterns of bone utilization at the artifact sites reflect neither the same intensity nor evidently the same range of activities as occurs at the camp or village sites of people today. Although bone fragmentation is clearly evident, the frequent occurrence of undamaged,

[16]In the case of the Nunamiut (Binford, 1978; 1981: 36), although extensive bone modification is carried out by the Eskimo, whole bone units are kept aside to feed the dogs. The entire effect, though, is extreme use and destruction of bone tissue, similar to activities described for the San and other peoples.

marrow-rich epiphyses implies that bones were not extensively processed by hominids. This point is especially clear when we remember that both hominids and carnivores had access to these bones. As suggested earlier for FLK "Zinj" (p. 117), tooth marks on pieces of limb bone shaft indicate that carnivores probably fragmented meat-bearing bones at least on occasion. Complete, un-damaged, limb bones that would have been rich in meat and marrow also occur at every site in Bed I. A comparison between the Olduvai sites and modern campsites in Botswana illustrates the point. In the five Olduvai artifact assemblages, an average of 9% of the total number of long bone specimens identified to family level ($N = 558$) consisted of unbroken long bones. These included all major kinds of long bone, meat-bearing and nonmeat elements. In contrast, only 1.9% of the total number of large mammal long bone pieces ($N = 162$) found at 16 !Kung San campsites were complete (Yellen, 1977b: 146–236). In contrast to these modern human campsites, Olduvai hominids apparently left whole bones and possibly other animal tissues potentially at-tractive to carnivores at the locus of bone accumulation. Evidently, carnivores that visited these sites were not left with merely finishing off scraps of bone.

By itself, a relatively low degree of carcass utilization by hominids need not have resulted in competitive interaction with carnivores. Nonetheless, the evidence from cut marks, tooth marks, and the remains of carnivores in the Olduvai assemblages suggests that hominids and carnivores overlapped in their use of carcasses and that there was ample potential for interaction— yet hominids apparently did not remove or process intensively remains that were possibly attractive to carnivores in the vicinity.


## Avoiding the Same Sites at the Same Time


A third possible means for reducing competition and the chances of pre-dation is an obvious one. This would have involved minimizing the temporal overlap of hominids and carnivores at these sites. Carnivores tend not to migrate but are all-year occupants of their home range areas. Therefore, car-nivores would have presented a persistent problem to hominids who foraged for animal tissues and transported them to particular spots on the landscape. The rapid processing of meat and of other resources from the carcass parts brought to these sites, followed by immediate abandonment of the site, would have helped to decrease the time hominids spent handling animal tissues, the time spent around the refuse, and the chances of interaction with carnivores. This idea will be considered in Chapter 9 as we explore the reasons why hominids transported and accumulated bones and artifacts in the first place.

# 8

# Obtaining Resources and Accumulating Debris

## Hunting and Scavenging

It is an understatement that hominid foraging, particularly hunting, has held a significant place in ideas about human ancestors. Reconstructions of early hominid activities can sometimes play a myth-like role in how we view ourselves and in defining concepts of human nature (Cartmill, 1983; Landau, Pilbeam, and Richard, 1982). The resulting scenarios of human evolution offer powerful symbols that feed our curiosities about our ancestry. Ideas about hominid hunting and other modes of foraging have helped greatly to mold such scenarios.

One of the best-selling books of the 1960s was *African Genesis* by Ardrey (1961), who began his dynamic tale of human origins with the stirring phrase "Not in innocence, and not in Asia, was mankind born." Ardrey went on to present findings from fossils and animal behavior in the context of the "killer ape" view of human ancestors. This view derives from Raymond Dart, who from his study of the fossilized bones of ungulates, carnivores, and primates from South African caves, envisioned ravenous, bipedal apes commiting violent acts of predation and butchery. As developed later by Ardrey (1976), humans owe their uniqueness in the primate world to an evolutionary history of hunting, use of weapons, and violence stretching back at least 3 million years. Whether it is a bone weapon transformed into an orbiting space craft in a blink of geologic time or some other symbol, Ardrey's presentation of the hunting hypothesis has left a poignant mark. In the paleoanthropological literature, Washburn and Lancaster (1968) presented the hunting hypothesis in less dramatic form. The point of their article, nonetheless, was that human aggression, cooperation, technological innovation, emotional states, and physiological functions have all been tuned by millions of years of hunting, by natural selection for efficiency as predators.

Diametric to that popular version of human evolution, the gathering of plant foods has also been advocated as the prime mover of early hominid evolution (e.g., Tanner, 1981; Zihlmann and Tanner, 1978). This outlook on human ancestors looks to the predominantly vegetarian diets of tropical hunter–gatherers and to the predominance of herbivory among living higher primates for evidence that plant foods were the staple of early hominid diets. In this regard, the uniqueness of humans lies in the gathering of fruits, nuts, berries, and other plant products, and the bringing of these to a common meeting ground where less successful foragers, or young and old individuals, can be assured of food. The socializing influence of gathering is a critical determinant of human uniqueness. Sometimes symbolized by the phrase "Woman the Gatherer," this view of human evolution has been fueled in part by a feminist response to the claims, sometimes even bare-faced boasts, of the hunting hypothesis, with its male orientation (Haraway, 1978). The tension between "Man the Hunter" and "Woman the Gatherer" reminds us, as we sometimes need to be, that reconstructions of our ancestors both express and influence social and ideological conceptions in the present. Yet these images beg the question whether it is possible to determine how much early hominids hunted or scavenged or gathered plant foods—not by reference to modern parallels (which are so easily filtered through existing beliefs about the past and the present) but by reference to the only real source of information about particular hominid ancestors—the fossil record.

In recent years, by examination of faunal remains from archeological sites, the "scavenger hypothesis" has begun to challenge the traditional hunting hypothesis (e.g., Binford, 1981, 1984; Blumenschine, 1986; Shipman, 1986a). The possibility that early hominids may have scavenged meat or other substances from animals already dead is not new. This idea was suggested by several earlier investigators (Bartholomew and Birdsell, 1953; Clark, 1960; Schaller and Lowther, 1969). However, the view that scavenging was the dominant and possibly only way hominids obtained food from animals (i.e., scavenging as an alternative exclusive of hunting) is a new idea. The issue of hunting versus scavenging is believed to be important because hunting is often portrayed as the critical factor underlying the hunting–gathering adaptation, home bases, food sharing, and other distinctive human traits. If early hominids were hunters, then these other traits can also be projected back into the past to characterize our ancestors. The elevation of hunting to such a central role is based on the following line of thinking: Hunting provides abundant food resources; in fact, the killing of large game offers a superabundance with enormous potential for sharing with members of the social group. The transport of this food, which with the aid of stone tools already comes in portable containers, to a home base provided the foundation for sharing and other forms of social cooperation. However, this portrayal of hunting and its implications has recently been contrasted with apparent evidence for hominid scavenging. According to this revised view, hominid scavenging involved picking up the leftovers from carnivore kills—scraps of food, disarticulated parts of carcasses—a practice that could not support food sharing much less home base activity (Binford, 1981; Shipman, 1983). Thus, recent formulations of the scavenging hypothesis hold significant implications for our views of early humans.

At Olduvai we have seen that hominids were collectors of animal bones and that they processed the bones for some reason. Access to carcasses by scavenging and/or hunting was obviously a prerequisite for bone transport to the artifact sites, and obtaining meat would appear to be the obvious reason. Some statements of the hunting hypothesis have pointed to the Olduvai evidence for support; but those arguments have been based upon the simplistic assumption that animal bones in association with stone tools (= weapons) imply hunting by hominids (e.g., Ardrey, 1976). Other accounts of Olduvai have also assumed hunting and have adopted parallels provided by modern hunters in evaluating seasonality or other aspects of hominid activities (e.g., Speth and Davis, 1976). M.D. Leakey, the excavator of the sites, has kept within the evidence, claiming no clear predominance for either hunting or scavenging, though both were probably practiced (1971: 259). This view coincides with that of Isaac, who leaves open the issue of hunting and scavenging (Isaac 1971: 289, 1978, 1984; Isaac and Crader, 1981). A flurry of analyses of the Olduvai remains has taken place over the past several years against this background of interpretation. The first part of this chapter will examine the results and points of agreement and controversy.

## Hunting and Scavenging Today

Hunting by modern carnivores[1] in African savannas achieves variable success depending on the predator species, the degree of social cooperation in the hunt, the prey species, and the overall ecological situation. For example, solitary lions may have a success rate in predation less than 29% (Schaller, 1972: 445), whereas success rates of 85% have been reported for packs of wild dogs (Estes and Goddard, 1967). Scavenging, in terms of access to carcasses, signifies a rather wider range of phenomena. Early access to an animal already dead (early scavenging) may permit the entire skeleton and all of its resources to be available. Late scavenging, in contrast, may allow access to skeletal elements only after much disarticulation and scattering has occurred. Porcupines, which seek dry bones (Brain, 1981), are good examples of late scavengers, whereas many of the large African carnivores combine early scavenging and hunting in varying proportions as their main strategy for acquiring meat. Early scavenging and hunting, then, are not easily distinguished in terms of the portions of carcasses available to carnivorous animals (Potts, 1982, 1983).

In the Serengeti Plain today, meat is accessible to carnivores in three ways:

1. Predation: Only approximately one-third of ungulate mortality (the main potential food supply for carnivores) is caused by hunting.

---

[1]Unless specified, the term *carnivores* refers to species of the mammalian order Carnivora, particularly the larger members ($\geq$ 10 kg). Vultures are referred to as carnivorous birds. Other bone collectors, such as the porcupine, are not considered carnivorous.

2. Feeding off of animals that have died by causes other than predation (e.g., starvation, disease): Roughly two-thirds of ungulate mortality occurs in this manner.
3. Locate and feed off of another predator's kill: This is said to be of minor importance in the Serengeti today since carnivores either consume their kills quickly (hyenas, wild dogs), guard them very effectively (lions), or carry them to protected areas (leopards). The cheetah is the only predator that leaves large portions of a carcass available to scavengers on a regular basis (Houston, 1979: 265–266).

Despite the fact that the majority of ungulates die by causes other than predation, the large carnivores of the Serengeti kill to obtain most of their food. An estimated 33% of the food of hyenas is scavenged, only 10–15% for lions, while cheetah, leopard, wild dog, and jackals appear to scavenge rarely (Bertram, 1979; Houston, 1979). A greater reliance on scavenging has been attributed to the brown hyena *(Hyaena brunnea)*, found today only in southern Africa. Yet the few studies carried out to date on this shy, nocturnal carnivore disagree about the relative degree of scavenging and hunting. On the one hand, brown hyenas are said to be efficient hunters (Pienaar, 1969). Information provided by Skinner (1976) seems to support this view; for example, hunting episodes are described, and other kinds of carnivores, such as spotted hyenas, do scavenge from carcasses originally in the possession of brown hyenas. Nonetheless, based on observations of hyenas at carcasses placed out for them, Skinner concludes that the brown hyena is not a competent hunter; rather, "it is an extremely efficient scavenger/omnivore, hunting small mammals where possible" (1976: 267). This latter view is supported by subsequent studies, which characterize the brown hyena as an omnivore and scavenger of all kinds of vertebrate remains, though this foraging strategy is acknowledged to be a response to arid conditions where large ungulates are thinly distributed (Mills and Mills, 1978; Owens and Owens, 1978). It seems safe to say that in the semidesert areas where they have been studied, brown hyenas do what they must to get by, whether it is scavenging or hunting. These two forms of access to meat do not seem to be exclusive of one another, though hunting focuses on small mammals. A predominance of scavenging has also been ascribed to striped hyenas *(Hyaena hyaena);* yet this finding again is based on observations of these carnivores around experimental carcasses in a desert habitat (Skinner *et al.*, 1980).

In brief, studies of large carnivores in high biomass savannas of Africa indicate that hunting and scavenging are complementary ways of acquiring carcasses and their products. Although the emphasis tends to be on hunting, the distinction between these two types of foraging does not appear to be critical. In more arid areas where ungulates are not so numerous, the hyenas at least show a tendency toward scavenging. Again, though, the distinction is not absolute and primarily expresses itself in a prey size bias, which may be related to prey population density.

Furthermore, lions and spotted hyenas of the Serengeti tend to scavenge from kills made by other predators and often from each other (Kruuk, 1972; Schaller, 1972). That is, few scavenging events were of animals that died from nonpredatory causes, such as disease and starvation. Predation and possession of a carcass seem to attract other carnivorous mammals and birds. Yet, as was pointed out in the last chapter, sometimes scavengers simply wait their turn while another carnivore eats a portion of it.

Yet what about the enormous number of ungulates that, at least in the Serengeti, die from causes other than predation? Indeed, some 67% of the ungulates in the Serengeti die from such causes and are mostly untouched by the large carnivores (Houston, 1979). The use of these carcasses (mostly migratory species such as the wildebeest) is the basis for the only clear case of 100% scavenging known in East Africa, the griffon vultures. The foraging of griffon vultures depends entirely on finding dead animals. They are able to locate scavengable carcasses by following the migratory herds. As a result of their long-distance gliding abilities, griffons focus exclusively on these herds and are thus able to keep away from predatory carnivores (Houston, 1974). The latter have relatively fixed ranges related to breeding areas and cannot move the great distances griffons do each day to keep up with the migratory ungulates. Serengeti hyenas and lions feed upon the migratory wildebeest, zebra, and Thomson's gazelle, but mainly during a few months out of the year when these great herds pass by. During other times of the year, carnivores hunt the wide diversity of resident (nonmigratory) prey species (Kruuk, 1972; Melton and Melton, 1982). When the source of meat is confined to resident ungulates, scavenging evidently becomes a highly competitive matter among carnivores, whereas the big migrations afford far greater scavenging opportunities (Potts, 1984a).

The issues surrounding early hominid meat eating and hunting arise not from the uniqueness of these behaviors among mammals but from their distinctiveness among primates. Therefore, this brief review of hunting and scavenging in modern habitats must also note evidence about how primates acquire meat. Given reports of predation by chimpanzees and baboons, there is no doubt that some higher primates do hunt small prey deliberately. Gazelles, small baboons, birds, and other animals under 10 kg in body weight comprise the focus of the prey items taken. It has also been claimed in these reports that nonhuman primates do not scavenge. However, the practice in chimps of "pirating" fresh kills from baboons (Goodall, 1986; McGrew, 1979) is the equivalent to early scavenging by carnivores. The distinction between pirating and scavenging in nonhuman primates is meaningless when viewed in terms of the variation in scavenging behavior among carnivores (Potts, 1984a). Besides this, the issue of early hominid meat-eating is founded on the fact that tropical latitude hunter–gatherers consume at least 10–20 times more meat (by weight) than is estimated for the relatively carnivorous chimpanzees at Gombe (Hayden, 1981; Lee and DeVore, 1968; Teleki, 1981: 321). Moreover, much of the meat intake of hunter–gatherers, recently and apparently in prehistoric times, derives from mammals over 10 kg in weight, often from animals much larger than this limit. This is a further distinction that defines a shift to eating more meat and doing more hunting, a transition that occurred at some point in hominid evolution. It should be pointed out, however, that scavenging is not unknown among recent hunter–gatherers. The Hadza, a group of savanna foragers in Tanzania, and the San of Botswana are two cases in which scavenging from carnivore kills is known (Yellen, 1977a; J. O'Connell, pers. comm.).

We have seen in this review of "foraging for meat" that hunting and scavenging by modern carnivores signify opportunistic, and not mutually exclusive, modes of obtaining carcasses. In addition, human hunters occasionally will scavenge when the opportunity presents itself; and we see that nonhuman primates engage in both activities. Finally, the appropriation of a carcass soon after a kill by a different carnivore or primate can offer an abundance of meat.[2] Given all of this, it might seem that the heat of debate devoted to the question "Were our ancestors hunters or scavengers?" is quite misplaced. Indeed, is this question even properly phrased? It is important to scrutinize this idea. However, the example of the griffon vulture illustrates that exclusive scavenging can occur. Under ecological conditions like the present-day Serengeti, a mostly scavenging mode of foraging is conceivable in a terrestrial, nomadic mammal that could exploit the large number of dead animals available from a few migratory ungulate species. In addition, the experiment on scavenging performed in the Serengeti by Schaller and Lowther (1969) suggests that a hominid living mainly on plant foods could have relied upon scavenging alone for its meat. Thus, conceivably, a scavenging niche that excluded predation was open to early hominids, such as those at Olduvai. The fact that several carnivores, such as the cheetah, obtain almost 100% of their food from hunting further suggests that an exclusively hunting mode of foraging was also a feasible strategy for gaining access to carcasses. We now turn to the various lines of fossil evidence related to this question.

## Inferences from Bed I Olduvai

A variety of methods have been proposed to discern hunting and scavenging based on prehistoric faunal assemblages (Behrensmeyer, 1987). Animals other than large mammals provide some examples relevant to Bed I Olduvai. For instance, the fragmentary nature of the elephant shrews in each level at FLK North has been taken as evidence that these animals were hunted (Butler and Greenwood, 1976). The fragmented condition of the bones indicates that

[2]In a study of hunting by cheetahs in the Serengeti, Schaller (1970) reports that 12% of the animals killed by this carnivore during the study period were appropriated by other carnivore species *before* cheetahs could feed from the carcass.

these insectivores did not die *in situ*, and usually very small animals ($< 12$ kg) are consumed in their entirety by carnivores (i.e., they are not available for scavenging). As we noted previously, though, the taphonomic effects on the remains of such small animals are unclear for the sites in Bed I. Sometimes, hunting has been suggested based on unusual characteristics of the faunal sample relative to the expected characteristics of natural, living populations. Auffenberg (1981) considers the turtle *Pelusios sinuatus* at site DK to have been selectively hunted based on its restricted size range relative to more widely varying natural turtle populations.

The question of hunting versus scavenging of large mammals from archeological and paleontological sites has been the target of a wider range of methods. For the late Stone Age of southern Africa, Klein (e.g., 1978) relates the age distributions of archeological faunas to selective predation. One type of age distribution (numerous very young individuals and few prime adults) typifies a natural pattern of attritional mortality, whereas the other distribution (mostly prime adults) is likely to have derived from some selective process, such as hunting. In a later view, Klein (1982) equates the latter age pattern to hunting, but the former distribution may occur by scavenging.

In contrast, other researchers suggest that predators often select juveniles and other animals that are easier to obtain than prime adults. Carnivores in some situations kill a higher proportion of juveniles than expected from the general prey population (Kruuk, 1972; Schaller, 1972). Further, Vrba (1975, 1980) posits that primary predation produces a high representation of juveniles (in terms of MNI) in fossil bone assemblages; the relative frequency of juveniles also should increase for larger bodied prey in a hunted faunal assemblage. In contrast, scavenged assemblages should have low percentages of juveniles.

Table 8.1 summarizes the frequencies of various broad age categories in populations of living mammals in Africa. The percentage of juveniles in such populations typically varies from 20–40% (approximately one-third, on the average), although higher and lower frequencies occur. Table 8.2 summarizes the percentage of immature individuals (based on MNI) for each site in Bed I Olduvai.[3] Generally, these percentages match the frequencies of juveniles in large mammal populations today, although the assemblage from FLKNN–3 is at the high end of the range of variation. At FLK North–6, immature individuals are represented about equally throughout the size classes, including very large animals (size class E). FLK "Zinj" shows the lowest overall representation of juvenile MNIs; yet there is an increase in the frequency of juveniles from 14% to 50% going from small to large bovids (Table D.3). The antelopes from FLKNN–2 show a clear decrease in juveniles with an increase in body size (Table C.3). Interestingly, FLKNN–3 exhibits an increase in

[3]More detailed data on the frequency of juvenile and adult individuals (MNIs) for various taxa are provided in Appendixes A–E.

**TABLE 8.1.** Data on the Frequency of Juvenile and Adult Age Classes in Living Populations of Mammals in Africa

| Animal | Location | Age-class percentages | Reference |
|---|---|---|---|
| Wildebeest | Serengeti ($N$ = 360,000) | 17% subadults<br>83% adults | Kruuk (1972:83) |
| | Ngorongoro ($N$ = 13,528) | 25% subadults<br>75% adults | Kruuk (1972:84) |
| Thomson's gazelle | Serengeti | subadult mean percentage<br>= 25% | Hvidberg-Hansen and de Vos (1971) |
| Ungulate populations | Zimbabwe | 25–50% immature | Dasmann and Massman (1962) |
| Impala | Southern Africa | 20–21% immature | Stewart and Stewart (1966) |
| Waterbuck | Sabi-Sand Game Reserve | 33% immature<br>59% adult<br>8% unclassified | Herbert (1972) |
| Giraffe | Wankie N.P. (Zambia)<br>Nairobi N.P. | 12–30% immature<br>44% immature<br>56% adult | Dagg and Foster (1976:144) |
| Rhinoceros | Amboseli-Ngorongoro-<br>Olduvai-Tsavo | Range: 39–44% immature | Western and Sindiyo (1972) |
| Black rhinoceros | Tsavo East Reserve<br>(5 counts) | 19–24% immature | Schenkel and Schenkel-<br>Hulliger (1969:38–40) |
| Hippopotamus | Queen Elizabeth Park | 31% immature | Laws (1968) |
| Lion | Serengeti plains | 17% cubs<br>26% subadult<br>57% adult | Schaller (1972) |
| | Serengeti woodlands | 27% cubs<br>20–25% subadult<br>50% adult | Schaller (1972) |
| | Manyara | 20–25% cubs | Schaller (1972) |
| | Nairobi N.P. | 25% cubs | Schaller (1972) |
| | Kruger N.P. | 33% cubs and subadults | Schaller (1972) |
| Hyena | Ngorongoro | 18% immature | Kruuk (1972) |
| Olive baboons | Laikipia, Kenya | 41% immature | Berger (1972) |

**TABLE 8.2.** Percentage Representation of Immature Individuals (MNI) for Mammal Macrofauna, Bed I Sites[a]

| Level | Percentage immature |
|---|---|
| FLK North–6[b] (N = 20) | 35 |
| FLK "Zinj" (N = 36) | 28 |
| FLKNN–2 (N = 23) | 35 |
| FLKNN–3 (N = 34) | 47 |
| DK–2 (N = 41) | 29 |
| DK–3 (N = 36) | 32 |
| Long K (N = 48) | 21 |

[a]The total sample of individuals from each level is provided.
[b]Excludes *Elephas recki* material.

juveniles with bovid body size, as expected by Vrba for a hunted assemblage (Table B.3). DK–3 shows the same trend, but DK–2 does not (Tables A.3, A.12).

The problems with this kind of analysis are several. First, MNI provides samples that are too small to place much confidence in the calculated percentages of immature individuals. In addition, young animals tend to undergo differential destruction and are grossly underrepresented in most modern and fossil assemblages (Behrensmeyer *et al.*, 1979; Western, 1980). Therefore, juveniles in general, especially among small-sized species, may be highly underrepresented in these fossil assemblages. This point especially holds for those Olduvai assemblages in which preferential attrition of bone is best documented (e.g., FLKNN–2, FLK "Zinj," and DK–2, see p. 120). Since juvenile and small animal bones are most open to mechanical and chemical destruction and winnowing, the percentages of juveniles in Bed I assemblages are open to several interpretations other than the mode of access to carcasses. As suggested by the preceding taphonomic analyses, information about the bones of juveniles is likely to be quite biased by effects unrelated to hominid or carnivore activity.

The amount of variance in prey body sizes has been suggested as another indicator of hunting versus scavenging (e.g., Vrba, 1975). A narrow range of species or body sizes is often predicted to result from a hunting strategy (see Behrensmeyer, 1987, for a review of this subject). However, a narrow or large range of body sizes in an assemblage could reflect either predator selection or simply the variance in the natural population of ungulates (Vrba, 1980). Another difficulty with this approach is that a broad range of body sizes or species preserved in a bone assemblage would not necessarily reflect a pure scavenger strategy, but possibly a mixed hunter/scavenger mode of foraging. In addition, some human hunters hunt a wide diversity of species and body sizes (e.g., San hunters; see Yellen, 1977b); thus, hunting does not necessarily result in a narrow range of variation in the faunal assemblage.

Another approach, often adopted by archeologists, involves estimating the predatory abilities of hominids armed with a particular stone technology. For example, scavenging is believed to have been more likely than hunting as the way early hominids obtained bones from medium and large-sized ungulates. The reason provided is the assumed simplicity of the technology (and, by implication, the strategies) of these hominids (Isaac and Crader, 1981). Of course, based on the same evidence, the staunchest proponents of the hunting hypothesis claim that these hominids were cunning and daring predators.

The methods proposed by previous researchers to illuminate the issue of hominid scavenging and hunting serve to illustrate the complexity involved in using the fossil record to infer foraging from faunal remains. In the past several years, other lines of evidence have been sought that avoid the problem posed by differential attrition of age classes and suppositions about the abilities of hominids. Study of the Olduvai remains and development of the scavenging hypothesis have spawned most of this new research, as we shall now see.

### The Scavenging Hypothesis

That early hominids at Olduvai were exclusively scavengers in the way they obtained bones and food from animals is a position strongly advocated by Binford (1981, 1985). According to his analyses, the only unambiguous pattern in the Olduvai faunal remains points decidedly to scavenging of bone marrow and perhaps incidental eating of tiny scraps of dessicated meat by hominids (1985: 302). Olduvai hominids scavenged from carcasses previously exploited by predators and other scavengers. The parts scavenged were primarily distal limb bones, which have little meat on them to begin with and little attraction to carnivores. Instead, the only edible component of such bones is the marrow inside, and the tool kit of hominids was equipped primarily to crack open these marrow bones. The low expectation of food from this activity, and the view that many of the Olduvai sites were ungulate death areas or scatters around such sites, suggest that hominids did not regularly carry bones away from death sites—and when they did, it was not to a social group convening at a home base (Binford, 1981: 292–294).

These conclusions concerning early hominids at Olduvai are based on Binford's analysis in the book *Bones*. We noted several problems with this analysis in Chapter 6, specifically with regard to the taphonomic inferences of particular sites. Furthermore, the interpretation of hominid activities presented in *Bones* is based upon an analytical approach in which the relative frequencies of different skeletal parts are construed to inform not only about the contributions of carnivores and hominids to the bone assemblages but also about the way hominids usually obtained animal bones. Binford's residual method refers hominid activity to those patterns of skeletal element representation that are unlike those found in assemblages produced by modern carnivores. The problem is that this method *a priori* associates hominids with scavenging since virtually all modern carnivores, and certainly those on which the *Bones* analysis is based, are primarily hunters. If overlap is prohibited between assemblages made by hominids and modern carnivores, the residual left over must inevitably be skeletal parts available only to a scrounging type of scavenger, that is, a behavior that does not characterize the carnivores (wolves, lions, and spotted hyenas) on which Binford's carnivore models are based. The attribution of scavenging to the hominids of Olduvai is partly an artifact of the method.

Furthermore, a focus upon distal limb elements and their breakage for marrow is simply not manifested in the bone assemblages from the artifact sites. Bunn and Kroll (1986) have illustrated this point with their in-depth identification of limb bone fragments from FLK "Zinj"; their analysis shows that meaty upper limb bones were abundant in that assemblage. Table 8.3 provides a breakdown of the major limb elements for bovids in each Olduvai assemblage examined here. At all of the sites, meat-bearing bones from the

**TABLE 8.3.** Frequencies of Proximal, Midlimb, and Distal Long Bones of Bovids Based on MNE[a]

| Site | Meat-bearing proximal long bones (humerus and femur) | Meat-bearing midlimb long bones (radius, ulna, and tibia) | Nonmeaty distal long bones (metacarpal and metatarsal) |
|------|------|------|------|
| FLKNN–2 | 16 | 26 | 20 |
| Long K | 35 | 38 | 28 |
| FLK North–6 | 11 | 21 | 10 |
| FLK "Zinj" | 27 | 39 | 31 |
| FLKNN–3 | 5 | 16 | 11 |
| DK–2 | 23 | 46 | 27 |
| DK–3 | 22 | 18 | 30 |
| All artifact sites: | 88 | 140 | 109 |
| Complete bovid skeleton | 4 | 6 | 4 |

[a]A division of bovid size class can be calculated by raw data in the appendixes.

proximal and middle segments of the limbs are clearly more abundant than the distal elements. The frequencies of proximal : mid-limb : distal elements can be compared to the ratio of these elements in living bovids, namely 4 : 6 : 4. According to this comparison, proximal bones (which yield the greatest quantity of meat) are about as numerous as expected relative to mid-limb bones.[4] At the artifact sites and in the FLKNN–2 assemblage, metapodials are more abundant than expected relative to meat bones (48% of the total number of meat-bearing bones versus 40% in living bovids), but this difference is not significant.[5] There is variation among the artifact sites: The number of metapodials at DK–3 is significantly greater than expected relative to meat-bearing bones; yet the proximal limb elements are unusually abundant compared with mid-limb bones. A slight opposite effect is evident at FLK North–6, where metapodials are underrepresented and mid-limb bones are over-represented.[6] The pattern of proximal, mid-limb, and distal representation seen at FLKNN–2 fits within the variation shown by the artifact sites, while the proportions at Long K are even more similar to those in living antelopes.

These comparisons do not substantiate the claim that hominids primarily selected nonmeaty distal limb segments for transport. The idea that such bones were all that was available to hominids is certainly incorrect. However, if we take into account Binford's calculations of differential bone preservation, the representation of metapodial bones in the Olduvai assemblages would be amplified relative to what is expected in a complete bovid skeleton. According to Binford's calculations for sheep and caribou bones, the survival percentage of metapodials ranges from about 50–70% of that of meat-bearing long bones. In other words, differential preservation should work against distal segment marrow bones relative to more proximal meat bones. Yet this factor does not appear to apply to the Olduvai assemblages. At the artifact sites, 38% of the unbroken long bones ($N = 58$) are metapodials; in addition, an average of 16% of the minimum number of metapodials from these sites are unbroken specimens (range 12–23%). These figures suggest that these nonmeat bones were not so subject to destruction or damage as were the other major limb bones. Moreover, these data do not support the view that hominids were collecting metapodials strictly for the purpose of smashing them for marrow, as proposed by Binford (1981).

A final point underlying the scavenging hypothesis presented in *Bones* concerns the artifact assemblages. One of the Olduvai sites also studied here,

---

[4]For all five artifact sites (combined) a ratio of 63% compared with 67% in living bovids.

[5]In one-sample $X^2$ tests: $X^2 = 2.46$; $df = 1$; $p > 0.10$, for the artifact sites; and $X^2 = 0.31$; $df = 1$; $p > 0.50$ for FLKNN–2 (compared with that expected in a complete bovid skeleton normalized for sample sizes). At Long K, nonmeaty metapodials occur in a frequency that is 39% of the number of meat-bearing bones.

[6]A one-sample $X^2$ test for distal bones versus meat bones at DK–3: $X^2 = 7.0$; $df = 1$; $p < 0.01$.

FLKNN–3, is claimed to exhibit a clear pattern of limb bone breakage by hominids to obtain marrow. The artifacts from this site are presented as almost exclusively a heavy-duty tool kit for smashing bones; this would help support the idea that hominids practiced a scrounging style of scavenging (Binford, 1981: 281). However, the information presented leaves out virtually all of the small, sharp-edged pieces known from this site (29 out of a total number of 48 modified artifacts: Leakey, 1971; Table B.10). These pieces are classified as broken flakes and core fragments (none of which fit together to form a single flake), and they represent the type of small "waste" flakes that are known to have been used as cutting tools at other Plio–Pleistocene sites (Keeley and Toth, 1981). Thus, heavy-duty bone breaking implements do not comprise the major component of the artifact assemblage from FLKNN–3.

In summary, meat-rich skeletal elements are neither rare nor especially underrepresented in the assemblages collected primarily by hominids; the cracking of metapodials for marrow was evidently not the focus of hominid activities at these sites; and the tool assemblages are dominated by small artifacts useful for cutting soft tissues. The faunal and artifact data from the sites of Bed I Olduvai examined here do not uphold the scavenging hypothesis as presented by Binford (1981, 1985).

A different approach to the foraging activities of hominids at Olduvai has been developed by Shipman in a series of intriguing articles devoted to the issue of hunting versus scavenging (1983, 1984, 1986a,b). Two main lines of evidence are examined by Shipman—the distribution of tool cut marks on animal bones and the feasibility of scavenging in the ancient environments of Bed I Olduvai. The feasibility study illustrates that, assuming certain energy requirements of hominids and consumption rates by carnivores, the environment of Bed I was capable of producing an adequate supply of scavengable matter that hominids could have utilized (Shipman, 1986a).

A potential problem here is that in Shipman's analysis, the availability of carcasses is directly related to the prediction of biomass from rainfall. An estimate of 900–1000 mm per year is taken to apply throughout Bed I times, which yields a high amount of biomass and a high mass of scavengable carcasses. This estimate is crucial in judging that scavenging was a feasible endeavor for Olduvai hominids. Although such rainfall estimates probably do apply to the early sites from Olduvai, sites FLK "Zinj" and FLK North–6 appear to have formed during relatively dry intervals—probably less than 800–350 mm per year based on faunal and pollen evidence. The mass of scavengable carcasses would have been considerably lower, according to this line of theoretical analysis; yet carcass materials transported to these sites (in terms of species, taxonomic diversity, and body parts) do not contrast appreciably with that found on sites formed during wetter periods. This hints that the collection of bones primarily by hominids in Bed I was not strictly tied to the availability of scavengable carcass material as expected from rainfall, following Shipman's method. Nonetheless, Shipman's approach, along with Blumenschine's observations (1986) of carcasses in the modern Serengeti, illustrates that hominid acquisition of carcass parts purely by scavenging is conceivable under certain conditions, as we saw earlier in the case of the griffon vultures.[7]

The second line of Shipman's analysis looks to the bovid remains from Bed I Olduvai and seeks to determine the distribution of cut marks and carnivore tooth marks on these bones. According to that analysis, Olduvai hominids did not regularly disarticulate carcasses; instead, they scavenged bones already disjoined and scattered by carnivores (Shipman 1984, 1986a). Though based on the analysis of different data, this conclusion is like Binford's in its content. In addition, scavenging and hunting are treated as modes of foraging that exclude one another (i.e., the results of Shipman's tests tend to favor either one foraging mode or the other). A brief summary of the predictions of Shipman's original hypothesis is as follows. First, hunting is linked specifically to the disarticulation of limb bones; accordingly, a hunted assemblage of bones is supposed to have a high percentage of cut marks near the articular ends of long bones but few at mid-shaft locations. In contrast, scavenging is expected to show the reverse pattern and, thus, is linked specifically to scrounging for bones already disarticulated. Second, an assemblage resulting from hunting will exhibit a high proportion of tool marks due to skinning the animal (i.e., on nonmeaty bones, where hide lies close to the bone). Since scavenging, according to this view, does not offer access to intact carcasses, cut marks made by scavenging hominids should occur much less frequently on nonmeat limb bones than meat bones; however, earlier access by carnivores to the latter type of bones means that carnivore tooth marks will be proportionately more abundant on meat bones than are hominid cut marks. This prediction is a complicated one that, Shipman points out, does not clearly distinguish hunted from scavenged assemblages.[8] A final prediction involves overlapping marks made by carnivore teeth and hominid tools. The occurrence of a tool mark overlying (made after) a carnivore tooth mark necessarily implies that hominids utilized that particular bone after carnivores had done so—hence, scavenging by hominids.

---

[7]In a system like the Serengeti, on which Shipman's model is based, scavenging opportunities are strongly linked with the migratory ungulates. Presumably scavenging hominids would have to deal with the shifting spatial focus of these opportunities by also becoming migratory, a strategy that is not adopted by any mammalian carnivore, including striped and brown hyenas. Alternatively, nonmigratory hominids could have acquired carcasses exclusively by scavenging if this activity were confined to certain seasons of the year (Blumenschine, 1986; see following). In other seasons of the year, hominids would have had to rely on plant foods, if hunting is disallowed (Shipman, 1986a: 31).

[8]This prediction modifies the view of Potts and Shipman (1981) that cut marks on nonmeat elements may be indicative of using nonmeat resources, such as hide or tendon.

As Shipman (1986b) has recently pointed out, there is a difficulty inherent in the first prediction. The comparison between Olduvai and any control assemblage (made by modern hunters) must ensure approximately equal ratios of articular ends to mid-shaft pieces. The initial comparison that Shipman made in this regard was to the Neolithic site of Prolonged Drift, Kenya (Gifford et al., 1981). Taking the identified bovids from FLK "Zinj" as an example, out of 200 limb segments (proximal end, distal end, or mid-shaft) represented at this artifact site, 30.5% are mid-shaft segments. In contrast, perusal of the data from Prolonged Drift suggests that far fewer mid-shaft areas are preserved (10% or less) relative to the ends of bones at this Neolithic site. In line with this observation, the Prolonged Drift assemblage exhibits a very large number of butchery marks near joints and few at mid-shaft, while the Olduvai bovid sample from Bed I shows a much smaller percentage of tool marks near joints. Instead, the distribution of cut marks and carnivore tooth marks in the Olduvai sample is very similar, which results *partly* from the fact that both types of mark are observed in exactly the same bone sample (i.e., with the same initial proportions of limb ends and mid-shaft segments). Although the Prolonged Drift comparison is now deemed inappropriate, a different set of predictions from that based on Prolonged Drift have now been proposed (Shipman, 1986b). These new predictions of the hunting and scavenging hypotheses derive from the pastoralist site at Ngamuriak, Kenya (Marshall, 1986). Differences between this site and Prolonged Drift, however, suggest that human butchery is variable, at least in the production of cut marks on bones. Hence, a model of hunting and systematic butchery should not rely upon a single case.

It must also be noted that the number of bones bearing tool cut marks are very few compared to the overall size of the bone accumulation at each site. If we accept that hominids were important collectors of bones at the artifact sites, researchers who deal with *frequencies* of cut marks might seriously consider whether, in fact, samples of cut-marked bones can ever be expected to reflect adequately hominid interaction with specific skeletal parts or species. An inevitable focus upon relatively complete, identifiable specimens also means that much of the search for and counting of cut marks is confined to a sample that does not reflect the most intensively utilized pieces at a site.

Shipman's detailed identifications of bone surface damage have shown, however, that hominid tool marks do (on rare occasions) overlie carnivore tooth marks. There is little doubt that hominids scavenged these particular bones. On the other hand, the few cases in which carnivore tooth marks overlie tool marks are more difficult to evaluate. It is possible that hominids scavenged these bones but still left something on them attractive to carnivores. In other words, this type of evidence (overlapping cut marks and tooth marks) permits us to recognize scavenging but not necessarily hunting.

The evidence that carnivores gnawed and broke bones *at the sites* where hominids appear to have been the primary bone collector further suggests that carnivores may have been attracted to materials collected by hominids. This, along with the data on overall skeletal part representation, implies that hominids were not always or consistently limited to scraps or leftovers from carnivore kills. In comparison with hunter–gatherer campsites (and given that both hominids and carnivores had access to the sites), the undamaged condition of some bones (see p. 202), including meaty and marrow-rich elements with cut marks on them, further indicates that hominids were not restricted to marginal scavenging. Unfortunately, the collection of scraps left by carnivores has become synonymous with the scavenging hypothesis. This dismisses the possibility that early scavenging can provide access to intact carcasses. In fact, early scavenging of intact carcasses is the norm among vultures that scavenge for most or all of the meat they consume; this is also practiced by mammalian carnivores during periods of abundant carcasses at the end of the dry season in the Serengeti (Blumenschine, 1986). Thus, a hominid relying on scavenging, as envisioned by Shipman (1986a), might be expected to monitor such carcasses. Finally, the relative abundance of certain skeletal elements (e.g., carpals and tarsals) at each of the Olduvai sites studied here suggests that articulated units were brought to these sites, not disarticulated bones or small units one at a time (Chapter 4).

### Scavenging in the Serengeti

Another recent development of the scavenging hypothesis stems from valuable observations of carcasses in the present-day Serengeti. In this study, Blumenschine (1986) has evaluated the scavenging opportunities available to early hominids by examining carcasses found in diverse habitats, in different seasons of the year, and utilized by a variety of predators and scavengers. In assessing the feasibility and various contingencies of scavenging in a modern environment, Blumenschine's goal is also to develop criteria whereby scavenged assemblages of bones can be recognized in the archeological record.

This study points out that the best scavenging opportunities are provided by medium-sized ungulates, such as wildebeest and zebra. This is due not only to their abundance relative to large species but also to the greater amount of edible tissues they offer compared to small animals. Generally, small species such as the gazelles are not available for scavenging because they are rapidly consumed by carnivores. In situations where carnivores do leave a carcass before it is completely consumed, all marrow bones of the limbs and the contents of the skulls tend to be available to scavengers. The best place to find such carcasses in the Serengeti today is in woodlands near water, where lions are the dominant predator. In these wooded riparian settings, carcasses persist longer because hyenas tend to avoid such areas and thus do not find these carcasses quickly or at all. The most favorable time of year is in the dry season, when migratory ungulates glut the Serengeti and become abundant in the riparian woodlands due to the availability of water (Blumenschine, 1986).

Based on these findings, scavenging opportunities are greatest under two sets of conditions: First, in the riparian woodlands during the dry season, edible tissues are available from medium-sized ungulates killed and then abandoned by felids; carcasses of these ungulates are also highly available due to natural mortality. Second, numerous animals also die of nonpredatory means on the open plains, especially at the end of the dry season. In this situation, many carcasses can be found relatively untouched by other carnivores. Blumenschine (1986) explores the differences between these two opportunities for scavenging and favors the first as that most likely to have been adopted by hominid scavengers. This conclusion is based on the proximity of known archeological sites to water (i.e., riparian settings); the lower risk of predation in such settings due to the availability of trees for hominids to climb; and the longer season of scavenging opportunity provided by riparian woodlands compared to the open plains.

This research furnishes a useful analysis of scavenging, based on the Serengeti analogue, against which to evaluate the bone assemblages collected at the Olduvai sites. How well do these sites correspond to the scavenging opportunities formulated by this approach? First, medium-sized ungulates do comprise the majority of animals in each of the Olduvai bone assemblages (Chapter 7). But we must take into account that, indeed, the majority of living ungulates in East African savannas are medium-sized ungulates. Predators, and potentially early hominid hunters, would also be expected to take advantage of the vast source of animals in this size range. Furthermore, the most important scavenging opportunities in the Serengeti result from the large migratory herds composed of just a few ungulate species. In the Serengeti study, a single species (wildebeest) accounted for 60% of the carcasses found, and 80% belonged to just two species of medium-sized ungulates (wildebeest and zebra) (Blumenschine, 1986). Thus, a very few species provide the best opportunities to scavengers. In contrast, the Olduvai assemblages are not dominated by one or a few species; instead, they are characterized by a wide diversity of animals (Tables 7.1 and 7.24). Although it is quite possible that during the Plio–Pleistocene more than two species contributed to seasonal gluts of carcasses, the Olduvai sites show ample evidence of species that surely were not migratory but were resident species generally unavailable to scavengers, at least in African savannas today (see p. 207). These resident species would include at least browsing ungulates, suids, and monkeys.

The fact that scavenging opportunities in the Serengeti are greatest in riparian woodlands affords a second way to assess scavenging by Olduvai hominids. Indeed, the Olduvai sites occur within the ancient lake margin zone. This facies, as defined by Hay (1976), was very broad, and the sites were not necessarily very close to the lake waters (see Chapter 2). Nonetheless, fossil rhizomes and other evidence do indicate that some of the sites examined here were very close at least to swamp or marsh. Wooded areas, as well as open plains and marsh, in the vicinity of these sites are further suggested by the murid rodents preserved at localities FLKNN and FLK. In contrast with Blumenschine's observation regarding hyena avoidance of woodlands near water in the modern Serengeti, there is ample evidence in the ancient faunal assemblages that bone-gnawing carnivores similar to spotted hyenas (in the way they modified and collected bones) were active in the lake margin zone at Olduvai. One or more species of carnivores were capable of inflicting considerable damage to bones, including marrow-rich elements. The carnivore-like assemblages from FLKNN–2 and Long K suggest that such a carnivore was not only active in this riparian setting but also lived there as an active bone collector. The presence of these carnivores, known from bone modifications from each of the Olduvai sites, means that (1) riparian zones at Olduvai were not necessarily prime settings for hominid scavengers, and (2) the timing and location of scavenging opportunities at Olduvai may have differed substantially from that in the modern Serengeti.

In addition, Blumenschine (1986: 139) defines several other characteristics that should typify scavenging by hominids in a situation like the modern Serengeti.[9] However, most of these predictions might apply to any behaviorally transported bone assemblage, including those formed by hunting and systematic butchery (e.g., cut marks on distal limb bones) or to assemblages affected by differential preservation (e.g., low proportion of juveniles).

Yet one characteristic that the artifact assemblages from Olduvai do match relates to the sequence of carcass parts consumed by carnivores. Based on feeding episodes at carcasses and the parts left over time, Blumenschine (1986) has been able to construct which parts of a carcass are consumed early and late by carnivores. A standard order emerges: viscera is generally first to be consumed, followed by hind flesh, forequarter flesh, head flesh, hindlimb marrow, forelimb marrow, and skull contents (last). Usually, all parts of one area are finished before portions of the next carcass region are begun. Because small ungulates go through this consumption sequence faster than a larger individual, small animals are likely to be represented in a scavenged bone assemblage primarily by parts left only late in the consumption sequence. This is the expectation relative to larger ungulates, which should have a higher representation of parts consumed early in the sequence (Blumenschine, 1986: 145). In fact, the bovids at four of the artifact sites from Olduvai exhibit this pattern (DK–3, FLKNN–3, FLK "Zinj," and FLK North–6). At DK–2 there are equal numbers of elements consumed early and late for both small and large bovids. At FLKNN–2, which is not associated with artifacts, small bovids are too scarce to determine the pattern. Yet larger bovids show a higher percentage of parts consumed late in the standard sequence. This might imply

---

[9]These characteristics include (a) a predominance of adults over juveniles in the bone assemblage; (b) predominance of fragmented limb bones and cranial parts over axial elements; (c) a higher proportion of cut marks on distal limb bones than on more proximal parts; and (d) small species represented mainly by parts consumed at the end of the carcass consumption sequence, while larger species are also represented by bones available earlier in the sequence.

scavenging even though the relationship with small bovids cannot be tested. At Long K, the trend from small to medium to large bovids does not accord with that predicted for a scavenger.

The interpretive problem here is that parts consumed late (metapodials and phalanges) may be transported with articulated limbs that are taken from a carcass and consumed elsewhere. This is the pattern at the Amboseli hyena den and is expected for carnivore bone collectors generally. Parts that are consumed early (especially vertebrae, pelvis, and ribs) are not detached from a carcass easily or quickly by carnivores, including the initial predator. Thus, these elements would tend to be underrepresented in any *transported* collection of bones made by predators or scavengers. Despite this important difficulty in applying consumption sequences at carcass sites to transported bone assemblages, the pattern seen at the Olduvai artifact sites hints that scavenging opportunities may have been taken advantage of by the hominids contributing to these sites.

Blumenschine's study establishes the critical variables that underlie scavenging in the Serengeti today. In doing so, it also establishes conditions under which a hominid scavenger could thrive by obtaining low utility leftovers (compared with parts eaten more quickly) and avoiding competition with carnivores. However, the most favorable conditions for scavenging in the Serengeti today are not clearly reflected at either the artifact sites or in the bone assemblages from FLKNN–2 or Long K.

In brief, none of the analyses of the scavenging hypothesis considered so far appears to offer definite evidence for scavenging by hominids. Does this mean that Olduvai hominids were not primarily scavengers? Does it mean that they were hunters?

## Timing of Hominid and Carnivore Access to Carcasses

A further attempt to investigate how Olduvai hominids obtained carcasses comes from comparing sites that had varying degrees of contribution from hominid and carnivore bone collectors. Since carnivores evidently played a greater role at two of the sites and hominids did so at the artifact sites, comparisons of the patterns of preserved skeletal parts in the "more carnivore" and "more hominid" assemblages may help indicate when carnivores and hominids gained access to carcasses.

The method summarized here (Potts, 1983) is based on generalizations about the ways African carnivores disarticulate and remove portions of carcasses. Carnivores, notably hyenas, that remove portions of carcasses from death sites tend to tear off and take away the limbs completely. In particular, the forelimbs, including the scapula, have been noted to be the first part carried away. Axial elements such as vertebrae, ribs, and pelvis and also the skull are most likely to remain at the death site. While these observations were made in passing by a variety of researchers (e.g., Kruuk, 1972; Shipman and Phillips-Conroy, 1977), a systematic study of carcass disarticulation and scattering confirms these impressions (Hill, 1975, 1979b; Hill and Behrensmeyer, 1984). Hill's study in a variety of East African game reserves and habitats has shown that the disarticulation sequence of ungulates is quite uniform. A highly consistent statistical sequence is detected not only in a diversity of environments but also in a variety of species (topi, zebra, wildebeest, Grant's gazelle, and domestic cow). In addition, in the earliest stages of disarticulation, as parts become separated from the axial skeleton, they tend to be scattered or removed from the carcass site (Hill, 1975). The general sequence is as follows: The forelimb (including the scapula) is the first unit to separate and to be removed from the axial skeleton; the disarticulation of the hindlimb (starting with the femur) follows, leaving the axial skeleton behind. Limb units are not always scattered from the carcass, and this allows study of the disarticulation sequence of bones within the forelimb and hindlimb units. Whether limbs stay with a carcass largely depends on the actions of predators and scavengers. Nonetheless, the large-scale pattern of forelimb disarticulation (and potential removal) followed by hindlimb disarticulation is seen in many species, overshadowing variations in the separation of individual bones within the larger units.

Based on these generalizations, I suggested that the proportions of forelimb, hindlimb, and axial elements in faunal assemblages would reflect the *relative* timing of access to carcasses by diverse bone collectors. In other words, the skeletal units available at animal death sites will constrain the skeletal parts transported away when more than one bone collector is involved. The collector having later access to a carcass (and, therefore, necessarily a scavenger) will have a different choice of carcass units available for removal than the carnivores or hominids with earlier access. If the *sequence* of carcass access is consistent and the earlier arriver tends to remove the same body parts each time, the bone assemblages made by both bone collectors should reflect the relative time of access (earlier versus later) of each to carcasses. At Olduvai we have evidence for at least two different bone accumulators—one or more carnivores and hominids. Hence, the comparison among assemblages in which the hominid and carnivore contributions are variable (e.g., artifact sites versus FLKNN–2 and Long K) can clarify this question about relative timing of access to carcasses.

The uniform sequence proposed by Hill implies that since forelimbs are removed earlier during natural disarticulation (especially aided by carnivores), the proportion of forelimb bones in a transported assemblage should be particularly indicative. A high number of forelimb elements relative to hindlimb bones means that the bone collector had access to the unit that usually disappears most rapidly from carcasses—the forelimb. Thus, a high forelimb to hindlimb ratio *(F/H)* suggests early access to carcasses if, in fact, more than one agent were responsible for removing bones from those carcasses. In addition, the ratio of axial elements to limb elements *(A/L)* was calculated because the removal of both fore and hindlimbs typically precedes removal of axial remains from death sites.

Figures 8.1 and 8.2, based on an earlier publication (Potts, 1983), depict these two ratios for small, medium, and large bovids from Olduvai. The most obvious pattern is the consistent prevalence of forelimb bones across all body size classes in the probable carnivore accumulation at FLKNN–2. The *F/H* ratio for all bovids from this site equals 2.8, compared with a range of 0.75–1.52 from the artifact sites. The data from FLKNN–2 suggest highly consistent early access to bovid carcasses of all sizes, prior to the removal of units by other bone collectors. In contrast, none of the artifact sites exhibits a consistent pattern of forelimb or hindlimb predominance throughout the different body sizes. Furthermore, there is considerable variation among the artifact sites in the *F/H* ratio for small and large bovids. For medium-sized bovids, though, all sites show a fairly high *F/H* ratio. If we grant that hominids were *primarily* responsible for manufacturing these broad patterns of skeletal representation, then hominids tended to gain access to medium bovids also before

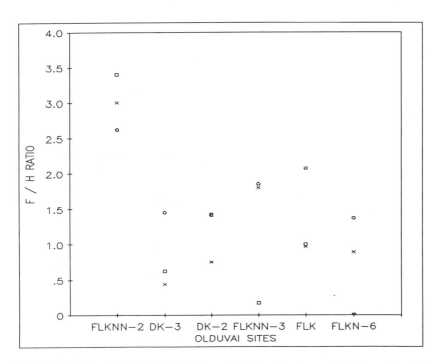

**FIGURE 8.1.** Forelimb to hindlimb bone *(F/H)* ratios for small (x), medium (circles), and large (squares) bovids at each Olduvai site (Long K not included). See Potts (1983) for data.

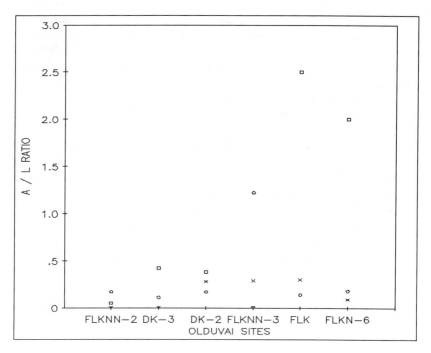

**FIGURE 8.2.** Axial to limb bone *(A/L)* ratios for small (x), medium (circles), and large (squares) bovids at each Olduvai site (Long K not included). See Potts (1983) for data.

the forelimbs were taken away by carnivores. The important distinction, however, is the consistently high proportion of forelimb elements at FLKNN–2 compared with the diverse, unspecialized pattern of forelimb and hindlimb elements at the "primarily hominid" sites.[10] As expected for behaviorally transported bone assemblages, the *A/L* ratio at all sites is low.[11] The large bovids from two sites, FLK "Zinj" and FLK North–6, are an exception. Based on small samples, the *A/L* ratio is higher than expected at these sites, both of which were formed during drier intervals of Bed I. However, this ratio is not so indicative as the *F/H* ratio about when access occurred. In the case of these two sites, for example, the high proportion of axial elements could

[10]The assemblage from Long K, which exhibits significant input from a carnivore bone collector, also shows forelimb predominance but not to the extent shown at FLKNN–2. *F/H* for all bovids equals 1.42. Like FLKNN–2, the *F/H* ratio at Long K is above 1.0 for both small bovids (1.13) and medium bovids (1.72). No limb bones of large bovids were found at the Long K site. These data also hint at the consistent availability of forelimbs and, thus, early access by the carnivores active at Long K relative to other bone collectors.

[11]Range for the artifact sites for *A/L* is 0.19–0.84.

reflect either very late access to carcasses (when only axial parts remained) or the removal of highly valued meaty regions from the axial areas of large carcasses (which could have occurred during early access).

This latter point brings up two problems with this method of analyzing the timing of carcass access. First, by virtue of having stone tools, hominids, like people today, were likely to have selected parts from a parent population of bones that may not be in proportion to what was simply available (Binford, 1985; Potts, 1983). This question of availability versus selective preference again rears its head (see p. 155). It suggests that the forelimb, hindlimb, and axial proportions at the artifact sites are not necessarily interpretable in terms of early or late access to carcasses. Nonetheless, the presence of forelimbs of medium bovids (and forelimbs of small bovids at FLKNN–3 and large bovids at DK–2) does imply that hominids tended to gain access to these carcasses before carnivore *bone collectors* had arrived.[12] Despite the fact that hominids did not necessarily select parts in proportion to their availability, the $F/H$ ratio, in particular, reflects the stage at which the possession of a carcass by hominids intersected the process of disarticulation and removal of bones by carnivores. The data from FLKNN–2 and Long K make clear that carnivores were involved in a sequence of removing skeletal units from carcasses; moreover, they transported bones from carcasses at which they had arrived early. A clear result from the comparison between the "primarily carnivore" assemblages and the artifact assemblages in Bed I is that the latter are rather unspecialized in the representation of skeletal units. If bone collectors other than hominids were present throughout Bed I times, this unspecialized pattern suggests that the primary bone collectors at the artifact sites, namely hominids, had a combination of relatively early and somewhat later access to carcasses. The occasional access to forelimbs (or, for medium-sized bovids, *regular* access to forelimbs) strongly indicates that bone collectors at the artifact sites did not scavenge by scrounging for disarticulated parts left by carnivore bone collectors.

A second problem is posed by Blumenschine (1986: 141). He posits that since disarticulation occurs mainly after the food value of a carcass is exhausted, the sequence of disarticulation is irrelevant to understanding the availability of carcass parts to scavengers. Instead, the important factor is the consumption sequence, which determines what is consumed at a carcass and what is later available for scavenging. The consumption sequence (summarized on p. 220) does not correspond with the disarticulation sequence. For example, in Blumenschine's study the forelimb marrow was available at

---

[12]This does not mean that carnivore bone collectors take away only forelimbs when they are the first ones at a carcass; it simply means that forelimbs are usually the quickest for carnivores to separate and the initial skeletal units to be removed by them.

carcasses until late in the consumption sequence. At the end of this sequence, the resource life of a carcass is essentially finished. Thus, how can the predominance of forelimbs in a bone collection signify early access to carcasses when such units are available at carcasses near the end of their resource life?

It is true that much of skeletal disarticulation takes place after the food value of a carcass is depleted. Yet when a carnivore drags a portion of a carcass away or takes it to a place of bone accumulation, that carcass certainly still possesses useful resources. The reason carnivores remove pieces from carcasses and from the death site is due to the fact that these pieces are valued. Further, reports by Hill (1975) of carcass disarticulation and removal during the first several days after death illustrate that forelimbs are separated and often removed from carcasses within the first day or by the second day, followed closely by hindlimbs. He reports that the earliest stages of carcass disarticulation and scattering often occur rapidly; when it does carnivores are largely responsible for this rapid removal of limbs (Hill, 1975; pers. comm.).

The question at Olduvai is how to account for the parts *removed* by hominids and carnivores from carcasses and then accumulated at sites—not how they were consumed at death sites. The availability of parts at a carcass must be affected by both consumption sequence *and* whether a specific carcass unit is present (i.e., has not been carried away by an earlier carcass user). Species such as the spotted hyena, known to collect bones in other places, evidently collect bones only rarely in the Serengeti (Kruuk, 1972). The fact that Blumenschine's consumption sequence for spotted hyenas can be followed completely, from viscera to head contents with no part of the sequence missing, suggests that hyenas were not active in removing parts from carcasses during the period of study. Thus, the disassociation between disarticulation and carcass value noted by Blumenschine is not surprising. If in the modern Serengeti valued carcass parts are not removed prior to depletion of carcass resources, that situation is not especially pertinent to explaining the transport and accumulation of carcass parts at the Olduvai sites. When carcass parts are removed by carnivores, the forelimbs generally go first followed by hindlimbs. To reiterate, carnivores were involved in transporting bones at Olduvai; in fact, the accumulations at FLKNN–2 and Long K appear to have been produced mainly by a hyena-like carnivore. The reason behind using the sequence of disarticulation and removal of bones to evaluate the timing of access to carcasses is that in the presence of carnivore bone collectors (or even those that simply remove parts away from the carcass but not to fixed points), the transport of carcass parts by hominids would have been affected by what earlier carcass users typically took away. The FLKNN–2 assemblage and, to a lesser degree, that from Long K are distinct from the artifact sites in their high forelimb representation over all body size classes. Based on the Serengeti consumption sequence alone, these assemblages would reflect late scavenging, since forelimbs in Blumenschine's study stayed around carcasses until late. However, in modern situations where parts are removed from carcasses, as previously stated, the forelimbs often go immediately or in a matter of a day or two. Thus, the "primarily carnivore" assemblages at Olduvai were made up of parts removed by carnivores from carcasses soon after death.

Inevitably, the parts collected by hominids would have been influenced by carnivores that had removed bones during a period of earlier access to the same carcasses. The unspecialized character of the bone assemblages at the artifact sites suggests that hominids did not *always* obtain a narrow range of choice parts; hence, hominids do not appear to have been the initial user of carcasses in every case. That means they scavenged sometimes. *Yet* nor did they always, or even most of the time, collect marginal parts of carcasses. The evidence from medium-sized bovids, in fact, implies that hominids had access to carcasses before any carnivores had removed bones. It is not that hominids necessarily preferred forelimbs, but simply that they were there to be taken away. While this leaves open the possibility that hominids hunted these ungulates, all it really implies is that hominids had relatively early access to carcasses of these animals, possibly by locating dead animals still untouched by carnivore bone collectors active in the vicinity.

In short, this analysis of foraging for animal parts suggests that hominids were not specialists in their timing of access to carcasses. The data pertain specifically to the question of early versus late access relative to other agents, notably carnivores, that also remove bones from carcasses. However, this does not resolve the question of hunting versus scavenging. The evidence from the Olduvai sites implies, though, that this latter dichotomy poses the wrong question. The varied, or nonspecialized, pattern of skeletal unit transport inferred for hominids (relative to that of carnivore bone collectors in Bed I) is consistent with the overall pattern of interaction with fauna implied by bones from the artifact sites. This nonspecialized pattern is evident in the wide diversity of taxa and varied body sizes of animals found in the faunal assemblages at these sites. We noted earlier that the bone assemblages do not consist mainly of a few species of herd animals available (possibly seasonally) during prime scavenging periods. At least a partial reliance on resident animals by the bone collectors active at the artifact sites is suggested. In just this type of situation, carnivorous mammals adopt a mixed foraging mode of hunting *and* scavenging; the practice of both activities enables them to exploit both resident and migratory species. In general, the analyses here of the Olduvai faunal assemblages imply a broad base of faunal exploitation and a varied mode of foraging for food from animals. At this point, there seems to be no basis on which to discount that either hunting or scavenging occurred. Indeed, there are various lines of evidence indicating that hominids occasionally had later access to carcasses (i.e., scavenging). But the division of this issue into either hominids as hunters or as marginal scavengers appears to be incorrect. It eliminates needlessly the possibility that hominids practiced both modes of access to carcasses.

## Diet and Eating Meat

Before conclusions are drawn about how hominids obtained bones, we need to examine what resources animals provided to hominids. As noted earlier, meat (i.e., protein from muscle tissue) has typically been assumed to be the reason why hominids acquired parts of carcasses. The accumulation of animal bones by hominids has usually been equated with the systematic processing and eating of meat. However, the various renditions of the scavenging hypothesis emphasize that carcasses also provide other resources, specifically bone marrow, fat, hide, and sinew. It now is important to keep these various resources separate in our minds, for each type of resource has rather different implications (in terms of nutrition, social feeding, etc.) about the activities of hominids. Four lines of evidence will be summarized here regarding the question of carcass resources used by hominids: (1) the presence of meat-bearing bones; (2) cut marks and evidence for butchery; (3) evidence for marrow processing; and (4) the duration of bone accumulation at sites.

### Meat-Bearing Elements

The proportions of meat-bearing limb bones in the Olduvai assemblages are presented in Table 8.4. Meat-bearing bones tend to be slightly better represented at FLKNN–2 and Long K than at the artifact sites. This accords with the inference that bone-collecting carnivores at Olduvai had consistently early access to carcasses; yet it is also true that the small phalanges and podials are often consumed entirely by hyenas, an activity that could have

**TABLE 8.4.** Ratio of Nonmeat Limb Bones (Metapodials, Carpals, Tarsals, and Phalanges) to Meat-Bearing Limb Bones (Scapula, Humerus, Radius, Ulna, Femur, and Tibia) for All Large Mammals: Olduvai and Amboseli

| Site | Ratio (nonmeat/meat bones) |
|---|---|
| Artifacts sites[a]: | |
| FLK North–6 | 1.7 |
| FLK "Zinj" | 1.4 |
| FLKNN–3 | 2.6 |
| DK–2 | 1.9 |
| DK–3 | 2.0 |
| FLKNN–2 | 1.5 |
| Long K | 1.2 |
| Amboseli hyena den | 1.3 |
| Living large mammals (approximate) | 4.0 |

[a]Mean ratio for artifact site assemblages = 1.9.

lowered the frequency of nonmeat bones at the "primarily carnivore" sites. Besides this, the difference in ratios between artifact and nonartifact sites is not substantial, and the ratio at FLKNN–2 falls in the range of variation shown by the artifact sites in the proportion of nonmeat to meaty elements. Overall, the abundance of meaty limb bones in all of these assemblages is considerably greater than occurs in living mammals. These data are in agreement with information presented earlier for bovid long bones and further suggest that the transport of meat-bearing bones was an integral part of the activities of hominid and other bone collectors at Olduvai.

### Cut Marks and Butchery

Hominids undoubtedly obtained meat from bones, as shown by the occurrence of tool-slicing marks on meat-bearing bones. The majority of such marks result from slicing actions. Besides the data presented in Table 5.2, research by Bunn and Kroll (1986) and Shipman (1986a) document more extensively the presence of cut marks on animal bones from Bed I Olduvai. However, problems in recognizing cut marks and discrepancies between these two data sets have clouded exactly what is implied by the marks on these bones.

In the initial SEM study of cut marks from Olduvai (Potts and Shipman, 1981) our goal was to define microscopic criteria that uniquely distinguish stone tool cut marks from other types of surface modification. There is general agreement now that microscopic (SEM), macroscopic, and sedimentary criteria must be satisfied when identifying cut marks. The sedimentary criteria arise from the fact that bones resting in sand or gravel or in the rock debris of caves are liable to have "pseudo-cut marks" simply from being cut by the sharp edges of sedimentary particles during disturbance (e.g., trampling) of the bones (e.g., Behrensmeyer et al., 1986). Nonetheless, based on all three kinds of criteria, the fine-grain sediments of the Bed I sites preserve bones with unambiguous cut marks that all researchers agree upon. As was evident in the SEM study by Potts and Shipman (1981), these marks made by hominids are found on a wide range of species and body parts. Agreement among researchers about criteria, though, does not mean that the causes of all or even most of the surface marks on fossil bones can be unambiguously identified.[13] Studies that attempt to quantify the frequency and distribution of cut marks assume that most types of marks can be referred to specific agents. The discrepancies between Shipman (1986a) and Bunn and Kroll (1986) perhaps illustrate that this is not the case. The quantification of cut marks on different

[13]In the SEM study by Potts and Shipman (1981), in which conservative criteria for recognizing cut marks was used, 8% of the surface marks on Olduvai bones could not be attributed to cause. These marks exhibited combinations of features that did not match the criteria separating cut marks, carnivore and rodent tooth marks, fossil excavation/preparation marks, and some kinds of sedimentary abrasion.

skeletal parts is one of the most ambiguous issues in studies of early archeological sites.

In a detailed study of skeletal parts from FLK "Zinj," Bunn and Kroll (1986) maintain that 24% ($N = 138$) of 582 major limb bones of mammals identified to specific skeletal element have cut marks. Of these specimens, 94 exhibited microscopic criteria for cut marks.[14] This latter sample accounts for 16% of the major limb bone pieces designated to skeletal element. The quantity and distribution of these marks on meat and nonmeat bones suggest that meat was removed from the bones of small and large ungulates *and* that this was accomplished by systematic butchery (Bunn and Kroll, 1986). In their view, the evidence indicates that large quantities of meat were processed by hominids at FLK "Zinj" in an amount consistent with cooperative food sharing at this site.

In contrast, Shipman's SEM study (1986a) indicates that less than 2.4% of all major limb bones of bovids from Bed I bear cut marks. During this study, over 2500 major limb bones of bovids were closely examined from all sites within Bed I; all surface marks suspected to have been made by stone tools were replicated for study by SEM. Not only do the frequencies of cut marks identified by these two studies differ dramatically, but earlier in this chapter we also noted that Shipman considers the distribution of cut marks to reflect a lack of systematic butchery and disarticulation, a view quite different from that of Bunn and Kroll.

Based on my own SEM studies of Olduvai surface marks, I would agree with remarks made by Shipman (1986a: 29) that slightly more than 50% of marks that "by eye" look like possible cut marks do not show the SEM criteria for such marks. This is partly due to the fact that many of such surface marks occur singly (i.e., isolated from other marks). Such marks are not so easily identified correctly by eye as are sets of narrow, parallel grooves on a bone. Furthermore, close scrutiny of the limb bones of *Equus* from Olduvai showed that only 2.9% of these bones ($N = 138$) bear cut marks, a figure in accord with Shipman's for the Olduvai bovids. While Bunn and Kroll's assessment may overestimate the number of cut marks, SEM criteria may be far too conservative in recognizing cut marks in situations (like Bed I Olduvai) where pseudo-cut marks caused by sedimentary particles would not appear to be a major factor. Conservatism, by discarding all ambiguous cases, may be preferred. However, this could severely limit the sample sizes of cut marks for certain types of analyses and preferentially eliminate from consideration actual cut marks in certain skeletal locations, for example, due to differential erosion or loss of diagnostic signs. The number of cut marks overall and in different areas of the skeleton remains unclear until these important issues are resolved.

[14]This does not necessarily refer to SEM inspection of these marks. Bunn (1981, 1982) relies on study of bones under the light microscope and methods of cut-mark identification involving the width and cross-sectional shape of marks.

The meaning of cut-mark distributions is, of course, affected by these un-resolved problems. Nonetheless, several lines of evidence are clear: The Ol-duvai sites show ample numbers of meat-bearing bones, tool-slicing marks occur on such bones, and hominids appear to have obtained early access to carcasses on some occasions. According to this evidence, butchery to obtain meat must have occurred, and it is likely that cut marks were inflicted in certain skeletal locations more than others. The food-sharing and home base interpretation, favored by Bunn and Kroll, stems from the assumption that hominids must have removed all or large portions of meat from bones pos-sessing cut marks. Exclusive attention to cut marks and to hominid activities at these sites has made this the preferred, in fact the only, interpretation for many years. However, as we will discuss in the next chapter, evidence for carnivore attraction to meat-bearing bones at the artifact sites implies that hominids did not eat or share all of the meat or other edible tissue on these bones. In short, the amount of meat taken from these bones by hominids versus carnivores remains difficult to estimate.

*Marrow Processing*

A third line of investigation into the resources used by hominids concerns bone marrow. The scavenging hypothesis has implied that exploitation of an-imal tissues by hominids was largely confined to bone marrow. Although the characterization of hominids as marginal scavengers in search of marrow is not defensible, the cracking of marrow bones with stone tools evidently oc-curred more frequently at the Bed I artifact sites than at FLKNN–2 and Long K. Observations of marrow processing by modern humans and carnivores indicate that carnivores enter marrow-bearing long bones by gnawing off the articular ends, whereas humans use tools to crack through the diaphysis. As was noted in Chapter 5, isolated ends of bones, which typically occur by cracking diaphyses for marrow, are more common at the Olduvai artifact sites than at the nonartifact sites (see Table 5.13). These pieces comprise an average of 70% of the long bone epiphysis specimens at the five artifact sites. In contrast, the type of marrow bone pieces usually derived from carnivore gnawing make up 52% or more of the specimens at FLKNN–2 and Long K.

On this relative scale, the artifact sites predominantly manifest patterns of marrow processing associated with tool use, though this is not the only pattern of limb bone damage represented. This evidence indicates that hom-inids obtained and consumed diaphysis marrow from limb bones brought to these sites. This inference, though, does not imply that bone marrow was the sole interest hominids had in animal tissues, given the strong evidence that hominids did also handle meaty tissues. The consumption of marrow does not preclude the eating of meat, and vice versa. Furthermore, data dis-cussed in Chapter 5 suggest that carnivores sometimes did have access to long bones at these sites that had not been broken beforehand by hominids.

## Duration of Bone Accumulation

Hominids cut up parts of carcasses, they had access to meat and marrow, and in the process they made sizeable accumulations of animal bones. Does this mean that the eating of animal tissues was a standard and significant part of hominid life at Olduvai? Traditionally, the similarities between the artifact sites and the campsites of hunter–gatherers suggested that the debris left on these ancient sites had accumulated in short order, perhaps in a season or within a year. Under this assumption, the sheer quantity of bones at each site meant that the pursuit of animal tissues was a critical part of early hominid foraging.[15] The accumulation of 20, 40, or more individual animals of varying size implied that meat and possibly other animal resources made a regular and significant contribution to the diet and activities of the hominids who occupied these sites.

However, evidence for prolonged periods of bone accumulation at the Olduvai sites requires second thought about these traditional assumptions and interpretations. Based on surface weathering features (Chapter 3), animal bones evidently were transported and left exposed at each site over a period longer than 1 or 2 years. A minimum of several years of accumulation is indicated, and bones were modified by hominids at the artifact sites over that period. Given this inference, the regularity and contribution of meat and marrow to the diet of these hominids become far more difficult to estimate based simply on the quantity of animal bones and the presence of cut marks on some of them. The calibration of bone weathering patterns is not fine enough to discern seasonal fluctuations in bone accumulation rates or even to estimate minimum annual rates of bone transport to these sites (Potts, 1984a, 1986). Estimates of the rate of meat consumption or the percentage of meat and marrow in the diet depend on knowing the amount of meat on the bones when hominids obtained them, the rate of bone accumulation at sites, the percentage of meat on bones consumed by hominids, and the number of hominids that fed on the meat. At the Olduvai sites at least, the rates of bone accumulation appear to be slower than originally assumed. Scavenging (as one mode of acquiring animal parts) means that not all or even most of the bones transported by hominids still possessed all or most of the meat originally present. Finally, carnivores also were attracted to these artifact sites and sampled meat and/or marrow from bones also touched by hominids. Beyond these few relevant points, there is not adequate evidence to calculate the importance of meat and marrow in the diets of Olduvai hominids.

## Plant Foods

In such discussions about early hominid diet, the lack of prehistoric evidence about plant foods must be avowed. The significance of plants to early hominids,

[15]This, of course, was under the unscrutinized assumption that all bones brought to the site were the result of hominid activity.

including those that ate meat, is acknowledged by all researchers who recently have considered the question of hunting and scavenging at Olduvai. This is so for the following reasons: (1) Plants represent a major feeding opportunity for a tool user. Tools make certain plant resources uniquely available to hominids (Sept, 1984). (2) All higher primates are omnivorous but use plants as their primary dietary base; there is no clear reason why obtaining meat would have involved abandoning this fundamental aspect of hominoid diets. (3) Studies of microscopic wear on the teeth of some Miocene hominoids suggests that a chimpanzee-like diet based primarily on fruits also characterized hominoid ancestors; SEM examination of the teeth of Olduvai Hominid 7, a mandible from FLKNN–3 ascribed to early *Homo*, shows a similar pattern of wear (Teaford and Walker, 1984; Walker, 1981 and pers. comm.).

Although stone flakes from sites at Koobi Fora, Kenya, were used to cut plant material (Keeley and Toth, 1981), the role of plant foods in the formation of the Olduvai sites is unknown, as is the contribution of plants generally to early hominid diets (e.g., see Sept, 1986). Consequently, due to the lack of any comparison with plant foods, the *relative* importance of animal resources in the diets of these Olduvai hominids (based on the evidence of fossil bone assemblages) becomes virtually a moot point. With this admitted, our investigation here must proceed with aspects of hominid behavior testable by the material remains that are preserved at these sites.

In summary, the transport and slicing of meat-bearing bones suggest strongly that Olduvai hominids ate meat. Evidently, they also broke bones for marrow. The traditional assumption is that because the animal bone assemblages are large, meat was a highly significant, abundant component in the diet. However, there must now be reservations about this assumption given (1) that the rates of bone accumulation at the artifact sites appear to be slower than originally assumed, and (2) that both hominids and carnivores fed from the portions of carcasses carried to these sites.

## Hunting, Scavenging, and Eating Meat: An Overview

A common ingredient in recent developments of the scavenging hypothesis is that scavenging by hominids involved locating and using scraps left over when a carcass was finally abandoned by predators and other scavengers. The emphasis on finding bones already disarticulated is a clear example of this point (Binford, 1981; Shipman, 1983, 1984). The distinctiveness of the scavenging hypothesis relies in part on the difference between this type of reconstructed mode of hominid foraging and the great abundance of food made available by hunting. The hypothesis draws attention to the social implications of having a lot of food (e.g., food sharing) versus scrounging for a small meal of marrow (e.g., no sharing).

The recent (and valid) interest in this hypothesis has generated revised images of human ancestors, symbols that are distinctive by their contrast to

the hunting hypothesis. The proponents of the scavenging view have sharpened the contrasts wherever possible. Recent analyses of data from Olduvai
have tended to phrase the hunting/scavenging issue as an "either–or" question.
Consequently, the predictions and analyses associated with the scavenging
hypothesis have either focused exclusively on this foraging mode or have
offered predictions that do not adequately distinguish hunting from scavenging. Research and ideas presented by Blumenschine, Shipman, and Binford
have helped to define a "scavenger niche" and the opportunities possibly open
to early hominids. Yet scavenging opportunities are usually evaluated without
reference to possible hunting opportunities, in whatever way these might be
defined for early hominids. A scrounging mode of scavenging by hominids
(marginal scavenger) is not indicated by the Olduvai evidence. This inference
is significant because marginal scavenging has provided the fundamental distinction between the hunting and scavenging hypotheses.

A mixed strategy of scavenging and hunting for carcasses is a possibility
that may not be accessible through these lines of inquiry. A wide variety of
carnivorous mammals and birds indicate that this is the norm in how animals
acquire carcass parts. More significantly here, a diversity of skeletal units
(i.e., variations in forelimb, hindlimb, and axial proportions) and a wide range
of species (i.e., no single or few species predominating) are exhibited at each
of the sites where hominids played an important role. The extent of this diversity suggests that hominids adopted no single approach to foraging for
carcass parts. The clearest evidence for this view comes from comparing the
artifact sites with "primarily carnivore" sites within the ancient Olduvai environment itself. The narrower focus on forelimbs in the latter contrasts with
the accumulation of a more diverse or unspecialized array of skeletal parts
at the artifact sites. Wider variation in the selection of parts and the timing
of hominid access to carcasses (compared to the carnivore bone collectors) is
implied.

A varied time of access further implies that hominids did scavenge on occasion. However, based on methods developed so far, scavenging is bound
to be more readily discerned in the fossil record than hunting. One reason is
that hunting and early scavenging are difficult, if not impossible, to distinguish
on the basis of skeletal parts. The study of overlapping tooth and cut marks
further illustrates this point (see p. 217). At present, we are more likely to
answer questions about early, intermediate, and late access to carcasses than
about the proportion of hunted versus scavenged animals represented in bone
assemblages (though the latter two periods of access mentioned do connote
scavenging). These two searching strategies require different abilities and
can lead to different feeding opportunities. Still, the distinction may not have
been so important to Olduvai hominids—a point that seems to be borne out
by most mammalian carnivores. That is, scavenging and hunting combined
would have furnished a broad, unspecialized way of responding to opportunities to acquire carcasses as they arose. The faunal assemblages at the Olduvai

artifact sites indicate that such a varied approach to finding and transporting bones was practiced by hominids.


## Stone Artifacts: Transport and Accumulation

Until now we have explored various issues of site formation and hominid activities chiefly with the faunal remains in mind. Although recent work on site formation and early human behavior tends to focus exclusively on animal bones, obviously the stone artifacts have a bearing on taphonomic and behavioral interpretations of the Olduvai sites. This section addresses an important point about site formation at Olduvai, namely, that hominids accumulated modified artifacts and unmodified pieces of rock in places where they also brought and accumulated animal bones. What are the ecological and adaptive implications of this behavior? Before examining this question, a few points should be made about more traditional lines of inquiry and speculation on stone tools, namely, technology and use.

### Manufacture and Uses of Tools

The stone artifacts from each Olduvai site exhibit a wide range of forms and degrees of modification by hominids. The categories of artifacts established for Olduvai in M.D. Leakey's classic monograph (1971) are tools, utilized material, debitage, and manuports. The latter are exogenous pieces of stone raw material that show no sign of artificial chipping or use. Utilized pieces range from battered cobbles, representing possible hammerstones and anvils, to small chipped flakes and rock fragments. These bear damaged edges, possibly resulting from their use as cutting implements, but no clear pattern of flake scars. Debitage refers to flakes or thin fragments of sharp stone that result from stone-on-stone percussion and to thicker pieces called core fragments. Finally, the "tool" category encompasses cobbles and other chunks of rock that bear certain patterns of flake scars and also sharp or battered edges in the areas of modification. According to traditional archeological classification, different patterns of scarring that result from stone percussion define distinctive tool types, such as choppers, scrapers, discoids, handaxes, and so on.

From a detailed investigation of the stone technologies dating 1.5 Ma from Koobi Fora, Kenya, Toth (1982, 1985; Toth and Schick, 1986) has noted that the various tool types in those early stone artifact assemblages do not represent predetermined goals of tool manufacture. Rather, they signify a continuous range of forms produced as a result of making flakes. To use Toth's term, choppers, discoids, and other tool types that characterize Oldowan technology are technological "paths of least resistance." The shape and edge features that define these classic tool types depend on the size and shape of the original pieces of raw material and the degree to which these pieces were subjected to flake production.

My own observations of the Olduvai stone assemblages confirm these ideas about early stone technology. Many of the Oldowan tool types comprise a continuum of metric and qualitative attributes (such as artifact dimensions, overall shape, weight, edge length and shape, and the number and boldness of flake scars). This continuum is portrayed in Figure 8.3. The tool types reflect different degrees of flaking inflicted on rocks of varied original shape available to hominids in the ancient Olduvai region (known from manuports and utilized pieces).

If a rounded lava cobble or a thick chunk of quartzite is struck to produce a few flakes and scars that overlap, the result is a chopper (Figure 8.3a). If flaking extends around most of the circumference of the original piece, a discoid is produced (Figure 8.3b). If the original piece is irregular in shape, affording flake production in more than one plane, a polyhedron may result (Figure 8.3d). Several pieces from Olduvai that fit the definition of "chopper" or "discoid" could have been modified into "polyhedrons" if percussion had been continued on other flakable surfaces of the stone. If a lava cobble broken in half is flaked, the resulting form is either a heavy-duty scraper (Figure 8.3c) or a unifacial discoid (if the flaking is continued around the flat broken surface). If discoid-like flaking is imposed on an oval cobble, or if flaking produces a constricted or pointed area, the term "proto-biface" may be applied (Figure 8.3f). This tool/core category thus includes borderline cases between the discoid, scraper, and polyhedron types.

The continuum of form and apparent transformation of one tool type into another implies that the shapes and edge characteristics of Olduvai tool types need not have been "target designs" or the primary goals of tool making. Instead, sharp edges—either flakes or cores—may have been the primary products of stone technology during the period of Bed I. This general view of early stone technology has been advocated by Isaac (1984).

The actual uses of artifacts from this very early time range, and from the Lower Paleolithic overall, are poorly understood. Keeley and Toth (1981) examined under the microscope 56 stone artifacts from Koobi Fora (1.5 Ma); only 9 of these had clear traces of microscopic wear, 4 from contact with meat, and 5 from cutting, sawing, and scraping plant matter. Unfortunately, none of the Olduvai artifacts has been subjected to this same edge wear analysis.[16] The fact that all of the pieces with visible microwear from Koobi Fora were unretouched flakes and flake fragments demonstrates the potential importance of flakes in the activities of early hominids. The majority of stone

[16]Keeley's technique is applicable to fine-grain siliceous rock, such as chert (Keeley, 1980). In the present study, such rocks make up only 3 out of the 3995 artifact specimens from Olduvai for which stone composition was determined. Sussman's (1986; pers. comm.) examination of quartzite illustrates the difficulties of applying existing edge wear techniques to this type of raw material.

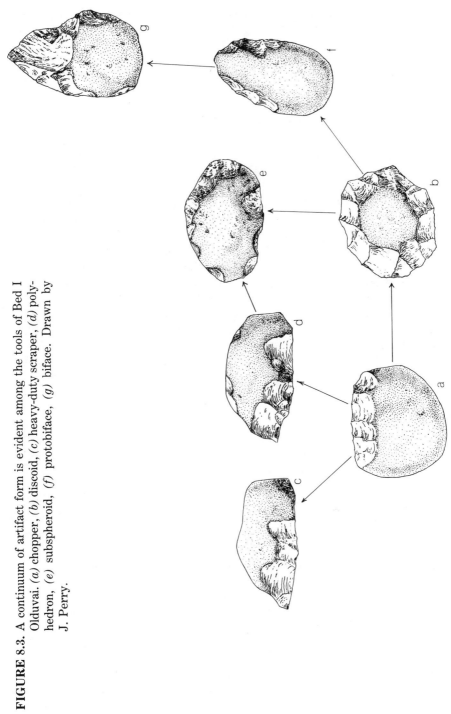

**FIGURE 8.3.** A continuum of artifact form is evident among the tools of Bed I Olduvai. *(a)* chopper, *(b)* discoid, *(c)* heavy-duty scraper, *(d)* polyhedron, *(e)* subspheroid, *(f)* protobiface, *(g)* biface. Drawn by J. Perry.

tool marks identified on animal bones from Olduvai are slicing and scraping marks; these indicate the use of sharp edges to remove outer soft tissue (Bunn and Kroll, 1986; Potts and Shipman, 1981). Chopping marks, related to the breakage of bones or possibly the disarticulation of joints, are rare. None-theless, the data on limb bones (see p. 231) do suggest that hominids removed marrow, in addition to outer soft tissue, from animal bones, undoubtedly aided by stone tools.

Apparently battered pieces of stone (classified as heavy-duty utilized ma-terial) would have been appropriate for processing bone marrow. However, such artifacts only comprise from 1% to 12% of the artifact assemblages at the five artifact sites studied here.[17] At the top of this range is the assemblage from FLKNN–3, characterized previously as a hominid marrow processing site (Binford, 1981; see p. 215). However, neither heavy-duty implements nor tool/cores with crushed edges can be said to typify this artifact assemblage or any of those examined here. Sharp stone flakes and cores that show fresh, unbattered edges constitute from 57% (FLKNN–3) to 84% (FLK "Zinj") of the artifact assemblages (Table 8.5). Therefore, sharp-edged pieces produced by percussion flaking were the most numerous artifacts in each of the Olduvai assemblages, and few of even the large artifacts exhibit signs of edge crushing. This implies that cutting functions (slicing, scraping, and sawing), though not necessarily confined to animal tissues, were an intimate part of stone tech-nology during Bed I times.

### Hominid Transport of Stone

Hominids were the only species at Olduvai considered to have made stone tools or to have carried rocks around in any great quantity. Since stones were one resource sought by hominids, at least on occasion, the acquisition and carrying of stone formed part of the time and energy budget of some (possibly not all) hominids at Olduvai. A few points on this matter are considered in this section.

Leakey (1971) and Hay (1976) have identified the variety of stone artifact raw materials introduced to the sites in Bed I. Table 8.6 summarizes the relative contribution of each material as a source for making artifacts.[18] While more artifacts are made out of quartzite than any other raw material, the dominant raw material by weight is usually a form of lava. Much of the small, light debitage from each level is quartzite.

Hay (1976) has also traced the origins of these rock types. The type of quartzite used at every Bed I artifact site is a basement rock that outcrops

[17]This calculation does not include manuports, since they show no evidence of use or flaking.

[18]Tables in the Appendix provide details about the number of artifacts made of specific raw materials and the weight of these materials recovered from each site.

**TABLE 8.5.** Relative Frequencies of Artifacts with Possible Crushing versus Cutting Functions

| Site | Number of artifacts (excluding manuports) | Percentage of hammerstones, anvils, and other heavy-duty utilized material | Number of heavy-duty cores | Percentage of heavy-duty cores with moderate to heavy crushing/chipping of edge | Percentage of entire assemblage made up of flakes and cores with fresh to slightly chipped edges |
|---|---|---|---|---|---|
| FLK North–6 | 114 | 8.8 | 5 | 20 | 76.3 |
| FLK "Zinj" | 2501 | 1.1 | 32 | 31.2 | 83.6 |
| FLKNN–3 | 49 | 12.2 | 4 | 0 | 57.1 |
| DK–2 and –3 | 1051 | 5.2 | 124 | 14.5 | 70.0 |
| Total | 3715 | 2.7 | 165 | 17.6 | 79.2 |

**TABLE 8.6.** Percentages of Different Raw Materials Used to Produce Stone Artifacts[a]

| Raw material | DK N (1162) | DK W (93,858 g) | FLKNN-3 N (70) | FLKNN-3 W (13,755 g) | FLK "Zinj" N (2647) | FLK "Zinj" W (72,403 g) | FLK North-6 N (116) | FLK North-6 W (12,012 g) |
|---|---|---|---|---|---|---|---|---|
| Basalt/trachyandesite | 17.7 | 20.3 | 35.7 | 57.3 | 0.8 | 1.2 | 9.5 | 30.0 |
| Nephelinite | 22.7 | 12.6 | 4.3 | 3.0 | 0.6 | 6.8 | 5.2 | 19.0 |
| Vesicular basalt | 17.8 | 38.3 | — | — | 4.7 | 44.7 | — | — |
| Lava indeterminate | 18.2 | 23.6 | 12.9 | 29.6 | 3.4 | 19.6 | 2.6 | 13.9 |
| Quartzite | 23.3 | 5.1 | 47.1 | 10.0 | 90.2 | 27.6 | 80.2 | 36.9 |
| Chert | 0.1 | .02 | — | — | — | — | 1.7 | 0.2 |
| Gneiss | — | — | — | — | 0.1 | 0.1 | — | — |
| Feldspar | 0.1 | 0.1 | — | — | 0.2 | .04 | — | — |
| Indeterminate | 0.1 | .003 | — | — | — | — | 0.8 | .02 |

[a] Percentages are calculated by number of specimens (N) and by weight (W).

closest to the excavated sites at the Naibor Soit inselberg (see Figure 2.1). Today, it consists of a ridge of coarse, tabular quartzite showing thin micaceous layers. It is located roughly 2 km to the north of the FLK complex of sites and 2–3 km northwest of DK. Trachyandesite and nonvesicular basalt are lavas derived from the volcanos Lemagrut, Olmoti, and Ngorongoro. The volcano Sadiman was the source for nephelinite. These raw materials were collected by Bed I hominids in the form of fine-grain, rounded cobbles, such as occur in dry stream channels running off the northern slopes of Sadiman and Lemagrut today. It is not known exactly how far away the excavated sites were located from such stream channels. Lava conglomerates and other evidence of stream action can be seen in the alluvial fan deposits in Bed I but not in the lake margin facies where sites have been found (see Figure 2.3). The FLK complex of sites was located over 1.5 km from the western extent of the alluvial fan facies reconstructed by Hay for middle Bed I. The vesicular, olivine basalt, of which some artifacts were composed, matches the lava flows that underlie the Bed I sedimentary sequence. This basal lava was likely exposed very close to some of the sites. At DK, for instance, this lava juts up above Level 3 and so was available right at the site. As the name implies, vesicular lava is irregular to flake, forms an edge interrupted by gaps (vesicles), and thus appears less useful as an edged tool than the fine, nonvesicular lava materials generally used for flaking. The origins of chert seem to be linked with the lake deposits (Hay, 1976). Therefore, this raw material, rarely found in Bed I levels, was probably available near the lake; yet its ancient distribution is unknown. The gneiss at the artifact sites is the type found at Kelogi (near the Side Gorge—Figure 2.1), 8–10 km away from the excavated sites in Bed I. Pieces of feldspar are also very rare in Bed I assemblages, and they may simply be pebbles derived from the northern part of the Olduvai basin.

Hominids evidently brought to these sites a variety of raw materials, some derived from highly localized, distant outcrops and others obtained from more widespread, less localized, and closer stone sources (e.g., stream channels, the basal lava flows). Clearly, some proportion of the places where hominids produced stone concentrations were located several kilometers away from the rock sources that they utilized. This proportion is unknown since sites found within the Olduvai basin are confined to the Gorge, the area of erosion, while sites closer to the stone outcrops would still be buried. Quartzite is one raw material consistently present in the Bed I artifact assemblages for which the source rock is confidently pinpointed. The 2–3 km, one-way distance involved in carrying quartzite to the sites could well have promoted traveling through at least several habitats in the area, and thus may have encouraged the ecological diversity of fauna transported and utilized by hominids (but within the lake margin zone).

Ethnoarcheologists (e.g., Gould, 1980) have reported that for some peoples procuring usable stone material (walking to the source and carrying material back) is the most time-consuming and laborious part of the tool-making process. An intensive use of stone artifacts, thus, may reflect well a relatively high cost for obtaining raw material. In this light, it is interesting that manuports occur at every artifact site investigated here. Furthermore, pieces classified as "utilized material" often show minimal modification, and flaked specimens typically show minimal flaking and edge wear. The most intensively modified pieces (by flaking and use) are spheroids and subspheroids. These objects often show flake scars characteristic of choppers, discoids, polyhedrons, and scrapers—but then have become modified sometimes extensively by battering and crushing of the edge. These forms, however, are quite rare in Bed I and become consistently more abundant in Bed II. If, as seems likely, the transport of stone over several kilometers to specific spots on the landscape was the most time-consuming and laborious part of the tool-making process, why was the modification and use of stone apparently far less intensive than would seem possible? Several answers might be entertained.

First, of the two known resources brought to sites, stone material was easier to obtain than animal tissues in the sense that stone sources, such as outcrops, are always found in the same places. Thus, access to stone raw material is highly predictable. Furthermore, even if more than one species of hominid used stone tools, competition between species for stone material would have been low compared to that among species of carnivorous mammals and birds for animal tissues. Therefore, the accumulation of some stone materials, especially manuports, which subsequently show no or little sign of utilization probably does reflect, in part, unhindered acquisition of a resource in high abundance. In this way, the occurrence of manuports and very slightly utilized pieces can be considered analogous to the bone-collecting tendencies of porcupines. Incisal gnawing is the only function ascribed to why porcupines collect bones; yet in virtually all porcupine collections studied, a high percentage of the bones show no gnawing or other modification by porcupines. As another example, hyenas are noted for consuming bones, from which they apparently derive some nutrition. Occasionally, hyenas transport bones to a den area, but many bones will not be consumed and some not even modified. Hence, an apparent "overcollection" of usable resources is not necessarily a rare phenomenon. It is possible that the collection but lack of use of some stone material by hominids can be considered in the same category as porcupine and hyena bone collecting in some contexts. This does not mean that this phenomenon has been adequately explained, but there do appear to be some common results produced by animals that transport resources to one or more fixed points.

Alternatively, it is possible that stone objects that bear no clear signs of use, in fact, were utilized but for activities that leave no traces at the macroscopic level examined so far.

A final hypothesis is that the transport of subsequently unused, or little used, stone materials reflects a strategy geared toward site reoccupation.

According to this idea, hominids accumulated numerous tools and unmodified rocks in one or more areas of their foraging range. An accumulation served as a useful source of stones to be carried around while foraging in that vicinity and to be used when food that required tool processing was brought to the site. This interpretation arises not only in light of the low degree of artifact modification but also from the evidence of bone weathering and damage, which indicates that hominids (as well as carnivores) made multiple visits to each of the Olduvai sites over a lengthy period of time. It may be significant that the excavated site in the entire Olduvai sequence that shows the highest frequency of manuports also shows clear evidence of reoccupation by hominids over the long term.[19]

None of these ideas proposed here to account for unutilized stone materials at Olduvai is adequately testable by data presently available. The apparent underutilization of stone, the mobility of hominids over at least several kilometers while acquiring stones, and the transport of many kilograms of stone to certain locations on the landscape would appear to be important aspects of site production from the viewpoint of the (long-term) time–energy budgets of early hominids at Olduvai. This matter will be brought up again in Chapter 9.

### A Dynamic Flow of Raw Materials

To account for the clustering of stone material at each of the artifact sites, much emphasis is placed on the transport of stone to these sites. The situation at Olduvai is not so simple, as indicated by the proportions of artifacts made of different raw materials. Table 8.7 presents the data on the frequency of pieces of different raw materials in each artifact class. The following observations summarize these data:

1. Leakey (1971) pointed out that lava debitage at Olduvai is scarce relative to quartz debitage, but the reverse is true for cores. While this point applies to the sites examined here, generally for lava raw materials, low numbers of cores are associated with low numbers of debitage, and high numbers of cores occur with high frequencies of lava debitage flakes.

2. Although this is also true for quartzite (positive relationship between cores and debitage), the data show huge discrepancies between the numbers of cores and debitage.

3. In general, other than quartzite, those materials represented by cores, utilized material, and debitage at a site are also represented by manuports. There is no particular positive or negative association between the number of manuports and the numbers of other artifacts of particular raw materials.

[19]This site, MNK Main Occupation located in Bed II, has six main archeological layers in a 1.5 m thick deposit. The layers are defined by concentrations of bones and artifacts, including over 800 manuports; a less dense scatter of artifacts and bones occurs between the layers.

**TABLE 8.7.** Number of Pieces of Different Raw Materials in Each Artifact Class

| Site | | Basalt/trachyandesite | Nephelinite | Vesicular basalt | Lava indeterminate | Quartzite | Chert | Gneiss | Feldspar |
|---|---|---|---|---|---|---|---|---|---|
| FLK North–6 | Manuports | 5 | 4 | 0 | 2 | 0 | 0 | 0 | 0 |
| | Utilized material | 1 | 1 | 0 | 1 | 8 | 2 | 0 | 0 |
| | Cores | 3 | 1 | 0 | 0 | 1 | 0 | 0 | 0 |
| | Debitage | 3 | 0 | 0 | 0 | 92 | 0 | 0 | 0 |
| FLK "Zinj" | Manuports | 1 | 3 | 86 | 33 | 21 | 0 | 1 | 0 |
| | Utilized material | 1 | 4 | 8 | 7 | 48 | 0 | 0 | 0 |
| | Cores | 1 | 6 | 3 | 5 | 26 | 0 | 0 | 0 |
| | Debitage | 20 | 4 | 31 | 56 | 2221 | 0 | 1 | 4 |
| FLKNN–3 | Manuports | 11 | 1 | 0 | 10 | 1 | 0 | 0 | 0 |
| | Utilized material | 4 | 0 | 0 | 0 | 5 | 0 | 0 | 0 |
| | Cores | 4 | 0 | 0 | 0 | 0 | 0 | 0 | 0 |
| | Debitage | 6 | 2 | 0 | 0 | 28 | 0 | 0 | 0 |
| DK | Manuports | 4 | 5 | —[a] | 8 | 9 | 0 | 0 | 0 |
| | Utilized material | 15 | 6 | 24 | 23 | 22 | 0 | 0 | 0 |
| | Cores | 45 | 39 | 29 | 26 | 16 | 0 | 0 | 0 |
| | Debitage | 140 | 211 | 109 | 138 | 198 | 1 | 0 | 0 |

[a]Numerous pieces of unmodified vesicular basalt occur naturally at DK.

4. On the other hand, quartzite manuports are very rare relative to the number of modified pieces and debitage. FLK "Zinj" may be an exception; 21 quartzite slabs with no evident modification occur there, a larger number than at any other site.

5. These observations suggest that quartzite was treated differently from the various types of lava at the Bed I sites. Except at "Zinj," pieces of unmodified quartzite usually did not accumulate at each site, unlike lava pieces. This suggests that transported pieces of quartzite were used immediately (except at FLK "Zinj"), whereas pieces of unmodified lava raw material still remained at each site at burial. Furthermore, percussion of quartzite resulted in the disintegration of cores, as in bipolar flaking. This is seen by the extremely high number of broken quartzite chips and "core fragments" that make up the debitage category.[20] In contrast, percussion of lava produced both cores and debitage.

6. FLK "Zinj" is unique among these four assemblages in the preponderance of quartzite cores over lava cores. Quartzite was treated differently at "Zinj," indicated by the occurrence of quartzite manuports and preponderance of cores and by the very large number of small quartzite flakes and core fragments. Evidently, there was variation in the transport and use of raw materials, which cannot be explained by factors such as the distance of the quartzite outcrop from the sites.

7. Frequencies of lava cores and debitage do indicate that the transport of stone was *not* confined to the introduction of unmodified stone to the site. Flaking and use of the manufactured pieces was not confined just to the site itself. For example, at FLK North–6, the higher number of lava cores ($N = 4$) than debitage ($N = 3$) suggests that flaking took place elsewhere. In other cases, cores are absent where debitage of that same stone material is present. Unfortunately, we do not know whether the "missing" material was just outside of the excavated area, left at the stone source, or transported and dropped by hominids some distance from the site. Other taphonomic factors, specifically water flow, may have had an effect on debitage at some sites (e.g., DK). But, overall, the geologic evidence argues against hydraulic factors having had a major influence over the proportions of different artifact classes or raw material types.

These general patterns of raw material abundance are pertinent to the movement of stones in and out of each site by hominids. Of course, it must be realized that each site only preserves the end product of perhaps many years of stone transport dynamics. Nonetheless, it is clear that each artifact assemblage represents a dynamic flow of stone in and out of the site at various points in the manufacturing process.

---

[20]Core fragments are small pieces of broken rock faceted by flaking but not having definite characteristics of flakes or cores, such as platforms.

## Overview

Aided by an array of analytical methods, we have seen that the Olduvai sites furnish varied opportunities to infer how hominids obtained animal parts, the importance of acquiring animal bones, and the nature of stone tool transport to and from sites. Since hominids were only one, albeit important, factor in the formation of the artifact sites, our analysis of hominid activities has focused on only the broadest or dominant characteristics of the faunas and stone artifacts. Comparisons of these sites to the nonartifact sites is critical in the assessment of hominid activities.

The artifact sites differ from the inferred carnivore site at FLKNN–2 in showing a more diverse, less specialized array of limb elements without exclusive focus on forelimbs or hindlimbs. The FLKNN–2 bone assemblage exhibits an exaggerated abundance of forelimbs; this same pattern is exhibited to a lesser degree at the Long K site, which also has a strong contribution from a carnivore bone collector. According to observations of carcass disarticulation and scattering in modern African habitats, comparisons between the "primarily carnivore" and "primarily hominid" sites suggest that the timing of carcass access by hominids was more varied than was that by carnivore bone collectors at Olduvai. That is, hominids acquired carcasses sometimes early and sometimes later in the sequence of removal of parts from carcasses relative to other animals that dispersed parts away from carcasses. This is consistent with scavenging and possibly some amount of hunting, though the distinction between hunting and early scavenging cannot yet be convincingly demonstrated. However, a marginal style of scavenging, in which hominids gained access largely to carcasses already disarticulated by carnivores, is not implied. Access to the bones of small ungulate species and juveniles, which are generally not available for scavenging but are present on the artifact sites, can probably be ascribed to a small degree of hunting. Moreover, species diversity and other features of the Olduvai assemblages do not indicate conditions such as are known in the modern Serengeti to favor an exclusively scavenger mode of obtaining animal parts.

The analysis of hominid foraging in this chapter supports the view that hominids did scavenge at least on occasion, an inference that has helped in recent years to debunk the hypothesis that hunting was the predominant attribute of early hominid behavior. However, the replacement of this hunting hypothesis with the view that early hominids were adapted exclusively or primarily to scavenging is likely to be just as incorrect.

The interpretation that Olduvai hominids ate meat is based on several lines of evidence: (1) The occasional appearance of tool slicing marks on meat-rich bones in areas of muscle attachment; (2) frequencies of meat-bearing limb bones that are similar to those collected at dens by hunting/scavenging carnivores that eat meat; and (3) occasional early access to carcasses by hominids. Thus, Olduvai hominids not only had meat available to them but also removed muscle tissue from bones they brought to the Olduvai sites. This means that hominids probably ate some unknown quantity of meat and that their use of animal parts went beyond the smashing of bones for marrow. However, the kind of bone modification associated with eating marrow is also represented at the Olduvai artifact sites.

The significance of meat (muscle tissue) and marrow in the hominid diet is unknown. Several lines of information now suggest that meat was probably less important in the diet than was once assumed: relatively long periods of bone accumulation at each site; evidence for incomplete processing of meat-rich and marrow-rich bones; clear signs that carnivores fed off of the meat-rich areas, occasionally without breaking inside the bones; and the possibility that hominids used nonedible tissues from these segments of carcasses.

Nonetheless, acquisition of meat from large mammals represented an important evolutionary development that had occurred by the time of Bed I Olduvai.

Based on the stone artifacts, we know that stone materials, including modified tools/cores and unmodified pieces, were brought to and left at the artifact sites. Pieces (flakes or cores) were also probably taken away from these sites, which must be considered part of a dynamic flow of artifacts and raw materials across the ancient landscape. That is, pieces underwent repeated modification and transport, much as Toth (1982) posits for the stone artifacts at Koobi Fora, Kenya. Any behavioral scenario must tie these inferences together with certain inferences about the bone assemblages at these sites (e.g., revisiting of sites and modifications to bones by hominids and carnivores).

This investigation is now at the point where we may examine *why* numerous stone tools, pieces of raw material, and animal bones were aggregated in specific locations at Olduvai. The home base hypothesis is one explanation. It proposes a social reason, the feeding of hominid social groups at campsites, as the salient cause for the accumulation of debris at the Olduvai artifact sites. In the next chapter, a variety of theoretical explanations are explored.

# 9

# Resource Transport: A Prelude to Home Bases

## The Home Base Concept

As noted in Chapter 1, the most widely embraced explanation for the archeological sites at Olduvai and other Plio–Pleistocene localities is that they represent home bases, or campsites. This traditional view has broad implications about early hominid behavior and, consequently, about the origins of several distinctive human characteristics. The home base is an interpretive concept invoked traditionally by archeologists to account for clusters of artifacts and animal bones uncovered by excavation. As Isaac (1983a) points out, the campsite interpretation of very old sites has been a simple, uncritical extension of the home base concept that applies to modern, including late Pleistocene, hunter–gatherers. In formulating ideas about home bases and overall land use patterns of ancient hominids, archeologists undoubtedly have been guided strongly by the studies of hunter–gatherers that commenced during the 1960s, especially research on the !Kung San in Botswana (Lee, 1979; Lee and Devore, 1976). Many researchers tend to treat the foraging of tropical latitude hunter–gatherers as a single type of adaptation, a unitary phenomenon shaped by a long evolutionary past. However, it appears inappropriate to characterize the land use patterns of all tropical foragers by reference to one or a few contemporary hunter–gatherer societies. Unfortunately, some of the generalizations that have emerged in the archeological literature concerning tropical hunter–gatherer land use are difficult to check due to limited ethnographic information.

This issue notwithstanding, home bases are a universal feature of all modern foraging peoples, playing a salient role in the organization of activities. Hunter–gatherers organize their activities around a campsite. The home base is a predetermined focus of activity to which members of a social group consistently return and meet. Foragers carry food from plants and animals to this specific location where the food is prepared and consumed. The home base is also the place where group members sleep, make tools, and perform other maintenance activities. It is the primary spatial arena of social activity: the exchange of stories and information, the redistribution of food, the rearing and protection of young, and the reciprocal exchange of other resources or services. A division of labor, notably along gender lines, is integral to the home base concept, for it is at the home base where resources obtained by diverse members of the social group can be exchanged (e.g., plants gathered mainly by women and large game hunted mainly by men). Based on observations of transient camps of tropical hunter–gatherers, a home base is not necessarily a single permanent location. It may be occupied for only a few days. Yet wherever it is located, a hunter–gatherer home base is the focus of social activity and a predictable place to which independently foraging members of the social group return. All of these features are highlighted in the home base concept developed by Isaac (e.g., 1976, 1978) and by Lee (1979: 489–494) and applied to Plio–Pleistocene hominids.

After they have been abandoned, the campsites of modern hunter–gatherers are recognized by accumulations of discarded cultural debris and food refuse. Sometimes structures, such as huts and hearths, may also be visible; in the case of the !Kung San, sets of huts and hearths signify traces of family units that made up the group that inhabited a campsite (Yellen, 1976).

A decade ago the analogy drawn between hunter–gatherer campsites and the accumulations of stone tools and animal bones from Plio–Pleistocene sites at Olduvai and elsewhere seemed quite appropriate. The basic pattern of all excavated Plio–Pleistocene sites classified as "Type C sites" (Isaac, 1978; Isaac and Crader, 1981), "living floors" (Leakey, 1971), or "campsites" consists of assemblages of broken bones from a varied array of species associated with a variety of stone artifacts. The tools and portions of animal carcasses traditionally signify the manufacture and use of tools at the site and the presence of food refuse, implying (within the context of the home base interpretation) a significant dietary reliance on animal foods. Abundant faunal remains found at some sites are believed to indicate that hominids consistently returned with food to the site and divided animal foods, as well as any plant foods collected, with other members of the social group that met at that place daily.

The link between the home base concept and the food sharing interpretation of early hominid subsistence has been explicitly stated by Isaac (1976, 1978, 1983b). Figure 9.1, based on Isaac's publications, summarizes the food sharing hypothesis. This hypothesis first states that certain aspects of hominid behavior are informed directly by archeological evidence. These are denoted by an asterisk in Figure 9.1: (1) the carrying of animal bones, stone tools and raw materials; (2) the manufacture of stone tools; and (3) the use of animal tissues by hominids, which connotes consumption of meat from large mammals. According to Isaac, animal tissues could have been obtained by hunting and/or scavenging. By carrying animal bones, hominids had evidently delayed their consumption of food—an important contrast with nonhuman primates, which tend to eat food as soon as they find it. The delayed eating of food is a distinctive feature of human economy.[1]

[1]Nonetheless, a sizeable (but undocumented) contribution to the diets of many hunter–gatherers is apparently obtained while foraging—the so-called "snack factor." These foods are eaten immediately upon obtaining them and are not shared at campsites (Hayden, 1981; Mann, 1981).

Food sharing/home base hypothesis:

   Carrying of food and implements
   Toolmaking
   Increased consumption of meat obtained
      by hunting or scavenging

   Food sharing
   Division of labor
   Organization of movements around a
      home base

   ?Pair-bonding/male investment in
      child rearing

   Partial developments
      Prolonged infant dependency
      Enhanced communicative abilities

**FIGURE 9.1.** Food-sharing hypothesis of G. L. Isaac.

This hypothesis then posits that an integrated set of behaviors and social characteristics emerged with these archeologically visible traits. These proposed features are the sharing of food and a division of labor, especially along gender lines. This postulate assumes that edible parts of plants were collected chiefly by females and animal foods particularly by males. The diet of these hominids resulted from this dual subsistence strategy. Food was returned to a central area, the home base, which was, as previously noted, the focus of social activity. This hypothesis implies that food sharing was a highly important, and possibly the earliest, expression of complex social reciprocity in humans. Features that also may have been part of this new complex of behaviors were pair-bonding and increased male investment in rearing offspring. Finally, prolonged infant dependency and enhanced communication abilities would also have contributed to, and been promoted by, these fundamental changes in human sociality.

The home base/food sharing hypothesis is thus a very attractive idea because it integrates many aspects of human behavior and social life that are important to anthropologists—reciprocity systems, exchange, kinship, subsistence, division of labor, technology, and language. Although this interpretation has gained widespread attention in the past 15 years or so, it actually has a long history as the dominant social and subsistence interpretation of Pleistocene hominids and sites. For example, Zuckerman (1933: 158–159) also envisioned "far reaching social and sexual consequences" as part of the shift from a general primate vegetarian pattern to one based on hunting and gathering in early hominids. These consequences included the sharing of meat at campsites and concomitant division of labor and pair-bonding. Zuckerman's portrait of early human behavior, however, did not rely on specific archeological data. Although recent restatements of the idea have tried to cast a nonhuman character on the activities of Plio–Pleistocene hominids, the home base (or "central place foraging") hypothesis still specifies only those aspects that are distinctively human, leaving the nonhuman aspects vague or nonexistent (Isaac, 1983a,b; 1984).

Observing that the terms "home base" and "food sharing" are charged with modern human connotations, Isaac substituted the term "central place foraging." "Central place" refers specifically to a home base (Isaac 1983a,b; 1984).[2] Hence, this renaming of the food sharing hypothesis stresses even further the importance of a home base in the activities of Plio–Pleistocene hominid activities. Although a central place need not imply an active redistribution of food, this revised statement of the home base idea still sees an important relationship between the delayed consumption of food (eating postponed until food is carried to a home base) and the focusing of social activity at a home base. The sharing of food is one of two fundamental aspects of the home base interpretation that has major implications for early hominid adaptation and the evolution of human behavior.

The second aspect concerns the safety afforded by a protected home base. As a common meeting place of the social group, a home base is assumed to provide protection. This notion about early hominid home bases was addressed even before the excavation of Plio–Pleistocene sites at Olduvai. For instance, Washburn and DeVore (1961) identified a significant difference between hominid base camps and primate sleeping trees: Elderly and infirm individuals are cared for at the campsite, and the young can play and develop skills encouraged by social care and cultural learning within the safe refuge of the home base. Thus, the increased dependence of hominids on culture[3] and the presumed prolonged maturation of early hominid infants required a home base (Lancaster 1978; Mann 1975).

Obviously, the home base interpretation, with its emphasis on safety, food sharing, and associated sociality, has played an enormously influential role

[2]Besides this archeological application of the term, "central place" has an established, but slightly different, zoological meaning as well. It refers to any fixed point in space to which a group of animals rhythmically disperses and returns. Thus, central place in this original broad sense also encompasses nest, sleeping, and den locations of a wide spectrum of animals, including many primates (Hamilton, William, and Watt 1970).

[3]In the thinking of paleoanthropologists, dependence on culture is often signified by the simple presence of stones modified by hominids. This partly inappropriate equation between culture and stone tool manufacture has undoubtedly contributed to the traditional view that the earliest archeological sites indicate that most distinctively modern human characteristics, including home bases, had already emerged.

in studies of human evolution. The question here is whether this particular explanation of the Olduvai sites is the only one possible, and whether the Olduvai data are consistent with the home base view.

## Critique of the Home Base Interpretation

Several characteristics of the faunal and artifact assemblages appear to conflict with the home base interpretation of the sites examined in this study. In this section, I will outline those aspects of Olduvai site formation that are inconsistent with the view that these sites served as home bases with the same social and economic functions as modern hunter–gatherer campsites.

### Safety?

To reiterate the key inferences about site formation, hominids were probably the primary (but not necessarily the only) collectors of animal bones and stone artifacts at five of the sites (FLKNN–2 and Long K are the exceptions). Nonetheless, both hominids and carnivores significantly modified the animal bones at these sites. As discussed earlier, the presence of cut-marked bones in association with stone artifacts strongly implies that hominids modified animal bones directly at these sites. While carnivore tooth marks might have been made prior to the accumulation of those modified bones, the evidence indicates otherwise. Fragments of individual bones, which show diagnostic signs of carnivore breakage (see Chapter 5), are preserved at each Olduvai site. It is evident that carnivores were attracted to these areas of bone accumulation and, in addition to hominids, were also causes of bone damage and attrition there.

The attraction of carnivores to specific areas where hominids had brought tools, raw materials, and animal bones was likely to have restricted the activities of hominids at these sites. As we noted at the end of Chapter 7, the Olduvai sites preserve evidence of a partial ecological overlap between hominids and carnivores. This idea of overlap is based on the following: (1) Carnivores and hominids were attracted at least occasionally to the same species, skeletal parts, and sometimes the same specific bones within any given site; (2) comparisons between the artifact sites and the "primarily carnivore" sites show that, although differences exist in the proportions of species and body parts collected at these two sets of sites, overall the bone assemblages are similar and some of the same species appear in each; (3) a competitive milieu surrounding animal tissues is hinted by the relative abundance of carnivores, especially of small size, preserved at the artifact sites.

It was also noted in Chapter 7 that animal bones were not processed completely at sites where hominid activity was prominent. The sharing of food at modern campsites usually results in efficient, intensive processing of carcasses. Scavenging by carnivores indeed can occur at such home bases. Yet, as noted previously, carnivore access to bones in human camp/village sites is mostly confined to dogs—a controlled, domestic scavenger. Group consumption of food by people, combined with the activities of dogs, are efficient in keeping campsites clean of uneaten animal food debris.

At Olduvai, there is evidence that marrow from limb bone diaphyses was processed to a greater extent at the stone tool sites than at carnivore sites. However, the presence of unbroken meat- or marrow-rich long bones at the artifact sites and of carnivore tooth marks on meat-bearing bones (see pp. 93 and 202) indicates that hominid consumption of edible tissues (and processing of the bones) was not so efficient as that generally practiced by living hunter–gatherers. It also suggests why carnivores were attracted to these sites of bone and artifact accumulation. Apparently, edible tissues were available.

Hence, the partial excursion of the Olduvai hominids into the feeding domain of carnivores resulted not only in a high *potential* ecological overlap but also an actual overlap in the use of food resources and of spatially focused areas. Instead of refuges of safety and protection, the Olduvai sites were places of potential interaction with carnivores. This implication of Olduvai site formation conflicts with the home base interpretation (i.e., that the artifact sites were the safe, primary foci of hominid social life). The basic principle that animals avoid predation when possible would seem to be particularly important in understanding the use of large mammal carcasses by early hominids. It is likely that strategies to cope with carnivore competition and potential predation were at a premium, though these selective factors would have been balanced against other factors (e.g., dietary, social) affecting survival and reproduction. I suggest here simply that, given the evidence for hominid–carnivore overlap in the use of space, certain fauna, and specific bones, the focusing of social life (in the sense of a hunter–gatherer home base) at these areas of bone and artifact accumulation was probably not a strategy adopted by the Olduvai hominids.

### Food Sharing?

Information pertinent to hominid and carnivore activities alone provides strong reasons to doubt that safety from predation, especially to young, old, or infirm individuals (as implied by the home base concept), was afforded by the sites at Olduvai. Moreover, the food sharing aspect of the home base interpretation does not necessarily hold up so well as previously envisioned. Among African hunter–gatherers meat is shared at the campsite primarily when large ungulates are killed (e.g., giraffes, hippopotamus, antelopes over 100 kg). Among modern hunter–gatherers throughout the world, the most extensive degrees of resource sharing within groups occur in those that exploit large game (Hayden, 1981: 386–390).[4] Animal food sharing at campsites is

[4]Hayden's review (1981) of animal food sharing shows that small game may also be shared, though often among a smaller number of people such as the hunter's immediate family.

**TABLE 9.1.** Average Percentage of Very Large Mammals (>820 kg) and Large Bovids (>320 kg) in the Faunas of the Five Artifact Sites[a]

|  | Specimens | MNE | MNI |
|---|---|---|---|
| Very large mammals[b] (Proboscideans, hippo, giraffids, rhinos) | 3.4 | 3.8 | 13.2 |
| Large bovids[c] | 8 | 10 | 21 |

[a]Three estimates of frequency are provided based on the number of specimens, minimum number of elements (MNE), and minimum number of individuals (MNI).

[b]Modern census range: 1–8%.

[c]Modern census range: 1–26%.

especially important among the !Kung San and Bisa of Africa, and in both cases hunters deliberately seek game over 100 kg (Lee, 1979; Marks, 1976). With regard to Plio–Pleistocene archeological sites, Isaac (1984: 53) remarks that animals weighing 115–340 kg tend to be the best represented in the faunal assemblages. This fact could be taken as support for the idea that faunal exploitation and carcass transport to sites was directed toward food sharing, as seen among modern hunters. However, as we explored in Chapter 7, the bone assemblages from the artifact sites consist of macromammal species of all sizes—from small (gazelles and monkeys) to large or very large (elephant, giraffe, hippo, and rhino)—and these are about as abundant as expected in a savanna—mosaic habitat. Table 9.1 and Figure 9.2 summarize the data pertaining to this point. Based on modern census data from African savannas (Chapter 7), the abundance of very large species rarely exceeds 8% of the large mammals. Given that MNI calculations tend to overestimate the frequency of rare taxa, the various estimations of very large mammal representation at Olduvai fall within this low range (Table 9.1). The relative abundance of small, medium, and large bovids also falls within the typical range of frequencies for these body size classes in modern savannas. The pattern seen in Figure 9.2 accords with that found in modern dry savannas: Medium bovids are most abundant, followed by small bovids, and then large bovids. Given the tendency of preservation biases to favor large animals, there is no evidence to suggest preferential transport of large ungulates to the stone artifact sites (i.e., beyond that expected in the environment in general). While this certainly does not refute the possibility of food sharing, the relative representation of fauna at Olduvai does not provide evidence of a deliberate strategy of animal exploitation and food transport devoted to the sharing of food. Foraging by scavenging and hunting without food exchange would seem just as likely to account for the body sizes of animals represented. The fact that carcass parts transported to the stone tool sites were processed in a way that left edible parts unused suggests that if hominids did share food,[5] it was

[5]Beyond the level of "tolerated scrounging" (Isaac, 1978) or "tolerated theft" (Blurton Jones, 1984).

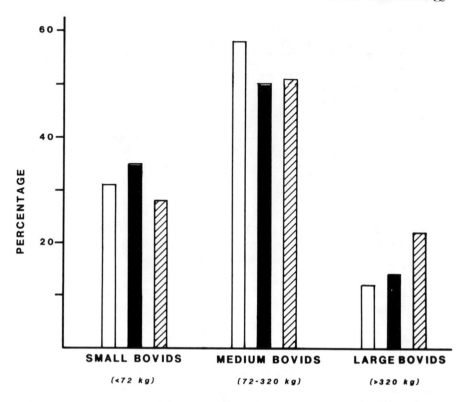

FIGURE 9.2. Relative abundance of small, medium, and large bovids from the
        artifact sites of Bed I Olduvai (averaged). Three estimates of tax-
        onomic abundance are used: E (white bar), MNE (dark bar), and
        MNI (striped bar).

not the kind seen among at least some hunter–gatherers. Intensive modification of bones brought to camps is the rule among modern foragers. As
noted previously, marrow bones are fragmented and often boiled, and all
edible soft tissues tend to be used. The sharing of animal tissues at the campsite promotes their efficient use and destruction. The incomplete processing
of meat and bones at the Olduvai sites and the attraction of carnivores to
these areas were complementary aspects of site formation and are complementary aspects of the argument against safety, extensive exchange of food
at the sites, and home bases at Olduvai.

*Brief Periods of Use of Spatially Confined Sites?*

A further point of conflict with the home base interpretation concerns the
duration over which bones were introduced to each stone tool site (Potts,
1986). Data on weathering discussed in Chapters 3 and 5 suggest that animal

bones were introduced to each of the Olduvai sites over minimum periods of at least 5–10 years. Furthermore, hominid modification of bones at the five stone tool sites appears to have been intermittent and spread out over the period of bone accumulation. In contrast, modern hunter–gatherers in the tropics (other than coastal and estuarine groups) tend to reuse specific, delimited campsites over a much shorter period. Due to the accumulation of refuse and infestation by insects attracted to camp debris, the use of campsites by hunter–gatherers is usually transient with reoccupation of the *exact same spot* occurring only up to a period of several months in total (e.g., Mulvaney, 1969: 67–68; Yellen, 1976). The larger vicinity of a given camp may be reoccupied over many years, but new camps are made in slightly different spots (e.g., around a watering hole). On rare occasions, the Hadza of Tanzania reoccupy the same delimited campsite up to a period of 2 years; clearing away of old debris usually accompanies these reoccupations (J. F. O'Connell, pers. comm.). Still, the relatively long-term accumulation of bones at each of the Olduvai sites contrasts even with this longest period of campsite use reported for tropical latitude hunter–gatherers; moreover, there is no evidence that large and/or complete bones that had been exposed longer (i.e., remaining from previous visits) had been cleared from the Olduvai sites.

*Shelters?*

A final issue that must be considered concerns the evidence for shelters at Olduvai. The construction of a shelter may be viewed as a fundamental development of modern home base activity. The roughly circular arrangement of unmodified basalt rocks at DK–3 is thus an important matter to consider (see p. 29). The popular interpretation of this cluster of stones (about 4 m in diameter) is that it formed the foundation of a shelter, making it the earliest known structure on an archeological site (Campbell, 1982; Leakey, 1971). This interpretation is based on the similarity of the DK stone configuration to rings of stone that support grass huts in southern Africa today and also to aboriginal hunting blinds in Australia (Gould, 1967; Leakey, 1971). The basalt stones at DK range in diameter from about 5–20 cm, and at first glance would seem to be similar to manuports introduced to the site by hominids. If this were the case, the arrangement of stones at DK–3 would be difficult to explain other than by hominid activity. Although the DK locality shows the clearest taphonomic effects from water action of any of the Bed I sites, the rocks forming the circle are too large to have been moved considerably by the degree of water action apparent at this site.

However, two points stand in the way of the hominid activity interpretation. First, the basalt stones that make up the circle come from the basalt layer that lies directly below DK–3 and that naturally protrudes through this horizon in various areas of the site. The irregular basalt rocks show no sign of hominid alteration and probably became detached from the layer below by weathering (Leakey, 1971: 24). An alternative hypothesis that has not been considered widely before is that the roughly circular arrangement of stones may have been produced by a radial distribution of tree roots, known in more recent contexts to penetrate and break up bedrock. Only a few small stone flakes and bone fragments were found within the DK circle, and these could have been introduced to the site by water flow. In cases where there are not yet criteria to infer the causes of unique archeological patterns such as the DK stone circle, alternative taphonomic interpretations must be placed at least on equal footing to ideas that stress hominid activity.

A second problem is indeed the uniqueness of this stone circle in the archeological record of the early Pleistocene. It is the only one known from Olduvai or anywhere else. Other than the DK–3 site, the earliest traces of a shelter are believed to come from Terra Amata, a locality around 300,000 years old. The resolution of the occupation levels at this locality has been disrupted by the vertical movement of stone artifacts (Villa 1982, 1983). Nonetheless, the presence of piled stones, large limestone slabs, and possibly post holes at this open air site has suggested that shelters may have been built at Terra Amata (de Lumley, 1969b). Even if this interpretation is correct, the lack of any older evidence of structures on archeological sites back until DK–3, a gap of 1.5 million years, makes the Olduvai site a truly isolated occurrence. Therefore, based on DK–3 alone, it seems unwise to think that building shelters was part of the behavioral repertoire of Olduvai hominids or any hominids prior to the Middle Pleistocene, at the earliest.

## Alternatives to the Home Base Hypothesis

The basic features of artifact site formation at Olduvai that need to be accounted for are: the transport and concentration of debris on the ancient landscape, that is, the transfer of carcass segments away from death sites to delimited areas, and the introduction of stone to these same areas from a distance of sometimes several kilometers away. One attraction of the home base hypothesis is that social factors, such as safe refuge and food sharing, seem to provide such compelling reasons why Olduvai hominids produced sites.

The various lines of evidence and inference discussed so far in this chapter cast doubts on the idea that social factors (imperative to the home base interpretation) adequately explain why resources were transported to the artifact sites at Olduvai. It may be unwise to assume that food sharing occurred at these sites. It is also clear that carnivores gained access to meat and marrow at these sites; thus, they probably were not places frequented by infants or other individuals incapable of defense. In addition, other behavior patterns (e.g., processing of all edible tissues, short-term use of sites) associated with hunter–gatherer home bases cannot be assumed to have been practiced at these sites. The available evidence suggests that hominids would have minimized the time spent at these sites rather than use them as the primary spatial focus of social activity.

Explanations other than "home bases" are useful to explore. In fact, several alternative ideas can be advanced based on the fact that a wide range of animals (e.g., various carnivores and birds) transport and accumulate objects found in their habitats. These alternative ideas are derived from (1) observations of particular resource collectors (especially bone accumulators), and (2) ecological strategies and adaptive problems that, theoretically, were encountered by hominids in transporting and accumulating bones and stone artifacts. The resulting hypotheses are not *ad hoc* explanations of data already encountered in this study. Rather, they are derived from theoretical consideration of the processes and results of collecting animal bones and stone artifacts in delimited spots. These ideas stand alongside the home base hypothesis (and the social factors it implies) as potential reasons why animals accumulate resources and leave debris. Each of these hypotheses is outlined below, and attention is drawn to data from the Olduvai sites that help to assess these ideas. The importance of this exercise is that, until recently, *behavioral* hypotheses other than the home base explanation simply had not been formulated to account for the contribution of hominids to the artifact sites at Olduvai or elsewhere.[6]

### Provisioning of Young

Provisioning of young is widely practiced by mammalian and avian species. It includes the regurgitation of meat (e.g., by wild dogs) at den sites by adults. Adult female hyenas have been observed to bring back portions of carcasses to their dens in order for their young to feed and gnaw (Hill, 1978, 1980b; Skinner *et al.*, 1980; L. Frank, per. comm.). In the case of the spotted hyena den at Amboseli, the accumulation of a large number of bones and bone fragments may be partly due to this behavior.

Bringing resources (e.g., food) to young and to other individuals unable to forage for themselves is one tenable way to explain the transport and accumulation of objects by hominids or other animals. Provisioning here does not mean "food sharing" in the sense conveyed by the home base hypothesis, because provisioning does not entail a reciprocal exchange of food among foragers.

In explaining the transport of bones and artifacts at Olduvai, the provisioning idea suffers from the same major problems as the home base interpretation. Potential carnivore attraction to sites posed an adaptive "problem"

---

[6]For the most part, *taphonomic* hypotheses involving water action and carnivore activity motivated the renewed studies of Koobi Fora and Olduvai during the 1970s. Only in the past 8 years have alternative interpretations of hominid behavior been discussed in detail (e.g., Binford, 1981, 1985; Isaac, 1983b, 1984; Isaac and Crader, 1981; Potts, 1980, 1982, 1984b; Shipman, 1983).

if, indeed, these were areas of infant care, campsite-type food exchange, and other maintenance activities. It is unlikely that such sites served as refuge for young or other individuals. Efficient methods of defending sites were possibly one way hominids dealt with this problem. However, efficient processing of potentially attractive animal tissues would have been a complementary strategy—but one evidently not practiced by hominids at these sites.

## Removal of Resources from Competitors and Predators

A second adaptive explanation, based on observations in many vertebrate species, is that resources are moved from where they are found to enable the collector to defend or protect those resources from competitors. Interference competition for animal tissues among carnivore species may be high (see Chapter 7). The search for prey, size of feeding groups, and other socioecological aspects of subsistence behavior may be greatly influenced by the need to minimize food losses to competing species (Curio, 1976; Kingdon, 1977; Lamprecht, 1978). Food transport and caching evidently represents one consequent strategy. Leopards, for instance, reduce losses of food by dragging carcasses to places inaccessible to scavengers. Carcasses too large for immediate or complete consumption are taken into trees, which permits the use of kills for several days without molesting by scavengers (Kruuk and Turner, 1967; Lamprecht, 1978). In situations where competition for carcasses with lions, jackals, and vultures is keen, hyenas return bones to their den sites. There, the bones often are dragged inside the den as far as possible to stave off loss of carcass portions to competitors (Brain, 1981: 62; Sutcliffe, 1973). To generalize from these examples, the transport of carcasses to areas hidden from or inaccessible to scavengers can account for the transport of faunal remains to specific locales within the habitat.

A related idea is that predator avoidance itself can have a significant influence on the foraging habits of animals that are themselves potential prey. Again, the use of den sites by hyenas serves as an example, since immature hyenas are known to retreat into the den during a period of danger (while the adults flee from the den) (Watson, 1965). The transfer of resources to an area safe from predation is, therefore, another adaptive reason for the accumulation of food debris.

Both of these ideas, competitor and predator avoidance, bear some of the features of the home base hypothesis—in particular, the notion of safe refuge. These ideas also have problems similar to the home base interpretation of the Olduvai sites. Hominids obviously did not transport faunal remains to places hidden from or inaccessible to carnivores. Based on tooth marks and other bone damage, large carnivores (e.g., hyenas) evidently visited these sites. It thus appears likely that predation was also a potential threat to hominids in these areas.

The removal of meat and articulated segments from the death site of an animal generally reduces the costs of competition (including the risk of predation) that may center at a fresh carcass. While this tenet may have applied to the transport of bones by early hominids away from death sites, the resulting concentrations of debris in the ancient Olduvai environment evidently still drew attention from carnivores and, thus, predatory risks. Therefore, the competitor and predator avoidance ideas do not appear to account adequately for the transport and accumulation of faunal remains by hominids at Olduvai.

Since all animal foragers must avoid predation to survive and since handling animal tissues would tend to increase such risks, how did Olduvai hominids manage to avoid predation? The facts of site formation and the inferences that follow from them regarding ecological overlap between hominids and carnivores imply that hominid strategies of predator avoidance were at a premium. Although we can infer nothing about social strategies of defense against predators, hominids apparently *lacked* other means that would have reduced the chances of carnivore interference at these sites. Examples would include the control of fire, domesticated carnivores, and relatively complete processing of bones (with attendent use of all edible tissues)—all of which are available to recent hunter–gatherers and are represented in the prehistoric record considerably later than the time period of Bed I Olduvai. This would leave the avoidance of predators itself as an important strategy, if not the primary means, by which Olduvai hominids coped with the attraction of carnivores to the sites of bone and artifact accumulation. That is, the chances of predation would have been reduced primarily by minimizing the time spent at these areas of bone accumulation and potential carnivore interference. By implication, the sites considered here were places to which parts of carcasses were taken and processed quickly; although hominids then abandoned these areas, the sites were reused over a period of time.

To reiterate, this basic strategy of predator avoidance only implies that hominids would have tended to minimize time spent at the sites. It does not explain why concentrations of debris were made in the first place. Other explanations for this must still be explored.

### Attraction to Immobile Valued Resources

It is well documented that animals locate sleeping locations, lairs, nests, etc., partly in relation to valued resources, such as particular food patches. Extending upon this principle, resources might be carried to a place where another, less movable, valued resource occurs. A relatively tight clustering of transported resources might result. In the case of early hominids, three immovable resources have been suggested as possible influences on site formation: water, sleeping trees, and shade. These will be considered in turn.

*Water Holes and Lake Margins.* Water attracts a variety of animals, including predators. The latter may focus their hunting at lakeside areas or water holes where game may be plentiful and possibly more vulnerable. Undoubtedly, hominids also required water, which suggests that hominid activity was in part spatially organized around watering areas. Accordingly, the Olduvai sites might have resulted from the concentration of activities near water; these activities would have included scavenging and processing of animal parts (Binford, 1984; Blumenschine, 1986), and plant foods may also have been most abundant around water sources (Sept, 1984).

With this idea we return to the question in Chapter 3 about the characteristics of assemblages formed at water margins. Lakesides, by themselves, do not appear to provide a focus delimited enough to account for the characteristics of bone and artifact clusters at the Olduvai sites (see p. 45). Although some of the excavated levels in Bed I have yielded small-scale, background-type assemblages of bones, the specific accumulations studied here exhibit a combination of dense concentrations of limb bones, high degrees of bone disarticulation and carcass mixing, and high species diversity, evidently unparalleled in predation arenas at water margins. This same combination of features also does not appear to characterize generally the lake margin facies in Bed I Olduvai (see Chapter 3). The repetitive use of the lake margin zone[7] certainly helps to explain why hominid archeological traces are visible in this area. Yet the basic matter of site formation that remains unaccounted for by this hypothesis is the repeated transport of bones (and artifacts) to specific spots within the lake margin zone.

*Trees as Shelter.*    Anatomical evidence that suggests that early hominids were quite capable of climbing may mean that these hominids climbed trees to feed and to escape predators (Isaac, 1981b, 1983a, 1984). Although this is not a new idea, in the context of archeological explanations it suggests a novel way to account for the transport of artifacts and bones by hominids to specific spots on the landscape. In short, these resources were brought to trees either because trees were where hominids slept (a home base with trees for security) or because they provided a means for avoiding competition during feeding (as is the case for leopards) (Isaac, 1983a; also see Blumenschine, 1986).

The difficulty with part of this hypothesis is essentially the same as that with the home base interpretation. The collection of animal bones (and incomplete processing of edible tissues) at a sleeping site would have attracted potential predators. The evidence for carnivore activity at these sites conflicts with the idea that these delimited areas of bone and artifact accumulation were also used as sleeping refuges by hominids. A positive point about this "trees as shelter" idea is that it gives attention to predator avoidance, an adaptive factor of evident importance once hominids entered partly into the

---

[7]The concentration of activities in the lake margin facies does not necessarily mean at the water's edge. As pointed out in Chapter 2, the Olduvai sites at DK and the FLK complex may have been up to 1–1.5 km from the waters of the perennial lake (Hay, 1976).

ecological realm of large carnivores. However, by accumulating animal bones, the transformation of sleeping trees into zones of potential interaction with carnivores would seem to be a dubious solution.[8]

*Trees as Shaded Areas.*     The home base and sleeping tree interpretations imply that these sites were *not* focal points for resources attractive to resident carnivores (such as meat, water, or shelter). It would follow that if carnivores were not attracted to these places, hominids were probably responsible for virtually every bone transported to these sites. As discussed in Part II and alluded to throughout Part III in this book, although we can assess the relative roles of particular agents of site formation (including bone accumulation), it is not yet possible to specify the percentage or the exact subset of bones brought by hominids to each site. This leaves open the possibility that nearly all the bones at the artifact sites were indeed collected by hominids (despite damage induced also by carnivores), but it also allows that carnivores contributed elements to these accumulations. Although water margins may not provide an adequate focus for highly delimited concentrations of bones and artifacts to develop, other locations attractive both to hominids and carnivores might do so. Shade provided by trees, as protection from the sun, is one such immobile resource that could have provided a common focus for the accumulation of materials used by hominids and carnivores (cf. "special-use location," Binford, 1984).

No direct evidence is available from the geologic record at Olduvai about the presence of trees at sites, specifically shade trees (the DK–3 stone circle could be an exception—see p. 258). However, as noted in Chapter 3, bone concentrations around trees attractive to carnivore bone collectors combine several of the distinctive characteristics of death sites and landscape scatters, as observed in modern savannas. In situations where trees are relatively rare, overlapping use of shaded areas by lions, hyenas, leopards, and cheetahs produces higher concentrations of bones from multiple ungulate species than occur on the landscape at large. But these locations are generally also distinguished by a relatively high degree of bone articulation, comparatively low species diversity, and/or a high proportion of axial parts or attritional elements (e.g., teeth, horn cores). As discussed earlier, the Olduvai bone accumulations do not exhibit these features. Recurrent transport of carcass parts by hominids to such shaded areas, where bones were processed with stone tools, may help to account for differences between the modern tree locations used by carnivores and the Olduvai sites, where both hominid and carnivore activity occurred. However, in the specific habitats of these sites, it appears unlikely that shade trees were at a premium. As discussed earlier (pp. 22 and 193), closed vegetation and arboreal habitats evidently were not rare in the lake

---

[8]The detrimental influence of a large carnivore at a sleeping tree site of a primate social group (chimpanzees) is exemplified by Goodall (1986: 557).

margin zone at Olduvai, even during the driest periods. It is also doubtful, therefore, that shade trees alone provided the kind of specific attraction that led to the recurrent, preferential transport of carcass parts by hominids to delimited spots, as the Olduvai sites represent.

In the next section, we will explore a final, theoretically important factor involved in the accumulation of debris—the energy expended in transporting resources. The transport of stone and bone to the same locations requires more detailed examination.

## The Energetic Effort of Site Production

As noted earlier, the home base interpretation of Plio–Pleistocene sites draws rather significant implications about social behavior from the transport of stones and fauna by hominids. For instance, Isaac (1978) emphasizes the importance of concentrations of animal bones, which signals the sharing of meat. On the other hand, Lee (1979: 493) has constructed his home base interpretation around the stone artifacts:

> The evidence from early living floors of tool-making man indicates that by Lower Pleistocene times, the life style predicated on carrying device, home base, and exchange was already well established. The proof is in the concentrations of exotic stones found at Bed I Olduvai in association with the remains of early man.

After he draws attention to the distance of several kilometers between stone sources and sites, Lee remarks that large energy and time inputs must have been involved in carrying stones to sites. This presumed large investment suggests to Lee that the living floors signify relatively permanent campsites to which members of a social group consistently returned. Food was brought to the site to feed those individuals involved in transporting stones and making tools.

The introduction of either bones or artifacts to delimited locations, then, has been pivotal to the view that Plio–Pleistocene sites were social and economic centers in the lives of early hominids.

Once stone tools became involved in the processing of animals or other food (whether sporadically or regularly), a new factor was introduced to hominid foraging—how to ensure or to facilitate the presence of food and tools together at the same places. By transporting, making, and using stone artifacts as part of the foraging process, hominids incurred an extra energetic cost not involved to any appreciable extent in the foraging behavior of any other primate. However, the cost of transporting stone must be viewed against the benefit of having stones in the vicinity of foraged resources that required processing with tools.

*Computer Simulation of Transport Energetics*

In order to better understand the energetic factors involved in accumulating fauna and artifacts at specific locations, a computer model of site production was developed.[9] The process of site production simulated here did not involve the transport solely of animal tissues or of stone resources. Instead, site production was viewed as a problem of bringing both of these resources together. Thus, this model is pertinent specifically to the five artifact sites in Bed I Olduvai. Energetic efficiency of carcass and stone transport to sites is the sole concern of the computer simulations. No assumption is made about the form of the stone material (shaped tools, blocks of raw material, or fragments). Although any form of collectable food could be considered as the other transported resource, animal carcasses (whether complete, partial, or as individual bones) are discussed here in view of their relevance to Olduvai site interpretation.

Since only the energetics of transport and site production are considered, no assumptions or conditions are made about the characteristics of hominid social groups. In creating a model based on energetics, it is necessary to assume that individuals adopt behaviors that maximize their *net* rate of energy intake while foraging (Emlen, 1966; Schoener, 1971; Smith, 1979). The site production model is this type of optimality model. It simulates the trade-offs between various stone transport and carcass transport strategies to ascertain the ways in which they are best linked to *minimize* energy expenditures of site production and, thereby, help to maximize the *net* rate of energy intake. The concept of site production "strategies" refers to an apparent anticipation of resource distribution such as occurs from prior foraging experience in animals that use learning and memory in foraging (Kamil and Sargent, 1981; Olton, Handelman, and Walker, 1981). The "strategies" of site production generated by the model have diverse implications concerning the efficiency of bringing stones and animal tissues together.

The parameters of the model are as follows:

1. *The number of sites:* Figure 9.3 depicts one site, symbolized by the cross in the center. This site represents an original stone source (e.g., an outcrop). The hexagon is the boundary of the foraging area. Each carcass is signified by a dot. In this case, the carcasses are carried back to this one source rock. Thus, no stones are carried in this situation; only faunal materials are moved. When stone material is carried away from the source to a new locus, new sites are represented. New sites, then, are used along with the original outcrop as a source of stone tools. Figure 9.4 depicts four different site production simulations involving 2 sites, 3 sites, 7 sites, and 19 sites. In the later case, stone is carried to produce 18 new sites, which are used along

---

[9]Alan Walker and Simon Walker, Johns Hopkins University, collaborated with the author in this effort (Potts and Walker, 1981).

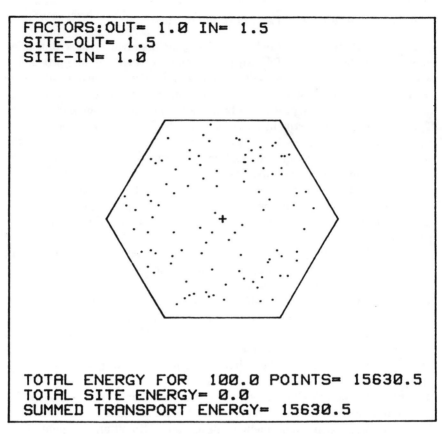

```
FACTORS:OUT= 1.0 IN= 1.5
SITE-OUT= 1.5
SITE-IN= 1.0
```

```
TOTAL ENERGY FOR  100.0 POINTS= 15630.5
TOTAL SITE ENERGY= 0.0
SUMMED TRANSPORT ENERGY= 15630.5
```

**FIGURE 9.3.** Site production simulation of 1 site ( + ), the original outcrop, in the center of a hexagonal foraging area. Carcasses (dots) are randomly spaced throughout the area. The stone and carcass transport factors equal 1.5, but since no stone is transported, the stone transport energy equals 0.

with the original outcrop. In each situation, sites are distributed in a tightly packed position around the original source, which minimizes the distance of stone transport. Site production simulations that generated up to 19 sites were examined.

2. *The number of carcasses available in the foraging area:* Carcasses are symbolized by dots dispersed randomly over the environment. The number of dots was varied from 1 to 100 in the simulations. In the case of 3 sites (Figure 9.4b), the border encompassing all three hexagons signifies the entire foraging area. Carcasses, whether hunted or scavenged, are obtained randomly over this area. Predator–prey experiments show that, although predators do not *seek* food by random walk, they usually do *encounter* it randomly. Predator–prey models with high predictive value have been based on spatially random food encounters (Krebs, 1978). Hence, random points form a rea-

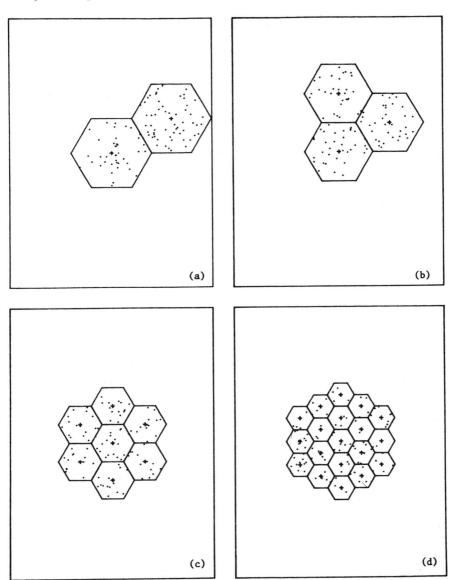

**FIGURE 9.4.** Four site production strategies: *(a)* 2 sites, *(b)* 3 sites, *(c)* 7 sites, and *(d)* 19 sites.

sonable way to represent the distribution of carcasses over time. As each point appears in succession, it is, in turn, transported back to the nearest site. The hexagon boundaries define which of the sites is nearest.

3. *Energy factors:* Energy in this model is a function of *distance traveled* multiplied by an energy factor. The energy factor for walking is fixed at 1. The factors for carrying objects are greater than 1. Factors for stone transport

and for bone transport are modified independently. Physiological studies have shown that well-conditioned humans carrying very heavy loads (up to 70 kg) for long periods of time do not expend more than two times the energy which is used during just walking (Givoni and Goldman, 1971; Goldman and Iampietro, 1962; Soule, Pandolf, and Goldman, 1978). Yet studies of Olympic athletes show that expenditures five times greater than walking are possible during fast running (Margaria, Cerretelli, Aghemo, and Sassi, 1963). This information provides some basis for setting the energy factors for stone and carcass transport. Factors of 1.5 and 2.0 were used most often in the simulations, although factors up to 5 were also considered.

- *Carcass transport energy* equals the distance walked from the site to a random point *plus* the energy expended in carrying the carcass material back. That latter quantity equals the distance multiplied by an energy factor.
- *Stone transport energy* equals the distance stone is carried (from the outcrop to the new site) multiplied by the energy factor. When more than one new site is created, multiple trips to the source rock are necessary. In that case, stone transport energy is calculated by summing the total walking energy (namely, the distance, since the energy factor is 1) with the total stone-carrying energy.

The hexagons provide a neat geometric solution to packing the sites always in the same area. That is, the total foraging area for 19 sites is the same as for 2 sites. It is essential to keep the foraging area the same size regardless of the number of sites because energy is related to the distance travelled. As the number of sites varies, the sites are packed together in different ways; these form different site production strategies (see Figure 9.4).

Changes in the number of sites affect the energetic trade-offs between stone and carcass transport. The animal remains are brought to the *nearest* site simply because it decreases the transport distance. In energy terms, this is the *only* reason to create new sites, that is, to take on the cost of transporting stones: to reduce the energy costs of transporting carcasses. Thus, as stone transport energy is increased due to the creation of more sites, carcass transport energy decreases. The most beneficial site production strategies are those with the lowest total energy expended. This quantity is called *summed transport energy* (STE), and it is obtained by adding the total energy *(E)* for stone transport and the total for carcass transport:

$$STE = E \text{ (stone)} + E \text{ (carcass)}$$

Each simulation consists of calculating the STE for *each* of the site production strategies (1 site–19 sites) for a given pair of energy factors (stone and carcass) and a given number of carcasses. Several questions, thus, can be assessed: Is it best energetically (lowest STE) to use only 1 new site at a time (a site to which every independently foraging group member returns)?

Is it optimal to make no new sites but to take all faunal material to the original stone source? Or is it most beneficial to produce and to use many sites at once, thus considerably reducing the distance animal remains must be transported?

*Results*

Figures 9.5–9.7 present the general shapes of the energy curves, obtained over numerous simulations, for the three quantities in the foregoing equation for STE. The E (stone) (Figure 9.5) when only 1 site—the original source—is used is 0 because no stones are moved. As the number of sites increases, the energy for transporting stones increases linearly. As more sites need to be stocked with stone, stones are carried a greater total distance.

In contrast, as the number of sites increases, each carcass (on the average) is transported a shorter distance (Figure 9.6). Energy for carcass transport

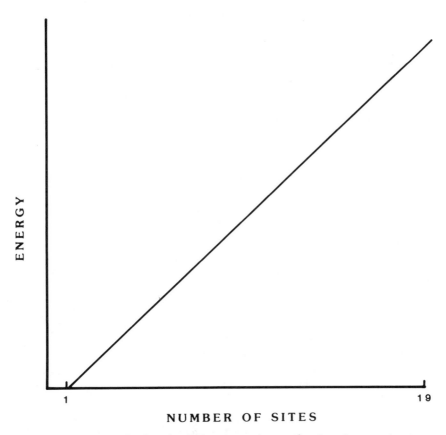

**FIGURE 9.5.** Site production simulation: general curve for stone transport energy.

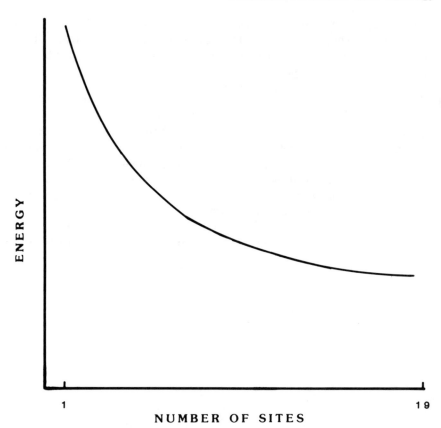

**FIGURE 9.6.** Site production simulation: general curve for carcass transport
        energy.

tends to decrease rapidly at first. But with the addition of sites, the saving
in carcass transport distance becomes less; thus, the energy curve levels off.

Finally, when the transport of energy factors are equal and the number
of points (carcasses) is 20 or more, STE decreases initially, levels off, and
often shows a slight rise as the number of sites is increased (Figure 9.7). The
total energy for using just the original stone source is usually the highest.
When only 1 new site is made and used in addition to the original source,
STE is reduced but is still relatively high. The minimum, or levelling off
point, generally occurs when anywhere from 5 to 15 sites are produced and
used at one time. Hence, up to a point, there exists an energetic advantage
for producing numerous sites.

The energy curves for an actual simulation are shown in Figure 9.8 for
100 random points (carcasses), and the stone and carcass energy factors both
equal to 1.5. Stone transport energy increases linearly. Bone transport energy

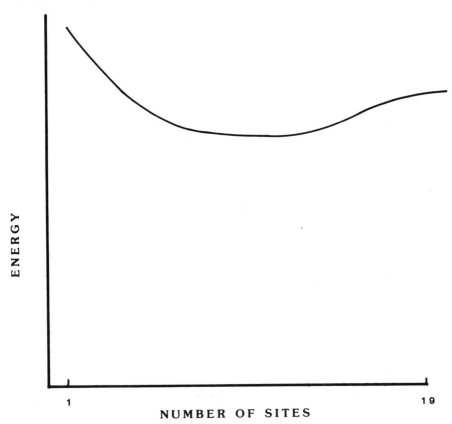

**FIGURE 9.7.** Site production simulation: general curve for summed transport energy (STE).

decreases quickly at first, then levels off. STE levels off at about 12 sites and starts to rise slightly at 18–19 sites.

There is, of course, a change in the minimum STE as the model parameters are varied in a controlled manner:

1. As the number of carcasses available in the area increases, it becomes energetically beneficial to produce more sites in the foraging area.
2. As the energy factor for stone transport is increased (and all other parameters are kept constant), fewer sites result in the best energy strategy. The stone energy factor is bound to be related to the mass of the stone carried. Efficient use of raw material in tool manufacture would decrease the amount of stone needed and, thus, decrease the total energy for the same number of sites (the difference between the two curves in Figure 9.9).

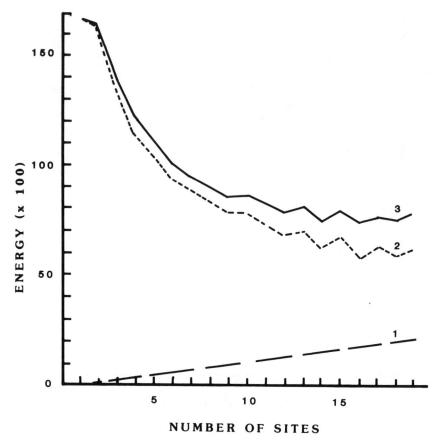

**FIGURE 9.8.** Results of an actual site production simulation: 100 points (carcasses); stone and carcass transport factors both equal 1.5. Curve 1 = stone transport energy; curve 2 = carcass transport energy; curve 3 = summed transport energy. STE levels off at about 12 sites.

3. As the bone transport factor is increased, STE becomes lower as more sites are used. This point is conceptually simple: When animal tissues are energetically expensive to carry, a short distance of transport is advantageous. This is achieved by packing more sites into the foraging area.

In summary, the model provides a way for creating varied assemblages of bone and stone material when *only* energetic considerations are operating. The results suggest that the production and use of many sites, instead of just one main site, at a time reduces the energy expended in bringing stone artifacts and animal bones together. This result is consistent with several inter-

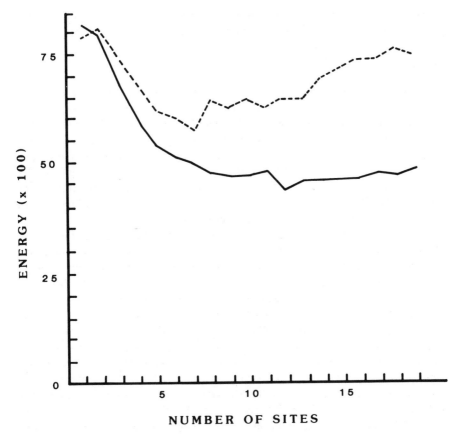

**FIGURE 9.9.** Site production simulation: Comparison of STE when only the stone transport factor is varied. This factor equals 1.5 (solid line) and 5.0 (broken line). Actual simulation involved 100 random points (carcasses); carcass transport factor equalled 1.5 (constant).

pretations of Plio–Pleistocene artifact sites. Since the production of sites may have been beneficial to hominids simply for energetic reasons, the presence of associated bone and artifact accumulations need not imply the existence of certain social behaviors among hominids or home bases (as also suggested by evidence from the Olduvai sites). According to the predictions of the model, stone artifacts and bones may become concentrated in specific locations by the repeated transport of stone and parts of carcasses (for processing with stone tools) to multiple places on the landscape. Sites are produced by transporting bones to nearby places where stone tools or raw materials had been left. The energetic benefits of such behavior may be considered separately from other possible adaptive reasons we have considered—social (e.g., food sharing), competitor avoidance, immovable resources—to explain the transport and accumulation of bones and artifacts in delimited locations.

### Some Predictions

Simplifying models often have their greatest value *not* by showing which processes actually occurred in real situations, but by guiding the interpretation of inconsistences between data and the model's expectations. The assumption and results of the site production model yield certain expectations about the modification of stone raw materials, the spatial distribution of sites, the number of times bones and stone material were transported to sites, and the energetic costs of transport. These expectations serve to focus attention on specific site data from Bed I Olduvai. Some of these data conform to the model, while other evidence provides subtle contradictions to it.

First, more than one stone raw material is present at each artifact site at Olduvai. The fact that the quartzite source (Naibor Soit to the north and northwest of the excavated sites) and the inferred sources of lava (streams from the volcanic highlands to the south and east) were in opposite directions from the sites indicates that more than one stone-gathering trip was involved. The quantity and volume of some raw materials also suggest this conclusion. For example, at FLK "Zinj," 20 kg of quartzite occur. This is well within the maximum load that well-conditioned (or airplane-traveling) humans can carry and at speeds that would have made the 6 km round trip to the quartzite source fairly rapid. This weight of quartzite also represents a volume of only 7556 cc (about 2 gallons). However, the largest unmodified piece of quartzite in this assemblage is 665 gm. Thirty rocks of this size would have to be transported to FLK "Zinj" to account for the total weight of quartzite. The irregular shape of quartzite blocks implies that the total volume of rocks carried would have surpassed the capacity of one trip by one hominid. The results of the initial simulations, which were based on only one stone-carrying trip for each site produced, can be appropriately modified by multiplying the stone transport energy by the number of trips. The result of this exercise is that when stone transport energy is multiplied by up to 10, and often more, the general results of the simulations still hold. For instance, Figure 9.10 depicts the same simulation as shown previously (Figure 9.8), but with the stone transport energy multiplied by 5 to represent 5 trips to stock each site with stone. The total energy expenditure (STE) is minimized when 7 sites are produced, that is, it is still energetically more efficient to create multiple sites. Only when 17 stone transport trips are required per site does it become more beneficial to produce only 1 new site rather than multiple sites. Yet, when that many trips are involved, the use of just the original source (no stone transport at all) becomes an even more advantageous strategy. A consideration of stone artifact quantities in Olduvai assemblages, then, does not substantially affect the conclusion that, when sites are produced, multiple, evenly spaced sites form the most efficient site production strategy.

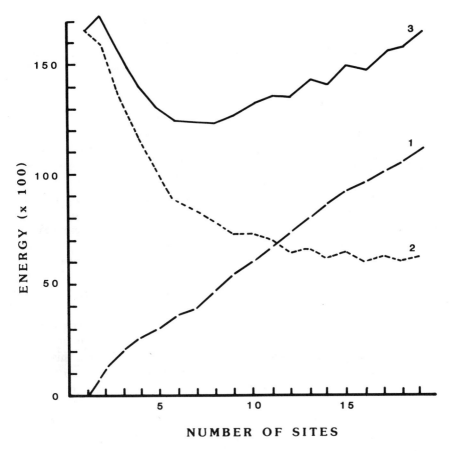

**NUMBER OF SITES**

**FIGURE 9.10.** Results of the same site production simulation as shown in Figure 9.8, but here the stone transport energy is multiplied by 5 to represent 5 stone-carrying trips to stock each new site produced. Curve 1 = stone transport energy; curve 2 = carcass transport energy; curve 3 = summed transport energy. STE reaches a minimum when 8 sites are produced and then increases.

A second consideration concerns the idea that parts of carcasses were taken to locations where stone tools or raw materials had already been placed. If stones useful for processing meat and bones did define the places to which animal tissues were brought, we would expect to find stones in abundance beyond that required to process the carcasses brought to the site. In fact, as noted in Chapter 8, unmodified rocks (manuports) of the same raw materials used for making sharp-edged flakes and cores were present at each artifact site at Olduvai. Furthermore, it is clear that many of the flaked pieces, which underwent transformations from one type to another (Figure 8.4), were not extensively modified. Generally, these pieces showed 2–5 flake scars, though many more flakes could have been obtained from most pieces; and many of the cores showed little or no chipping such as might have occurred from utilization (Table 8.5). Thus, in addition to the unmodified manuports, there is little evidence that the flaked pieces were exhausted in their use as either implements or as cores for producing sharp flakes. These findings indeed suggest that stones were accumulated at the Olduvai sites beyond that required to process animal tissues (and possibly plant foods) transported to these same places.

A related expectation based on the simulation model is that if stone were transported only to sites and nowhere else, there should be a positive relationship between the cores and debitage of different raw materials. With regard to lava materials at the 5 artifact sites, low numbers of cores are associated with low numbers of debitage, and high frequencies of cores are associated with high frequencies of debitage. However, it is clear that the transport, flaking, and use of stone were not confined just to the sites themselves. Rather, in some situations, cores and, in other cases, flakes evidently were removed from or contributed to sites in a biased manner (see p. 243). This biased "flow" of flakes and flaked pieces in and out of sites—at least part of which can only be ascribed to behavior rather than to other taphonomic factors (e.g., water action)—suggests that foraging hominids carried around pieces of useful stone material obtained during visits to the accumulations of stone. Although not incorporated into the computer simulations, this aspect of stone transport, if it involved small pieces of stone, would not substantially alter the energetics of concentrating stones and carcass parts in the same delimited places.

Another implication of the site production model concerns the ecological diversity of the fauna at each site. According to the model, sites created in an area possessing a diversity of habitats (Figure 9.11) should each sample a narrow environmental range relative to that which occurs over the entire foraging area. This expectation results from the fact that each site samples only those species that are found closest to it. Sedimentological, pollen, and microfaunal evidence from Bed I Olduvai suggests that at any one time a mosaic of habitats did exist. Thus, if macrofauna were returned only to the closest site out of many existing sites, representation of a narrow range of habitats may be expected from each site.

The large mammal assemblages from the five artifact sites in Bed I do show some differences in taxa that are good habitat indicators. For example, bovids of the dry plains dominate the assemblage at FLK North–6, whereas a bovid *(Kobus)* that preferred a moist, marshy habitat characterizes the FLKNN–3 assemblage. Nevertheless, none of the Bed I faunal assemblages represents a narrow range of habitats. As noted earlier, a wide spectrum of taxa from a diversity of habitats characterizes each of the large mammal assemblages examined here. The fauna introduced to sites do not appear to reflect narrow samplings of specific habitats in the Olduvai area (Chapter 7).

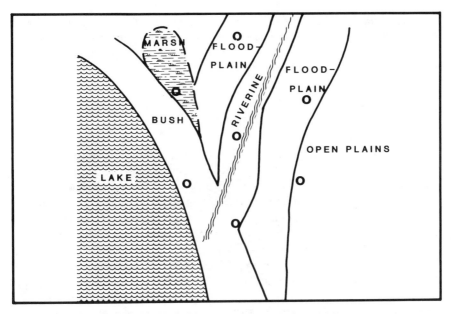

**FIGURE 9.11.** Stone cache idea placed in the environmental context of Bed I Olduvai. Circles represent sites, which could have been situated in a variety of habitats.

This conclusion somewhat conflicts with the idea that multiple sites, evenly spaced throughout a patchy environment, sampled only those species occurring closest to each site.

Optimality models can be criticized on a number of grounds. Obviously, the lowest STE in any simulation represents an optimal site production strategy only within the framework of the few parameters considered. Even manipulation of these very few parameters has generated a huge number of site production simulations. The addition of a single extra variable would make the model extraordinarily complex. In the reality of site production at Olduvai, however, intervening variables undoubtedly occurred. For example, the presence of some raw material sources close to the lake probably prohibited a geometric pattern of site production around one main outcrop, partly due to the lake's physical boundary. In addition, the spatial distribution of other resources, such as water or plant foods, and the effects of predation may have limited site production to certain areas. Again, an "optimal" spacing of sites through the foraging area would be disrupted by these factors. Moreover, the costs and benefits of site production could be measured in various ways (e.g., time, habitat preferences, predation risks); *energy* is only one of them. Ecological fluctuations during the formation period of each site may have led to changing "optimal" solutions to the energetic problem of bringing stone artifacts and animal resources together. Unfortunately, the time resolution of any faunal or artifact assemblage is insufficient to indicate such variations, that is, time averaging tends to mask variations in ecology and in consequent strategies of resource accumulation.

## Resource Transport

The computer model of site production simplifies in order to see the interplay between two fundamental factors known about the formation of the Olduvai sites—transport of bones and of stones. The results suggest that energetic efficiency in stone and carcass transport may have led to the concentration of these two kinds of resources at the same spots on the ancient landscape. Behaviorally, such places would represent reusable processing sites. This interpretation does not require that certain social behaviors were focused at these sites. Furthermore, this interpretation does not require other factors that are unknown or difficult to evaluate, such as the attraction of hominids to water or shade trees, to explain the spatially delimited concentration of stone artifacts and bones. The resource transport interpretation, however, does not exclude the possibilities that such factors influenced the location of carcass processing sites (see p. 280). The important point underlying the resource transport idea is that once stone tools and the processing of animal tissues became linked, the availability of transported tools and stone raw materials governed where in the foraging range hominids also carried parts of carcasses for processing. We know that at Olduvai the two resources, tools and animal tissues, were linked. The site production simulations imply that the creation of concentrations of stone and bone debris was possibly an effect of bringing these two resources together in an efficient manner.

### The Stone Cache Interpretation

In several publications, I have advanced the idea that the artifact sites in Bed I Olduvai were quick-term, processing sites where hominids had deposited stone material useful for processing animal tissues. This is the stone cache interpretation (Potts, 1982, 1984a,b, 1987). The idea of a stone cache fuses together two fundamental ideas: (1) The availability of stone was an essential element in the processing of animal tissues by hominids; and (2) the avoidance of predators was critical in handling carcass parts that were also potentially attractive to large carnivores. In other words, the stone cache idea conveys, in behavioral terms, the principle or strategy of resource transport explored in the previous sections. It also considers the role of hominid avoidance of predators on aspects of site formation (see p. 202). This interpretation explains the production of sites at Olduvai in the light of these two "principles" and under the constraints posed by prior inferences about site formation at Olduvai.[10]

A "stone cache" refers to an aggregation of transported stone, including modified and unmodified pieces, which was repeatedly visited to obtain or manufacture tools and to use them in processing food. Stone raw materials and tools left in various places in the foraging area provided useful materials for processing parts of carcasses and, possibly, other foods acquired during the forage. Tools and bones could have been brought together in three ways. First, once an animal was obtained, the carcass was abandoned temporarily to get stone necessary for processing it. Second, sufficient stone tools were carried during the forage to carry out the processing of a carcass where it was found. Finally, dissociated units lying at a death site or parts that could be cut from the carcass were carried to places where stones were available for further processing. While the first two means for bringing stone tools and bones together cannot be discounted, the Olduvai sites examined here were not primarily death sites but places where the bones of many animals were transported and accumulated. Only the third strategy produces such accumulations. The transport of portions away from death sites to spots where stone was available also would have limited the time spent at such sites, where competition or interaction with carnivores was potentially the greatest. In addition, the time and energy spent in handling and transporting portions of meat and marrow was minimized by taking bones to the nearest source of stone, where artifacts and bones from previous visits remained. Time spent at a stone cache site apparently was also minimized. In response to the occasional attraction of carnivores to these same places and utilization of some of the same bones, the new carcass parts brought to the stone cache by hominids were processed quickly to obtain whatever edible matter (meat or marrow) or other resources (e.g., sinew or hide) were needed or were available.

[10]Binford (1985) criticizes the stone cache idea on the basis that it is a *post hoc* argument that simply accommodates the evidence already at hand. In fact, the stone cache idea was originally derived from considering actual and theoretical strategies of resource transport and collection. One of these basic strategies concerns the assurance that stone is available when food requiring stone tool use is obtained. This is the basis of the stone cache idea, as presented here and earlier (Potts, 1982). This idea is not a *post hoc* argument in that it was developed from prior theoretical considerations of transport energetics. Nonetheless, it is also the case that the stone cache idea is consistent with prior inferences about artifact site formation at Olduvai, including those that appear to conflict with the home base hypothesis. It is necessary to discuss (here and Potts, 1984b) how the stone cache idea (indeed) accommodates the various prior inferences about site formation, including the activity of carnivores. This serves principally to support the idea that stone caches do plausibly account for Olduvai site formation. Although discourse on plausibility may seem like an attempt to simply accommodate the evidence, it needs to be shown whether evidence about site formation does or does not conflict with a new idea developed from theoretical considerations.

By abandoning the site immediately, hominids could probably often avoid direct competition with carnivores, thus establishing their role in the utilization of animal tissues in the ancient environment at Olduvai.

Unmodified and minimally modified pieces of stone, derived from sources some distance away, were deposited in delimited spots. This practice made these spots reusable over long periods of time for the processing of carcass parts obtained in the vicinity. Due to long-term, recurrent use of these sites, the associated artifacts consisted of stones flaked in an irregular manner, unshaped rocks utilized in various ways, and stone raw material that was not modified before burial by expansion of the lake. The concentrations of stones would also provide a readily available selection of cores and/or flakes to be removed from the site by hominids foraging in the immediate vicinity.

What factors would have governed the locations of stone caches in the Olduvai environment? According to the computer model of site production, an equal spacing of stone concentrations through the foraging range, blind to the features of the landscape, would have been advantageous. However, in practice, animals (including humans) forage and use the land in terms of regular or transient features of the landscape, usually not geometry. In fact, evidence from certain sites at Olduvai suggests that factors other than geometric spacing influenced the transport and concentration of artifacts and animal bones.

The first case concerns the presence of much of a skeleton of the bovid *Kobus sigmoidalis* at FLKNN–3 and the elephant skeleton at FLK North–6. If delimited concentrations of stones had been made at these two sites prior to the death of these animals, it would seem highly improbable that the animals happened to die later (either naturally or by predation) right at a stone cache. FLK North–6 represents the death site of the huge *Elephas recki;* and the medium-sized *Kobus sigmoidalis* at FLKNN–3 would have been very heavy to drag even a short distance as a complete skeleton. In these cases, the initial deposition of stone tools at a carcass may have prompted hominids to return to these places with parts of other carcasses to carry out quick-order processing.

A second case concerns the relation between Level 2 and the subjacent Level 3 at locality FLKNN. If the inferences in Chapter 5 about site formation are correct, an assemblage of bones made primarily by carnivores is located stratigraphically above what is judged to be an area where hominid activity played a much more important role. This stratigraphic relationship suggests that this locality was unusually attractive, leading to separate periods of activity first by hominids and carnivores (in Level 3) and then more exclusively by carnivores (Level 2). In this example, we must recall the alternative explanations for the transport of resources to particular places. The attraction provided by an immobile resource, such as a shade tree or shelter, would appear to be the only factor that could account for the superpositioning of one bone concentration upon another. In this second case, therefore, the presence of a third unknown resource is likely to have governed where hom-inids concentrated stone material useful for processing carcasses. At the FLKNN locality, the deposition of stone by hominids was later abandoned, and carnivores, probably hyenas, became more exclusive users of this location.

Although the attraction afforded by immobile resources is likely to have influenced where hominids deposited stone tools and raw materials, according to the stone cache interpretation it was the presence of these stones that prompted hominids to return with animal tissues over a period of years to these delimited places on the ancient landscape at Olduvai. Accordingly, the availability of stone material for processing carcasses outweighed the potential danger of visiting places where carnivores also may have been active.

## Potential Problems with the Stone Cache Interpretation

Two major concerns have greeted this proposed interpretation of the sites in Bed I Olduvai. The first issue focuses on premeditation, or planning for the future, which appears to be invoked by the stone cache idea. The second problem involves the testability of this interpretation.

The creation of stone caches would have involved moving flaked tools and raw materials from their sources to convenient locations in the foraging range. Over a period of time, food that required processing with stone tools would be brought to these "stockpiles" of stone. On the surface, this activity would appear to involve an extensive degree of forethought and planning—"thinking ahead" (Pfeiffer, 1985). In fact, the cache idea is claimed to imply a degree of strategic anticipation that is known only among complex, logistically or-ganized groups of modern hunter–gatherers—a behavioral characteristic un-likely to have occurred in early hominids (Binford, 1985).

However, neither the computer model of site production nor the stone cache interpretation assumes strategically complex planning as seen in modern humans. It does assume that hominids, like other primates or other animals, had a range of information about their environment and could recall the dis-tributions of resources and promising areas for foraging. Although field studies do not always demonstrate optimality in the ranging habits of animals, foraging studies of animals from insects to birds and mammals are based on the as-sumption that animals forage as if they applied stored information about their environments. The importance of knowledge about the environment and the excellent spatial learning and memory animals portray in response to patterns of food distribution have been documented by field and laboratory research (e.g., Kamil and Sargent, 1981; Olton et al., 1981). In studies of animal for-aging, it has been deemed reasonable to equate the way an animal uses its habitat (e.g., patch choice) with its expectation (mediated by learning and memory in some species) about the food sources in its habitat (Charnov, 1976; Orians, 1981).

The stone cache interpretation relies upon the observation that stone tools became an integral part of foraging for certain foods: Tool use and stone transport, as documented at Olduvai, must have affected the costs of searching for and handling those foods. Given the link between stone tools and food processing, the transport of stone (one aspect of the way Olduvai hominids used their habitat) was likely tied to expectations about food distribution. The computer simulations indicated that a geometric spacing between patches of transported stone in the area where carcasses could be obtained would have lowered foraging costs. However, as considered in the previous section, under actual conditions immobile resources like trees or large animal carcasses could have affected the initial deposition of stone in a portion of the foraging range. Unlike these latter factors when considered alone (p. 262), it is the link between the availability of stone material and the processing of carcasses that directs the concentration of artifacts and bones in the same delimited places. As indicated by the computer model, the introduction of stone to particular spots in the foraging area not only reduces total foraging costs over the use of a single "central place," it also creates the conditions for repeatedly transporting bone and more stone to that location. Thus, these spots are reused. The cognitive or organizational complexity that this behavior would entail is not far removed from that documented among chimpanzees at nut-cracking sites. Studies of chimpanzees in western Africa suggest that *(a)* temporary discard and later reuse of tools and *(b)* locating tools in relation to food sources are matters of past experience and memory rather than complex planning for the future. A brief aside on this intriguing behavior is worthwhile.

## Nut-Cracking Sites of Chimpanzees

At Bossou, Guinea, and in the Tai Forest, Ivory Coast, researchers have observed common chimpanzees *(Pan troglodytes verus)* to carry pieces of stone or large sticks that are then used as hammers and anvils to crack open nuts. At Bossou, pairs of loose stones are left at certain nut trees. Individual chimpanzees or small groups independently visit these trees, collect the nuts, and crack them for a period of time at the food source itself. By breaking the hard nut shells of oil-palm nuts *(Elaeis guineensis)*, the edible kernels are extracted. The cracking stones are left behind with associated nutshells. The nut trees are visited repeatedly when nuts are available, and the hammer and anvil stones are reused, apparently over many years. The Bossou chimpanzees engage in this activity only at trees where stones have been left; all nuts processed at a nut-cracking station come from that particular tree. Multiple pairs of nut-cracking stones occur at some sites, which allows more than one chimpanzee to break nuts at a time. Only one pair of stones is present at other trees. In that case, stones may be used by a few individuals in succession during a 20–60 minute period (Sugiyama, 1981; Sugiyama and Koman, 1979).

In Tai National Park, 200 km away, chimpanzees appear to take a slightly different approach toward the transport of nut-cracking tools. Either exposed tree roots or outcrops of granite or laterite situated near the nut tree are used as anvils. While the anvils are immobile, hammers of wood (sticks or broken roots) and stone (granite or laterite) are frequently carried from one anvil/nut tree location to another and are sometimes carried considerable distances. Like at Bossou, individuals or pairs of chimpanzees collect nuts in a tree (coala nuts) or on the ground (panda nuts). They then either crack the nuts at an anvil located within the area of the tree (ca. 10 m diameter) or carry the nuts up to about 30 m away to better anvils (often rock outcrops) than are available right at the tree. Hammers are brought to the anvils usually over a short distance (5–20 m). Yet out of 603 observations of hammer transport, 21 (3.5%) involved distances of 200–500 m (stones weighing up to 9 kg), and 3 cases (0.5%) involved movement of hammer stones (weighing up to 3 kg) over 500 m (Boesch and Boesch, 1984). Unlike the Bossou example, the Tai chimpanzees do not always leave hammers at the nut-cracking sites; rather they often transport them from one anvil/nut tree spot to another. Since panda trees are widely scattered in the Tai Forest, the distance hammers are transported between panda nut-cracking sites (preferentially granite hammer stones) may be especially long.

Interestingly, the Tai chimpanzees will collect nuts at an anvil only if a hammer is already present. When chimpanzees require a stone hammer at a cracking site (usually ascertained by visiting the site first), they will take one from a site where a hammer is available. This latter site tends to be the nut-cracking site (with a hammer) nearest to the site previously visited by the chimpanzees, thus minimizing the distance of hammerstone transport. The researchers who have analyzed the nut-cracking activities at Tai suggest that these chimpanzees remember where nut-processing stones are located in their foraging range and transport stones between nut trees based on past experience, or a "mental map" (Boesch and Boesch, 1984). Similar to Bossou, the sites at Tai are not "possessed" by any particular individual or group of chimpanzees; rather, they are visited by different individuals from time to time. Since several different chimpanzees independently use the nut-cracking stones at Tai, individuals may not know of previous stone transports and, thus, sometimes do not take the most efficient transport distances.

These examples of nut-cracking and tool use in two populations of chimpanzees illustrate how the processing of food (nuts) and transport behavior depends on the availability of tools. At Bossou, both hammer and anvil stones are transported to the most easily accessible place (the nut tree) and left for later use. In the Tai situation, hammers are brought to stationary anvils located near the tree prior to collection and processing of the nuts.

Although there are parallels, it must be realized that these two examples are not analogous to inferences about the role of hominids at the Olduvai sites. Chimp nut-cracking sites and the Olduvai artifact sites differ in ways that probably signify important evolutionary differences between chimpanzees and early tool-using hominids, at least those at Olduvai. These differences are discussed on p. 288. However, chimpanzee nut-cracking activities do exhibit two features that are integral to the stone cache interpretation of Olduvai. First, in chimpanzees we see a hint that stone transport may involve apparent anticipation of processing of a certain kind of food. Second, it is the presence of implements (anvils and hammers) at nut trees or nearby that focuses food processing activities and defines where refuse (nutshells and implements) becomes concentrated.

Similar to the connection made by chimpanzees between implements and the cracking of nuts, hominids at Olduvai had made a link between stone tools (especially sharp-edged pieces) and the processing of animal tissues. One difference between the two situations is that nut trees are immobile, whereas carcasses would have been obtained in different places from time to time. Under this later condition, I suggest that the transport of stones by Olduvai hominids to specific places in a general area where carcasses were known to be accessible (by scavenging or hunting), and the subsequent return of animal tissues to these places where stones had been left, amplify only slightly two features exhibited by chimpanzee nut-cracking activities: (1) anticipation based on past experience in foraging, and (2) the fact that tool availability guides the concentration (production) of food debris.

The stone cache interpretation proposed here for Olduvai suggests that early hominids anticipated finding food that required processing with stone tools. Anticipation, though, largely entails remembering the past in some detail, not necessarily complex planning ahead. With regard to foraging, the anticipation of future requirements, on the one hand, and learning and memory, on the other, are two aspects of the same phenomenon. The formation of stone caches would have required memory of past experience, particularly precise spatial locations and areas of successful foraging. This kind of memory appears to be represented in the behavioral repertoires of chimpanzees and of a wide range of animals observed in the light of optimal foraging theory. The assertion that stone caches would have required cognitive and strategic skills known only among logistically organized, future-thinking modern humans inappropriately extrapolates behaviors of modern people onto the ancient context at Olduvai and onto the interpretive possibilities (including energetics) explored in this chapter.

*Testability of the Stone Cache Hypothesis*

A second potential problem with the stone cache interpretation is that it simply leaves us with yet another untestable scenario, replacing the home base hypothesis, which originally also seemed untestable. Two points must be made in response to this critique.

First, the computer model of energetics, on which the stone cache idea is partly based, explores one of several adaptive factors related to the transport of resources. The significance of the stone cache idea is that it outlines a set of adaptive advantages and costs underlying the transport and concentration of bones and artifacts in the same places but without invoking a hunter–gatherer form of sociality focused at home bases. As such, the stone cache interpretation provides a *behavioral* alternative to the home base hypothesis. Although *taphonomic* interpretations (e.g., carnivore activity at death sites) have been considered by other researchers as an alternative to the home base explanation of the sites at Olduvai, alternative ideas involving hominid behavior that explain the transport of bones and artifacts have not been given due consideration.

Moreover, each of the factors we have explored to account for the transport of resources can be compared against prior inferences about the Olduvai sites. The stone cache interpretation originates from considering two fundamental influences on behaviors that led to the production of sites. First is the energetics of transporting bones and artifacts. According to the simulation model developed in this chapter, stone is brought into a foraging area, and carcass parts are brought for processing to places where stone is available (i.e., where it has been left). Two features of site formation at Olduvai are particularly pertinent to these aspects of the energetics model: the presence of manuports and long-term revisiting of these sites by hominids. Manuports are consistent with the view that stones were introduced to sites based not just upon expedient need for tools. Periodic reuse of particular, delimited spots over lengthy periods (based on bone weathering), in combination with the evidence for manuports, is consistent with the idea that stone resources provided an attraction for the repeated transport of animal parts to the sites.

The stone cache idea also develops from considering the avoidance of predators by hominids involved in handling parts of carcasses. Based on evidence that hominids and carnivores overlapped ecologically (i.e., in their use of space and carcasses), avoidance of carnivores was one of several theoretically important means identified in Chapter 7 (p. 202) to circumvent potential competition. One aspect of site formation that bears on this matter is the incomplete processing of meat- and marrow-rich bones, some of which bear tool cut marks. This suggests that transitory use of these processing sites may have been important in reducing the risks of interaction with potential predators. Other behavioral mechanisms, such as removal from these sites of pieces attractive to carnivores, evidently did not take place.

Thus, the stone cache/processing site interpretation is founded on a suite of requisite criteria:[11] (1) the tight concentration of transported artifacts and bones; (2) presence of cut marks (or other tool modifications) indicating a link between transported stones and the processing of animal tissues; (3) incomplete processing of bones that are rich in meat or marrow; (4) traces of carnivore gnawing on bones indicating the activity of carnivores at these same spots to which hominids transported stone artifacts; (5) evidence, such as

[11]No single criterion is characteristic *only* of the stone cache interpretation.

from bone weathering, for repeated visits to sites over the long term by hominids and carnivores; and (6) the presence of unmodified and unutilized pieces of stone that can only have been transported by hominids (manuports). This last criterion, in particular, signifies that the introduction of stone anticipated the transport and processing of animal tissues and possibly other foods. Given this set of criteria, the stone cache interpretation can indeed be evaluated relative to the other behavioral explanations defined in this chapter; it adds a behavioral hypothesis that may be either implied or contradicted by archeological data.

## Implications for the Origin of Home Bases

We noted earlier that home bases are an integral feature in the activities of modern hunter–gatherers. The socioecology of hunter–gatherers, which involves the exchange of food and the existence of secure locations for social activities, sleeping, and other maintenance behaviors, is organized around campsites. A decade ago, when home base activity was the inevitable interpretation of Plio–Pleistocene archeological sites such as those at Olduvai, it appeared that home bases were present rather early in human evolution. They coincided with the origin of the genus *Homo* and with the earliest manufacture of stone tools. This meant that hunter–gatherer home bases had no antecedent that was archeologically detectable.

However, the critique of the home base hypothesis for Olduvai and the alternative ideas about resource transport examined in this chapter imply a different view about the origin of home bases. The foraging patterns of nonhuman primates are characterized by feeding on the move, a tendency to consume food immediately where it is located; little or no transport of food takes place (Isaac, 1981a, 1983a). Although hammerstones and nuts are moved to nut-cracking sites by chimpanzees living in the Tai Forest, foraging by chimpanzees, for the most part, and by other apes and monkeys follows the pattern of immediate food consumption.

Inferences about the Olduvai sites suggest a hypothetical course for the development of home base activities from this baseline primate pattern of foraging. In situations where sources of stone and food were widely separated, early hominids introduced tools (and raw materials for their manufacture) into areas where foods could be obtained that typically required tool processing. One such food consisted of animal tissues that were acquired in various parts of the foraging range, not in one stationary location. It is clear that by 1.85 Ma at Olduvai, and perhaps earlier in other places, hominids began using stone tools to process animal bones. When acquired, animal parts that required processing were also moved to places where stone material had been deposited on a previous occasion. Hominids thus produced sites, but probably also foraged in ways generally exhibited by higher primates, with limited social activity at any site of stone/bone accumulation. By foraging for and consuming foods from a wide size range of animals, whether done regularly or sporadically, hominids had ventured into the ecological domain of carnivores. This placed a premium on avoiding potential predators. Since transported animal bones were not completely protected from carnivores, at least at Olduvai, the chances of interaction with carnivores probably would have been lowered if visits by hominids to these processing sites were brief. The attraction of carnivores to these same spots, either to bones and any meaty tissues left by hominids or as agents of bone transport in their own right, suggests that hominid social activity was not focused at these sites as it is at the campsites of modern hunter–gatherers.

The later development of home bases involved focusing both social activity and resource transport in the same places. More specifically, the appearance of home bases involved changes in the spatial dimension of hominid social life and feeding. Obviously, sociality, including foraging and consuming foods together, is characteristic of many primate species. One of the striking innovations of home base activity, however, is that feeding and sociality become focused at a predetermined point. Analysis of the Olduvai sites indicates that recurrent visiting of, and transport of resources to, fixed points were already aspects of hominid behavior by 1.8 Ma. The development of home bases required that this pattern of occasional visits to processing sites (to which stones and animal tissues were brought) became integrated with, and transformed by, a social pattern of return every day by independent foragers to a specific place. Focusing social activities at these predetermined places would have shifted the spatial and temporal patterns of transporting resources. For instance, rather than depositing stone materials in various locations of the foraging range, the transport of resources would have become mapped on to the *transient occupation* patterns that typify nonhuman primates (e.g., use of sleeping trees) and modern hunter–gatherers (in response to distributions of food and other resources). In other words, stone and food transport would have begun to follow social group movements. In some situations, this may have made obsolete both the accumulation of excess stone in specific locations and the long-term, occasional use of particular processing sites.

These ideas comprise only a rough, hypothetical outline of the shifts associated with the origin of home bases. At present, this scenario may be summarized in two steps. First, stone and certain food resources (including animal parts) were introduced to specific places, but these processing areas were not preferential foci of social activity. Second, social activity, the processing of food with tools, and, thus, the transport of resources became focused at the same spots on the landscape (Potts, 1984b).

### Further Behavioral Implications of Stone Cache/Processing Sites

The ideas developed in this chapter suggest that very old archeological sites from Olduvai tell us less about early hominid behavior and social grouping than has been traditionally suggested by the home base hypothesis (Potts, 1984b). From data and inferences derived about the formation of the Olduvai artifact sites, it would appear that social functions that typify the campsite activities of recent hunter–gatherers were *not* focused at these ancient sites. Since home bases (with their social *and* resource transport functions) are integral to the socioecology of recent hunter–gatherers, the latter probably do not adequately portray the socioecological characteristics of tool-making hominids at Olduvai. This idea, of course, contrasts with traditional assumptions.

Are there other living primates that serve as models for reconstructing the socioecology of early hominids at Olduvai?

First, the nut-cracking chimpanzees, discussed on p. 282, do not provide an adequate analogy for the activities of Olduvai hominids, despite the similar link between tools and food processing in both cases. The initial formulation of the stone cache and animal ~~processing~~ interpretation of the Olduvai sites (Potts, 1982) preceded detailed reports of stone transport and nut-cracking by chimpanzees in the Tai Forest (Boesch and Boesch, 1983, 1984). The latter activities illustrate the end of the range of variation in foraging among living nonhuman primates closest to that inferred for hominids at Olduvai. One of the intriguing aspects of nut-cracking behavior is that it produces areas that resemble archeological sites—implements associated with food debris. The nut-cracking stations are revisited, and the hammers and anvils are reused over considerable periods of time. These features are like those inferred for hominids at the Olduvai sites.

However, the degree of transport at Olduvai is of a different order from that exhibited by chimpanzees. This greater reliance on transporting implements and food implies a considerably greater delay in the use of stone and consumption of food than is the case in chimpanzee nut-cracking activities. Although chimpanzees at Tai National Park have been seen to carry stone hammers over 500 m, pieces of raw material on the Olduvai sites were 2–3 km from one main source (quartzite) and up to at least 11 km from one minor source (gneiss). Even though vesicular basalt was available right at locality DK, other types of stone were brought to this locality over a distance of 3 km or more. This does not mean that a given stone was carried such distances in a single trip. Nonetheless, the final distance from source, especially for pieces like the unmodified manuports, suggests a delay in the use of stone that contrasts with the more immediate transport and use of hammers by chimpanzees.

Moreover, the distances over which food is carried by chimpanzees are minimal. Interestingly, nuts are sometimes taken away from the immediate vicinity of a tree to an outcrop anvil. But the vast majority of nut-cracking stations described so far are located at the source of the food itself. In contrast, the Olduvai sites investigated here were not located at the source of animal food (i.e., death sites). Rather, the bones signify primarily animal tissues transported from death sites specifically to places where stone artifacts were also concentrated. The processing of animal tissues, thus, entailed a delay in food consumption. Although the amount of time delay involved is unknown, it would have far exceeded that typically exhibited in chimpanzee nut-cracking behavior. Because animals are mobile, the locations of death sites are not precisely predictable. The transport of animal foods at Olduvai must have revolved around this fact, even though animals may be more likely found, either living or already dead, in certain vegetation zones within an area. Recurrently used processing sites could not have been located directly at the food source as is the case with the nut-cracking sites of chimpanzees.

That aspect of hominid foraging represented by the Olduvai sites is different in kind from the nontool assisted foraging of nonhuman primates and different by degree from the tool-assisted, tool transport type of foraging represented by chimpanzee nut-cracking activity. Besides this difference in foraging, Olduvai hominids probably overlapped ecologically with carnivores and had to respond behaviorally to potential predators in ways not usually faced by nonhuman primates or by modern hunter–gatherers. Although they may rarely have visited the same site at exactly the same time, hominids and carnivores did overlap in the use of space and in modifying particular sets of bones at the Olduvai sites.

Foraging (i.e., how resources are acquired) and predator pressure are generally considered to exert a major influence on the social adaptations of primates and other mammals (e.g., Bernstein and Smith, 1979; Jolly, 1985; Richard, 1981; Wrangham, 1983). If, as suggested here, Olduvai hominids differed from nonhuman primates and hunter–gatherers in these ecological variables, it is possible—perhaps likely—that Olduvai hominids also differed in their social organization and demographic characteristics (Potts, 1987). Based on modern analogues, we could envision a broad range of possible reconstructions of hominid socioecology that are consistent with the inferences about Olduvai site formation. These analogues range from solitary or small groups of foragers to cohesive but shifting family units or multiple male/female groups. The only requirement is that they contribute stone and animal tissues to sites. Were we to demand, as has been the consistent goal in this study, that diagnostic criteria be defined or proposed to recognize, say, one kind of social system from another for the early hominids at Olduvai, there would be immediate agreement that we cannot yet make such a distinction based on material evidence from ancient Olduvai. The site formation processes and inferred activities of hominids at Olduvai do not necessarily point toward any specific socioecological strategy or reconstruction.

I would venture, however, that one aspect of sociality is implied by the processes of site production inferred for Olduvai hominids. The creation of sites was based on the use of two resources together, one of which provides no direct caloric benefit (stones). Given the occurrence of a population of tool-using hominids in a foraging area, if there had been no shared use of these two resources, those individuals who carried stone to one or more locations could have lost them to other individuals who concentrated their efforts on finding animal tissues or other foods. Thus, even without assuming any particular set of social group characteristics, the process of bringing food to places where stone was available (caches) would seem to imply a communal use of stone materials and, possibly, animal tissues. At the very least, the collective, cooperative transport of stone material to particular spots on the landscape would have been necessary. Stone transport (e.g., the distances involved) would imply an expectation of shared use and a predictability about the location of stones at least as great as occurs in the communal use of nut-cracking stones by living chimpanzees.

This proposed incipient reciprocity in foraging is a fundamental aspect of the home base concept. Yet, as suggested in this chapter, it does not imply the presence of home base activity. Such reciprocity also would have played an integral role in the creation of long-term, reusable processing sites—stone caches. That is, reciprocity without home bases is conceivable. Delayed use of resources; anticipated use of stone for processing animal tissues acquired later in time; and mutual, shared access to stone resources at processing sites are all implied by the stone cache interpretation. The home base interpretation also implies delayed use of resources and an ability to anticipate by acting on past experience. Members of the social group return to an acknowledged base camp, food may be brought there for redistribution, and sharing of food is often reciprocated in the future. I suggest that stone caches, that is, the deposition, in specific places, of stone material that was useful for processing food, preceded these social developments associated with home bases and made them possible at some later point in time.

### Recognizing an Ancient Home Base

According to the home base hypothesis, it is the "social focus" of a home base that induces foragers to bring food and tools to a specific place and to carry out important maintenance tasks there. However, factors other than a "social focus" have been explored in this chapter to account for accumulations of bones and artifacts transported in part by hominids. If the hominid contribution to the sites at Olduvai represents something other than home base behavior, this leaves open to question exactly how home bases may be identified in the prehistoric record.

According to the usage adopted by ethnologists, archeologists, and this study, home bases (as known among recent hunter–gatherers) occur when the main location to which resources are brought is also the central place of social activity.[12] At present, a few conditions necessary for home base activity

[12]Central place, or refuge, as defined and analyzed by Hamilton *et al.* (1970), Morrison (1978), Andersson (1978), and Orians and Pearson (1979).

can be proposed that may help to identify home bases in the Pleistocene archeological record. Each of these potential indicators apply only to those situations where clear taphonomic evidence exists for repeated transport of animal bones to a site, for hominid involvement at the site (stone tools in relatively undisturbed context), and hominid activity with the animal bones (e.g., tool cut marks). These indicators are: (1) controlled use of fire, or hearths; (2) extensive processing and consumption of animal tissues by hominids, as indicated by bone breakage; and (3) exclusively hominid modification of bones.

Hominid control over fire and the extensive fragmentation/destruction of animal tissues brought to a site would have, first, limited the attraction of carnivores to sites during periods of hominid occupation and, second, enabled the extraction of all edible tissues from bones (beyond that apparent at the Olduvai sites). Thus, evidence for controlled use of fire, extensive destruction of bones that bear edible tissues, or exclusively hominid modification of bones (i.e., no carnivore modification) would indicate the presence of behaviors essential for home base activity.[13] I propose that these signify requisite conditions, though not necessarily sufficient indicators, for home bases.

What is the earliest evidence for such activities? At present, there is no concensus about the evidence. According to some researchers, baked sediments at Chesowanja and at Site 20, Koobi Fora, Kenya, indicate the occurrence of concentrated fires in Africa back to 1.5 Ma (Clark and Harris, 1985; Gowlett, Harris, Walton, and Wood, 1981).[14] It is unclear, however, that this represents controlled use of fire by hominids as opposed to natural landscape fires (e.g., Isaac, 1982). According to traditional interpretations, hominids had control over fire by at least 400,000 years ago, as indicated by hearths, ash layers, or burned bones from temperate zone localities, notably Zhoukoudian, Vertesszollos, and Terra Amata. Evidence for hominid control over fire at Zhoukoudian has been disputed, and carnivore activity is well represented at this cave site (Binford and Ho, 1985; Binford and Stone, 1986). Further taphonomic analysis is needed to determine whether Middle Pleistocene hominids were able to use fire in order to occupy cave sites and other natural shelters for certain periods to the exclusion of carnivores.

Man-made shelters in the open air, especially in association with hearths, have also been deemed to be a good indication of hunter–gatherer campsites. The shelter–hearth association has been claimed for sites back to about 300,000 years ago—for example, at Terra Amata, France (de Lumley, 1969b). Yet an artificial structure and hearth may also be constructed at a hunting blind or special purpose site, and thus these features are not necessarily direct

[13]The prevelance of hunting is not considered an essential condition of home base activity since the social functions that take place at a home base would not appear to depend on food obtained only from hunted animals.

[14]See Clark and Harris (1985) for a critical review of evidence concerning traces of fire at Lower Pleistocene archeological sites in Africa.

signs of a campsite. Clear evidence of multiple huts and hearths, which do typify recent hunter–gatherer campsites, is not prevalent in the archeological record prior to the Upper Paleolithic (e.g., Klein, 1973).

Intensive processing of animal bones by early hominids is also a matter open to dispute. For example, processes such as trampling, weathering, and decay prior to mineral replacement affect the degree of fragmentation and destruction of bones originally deposited at a site. The fragmentary nature of bones excavated from several of the early archeological sites at Koobi Fora, 1.5 Ma (Bunn, 1982), and those excavated from Upper Pleistocene sites in southern Africa (Klein, 1977, 1980) may have resulted from such processes, not primarily from the extractive tasks of hominids.

An absence of carnivore modification to transported bones processed by hominids would indicate that home base activities were not constrained by carnivores attracted to a site used by hominids. This, of course, does not mean that hominids had home bases in the modern sense, simply that a condition had been met for focusing social activity and meat transport at the exact same locations. Carnivore gnawing appears in all major bone assemblages associated with stone tools that have been studied from Bed I Olduvai and Koobi Fora (Bunn, 1982; this study). Therefore, during the Lower Pleistocene, hominids and carnivores seem to have overlapped in the use of space (in the open air) and in their attraction to bones of particular body sizes and species. The same would appear to be true of cave sites in Europe and Asia during the Pleistocene. The degree to which hominids were able to deter carnivores from coming to these natural shelters (e.g., by the use of fire or by consuming or removing food morsels attractive to carnivores) probably determined whether hominids used these caves as home bases. In an open air situation, bones recently excavated from Olorgesailie, Kenya, dated 700,000–900,000 years old, show tool cut marks but very few damage patterns indicative of carnivore activity, based on preliminary study. In contrast, at Lainyamok—a site probably slightly younger than Olorgesailie and only 45 km away—carnivores were major accumulators of the fossil animal bone assemblages in an area where traces of early hominid activity are very rare. This evidence from the Middle Pleistocene of East Africa contrasts dramatically with the overlap of carnivore and hominid activities from Olduvai and suggests that at least one condition for the development of home bases—the exclusion of carnivores from central areas of hominid activity—may have been met by the early Middle Pleistocene in East Africa (Potts, in press).

Two other pieces of information pertinent to home bases should be noted. First, domesticated carnivores, especially dogs, play a role in fragmenting and destroying bones in the camps of modern hunter–gatherers, and in some cases they keep wild carnivores away from campsites (see p. 201). Domesticated dogs, therefore, could be important in excluding carnivores from areas of hominid activity and in maintaining a home base. However, the earliest domesticated dogs are only about 10,000 years old, which suggests that the behavioral shift to a symbiotic relationship between humans and relatively docile carnivores did not occur much before this time.

Second, archeological sites 1.5 Ma from the Karari Escarpment at Koobi Fora indicate that early hominids transported bones and tools to sites that do not appear to be stone caches (see p. 310). Although this does not necessarily imply that these sites were home bases, tools at one of the sites (Site 50) were evidently used for at least two purposes, based on tool edge microwear: cutting both meat and soft plant material (Keeley and Toth, 1981). The use of tools for diverse purposes at a single site may be considered by some archeologists as reasonably good evidence for the activities of a social group in one spot. However, a clear link has yet to be made between certain diverse ranges of artifact use and the kind of behaviors (e.g., reciprocal sharing, sleeping, maintenance activities) that characteristically take place at human home bases. The demonstration of multiple tool functions at a site is not sufficient evidence for home base activity since diverse tool-using behaviors might be represented at other kinds of sites, including stone caches.

In summary, the present evidence for the development of home bases during the Pleistocene is somewhat blurred. I have suggested some possible indicators of a home base. However, none of these is a sufficient criterion alone for recognizing a home base in the early archeological record. Furthermore, taphonomic analysis of Pleistocene sites, both recently excavated and those known for a long time, has not yet been able to resolve disputed claims about the control of fire by hominids, the means of bone fragmentation at many sites, or the exact relationship between hominid and carnivore modification of bone remains. At least one condition that encouraged the spatial overlap of social activities and resource transport, namely the exclusion of carnivores from areas of hominid activity, apparently existed in some regions inhabited by hominids during the Middle Pleistocene. A degree of hominid control over fire by about 400,000 years ago still seems a reasonable, but not absolutely certain, interpretation, and this innovation also would have helped to protect a home base and would have served to congregate individuals. The origin of home bases may thus date to at least 400,000–700,000 years ago. Yet this proposal remains at the level of a speculation or assertion until a better foundation for inferring home base activities is developed. Whether home base behaviors in the modern hunter–gatherer sense were typical of early hominids before the late Paleolithic also remains to be determined.

## Implications of Late Origins of Home Base Behavior

The sites of Bed I Olduvai are commonly used to illustrate that early hominid social groups were organized around home bases. However, these "best case" examples do not necessarily support that view. It is still possible that sites that preserve only small accumulations of animal bones and artifacts, unlike the sites examined here, served as the home bases of early hominids, and that such sites have yet to be recognized as campsites by archeologists. Another possibility was explored in the previous sections: The kind of sites formed primarily by hominids at Olduvai represent an antecedent to modern home bases, which originated at a later time.

There are two significant points related to this latter possibility. The first concerns the role of the home base concept in scenarios of hominid origins. For example, the hypotheses of Lovejoy (1981) and Tanner (1981), although diametric in the economic roles they posit for male and female protohominids, both state that home bases, areas of food sharing and relative safety, were an integral part in the lives of the first hominids more than 4 Ma. By postulating a very early origin for home bases, these researchers imply that the social and economic arrangements believed to typify the home base activities of hunter–gatherers were prime movers in the origin of hominids in the Pliocene or before. So, for instance, monogamous mating and the return of males to the home base with food are prime movers in Lovejoy's scenario, whereas the gathering and sharing of staple foods by females form the basis of hominid origins in Tanner's view.

The home base has largely served as a theoretical construct in scenarios of human evolution, not contingent upon evidence in the fossil record. There is no evidence from the geologic record for the existence of home bases back to 4 million years or more. Undoubtedly, the presumed importance of home bases for the earliest hominids is fueled by the view that archeologists have *demonstrated* that home bases were a well-developed phenomenon by 2 Ma. It is possible that hominids at Olduvai took food from stone caches or processing areas to other places where the social group was focused. Yet this means that social activity and feeding were not located at the primary places of bone and stone tool transport and accumulation. We are still left with something different from home bases in the modern hunter–gatherer sense of the term. This research on Olduvai indicates that the existence of such home bases has not yet been demonstrated archeologically. It calls for reevaluation of the home base model for all early archeological sites and for caution in assuming that home bases (i.e., something different from the sleeping sites and feeding locations that typify other primates) were a component in the lives of the earliest hominids.

A second, related point is that the home base interpretation links together several crucial changes in hominid evolution, for example, increased consumption of meat, changes in foraging strategy (to include hunting and scavenging), tool manufacture and increased dependence on technology, economic interdependence among adults in the manner of recent hunter–gatherers, language as an aid in the complicated network of social relations typical of home base activities, and brain size increase. The critique here of what has been construed to be the best material evidence for home bases at Olduvai 1.8 Ma and the possibility of viable alternative interpretations (e.g., stone caches), suggests that the events and changes integrated by the home base hypothesis were not necessarily all kicked into motion by the time of the earliest archeological sites. Based on discussion in the previous section, let us say that home bases in the modern human sense did not begin to typify the socioecology of hominids until, say, 700,000 years ago. In that case, we may have to separate in time such events as the first major increase in brain size and earliest production of stone tools, on the one hand, from the development of language or complex reciprocity, systems of hunter–gatherer band organization, and other features that were probably furthered by the spatial focusing of social life and resource transport in the same places. Moreover, a significant change by 2 Ma in foraging strategy and diet, involving animal foods, need not imply that forms of social organization found among tropical hunter–gatherers had also developed by then.

Investigations of modern hunter–gatherers and the adoption of the home base concept by many archeologists have helped to build an important evolutionary relationship between modern hunter–gatherers and the way of life of early human ancestors. The hunter–gatherer mode of adaptation, at least in the tropics and subtropics, is commonly viewed to be an ancient adaptation, extending back to at least 2 Ma (Lee and DeVore, 1968: 3). The persistent characterization of the lives of all hunter–gatherers as *exclusively* one thing ("nasty, short, and brutish") or another ("original affluent society") undoubtedly arises out of the belief that hunting–gathering is a unitary phenomenon honed by a very long evolutionary past (Smith and Winterhalder, 1981: 4). The general model of band society (Service, 1962) is essentially a statement about human ancestry. Extention of the study of a single hunting–gathering people to characterize hunter–gatherers in the past, as might be claimed in the case of the San studies, is similarly meant to convey something universal about human evolution (Lee, 1979: 490–494). According to that view, the Pleistocene evolutionary past shared by all humans is largely that of a hunter–gatherer, a way of life that has shaped our sociality and our anatomical, physiological, mental, and emotional makeup (Ardrey, 1976; Konner, 1982; Morris, 1969; Washburn and Lancaster, 1968; Wilson, 1978).

The proposal that home bases, as a fundamental component of hunter–gatherer adaptation, developed later in human evolution than originally believed opens these ideas about human nature to question. Revised thinking about home bases, in retrospect, parallels several recent independent studies that claim that fundamental biological and behavioral variables such as maturation rate, secondary altriciality, hunting and its social correlates (e.g., sexual division of labor), and the ability to generate stylistic heterogeneity so characteristic of cultures today, all underwent significant changes later in hominid evolution than usually recognized (Binford, 1985; Bromage and Dean, 1985; Dean, 1985; Dunnell, 1986; Lewin, 1987; Shipman, 1983; Smith, 1986; Tague and Lovejoy, 1986; White, 1982). *If this is so*, then the behavioral, social, and reproductive features that appear to typify humans probably do not represent a coherent package ingrained in our biology by virtue of *millions* of years of natural selection. Rather, they would reflect a mosaic pattern of change, similar to the varying rates of evolution in different aspects of hominid anatomy, that is, a series of changes laid on top of one another through time, under varied conditions of survival and reproduction. In this case, the study of hominid behavior and ecology during the past 2 million years or more may attempt to document the trajectory of human origins rather than simply convey the fine tuning of a hunter–gatherer adaptation that is supposed to have evolved nearly full blown by at least 2 Ma and has stuck with us ever since.

# 10

# Conclusion

## A Hierarchy of Inferences

What we know about early hominids at Olduvai (and elsewhere) is tightly linked to the process and structure of making inferences. Ideas about hominid activity are based on a hierarchy of conditional inferences, which corresponds to the levels of analysis mentioned in Chapter 1. Thus, for example, the stone cache interpretation is one of several ideas we can consider to explain why hominids carried resources to particular spots on the landscape. Yet this is what might be called a third-order inference, which depends on a set of prior interpretations. The latter include taphonomic (first-order) inferences (e.g., that the bones and artifacts indeed represent behaviorally transported remains and that hominids played a role in this) and second-order inferences concerning the specific activities of hominids at these sites and the ecological milieu (e.g., carnivore activities). There is also a conditional, or interdependent, set of inferences that pertains to site taphonomy alone. To distinguish agents of bone transport as "primarily hominid" and "primarily carnivore" depends on accurate recognition of stone tool and carnivore damage, contextual inferences based on the accumulations of stone artifacts and bone concentrations made by carnivores, as well as other lines of evidence and interpretation. On the one hand, some inferences are directly drawn from controlled experiments and "first principles." Winnowing of small objects by water flow is one example, and marks on bone surfaces can also be related to basic differences between, say, the effect of stone versus enamel on bone. In contrast, other inferences are based on multiple lines of data and on theoretical ideas or recurrent observations from one or more disciplines that offer an interpretation of those data. The idea that the relative frequency of carnivores in a faunal assemblage corresponds to the degree of interference competition over carcasses is an example of this type of inference. The validity of higher order inferences relies upon an intersecting web of lower order inferences of various kinds. The latter serve as the foundation for interpreting hominid activities and paleoecology.

No progress is likely to be made in the interpretation of excavated sites if we fail to recognize this inferential hierarchy and, thus, confuse diverse levels of inference. The view that the Olduvai sites represent behaviorally transported assemblages, for instance, must not be confounded with higher order interpretations, such as about stone caches. Hence, the latter interpretation cannot be correct if key, prior inferences, such as behavioral trans-

port of the assemblages or the presence of tool cut marks and carnivore damage
at the site, were shown to be incorrect. However, if the stone cache viewpoint
proves to be unlikely, this would not invalidate prior inferences about bone
damage or behavioral transport.

Other examples can be given. Surprisingly, the debate about whether
hominids at Olduvai were scavengers or hunters hardly ever concerns whether
these hominids scavenged or hunted. It usually concerns discrepancies in more
fundamental levels of observation and inference. First-order inferences accepted by one researcher are not necessarily accepted by another, which is
why I refer to these as conditional inferences. Discrepancies may arise in
whether a bone assemblage represents a palimpsest of death sites or bones
transported to specific places, or whether skeletal element frequencies result
mainly from hominid activities or carnivore activities. These discrepancies
manifest themselves up the hierarchy into different ideas about hominid foraging. What would appear to be very basic first-order inferences are still a
matter of debate in some cases (e.g., the frequency and anatomical distribution
of tool cut marks on bones from a site). There are also problems with researchers working with different data sets from the same site (e.g., skeletal
parts considered by Bunn and Kroll [1986] and Binford [1981, 1986]). Data
associated with lower order interpretations, then, form the basis for moving
on to a higher level in the hierarchy (hominid foraging) *and* thus form the
basis for disagreements about hominid activities. Resolving these differences
will depend on rigorously tested, standardized methods of observation and
analysis. At present, each researcher looks at sites and faunal remains in a
different way; the results have tended to get us nowhere quite rapidly.

The hierarchy of inferences about early hominids means that certain kinds
of interpretations need to be kept separate from others (Potts, 1984a). For
instance, although the causes of bone modification inform about the causes
of bone accumulation at a site, they are not necessarily equivalent. A hierarchical approach distinguishes questions about hominid versus carnivore
modification of bones from the relative roles these different agents may have
played in accumulating bones at a site (p. 143). The latter issue, in turn, is
considered separately from questions about the nature of hominid activities
at sites. This approach, thus, avoids the pitfalls of trying to assess all at once
ideas about hominid diet, hunting and scavenging, the home base issue, and
the relative degree of hominid versus carnivore involvement at sites. The
problem of merging these various, separable issues is exemplified by the
analysis of Olduvai in the book, *Bones* (Binford, 1981). Binford's analysis uses
the representation of skeletal parts *(a)* to identify carnivore and hominid activity, *(b)* to evaluate predation versus marginal scavenging (the latter is
equated with the availability of a particular kind of food—bone marrow), and
*(c)* to critique the matter of hominid home bases. The critique of home bases
is inextricably tied to the interpretation that hominids were marginal scavengers, which is equated with the inference that hominids only had access to

bones of low food utility, essentially only marrow. The reasoning is that food sharing at home bases cannot be supported by an occasional morsel of marrow. However, as noted in Chapter 8, the interpretation that hominids were marginal scavengers of bones of low food utility results inevitably from associating high quality parts with the activity of carnivore predators. When these aspects of skeletal part composition are factored out, the residual attributed to hominids can only be as a marginal scavenger. Binford's ideas about determining the unambiguous contributions of carnivores and hominids to bone assemblages represent a significant intellectual challenge. However, his specific view about hominid diet and foraging and the critique of the home base hypothesis are an inevitable outcome of the method used to assess hominid versus carnivore roles in site formation. This logical flaw arises from confounding different levels of inferential hierarchy and confusing too many separable issues.

In contrast, the hierarchical approach presented here, using criteria defined in Part II of this book, first examines the contributions of various agents in site formation. Acknowledging that different processes of transport, modification, and attrition often yield similar patterns of faunal/skeletal composition, the degree of fit between site data and the criteria defined for each process helps to assess relative contributions of agents of site formation. General acceptance of only two diagnostic features of hominid activity, tool cut marks and the transport of stone artifacts, means that contextual information becomes particularly helpful in evaluating the role of hominids at sites. The process of artifact transport and extreme degree of concentration of stone artifacts parallels the accumulation of bones (some with cut marks) at five sites we have examined. The *relative* importance of hominids as bone collectors at these sites is clear when contrasted to sites where artifacts were not concentrated and the bones overwhelmingly exhibit damage and preservation patterns distinctive of assemblages made by particular carnivores. Once these relative contributions are defined, *different* kinds of data concerning, for example, species or skeletal part representation, may be used to assess higher order questions: To what degree do "primarily hominid" and "primarily carnivore" assemblages differ or overlap? Did hominid and carnivore bone collectors differ consistently in their relative timing of access to carcasses? Do "primarily hominid" sites represent home bases? Indeed, higher order inferences are made assuming that prior taphonomic inferences are valid. Nonetheless, analysis of diverse questions about hominid activity and ecology must be based at least somewhat on independent criteria and data from those used to infer basic aspects of site taphonomy. Accordingly, the simple presence of cut marks on bones will not automatically mean that sites represent home bases where food was shared. Inferences about scavenging will not automatically relate to nonhome base explanations. The mere presence of stone tools will not necessarily imply hominid transport of bones found in the vicinity, and so on.

Taphonomy has been called a "science studying unique events," namely episodes in the past each with its own peculiar combination of events which we call site formation. Yet this definition leaves us with a contradiction since science is founded on repeatable observations under controlled conditions. The study of sites like those at Olduvai relies upon repeatable observations and comparisons in the present that yield information about the *variables* of site formation. Here the emphasis is upon processes, not on simply replicating static results (Binford, 1977). For instance, defining diagnostic criteria for transported assemblages of bones versus attritional landscape assemblages requires understanding the processes of animal death, disarticulation, scattering, and burial. And this requires repeated observation of carcasses in modern habitats.

But what about higher order ideas—aspects of hominid behavior now being considered by paleoanthropologists for which there are not closely analogous phenomena in the present to study? Scavenging as a regular mode of access to carcasses by stone tool-using hominids does not exist today. However, the variables that make scavenging possible are available for study (Blumenschine, 1986; Schaller and Lowthar, 1969). Moreover, ecological and even social processes by which a primate group may adopt a greater role in eating meat and hunting may also be investigated, as exemplified by field studies of baboons (Strum, 1981). Stone caches represent a strategy that facilitates bringing food and tool resources together in the same places—a strategy that, in its specific form, is not known in the present. However, resource transport by a variety of species can be studied, including the informative case in which chimpanzees reuse nut-cracking sites and transport hammerstones. Such studies provide data and insights about the ways that materials from the environment are collected in particular places and the ecological contexts in which this occurs. It is doubtful that simple, diagnostic signs of one possible behavior system versus another can be defined. Nonetheless, detailed inferences about site formation, ecological settings, and smaller scale aspects of hominid activity do permit evaluation of broad features of hominid behavioral ecology that relate specifically to producing sites.

## Hominid Behavior and Paleoecology at Olduvai

Given these ideas about the process of inference, I wish to summarize the results of this investigation on the sites of Bed I Olduvai.

In habitats that resembled modern savanna mosaics, tool-making hominids carried artifacts and parts of carcasses to specific places on the landscape. At least one species of carnivore also collected bones during the period of Bed I deposition, 1.85–1.70 Ma. We can begin to separate out environment (i.e., availability of fauna) from habitat use by particular bone collectors by comparing bone assemblages made mainly by different species. Thus, relatively low numbers of equids transported to the artifact sites (compared with zebra frequencies in modern savannas) seem to reflect poorer sampling of such animals, and possibly of plains habitats, than in the "primarily carnivore" assemblage at FLKNN–2 and also at artifact sites later in the Olduvai sequence. This hints that Bed I hominids transported few equids to their sites, though the relative abundance of this group probably did not fall outside of the range of modern savannas. There is a suggestion, though, that suids were relatively more abundant than occurs in any savanna known today.

Hominids were dependent on stone implements for certain tasks, as evidenced by cut marks on animal bones. However, it is not known how often such activities involving tool manufacture and use were performed. The manufacture of tools was extremely conservative. It largely involved (1) manufacture of sharp-edged pieces through stone-on-stone percussion and (2) transformations between diverse tool/core forms as flaking was initiated, stopped, proceeded, and finally halted by burial or other loss of the stone core. At each site, stone raw materials were left that were obtained several kilometers (Naibor Soit quartzite) to many kilometers away (Kelogi gneiss) from their sources. This indicates considerable mobility (wide home ranges) among stone tool-carrying hominids. Movement over such distances probably promoted the diversity of habitats and animal species sampled (and transported) by hominids. Although we have keyed in on the interpretation of spatially delimited sites, this unit of analysis is undoubtedly a small part of a larger pattern of hominid movement, foraging, and stone artifact deposition. Hominids revisited these particular places to process parts of carcasses with stone implements. However, these sites do not represent static depots of debris. Artifacts were undoubtedly carried and discarded in the foraging range some distance from the places of concentrated debris. In the absence of extensive excavation of individual paleosols, it is not possible to test directly ideas about spatially broad (and time-averaged) patterns of artifact discard and related land use.

The evidence of cut marks (slicing marks predominate), meat-bearing bones, and overall site taphonomy indicate about as clearly as possible that particular hominids were eating meat from large ungulates. Patterns of bone damage at the artifact sites also indicate that marrow was processed to a greater degree by percussion of limb bone diaphyses than occurred at FLKNN–2 and Long K, where the technique of access to limb bone marrow typifies that of carnivores.

Viewpoints about early hominid foraging tend to fall into extreme categories: man the hunter; woman the gatherer; and, more recently, hominid the scavenger. Such views are in curious conflict with broad behavioral variation in food consumption and ways of collecting food in apes and tropical latitude hunter–gatherers (Harding and Teleki, 1981; Jolly, 1985; Lee, 1979; Richard, 1985). They also conflict with evidence from the Olduvai faunal assemblages. Since these assemblages were transported behaviorally, they provide information about the variety of animals obtained and the relative timing of access by hominid and carnivore bone collectors. One consistent aspect of site production in Bed I Olduvai was *diversity*—both in the faunas and stone resources brought to the artifact sites. Animal bones transported to the artifact sites point toward a diversified, or nonspecialized, means of foraging; hominids represent the predominate agent of transport to these sites. The diversity of faunal body sizes, for example, was greater than the range of body sizes exploited by any mammalian carnivore today or by carnivore bone collectors in Bed I Olduvai. In addition, the artifact sites display a less specialized array of skeletal units (forelimb, hindlimb, and axial), whereas carnivore bone collectors at Olduvai produced assemblages with narrower skeletal diversity. The latter can be related to consistently early access to carcasses relative to other bone collectors; the patterns at the artifact sites appear to reflect *mixed* timing of access to carcasses and selection of carcass parts, primarily by hominids. Scavenging was probably part of the foraging repertoire, though a marginal, scrounging style of scavenging is not indicated. Altogether, none of these data can support any of the extreme, or narrow, views of hominid foraging.[1] It is not possible to assess the significance of acquiring animal tissues by hominids compared with plant foods. The fact that the production and location of artifact sites may have been guided by the acquisition of plant foods is a problem of interpretation that must be acknowledged.

Comparisons between "primarily hominid and carnivore" assemblages suggest that these two agents overlapped in the use of ungulate body sizes, particular species, and types of skeletal elements. By itself, this evidence for use of similar resources does not imply that hominids and carnivores interacted frequently or that competition determined the behavioral ecology of these species. Nonetheless, evidence from the artifact sites alone shows that hominids and carnivores visited these same delimited spots on the landscape *and* had access to at least some of the same carcass parts left there. This aspect of site formation strongly suggests that avoidance of predators by those hominids that helped to generate these sites was important. Critique of the home base hypothesis is largely based on the idea that hominids engaged in very brief visits to these sites and avoided them during likely periods of carnivore activity. Since there are no indications that other strategies were employed to minimize carnivore attraction to these sites, it appears unreasonable to posit that these sites were safe refuges or that the prominent activities at

---

[1]Based on taphonomic inferences drawn in Part II, the circumstances of preservation of Olduvai microfauna are difficult to evaluate. Andrews (1983) reports that the body parts of small mammals found at FLK North-1/2 (not included in this study) are typical of those produced by small mammalian carnivores. Leakey (1971) suggests that some of the small mammal assemblages could be due to hominids. Poor understanding of microfauna taphonomy and the influence of water at each site examined here, however slight, means that the exact processes by which the microfauna was introduced are difficult to infer. The contribution of small vertebrates to hominid diets, thus, remains unclear.

such places encouraged social grouping to become focused there. Taphonomic study of the South African cave sites indicates that early hominids (represented in Member 4 at Sterkfontein and Member I at Swartkrans) were highly susceptible to predation by carnivores (Brain, 1981). In fact, Brain (1981: 271) suggests that predators may have taken advantage of unsafe sleeping sites of hominids to obtain hominid prey. Given this background of hominid–carnivore interactions prior to and overlapping with the time range of Bed I Olduvai (albeit in a different region), predator avoidance by hominids involved in transporting and processing large mammal carcasses would evidently be at a premium. Repeated, but brief, visits by hominids that were not oriented specifically toward social activity would also have served to circumvent competition with carnivores interested in large mammal carcasses.

The Olduvai evidence indicates stability through time in the activities of hominids that led to the production of sites. All of the artifact sites show a consistent accumulation of diverse raw materials (at least four different types), a diversity of large mammal taxa and body sizes, and highly consistent relative frequencies of taxa. This consistency among the sites is striking, given that faunal and artifact resources were collected during periods representing highly varied environmental conditions over perhaps 150,000 years. Environmental settings evidently ranged from highly arid (FLK North–6) to rather moist (FLKNN–3 and DK). Apparently, the production of sites was not a response to narrow climatic conditions. Despite paleoclimatic variations, indeed there is little evidence for any faunal change within Bed I Olduvai (Gentry and Gentry, 1978). These considerations suggest that hominid transport of artifacts and animal parts to sites may have been one feature of ecological equilibrium that existed in the Olduvai region back through the earliest known sites. Given the possible taphonomic differences at site DK, the pattern of site production there appears to have been comparable to that evident in upper Bed I.[2] The apparent lack of influence of climatic (abiotic) factors on site production activities, but the suggested influence of carnivores (a biotic factor) on hominid site production, are expected in a behavior system that is largely "K-selected." Such systems are characterized by increased investment in survival of the young and by open, or learned, behavior programs that are more responsive to contingencies in the biotic environment than to those in the physical environment (Mayr, 1974; Wilson, 1975: 101; Wilson and Bossert, 1971).

The transport of stones and animal bones at Olduvai means that hominids delayed their consumption of meat/marrow and their use of stone resources. However, this does not imply that these hominids lived at home bases, in the sense of modern hunter–gatherer campsites. This conclusion is illustrated by the computer model of site production we explored in Chapter 9. More

[2]We have noted that the consistency in taxonomic abundance among the Olduvai sites probably results from time-averaging. This corresponds with the inference, based independently on bone surface weathering, that each site samples carcasses over at least a several year period of time.

important, this conclusion also stems from the evidence of site formation itself. When energetics or other nonsocial influences on resource transport are explored (Chapter 9), it is not meant to conflict with the idea that these hominids lived in social groups. It is almost certain that hominids did form social groups for the following reasons: (1) Social groupings are a general part of higher primate life; (2) tool use and manufacture were undoubtedly learned in a social setting; and (3) the feasibility of site production would seem to depend on communal use of stone materials at sites. Comparative socioecology among African hominoids may even serve to point out some likely features of early hominid social groups, such as relatively closed social networks and female exogamy (Wrangham, 1987).

In primates, associations have been suggested between wide home ranges and large social groups and between predator pressure and group defense. In addition, large home ranges and predator pressure have been linked to relatively large body sizes (Bertram, 1978; Clutton-Brock and Harvey, 1977; Krebs and Davies, 1981). We have noted that hominids ranged far to transport stone materials and that predator avoidance was important. Yet the nature of these correlations helps little to understand specific selective forces acting on hominids or to reconstruct the particulars of social grouping. The reason is that fundamental ecological variables, such as the detailed distribution of foods, intervene and disrupt the simple socioecological links between, say, predator pressure and social group characteristics (e.g., Clutton-Brock, 1974). When interactive, causal links among ecological and social variables become better understood, inferences about the range of habitats from which hominids carried resources, about the distance of movement, and about carnivore–hominid relationships may suggest specific ideas regarding group size, possibly group fission–fusion, and group foraging strategies.

Important shifts in social behavior may well have accompanied the carrying of stones, processing of food with stone implements, and consumption of meat. The conclusion reached here, however, is that home base social behaviors were not focused at the particular sites we have examined. Moreover, the apparent absence of evidence for a home base (resource transport and social activities focused in the same place) suggests that key ingredients in the socioecology of modern hunter–gatherers did not exist. In no way does this imply that the socioecology of chimpanzees or other nonhuman primates better portrays these hominids of Bed I Olduvai. The Olduvai sites do represent a shift from a nonhuman primate type foraging system. Foods found in nonstationary locations (i.e., carcasses of mobile animals) required processing with stone tools. Stone implements had to be available in the foraging area and especially nearby when carcasses were acquired. It is likely that hominids did carry tools with them through the foraging range (see p. 243), and it is possible that they carried stone tools most of the time. However, we know that these hominids deposited stones in certain places on the landscape that were revisited over lengthy periods of time; some of these stones were unmodified and minimally modified pieces some distance from their sources. In trying to understand the role of hominids in forming sites, the stones themselves signify an attractive "magnet" to account for the repeated introduction of animal carcasses by hominids to these sites for processing.

The transfer of stone tools and chunks of unused raw material to particular areas in the foraging range—perhaps originally at the site of an animal carcass or at a spot where shade or other foods were available—defined a focus for transport and processing of a wide diversity of animal parts and for further transport of stone. As envisioned here, this behavior pattern was similar to activities carried out by certain chimpanzees that over a lengthy period revisit nut-cracking locations defined by the presence of nut-cracking stones. The primary difference is that in chimpanzees the food source itself (the nut trees) determines where processing takes place, whereas hominids at Olduvai transported both the implements and the food source that required processing.

Past experience and memory, on the one hand, and anticipation and planning, on the other, are flip sides of the same coin in the foraging behavior of animals and are integral aspects of cognition (Menzel and Wyers, 1981). Thus, resource transport by Olduvai hominids, which involved bringing two resources obtained in different places to the same spot, probably entailed cognitive mechanisms enhanced over those signified by the nut-cracking sites of chimpanzees (cf. "mental maps," Boesch and Boesch, 1984). However, this does not imply planned, logistically organized storage, as evidenced in many human groups (Binford, 1980). In contrast to "central place foraging" (in the sense of Isaac, 1983a, 1984), it is possible that the processing of carcasses became linked with the availability of stone tools through "multiple place foraging." The latter type of foraging need not postulate the social correlates implicit in the home base view. In multiple place foraging, sites represent the primary places on the landscape to which resources were transported. The animal bones signify that the consumption of foods requiring stone tool processing was necessarily delayed. In addition, shared use of stone resources represents an incipient form of reciprocity. In these ways, multiple place foraging foreshadows the development of home bases.

Whether one or multiple sites were used by hominids at any given time, this nonhome base interpretation is founded upon certain criteria that may ultimately permit tracing the development of hunter–gatherer home bases from their antecedents. A distinction between home bases and the type of processing site inferred for Olduvai may be based, for example, upon the following: (1) evidence of activities that made the places of bone transport unattractive to carnivores (see p. 291) and (2) evidence that bone and stone transport had become grafted on to the movements of social groups, characterized in tropical hunter–gatherers by transient use of resources and short-term periods of reoccupation of specific, delimited spots.

## Differences among Researchers

In previous chapters, I have explained how certain views and inferences presented here contrast with those of other researchers who have discussed the sites of Bed I Olduvai. These differences have largely concerned inferences about site taphonomy or specific aspects of hominid activity. Researchers also diverge in their overall interpretations of the Olduvai sites. I wish to briefly summarize and comment on these in order to clarify the alternatives that are currently contemplated.

The food sharing hypothesis, and indirectly the home base interpretation, receives support from Bunn and Kroll (1986). A point of evidence in favor of the home base view is that hominid foraging for meat was not confined to scrounging for disarticulated scraps leftover from carnivore kills. Based on evidence for hominid butchery of carcasses, it can be argued that hominids had access to large quantities of meat and marrow. According to Bunn and Kroll (1986), this seems to imply cooperative food sharing. In earlier articles, Bunn (1981, 1983a) has suggested similarly that the presence and distribution of tool cut marks on bones from FLK "Zinj" indicate social acquisition and consumption of meat and marrow at these sites. The evidence of bone weathering for long periods of bone accumulation at the Olduvai sites is also rejected by these researchers, apparently in favor of a period of site use closer to that exhibited by modern hunter–gatherers. Thus, each view adopted about the Olduvai sites, specifically FLK "Zinj," is in accord with the home base, or central place foraging, interpretation.

Some comments were made in Chapter 8 pertinent to the sharing of meat and the amount of meat available at these sites. The representation of medium and large ungulates is not greater than expected in the environment at large; thus, animals with large yields of meat were not necessarily selected preferentially. In addition, as Hill (1984) has pointed out, the transport and accumulation of meat-bearing bones of a wide size range of animals occurs at hyena dens. Yet these represent neither foci of adult social life nor places where food is known to be exchanged among foraging hyenas. In other words, there is no necessary connection between transport of meat- and marrow-rich carcass parts and home base activities.

The most important difference from the present investigation, however, concerns how Bunn and Kroll treat the evidence for carnivore damage. Although they acknowledge it, the carnivore contribution to site formation is largely ignored and overshadowed by their attention to tool cut marks. As noted repeatedly here, carnivore damage to the bones indicates not only the presence of large and small scavenger/predators at the sites but also suggests that hominids were not responsible for consuming some portion of the edible tissues represented at these sites. From one point of view, carnivore activities can be thought to mask evidence of hominid activities. Carnivore damage to bones simply limits our abilities to discern the nature of hominid activities at sites. The butchery and food sharing interpretation adopts this view. In contrast, the view adopted here is that the action of carnivores, as one element of site formation, is an important, consistent part of the context of hominid activities at Olduvai and, in fact, *informs* about the nature of hominid activities at these sites.

It is important to acknowledge that home bases and food sharing remain important ingredients in our ideas about the development of human behavior and social life. Yet there are now clear alternatives to the home base explanation of the Bed I sites, believed until recently to provide textbook examples of home bases in the early archeological record. These alternatives appear to account for evidence about hominid and carnivore activities and other aspects of artifact site formation that the home base hypothesis has tended to ignore. Hominid transport and processing of animal bones represent an obvious similarity to the activities of present-day foragers. But this similarity does not provide grounds for ignoring ways in which the Olduvai sites and hominid activities differ, however subtly, from the present.

As proposed by Isaac, the term "central place foraging" may be preferred over "home base" and "food sharing." However, this concept of central place foraging connects together the same set of features distinctive of the home base hypothesis—particularly the focusing of social activity and debris accumulation at the same places. In zoological use of the term, "central place" need not have these connotations of a home base. For example, Blumenschine (1986: 147–148) suggests a central place interpretation of hominid land use that does not carry with it the connotations of hunter–gatherer home bases. He envisions larger foraging groups than occur among modern hunter–gatherers, which did not necessarily undergo daily fission and fusion nor were characterized by sexual division of labor. Moreover, return of the hominid foraging unit to safe refuge was important in minimizing the risks of predation. This version of central place foraging is compatible with the critique of the home base hypothesis pertinent to Olduvai. However, it leaves open for explanation the precise ways in which sites were produced, that is, why artifacts and bones were transported to a specific spot on the landscape, since this did not serve as a safe, social refuge. Repeated attraction to a stone cache/processing site or another valued resource location again must come into play.

Finally, various points of difference have been noted previously between the analyses and findings presented by Binford (1981) and those presented here. Based on analyses in his book *Bones*, most of the Olduvai artifact sites examined here are interpreted to be palimpsests of carnivore kills from which hominids were able to obtain marrow bones. This interpretation is countered in at least two respects by the analyses in this book. First, the transport of animal bones and stone artifacts is a fundamental inference, one which the analysis in *Bones* misses for most of these sites (see Chapter 3). Second, a scrounging style of late scavenging is not warranted by the evidence of either skeletal parts or tool cut marks (see Chapter 8).

In a later book, Binford (1984) summarizes his views about hominid foraging. He states that marrow bones were scavenged from carnivore kills in areas that hominids visited during mid-day, particularly water margins that attract game and carnivores. These bones were then taken short distances for processing of marginal food bits with stone tools. The Olduvai sites, thus, are now claimed to represent hominid transported assemblages in such mid-day rest locations (Binford, 1984: 255, 266). "In any event, once collected, a potential food requiring processing would be carried to the place where the processing could be readily performed. In the case of the animal parts remaining at sites of ravaged carcasses, at least one processing prerequisite would be usable hammers and probably anvils" (1984: 260). The latter view certainly converges on the concept of the stone cache presented here and earlier (Potts, 1982, 1984b). Neither this idea nor the view that the Olduvai sites strongly reflect hominid transport of bones is foreshadowed by the analysis and conclusions offered in *Bones*. Nonetheless, it is still claimed that carnivore kill sites form a strong component of the Olduvai bone assemblages (Binford, 1984: 249–255).

Binford (1984: 263–264) provides a useful general model of early hominid land use that involves routed feeding. Hominid movement over the landscape was guided by the presence of locations in the local habitat where important natural resources were available (e.g., water, protected sleeping area, outcrops of stone raw material). Due to the value of these resources, hominids used these locations on a regular, repetitive basis. Accumulations of debris were produced at some of these places. In the case of Olduvai, these sites largely resulted from the common attraction of hominids and carnivores to water sources, in particular.

As pointed out by Isaac (e.g., 1983a, 1984) and as discussed in Chapter 9, attraction to valued resources must be an important factor to consider in hominid land use. This factor indeed may account for the accumulation of bones in a general area and also identifies conditions leading to the activity of carnivore predators and hominids in the same vicinity. However, an array of taphonomic studies of modern East African habitats (Chapter 3) suggest that the Olduvai bone concentrations do not have a strong "kill site" component and that they (along with the artifact concentrations) are too delimited to be explained by attraction to general "preferred locations," such as lake margins. Instead, resource locations that are spatially more confined might offer conditions for transporting artifacts and raw materials to more specific places where animal carcasses are processed. Other than social factors (as in the home base hypothesis), the leading alternative factors thought to guide the repeated use of sites by hominids are the availability of stone itself used in processing (stone cache) and the presence of other (unidentified) valued resources that are spatially delimited. As suggested earlier and also by Shipman (1986a: 37), these two factors are not mutually exclusive. Repeatedly used sources of transported stone may have been produced at places such as trees providing shade, small waterholes, or plant food sources.

This brief summary of alternative viewpoints reflects the need to entertain and constantly reassess a diversity of ideas about early hominid sites and activities—a type of research exemplified by Isaac with tremendous influence (e.g., 1983a, 1983b; 1984). As I discussed on a rather preliminary basis in Chapter 9, the key will be to define criteria that distinguish among the behavioral alternatives. Such criteria are likely to derive from (1) considering fundamental factors that potentially affected hominid behavior—such as avoidance of predators, social sharing of large portions of food, and availability of stone for processing food—and (2) defining suites of features of site formation that uniquely reflect the impact of such factors. Thus, the transport of bones (delayed consumption) and processing of meat and marrow are expectations of the home base and food sharing ideas. Yet these features *in combination with* others that indicate the importance of predator avoidance (e.g., carnivore activity at sites, lack of intensive carcass processing) suggest that the home base interpretation does not apply and that hominids were not the only ones to have a "share" of the meat. Moreover, long-term reuse of sites at which pieces of raw material had been left implies that the availability of stone to carry out processing tasks was of added significance. In this way, we may be able to assess the importance of ecological, foraging, social, and other factors around which broad interpretations of hominid sites (and critiques of those ideas) are based.

## Behavioral Variation in Time and Space

In the last chapter, we considered several broad, evolutionary implications that arise from this study of Bed I Olduvai. Nevertheless, inferences drawn from the analysis of a small sample of sites, spanning possibly 150,000 years, from one sedimentary basin must not be expanded to fill the whole adaptive picture for tool-making hominids of the Plio–Pleistocene. Situational factors, such as the density of ungulates and carnivores and the distribution of stone sources, undoubtedly varied from region to region, and we have examined in some detail how such factors may have influenced hominid activities and patterns of site formation. Therefore, instead of uniformity, it is reasonable to expect that site formation and associated hominid activities varied in response to diverse contexts. Such is the case when we compare, for instance, the archeological sites of Bed I Olduvai and Koobi Fora, Kenya.

The best studied sites from Koobi Fora are located on the Karari Escarpment, 20 km east of Lake Turkana, and dated 1.6–1.3 Ma (Harris, 1978; Isaac, in press; Isaac and Harris, 1978). Compared with Olduvai, the Karari situation is characterized by an overall smaller size of artifacts (especially away from the basin margin where stone cobbles for making tools were less available), extensive curation of core forms, much lower frequencies of manuports, and an apparent dropoff in the number of sites away from the basin margin (Harris, 1978; Isaac, 1984; Toth, 1982). These facets of site formation and distribution do not seem to correspond to stone-caching behavior. Regardless of specific interpretations, it is evident that the relationships among habitats, stone material sources, hominid site locations, and hominid habitat use created an adaptive and ecological milieu for site production at Koobi Fora that differed from that at Olduvai. In addition, sites containing rich clusters of artifacts but no bones are known from the Karari, but these are nonexistent in Bed I Olduvai. Although the extent of decay of bones is difficult to evaluate, these sites at Karari may represent a further departure in site formation from that at Olduvai.

The point of this brief comparison is that behavioral and ecological variability in hominids needs to be documented. Early hominid behavior, whether that of *Australopithecus* 3 Ma or early *Homo* from 2.5 to 1.5 Ma, has typically been viewed as a unitary, singular phenomenon. By implication, Olduvai has stood for what all early hominids were like, and what occurs at Olduvai must also occur at Koobi Fora and elsewhere. Moreover, these behaviors should be consistent with views about the behavioral ecology of australopithecines and early *Homo* in southern Africa. This classic viewpoint is evoked by questions such as "Did early hominids hunt or scavenge, or was gathering plant foods most important to the diets of early hominids?" What applies for one direct human ancestor of the Plio–Pleistocene is treated as though it applies for all.[3]

This viewpoint is probably incorrect for two reasons. First, hominids appear to have undergone a minor radiation of species during the Late Pliocene, and variation in behavioral ecology is likely to have accompanied this process. Second, and more pertinent to this study, the role of hominids in site formation—the activities they engaged in that left us with an archeological record—appears to be tied to particular ecological and geographic contexts, that is, to situational factors that are bound to have varied from region to region. Thus, the activities of tool-making hominids at Olduvai 1.8 Ma does not necessarily correspond to what hominids did at Koobi Fora 1.5 million years ago, or even at Olduvai during later periods as the environment became drier overall and the physical geography of the basin changed (Cerling and Hay, 1986; Hay, 1976). I suggest that our understanding of early hominid socioecology will be enhanced by searching for spatial and temporal differences in these types of variables and exploring how they are associated with detailed aspects of site formation (Potts, 1987).

---

[3]Robust australopithecines, on the other hand, are generally believed to have been different in behavior, diet, and ecology from other Plio–Pleistocene hominids.

When archeological sites are scrutinized from an evolutionary perspective, variation in hominid activities and ecology through time and space becomes an important focal point. This perspective directs us toward certain behavioral complexes that relate to significant aspects of hominid paleobiology. These complexes include:

- The occurrence, maintenance, and strategy of site production
- Selection and transport of fauna and stone material
- Habitat use, as evaluated from the resources brought to sites
- The uses of artifacts
- The treatment and use of different stone raw materials
- Socioecological characteristics that correspond to the transport and modification of resources

Archeological data have a bearing upon these behavioral complexes only when detailed analysis of site formation shows that we can consider hypotheses about hominid activities. This line of detective work, although varying from traditional archeological approaches, generates a set of questions, data, and explanations that may contribute significantly to comprehending hominid evolution.

# Bibliography

Andersson, M., 1978, "Optimal Foraging Area: Size and Allocation of Search Effort," *Theoretical Population Biology*, vol. 13: 397–409.

Andrews, P., 1983, "Small Mammal Faunal Diversity at Olduvai Gorge, Tanzania" in J. Clutton-Brock and C. Grigson, eds., *Animals and Archaeology: 1. Hunters and Their Prey*, BAR International Series 163, Oxford, pp. 77–92.

Andrews, P., and J. Cook, 1985, "Natural Modifications to Bones in a Temperate Setting," *Man*, vol. 20: 675–691.

Andrews, P., J. M. Lord, and E. Nesbit Evans, 1979, "Patterns of Ecological Diversity in Fossil and Modern Mammalian Faunas," *Biological Journal of the Linnean Society*, vol. 11: 177–205.

Ardrey, R., 1961, *African Genesis*, Dell, New York.

Ardrey, R., 1976, *The Hunting Hypothesis*, Bantam, New York.

Auffenberg, W., 1981, "The Fossil Turtles of Olduvai Gorge, Tanzania, Africa," *Copeia*, no. 3: 509–522.

Bakker, R. T., 1972, "Anatomical and Ecological Evidence of Endothermy in Dinosaurs," *Nature*, vol. 238: 81–85.

Bartholomew, G. A., and J. B. Birdsell, 1953, "Ecology and the Protohominids," *American Anthropologist*, vol. 55: 481–498.

Bearder, S. K., 1977, "Feeding Habits of Spotted Hyaenas in a Woodland Habitat," *East African Wildlife Journal*, vol. 15: 263–280.

Behrensmeyer, A. K., 1975, "The Taphonomy and Paleoecology of the Plio–Pleistocene Vertebrate Assemblages East of Lake Rudolf, Kenya," *Bull. Museum Comparative Zoology Harvard*, vol. 146: 473–578.

Behrensmeyer, A. K., 1978, "Taphonomic and Ecologic Information from Bone Weathering," *Paleobiology*, vol. 2: 150–162.

Behrensmeyer, A. K., 1983, "Patterns of Natural Bone Distribution on Recent Land Surfaces: Implications for Archaeological Site Formation" in J. Clutton-Brock and C. Grigson, eds., *Animals and Archaeology: 1. Hunters and Their Prey*, BAR International Series 163, Oxford, pp. 93–106.

Behrensmeyer, A. K., 1987, "Taphonomy and Hunting" in *The Evolution of Hunting*, Spring Symposium, Field Museum of Natural History, Univ. of Chicago Press, Chicago.

Behrensmeyer, A. K., and D. E. Dechant Boaz, 1980, "The Recent Bones of Amboseli Park, Kenya, in Relation to East African Paleoecology" in A. K. Behrensmeyer and A. Hill, eds., *Fossils in the Making*, Univ. Chicago Press, Chicago, pp. 72–92.

Behrensmeyer, A. K., D. Western, and D. Dechant Boaz, 1979, "New Perspectives in Vertebrate Paleoecology from a Recent Bone Assemblage," *Paleobiology*, vol. 5: 12–21.

Behrensmeyer, A. K., K. D. Gordon, and G. T. Yanagi, 1986, "Trampling as a Cause of Bone Surface Damage and Pseudo-Cutmarks," *Nature*, vol. 319: 768–771.

Berger, M. E., 1972, "Population Structure of Olive Baboons in the Laikipia District of Kenya," *East African Wildlife Journal*, vol. 10: 159–164.

Bernstein, I. S., and E. O. Smith, eds., 1979, *Primate Ecology and Human Origins*, Garland STPM Press, New York.

Bertram, B., 1978, "Living in Groups: Predators and Prey," in J. R. Krebs and N. B. Davies, eds., *Behavioural Ecology*, Sinauer, Sunderland (Mass.), pp. 64–96.

Bertram, B., 1979, "Serengeti Predators and Their Social Systems" in A. Sinclair and M. Norton-Griffiths, eds., *Serengeti*, Univ. Chicago Press, Chicago, pp. 221–248.

Biberson, P., and E. Aguirre, 1965, "Experiences de Taille d'Outils Prehistoriques dan des Os d'Elephant," *Quaternaria*, vol. 7: 165–183.

Biddick, K. A., and J. Tomenchuk, 1975, "Quantifying Continuous Lesions and Fractures on Long Bones," *Journal of Field Archaeology*, vol. 2: 239–249.

Binford, L. R., 1977, "Olorgesailie Deserves More Than the Usual Book Review," *Journal of Anthropological Research*, vol. 33: 493–502.

Binford, L. R., 1978, *Nunamiut Ethno-archaeology*, Academic Press, New York.

Binford, L. R., 1980, "Willow Smoke and Dogs' Tails: Hunter–Gatherer Settlement Systems and Archaeological Site Formation," *American Antiquity*, vol. 45: 4–20.

Binford, L. R., 1981, *Bones: Ancient Men and Modern Myths*, Academic Press, New York.

Binford, L. R., 1982, "The Archaeology of Place," *Journal of Anthropological Archaeology*, vol. 1: 5–31.

Binford, L. R., 1984, *Faunal Remains from Klasies River Mouth*, Academic Press, Orlando.

Binford, L. R., 1985, "Human Ancestors: Changing Views of Their Behavior," *Journal of Anthropological Archaeology*, vol. 4: 292–327.

Binford, L. R., 1986, Commentary to Bunn and Kroll, *Current Anthropology*, vol. 27.

Binford, L. R., and J. B. Bertram, 1977, "Bone Frequencies and Attritional Processes" in L. R. Binford, ed., *For Theory Building in Archaeology*, Academic Press, New York, pp. 77–153.

Binford, L. R., and C. K. Ho, 1985, "Taphonomy at a Distance: Zhoukoudian, 'The Cave Home at Beijing Man'?," *Current Anthropology*, vol. 26: 413–442.

Binford, L. R., and N. M. Stone, 1986, "Zhoukoudian: A Closer Look," *Current Anthropology*, vol. 27: 453–475.

Blumenschine, R., 1986, *Early Hominid Scavenging Opportunities*, British Arch. Reports International Series 283.

Blurton Jones, N. G., 1984, "A Selfish Origin for Human Food Sharing: Tolerated Theft," *Ethology and Sociobiology*, vol. 5: 1–3.

Boaz, N. T., and A. K. Behrensmeyer, 1976, "Hominid Taphonomy: Transportation of Human Skeletal Elements in an Artificial Fluviatile Environment," *American Journal of Physical Anthropology*, vol. 45: 53–60.

Boesch, C., and H. Boesch, 1983, "Optimisation of Nut-cracking with Natural Hammers by Wild Chimpanzees," *Behavior*, vol. 83: 265–288.

Boesch, C., and H. Boesch, 1984, "Mental Map in Wild Chimpanzees: An Analysis of Hammer Transports for Nut Cracking," *Primates*, vol. 25: 160–170.

Bonnefille, R., and G. Riollet, 1980, "Palynologie, Vegetation et Climats de Bed I et Bed II a Olduvai, Tanzania," *Proceedings of the Eighth PanAfrican Congress of Prehistoric and Quaternary Studies*, Sept. 1977, Nairobi, pp. 123–127.

Bonnefille, R., D. Lobreau, and G. Riollet, 1982, "Pollen Fossile de *Ximenia* (Olacaceae) dans le Pleistocene Inferieur d'Olduvai en Tanzanie: Implications Paleoecologiques," *Journal of Biogeography*, vol. 9: 469–486.

Bonnichsen, R., 1973, "Some Operational Aspects of Human and Animal Bone Alteration," in B. M. Gilbert, ed., *Mammalian Osteo-Archaeology: North America*, Missouri Arch. Society, pp. 9–24.

Bonnichsen, R., 1978, "Critical Arguments for Pleistocene Artifacts from the Old Crow Basin, Yukon: A Preliminary Statement" in A. L. Bryan, ed., *Early Man in America*, Occasional Papers No. 1 of the Dept. Anthro., Univ. Alberta, pp. 102–118.

Bonnichsen, R., 1979, *Pleistocene Technology in the Beringian Refugium*, Archaeological Survey of Canada, Paper No. 89.

Bonnichsen, R., and M. H. Sorg, eds., in press, *Bone Modification*, Center for the Study of Early Man, University of Maine, Orono.

Bourliere, F., 1965, "Densities and Biomasses of Some Ungulate Populations in Eastern Congo and Rwanda," *Zoologica Africana*, vol. 1: 199–207.

Brain, C. K., 1967, "Hottentot Food Remains and Their Bearing on the Interpretation of Fossil Bone Assemblages," *Scientific Papers of the Namib Desert Research Station*, no. 32.

Brain, C. K., 1969a, "The Contribution of Namib Desert Hottentots to an Understanding of Australopithecine Bone Accumulations," *Scientific Papers of the Namib Desert Research Station*, no. 39, pp. 13–22.

Brain, C. K., 1969b, "Faulnal Remains from the Bushman Rock Shelter, Eastern Transvaal," *South African Archaeological Bulletin*, vol. 24: 52–55.

Brain, C. K., 1969c, "The Probable Role of Leopards as Predators of the Swartkrans Australopithecines," *South African Archaeological Bulletin*, vol. 24: 170–171.

Brain, C. K., 1980, "Some Criteria for the Recognition of Bone-Collecting Agencies in African Caves" in A. K. Behrensmeyer and A. Hill, eds., *Fossils in the Making*, Univ. Chicago Press, Chicago, pp. 107–130.

Brain, C. K., 1981, *The Hunters or the Hunted*, Univ. Chicago Press, Chicago.

Bromage, T. G., and M. C. Dean, 1985, "Re-evaluation of the Age of Death of Immature Fossil Hominids," *Nature*, vol. 317: 525–527.

Brooks, A. S., and J. E. Yellen, 1987, "The Preservation of Activity Areas in the Archaeological Record: Ethnoarchaeological and Archaeological Work in Northwest Nganiland, Botswana" in S. Kent, ed., *Method and Theory for Activity Area Research: An Ethnoarchaeological Approach*, Columbia Univ. Press, New York, pp. 63–106.

Bunn, H. T., 1981, "Archaeological Evidence for Meat-Eating by Plio–Pleistocene Hominids from Koobi-Fora and Olduvai Gorge," *Nature*, vol. 291: 574–577.

Bunn, H. T., 1982, *Meat-eating and Human Evolution: Studies on the Diet and Subsistence Patterns of Plio–Pleistocene Hominids in East Africa*, Ph.D. Dissertation, Dept. of Anthropology, Univ. California, Berkeley.

Bunn, H. T., 1983a, "Evidence on the Diet and Subsistence Patterns of Plio–Pleistocene Hominids at Koobi Fora, Kenya, and at Olduvai Gorge, Tanzania" in J. Clutton-Brock and C. Grigson, eds., *Animals and Archaeology: 1. Hunters and Their Prey*, BAR International Series 163, Oxford, pp. 21–30.

Bunn, H. T., 1983b, "Comparative Analysis of Modern Bone Assemblages from a San Hunter–Gatherer Camp in the Kalahari Desert, Botswana, and From a Spotted Hyena Den Near Nairobi, Kenya" in J. Clutton-Brock and C. Grigson, eds., *Animals and Archaeology: 1. Hunters and Their Prey*, BAR International Series 163, Oxford, pp. 143–148.

Bunn, H. T., and E. M. Kroll, 1986, "Systematic Butchery by Plio–Pleistocene Hominids at Olduvai Gorge, Tanzania," *Current Anthropology*, vol. 27: 431–452.

Butler, P. M., and M. Greenwood, 1973, "The Early Pleistocene Hedgehog from Olduvai, Tanzania" in L. Leakey, R. Savage, and S. Coryndon, eds., *Fossil Vertebrates of Africa*, vol. 3, Academic Press, London, pp. 7–42.

Butler, P. M., and M. Greenwood, 1976, "Elephant-shrews (Macroscelididae) from Olduvai and Makapansgat" in R. Savage and S. Coryndon, eds., *Fossil Vertebrates of Africa*, vol. 4, Academic Press, London, pp. 1–56.

Cahen, D., and J. Moeyersons, 1977, "Subsurface Movements of Stone Artifacts and Their Implications for the Prehistory of Central Africa," *Nature*, vol. 266: 812–815.

Campbell, B. G., ed., 1982, *Humankind Emerging*, Little, Brown and Co., Boston.

Cartmill, M., 1983, "Four Legs Good, Two Legs Bad," *Natural History*, vol. 92: 65–79.

Cerling, Thure E., and R. L. Hay, 1986, "An Isotopic Study of Paleosol Carbonates from Olduvai Gorge," *Quaternary Research*, vol. 25: 63–78.

Cerling, T., R. L. Hay, and J. O'Neil, 1977, "Isotopic Evidence for Dramatic Climatic Changes in East Africa during the Pleistocene," *Nature*, vol. 267: 137–138.

Charnov, E. L., 1976, "Optimal Foraging: The Marginal Value Theorem," *Theoretical Population Biology*, vol. 9: 129–136.

Chow, V. T., 1959, *Open-Channel Hydraulics*, McGraw-Hill, New York.

Churcher, C. S., and M. L. Richardson, 1978, "Equidae" in V. Maglio and H. B. S. Cooke, eds., *Evolution of African Mammals*, Harvard Univ. Press, Cambridge (Mass.).

Clark, J. D., 1960, "Human Ecology During Pleistocene and Later Times in Africa South of the Sahara," *Current Anthropology*, vol. 1(4): 307–324.

Clark, J. D., 1970, *The Prehistory of Africa*, Praeger Publishers, New York.

Clark, J. D., 1977, "Bone Tools of the Earlier Pleistocene," *Eretz-Israel*, vol. 13: 23–37.

Clark, J. D., and J. W. K. Harris, 1985, "Fire and Its Roles in Early Hominid Lifeways," *African Archaeological Review*, vol. 3: 3–27.

Clarke, R. J., F. C. Howell, and C. K. Brain, 1970, "More Evidence of an Advanced Hominid at Swartkrans," *Nature*, vol. 225: 1219–1222.

Cleveland, G. C., J. J. Flenniken, D. R. Huelsbeck, R. Mierendorf, S. Samuels, and F. Hassan, 1976, *Preliminary Archaeological Investigations at the Miller Site, Strawberry Island, 1976: A Late Prehistoric Village Near Burbank, Franklin County, Washington*, Washington Arch. Research Ctr., Project Report No. 46.

Clutton-Brock, J., 1974, "Primate Social Organisation and Ecology," *Nature*, vol. 250: 539–542.

Clutton-Brock, J., and P. Harvey, 1977, "Primate Ecology and Social Organisation," *Jour. Zool. London*, vol. 183: 1–39.

Coe, M., 1980, "The Role of Modern Ecological Studies in the Reconstruction of Paleoenvironments in Sub-Saharan Africa" in A. K. Behrensmeyer and A. Hill, eds., *Fossils in the Making*, Univ. Chicago Press, Chicago, pp. 55–67.

Cooke, H. B. S., and A. F. Wilkinson, 1978, "Suidae and Tayassuidae" in V. Maglio and H. B. S. Cooke, eds., *Evolution of African Mammals*, Harvard Univ. Press, Cambridge (Mass.).

Crader, D. C., 1974, "The Effects of Scavengers on Bone Material from a Large Mammal: An Experiment Conducted Among the Bisa of the Luangwa Valley, Zambia," *Ethnoarchaeology*, monograph IV, C. Donnan and C. Clewlow, eds., Inst. Arch., UCLA, pp. 161–176.

Crader, D. C., 1983, "Recent Single-Carcass Bone Scatters and the Problem of 'Butchery' Sites in the Archaeological Record" in J. Clutton-Brock and C. Grigson, eds., *Animals and Archaeology: 1. Hunters and Their Prey*, BAR International Series 163, pp. 107–141.

Curio, E., 1976, *The Ethology of Predation*, Springer-Verlag, Berlin.

Curtis, G. H., and R. L. Hay, 1972, "Further Geological Studies and Potassium–Argon Dating at Olduvai Gorge and Ngorongoro Crater" in W. W. Bishop and J. A. Miller, eds., *Calibration of Hominoid Evolution*, Scottish Academic Press, Edinburgh, pp. 289–301.

Dagg, A. I., and J. B. Foster, 1976, *The Giraffe*, Van Nostrand Reinhold, New York.

Dart, R. A., 1956, "The Myth of the Bone-accumulating Hyena," *American Anthropologist*, vol. 58: 40–62.

Dart, R. A., 1957, *The Osteodontokeratic Culture of Australopithecus prometheus*, Transvaal Museum Memoirs, no. 10.

Darwin, C., 1871, *The Descent of Man*, Modern Library, New York.

Dasmann, R., and A. S. Massman, 1962, "Abundance and Population Structure of Wild Ungulates in Some Areas of Southern Rhodesia," *Journal of Wildlife Management*, vol. 26: 262–268.

Davis, D. D., 1976, *Spatial Organization and Subsistence Technology of Lower and Middle Pleistocene Hominid Sites at Olduvai Gorge, Tanzania*, Ph.D. dissertation, Yale University, New Haven, Connecticut.

Day, M., 1976, "Hominid Postcranial Material from Bed I, Olduvai Gorge" in G. Isaac and E. McCown, eds., *Human Origins*, Benjamin Press, Menlo Park, California, pp. 363–374.

Dean, M. C., 1985, "The Eruption Pattern of the Permanent Incisors and First Permanent Molars in *Australopithecus (Paranthropus) robustus*," *American Journal of Physical Anthropology*, vol. 67: 251–257.

Delany, M. J., and D. Happold, 1979, *Ecology of African Mammals*, Longman, London.

Dennell, R., 1986, "Needles and Spear-throwers," *Natural History*, vol. 95: 70–78.

de Lumley, H., ed., 1969a, "Une Cabane Acheuleenne dans la Grotte du Lazaret," *Memoires de la Societe Prehistorique Francaise*, vol. 7.

de Lumley, H., 1969b, "A Paleolithic Camp at Nice," *Scientific American*, vol. 220: 42–50.

Dodson, P., 1973, "The Significance of Small Bones in Paleoecological Interpretation," *Contrib. Geol.*, vol. 12: 15–19.

Dodson, P., and D. Wexlar, 1979, "Taphonomic Investigations of Owl Pellets," *Paleobiology*, vol. 5: 275–284.

Dorst, J., and P. Dandelot, 1970, *A Field Guide to the Larger Mammals of Africa*, Collins, London.

Eaton, R. L., 1974, *The Cheetah*, Van Nostrand Reinhold, New York.

Emlen, J. M., 1966, "The Role of Time and Energy in Food Preference," *American Naturalist*, vol. 100: 611–617.

Estes, R. D., 1967, "Predators and Scavengers," *Natural History*, vol. 76: (2) 20–29; (3) 38–47.

Estes, R. D., and J. Goddard, 1967, "Prey Selection and Hunting Behavior of the African Wild Dog," *Journal of Wildlife Management*, vol. 31: 52–70.

Evernden, J. F., and G. H. Curtis, 1965, "Potassium–Argon Dating of Late Cenozoic Rocks in East Africa and Italy," *Current Anthropology*, vol. 6: 343–385.

Fiorillo, A. R., 1984, "An Introduction to the Identification of Trample Marks," *Current Research*, vol. 1: 47–48.

Fitch, F. J., P. J. Hooker, and J. A. Miller, 1978, "Geochronological Problems and Radioisotopic Dating in the Gregory Rift Valley" in W. W. Bishop, ed., *Geological Background to Fossil Man*, Scottish Academic Press, Edinburgh, pp. 441–461.

Fleischer, R. L., P. B. Price, R. M. Walker, and L. S. B. Leakey, 1965, "Fission-track Dating of Bed I, Olduvai Gorge," *Science*, vol. 148: 72–74.

Foley, R., 1981, "Off-site Archaeology: An Alternative Approach for the Short-sited" in I. Hodder, G. Isaac, and N. Hammond, eds., *Pattern of the Past*, Cambridge Univ. Press, Cambridge.

Foster, J. B., 1967, "The Square-Lipped Rhino," *East African Wildlife Journal*, vol. 5: 167–170.

Foster, J. B., and D. Kearney, 1967, "Nairobi National Park Game Census, 1966," *East African Wildlife Journal*, vol. 5: 112–120.

Foster, J. B., and R. McLaughlin, 1968, "Nairobi National Park Game Census, 1967," *East African Wildlife Journal*, vol. 6: 152–154.

Frison, G. C., 1971, "Shoshonean Antelope Procurement in the Upper Green River Basin, Wyoming," *Plains Anthrop.*, vol. 16: 258–284.

Frison, G. C., 1974, *The Casper Site*, Academic Press, New York.

Frison, G. C., D. N. Walker, S. D. Webb, and G. M. Zeimans, 1978, "Paleo–Indian Procurement of *Camelops* on the Northwestern Plains," *Quaternary Research*, vol. 10: 385–400.

Geist, V., 1971, *Mountain Sheep*, Univ. Chicago Press, Chicago.

Gentry, A. W., 1976, "Bovidae of the Omo Deposits" in Y. Coppens *et al.*, eds., 1976, *Earliest Man and Environments in the Lake Rudolf Basin*, Univ. Chicago Press, Chicago, pp. 275–292.

Gentry, A. W., and A. Gentry, 1978, *Fossil Bovidae (Mammalia) of Olduvai Gorge*, British Museum, London.

Gifford, D. P., 1977, *Observations of Modern Human Settlements as an Aid to Archaeological Interpretation*, Ph.D. dissertation, Univ. California, Berkeley.

Gifford, D. P., 1980, "Ethnoarchaeological Contributions to the Taphonomy of Human Sites" in A. K. Behrensmeyer and A. Hill, eds., *Fossils in the Making*, Univ. Chicago Press, Chicago, pp. 93–106.

Gifford, D. P., 1981, "Taphonomy and Paleoecology: A Critical Review of Archaeology's Sister Disciplines" in M. B. Schiffer, ed., *Advances in Archaeological Method and Theory*, Academic Press, New York, pp. 365–438.

Gifford, D. P., and D. C. Crader, 1977, "A Computer Coding System for Archaeological Faunal Remains," *American Antiquity*, vol. 42: 225–238.

Gifford, D., G. Isaac, and C. Nelson, 1981, "Evidence for predation and pastoralism at Prolonged Drift," *Azania*, vol. 15: 57–108.

Givoni, B., and R. Goldman, 1971, "Predicting Metabolic Energy Cost," *Journal of Applied Physiology*, vol. 30: 429–433.

Goldman, R., and P. Iampietro, 1962, "Energy Cost of Load Carriage," *Journal of Applied Physiology*, vol. 17: 675–676.

Goodall, J., 1986, *The Chimpanzees of Gombe*, Harvard Univ. Press, Cambridge.

Gould, R. A., 1967, "Notes on hunting, butchering and sharing of game among the Ngatatjara and their neighbors in the West Australian Desert," *Kroeber Anthropological Society Paper*, vol. 36: 41–66.

Gould, R. A., 1980, *Living Archaeology*, Cambridge Univ. Press, Cambridge.

Gowlett, J. A. J., J. W. K. Harris, D. Walton, and B. A. Wood, 1981, "Early Archaeological Sites, Hominid Remains, and Traces of Fire from Chesowanja, Kenya," *Nature*, vol. 294: 125–129.

Grayson, D. K., 1978, "Minimum Numbers and Sample Size in Vertebrate Faunal Analysis," *American Antiquity*, vol. 43: 53–65.

Gromme, C. S., and R. L. Hay, 1967, "Geomagnetic Polarity Epochs: New Data from Olduvai Gorge, Tanganyika," *Earth and Planetary Science Letters*, vol. 2: 111–115.

Gromme, C. S., and R. L. Hay, 1971, "Geomagnetic Polarity Epochs: Age and Duration of the Olduvai Normal Polarity Epoch," *Earth and Planetary Science Letters*, vol. 10: 179–185.

Guilday, J. E., P. W. Parmalee, and D. P. Tanner, 1962, "Aboriginal Butchering Techniques at the Eschelman Site (36 La 12), Lancaster County, Pa.," *Penna. Archaeologist*, vol. 32: 59–83.

Hamilton III, W. J., J. William, and K. E. F. Watt, 1970, "Refuging," *Annual Review Ecology and Systematics*, vol. 1: 263–297.

Hanson, C. B., 1980, "Fluvial Taphonomic Processes: Models and Experiments" in A. K. Behrensmeyer and A. Hill, eds., *Fossils in the Making*, Univ. Chicago Press, Chicago, pp. 156–181.

Haraway, D., 1978, "Animal Sociology and a Natural Economy of the Body Politic," *Signs*, vol. 4: 21–60.

Harding, R., and G. Teleki, 1981, *Omnivorous Primates*, Columbia Univ. Press, New York.

Harris, J. W. K., 1978, *The Karari Industry*, Ph.D. Dissertation, Univ. California, Berkeley.

Hay, R. L., 1976, *Geology of the Olduvai Gorge*, Univ. California Press, Berkeley.

Hayden, B., 1981, "Subsistence and Ecological Adaptations of Modern Hunter-Gatherers" in R. Harding and T. Teleki, eds., *Omnivorous Primates*, Columbia Univ. Press, New York, pp. 344–421.

Haynes, G., 1980a, "Evidence of Carnivore Gnawing on Pleistocene and Recent Mammalian Bones," *Paleobiology*, vol. 6: 341–351.

Haynes, G., 1980b, "Prey Bones and Predators: Potential Ecologic Information from Analysis of Bone Sites," *OSSA*, vol. 7: 75–97.

Haynes, G., 1983, "On Watering Holes, Mineral Licks, Death, and Predation" in J. Mead and D. Meltzer, eds., *Environments and Extinction in Late Glacial North America*, Center for the Study of Early Man, Univ. of Maine, Orono, pp. 53–71.

Hendey, Q. B., and R. Singer, 1965, "The Faunal Assemblages from the Gamtoos Valley Shelters," *South African Archaeological Bulletin*, vol. 20: 206–213.

Herbert, H. J., 1972, *The Population Dynamics of the Waterbuck Kobus ellipsipymnus (Ogilby, 1833) in the Sabi-Sand Wildtuin*, P. Parey, Hamburg.

Henschel, J. R., R. Tilson, and F. von Blottnitz, 1979, "Implications of a Spotted Hyaena Bone Assemblage in the Namib Desert," *South African Archaeological Bulletin*, vol. 34: 127–131.

Hill, A., 1975, *Taphonomy of Contemporary and Late Cenozoic East African Vertebrates*, Ph.D. Dissertation, Univ. London, London.

Hill, A., 1978, "Hyaenas, Bones, and Fossil Man," *Kenya Past and Present*, vol. 9: 9–14.

Hill, A., 1979a, "Butchery and Natural Disarticulation," *American Antiquity*, vol. 44: 739–744.

Hill, A., 1979b, "Disarticulation and Scattering of Mammal Skeletons," *Paleobiology*, vol. 5: 261–274.

Hill, A., 1980a, "Early Postmortem Damage to the Remains of Some Contemporary East African Mammals" in A. K. Behrensmeyer and A. Hill, eds., *Fossils in the Making*, Univ. Chicago Press, Chicago, pp. 131–152.

Hill, A., 1980b, "Hyaena Provisioning of Juvenile Offspring at the Den," *Mammalia*, vol. 44: 594–595.

Hill, A., 1981, "A Modern Hyaena Den in Amboseli National Park, Kenya," *Proceedings of PACPQS: Nairobi*, pp. 137–138.

Hill, A., 1983, "Hyaenas and Early Hominids" in J. Clutton-Brock and C. Grigson, eds., *Animals and Archaeology: 1. Hunters and Their Prey*, BAR International Series 163, Oxford, pp. 87–92.

Hill, A., 1984, "Hyaenas and Hominids: Taphonomy and Hypothesis Testing" in R. Foley, ed., *Hominid Evolution and Community Ecology*, Academic Press, London, pp. 111–128.

Hill, A., and A. K. Behrensmeyer, 1984, "Disarticulation Patterns of Some Modern East African Mammals," *Paleobiology*, vol. 10: 366–376.

Hooijer, D. A., 1969, "Pleistocene East African Rhinoceroses" in L. Leakey, ed., *Fossil Vertebrates of Africa*, vol. 1, Academic Press, New York, pp. 71–98.

Houston, D. C., 1974, "Food Searching in Griffon Vultures," *East African Wildlife Journal*, vol. 12: 63–77.

Houston, D. C., 1979, "The Adaptations of Scavengers" in A. Sinclair and M. Norton-Griffiths, eds., *Serengeti*, Univ. Chicago Press, Chicago, pp. 263–286.

Hvidberg-Hansen, H., and A. de Vos, 1971, "Reproduction, population and herd structure of two Thomson's gazelle (*Gazella thomsoni* Gunther) populations," *Mammalia*, vol. 35: 1–16.

Hughes, A. R., 1954, "Hyenas versus Australopithecines as Agents of Bone Accumulation," *American Journal of Physical Anthropology*, vol. 12: 467–486.

Isaac, G. L., 1967, "Towards the Interpretation of Occupation Debris: Some Experiments and Observations," *Kroeber Anthrop. Soc. Paper* 36: 31–57.

Isaac, G. L., 1969, "Studies of Early Culture in East Africa," *World Archaeology*, vol. 1: 1–28.

Isaac, G. L., 1971, "The Diet of Early Man: Aspects of Archaeological Evidence from Lower and Middle Pleistocene Sites in Africa," *World Archaeology*, vol. 2: 278–295.

Isaac, G. L., 1972a, "Chronology and Tempo of Cultural Change during the Pleistocene" in W. W. Bishop and J. A. Miller, eds., *Calibration of Hominoid Evolution*, Scottish Academic Press, Edinburgh, pp. 381–430.

Isaac, G. L., 1972b, "Early Phases of Human Behavior: Models in Lower Paleolithic Archaeology" in D. L. Clarke, ed., *Models in Archaeology*, Methuen, London, pp. 167–200.

Isaac, G. L., 1976, "The Activities of Early African Hominids" in G. Isaac and E. McCown, eds., *Human Origins*, Benjamin, Menlo Park (California), pp. 483–514.

Isaac, G. L., 1977, *Olorgesailie*, Univ. Chicago Press, Chicago.

Isaac, G. L., 1978, "The Food-sharing Behavior of Protohuman Hominids," *Scientific American*, April.

Isaac, G. L., 1979, "Comment" in S. T. Parker and K. R. Gibson, 1979, *Behavioral and Brain Sciences*, vol. 2: 367–408.

Isaac, G. L., 1981a, "Stone Age Visiting Cards: Approaches to the Study of Early Land Use Patterns" in I. Hodder, G. Isaac, and N. Hammond, eds., *Pattern of the Past*, Cambridge Univ. Press, pp. 131–155.

Isaac, G. L., 1981b, "Archaeological Tests of Alternative Models of Early Hominid Behavior: Excavation and Experiments," *Phil. Transactions Royal Soc. London*, vol. B292: 177–188.

Isaac, G. L., 1982, "Early Hominids and Fire at Chesowanja, Kenya," *Nature*, vol. 296: 870.

Isaac, G. L., 1983a, "Bones in Contention: Competing Explanations for the Juxtaposition of Early Pleistocene Artifacts and Faunal Remains" in J. Clutton-Brock and C. Grigson, eds., *Animals and Archaeology: 1. Hunters and Their Prey*, BAR International Series 163, Oxford, pp. 3–19.

Isaac, G. L., 1983b, "Some Archaeological Contributions Towards Understanding Human Evolution," *Canadian Journal of Anthropology*, vol. 3: 233–243.

Isaac, G. L., 1984, "The Archaeology of Human Origins: Studies of the Lower Pleistocene in East Africa 1971–1981," *Advances in World Archaeology*, vol. 3: 1–87.

Isaac, G. L., in press, *Koobi Fora Research Monograph*, vol. 3.

Isaac, G. L., and D. Crader, 1981, "To What Extent Were Early Hominids Carnivorous? An Archaeological Perspective" in R. Harding and G. Teleki, eds., *Omnivorous Primates*, Columbia Univ. Press, New York, pp. 37–103.

Isaac, G. L., and J. W. K. Harris, 1978, "Archaeology" in M. G. Leakey and R. Leakey, eds., *Koobi Fora Research Project*, vol. 1, Clarendon Press, Oxford, pp. 64–85.

Isaac, G. L., R. Leakey, and A. K. Behrensmeyer, 1971, "Archaeological Traces of Early Hominid Activities, East of Lake Rudolf," *Science*, vol. 173: 1129–1134.

Jaeger, J.-J., 1976, "Les Rongeurs (Mammalia, Rodentia) du Pleistocene Inferieur d'Olduvai Bed I" in R. Savage and S. Coryndon, eds., *Fossil Vertebrates of Africa*, vol. 4, Academic Press, London, pp. 57–120.

Jelinek, A. J., 1977, "The Lower Paleolithic: Current Evidence and Interpretations," *Ann. Rev. Anthro.*, vol. 6: 11–32.

Jolly, A., 1985, *The Evolution of Primate Behavior*, Macmillan, New York.

Jolly, C. J., 1970, "The Seed-eaters: A New Model of Hominid Differentiation Based on a Baboon Analogy," *Man*, vol. 5: 5–26.

Kamil, A. C., and T. D. Sargent, eds., 1981, *Foraging Behavior*, Garland Press, New York.

Kappelman, J., 1984, "Plio–Pleistocene Environments of Bed I and Lower Bed II, Olduvai Gorge, Tanzania," *Palaeogeography, Palaeoclimatology, Palaeoecology*, vol. 48: 171–196.

Keeley, L. H., 1980, *Experimental Determination of Stone Tool Uses*, Univ. Chicago Press, Chicago.

Keeley, L. H., and N. Toth, 1981, "Microwear Polishes on Early Stone Tools from Koobi Fora, Kenya," *Nature*, vol. 293: 464–465.

King, F. B., and R. W. Graham, 1981, "Effects of Ecological and Paleoecological Patterns on Subsistence and Paleoenvironment Reconstructions," *American Antiquity*, vol. 46: 128–142.

Kingdon, J., 1977, *East African Mammals*, vol. III, part A, Academic Press, London.

Klein, R. G., 1971, "The Pleistocene Prehistory of Siberia," *Quaternary Research*, vol. 1: 133–161.

Klein, R. G., 1972, "The Late Quaternary Mammalian Fauna of Nelson Bay Cave (Cape Province, South Africa): Its Implications for Megafaunal Extinctions and Environmental and Cultural Change," *Quaternary Research*, vol. 2: 135–142.

Klein, R. G., 1973, *Ice-Age Hunters of the Ukraine*, Univ. Chicago Press, Chicago.

Klein, R. G., 1975, "Paleoanthropological Implications of the Nonarchaeological Bone Assemblage from Swartklip I, South-Western Cape Province, South Africa," *Quaternary Research*, vol. 5: 275–288.

Klein, R. G., 1977, "The Mammalian Fauna from the Middle and Later Stone Age (Later Pleistocene) Levels of Border Cave, Natal Province, South Africa," *South African Archaeological Bulletin*, vol. 32: 14–27.

Klein, R. G., 1978, "Stone Age Predation on Large African Bovids," *Journal of Archaeological Science*, vol. 5: 195–217.

Klein, R. G., 1980, "The Interpretation of Mammalian Faunas from Stone Age Archaeological Sites, with Special Reference to Sites in the Southern Cape Province, South Africa" in A. K. Behrensmeyer and A. Hill, eds., *Fossils in the Making*, Univ. Chicago Press, Chicago, pp. 223–246.

Klein, R. G., 1982, "Age (Mortality) Profiles as a Means of Distinguishing Hunted Species from Scavenged Ones in Stone Age Archaeological Sites," *Paleobiology*, vol. 8(2): 151–158.

Klein, R. G., and Cruz-Uribe, K., 1984, *The Analysis of Animal Bones from Archaeological Sites*, Univ. of Chicago Press, Chicago.

Konner, M., 1982, *The Tangled Wing*, Holt, Rinehart and Winston Publ., New York.

Krebs, J. R., 1978, "Optimal Foraging: Decision Rules for Predators" in J. R. Krebs and N. B. Davies, eds., *Behavioural Ecology*, Sinauer Ass., Inc., Sunderland, Mass., pp. 23–63.

Krebs, J. R., and N. B. Davies, eds., 1978, *Behavioural Ecology*, Sinauer Ass., Inc., Sunderland (Mass.).

Krebs, J. R., and N. B. Davies, 1981, *An Introduction to Behavioural Ecology*, Blackwell, Oxford.

Kroll, E., and G. Isaac, 1984, "Configurations of artifacts and bones at early Pleistocene sites in East Africa" in H. J. Hietala, ed., *Intrasite Spatial Analysis in Archaeology*, Cambridge University Press, Cambridge, pp. 4–31.

Kruuk, H., 1972, *The Spotted Hyena*, Univ. Chicago Press, Chicago.

Kruuk, H., 1975, *Hyaena*, Oxford Univ. Press, London.

Kruuk, H., and M. Turner, 1967, "Comparative Notes on Predation by Lion, Leopard, Cheetah and Wild Dog in the Serengeti Area, East Africa," *Mammalia*, vol. 31: 1–27.

Kurten, B., 1953, "On the Variation and Population Dynamics of Fossil and Recent Mammal Populations," *Acta Zool. Fennica*, vol. 76: 1–122.

Lamprecht, J., 1978, "The Relationship between Food Competition and Foraging Group Size in some Larger Carnivores," *Z. Tierpsychol.*, vol. 46: 337–343.

Lamprey, H. F., 1963, "Ecological Separation of the Large Mammal Species in the Tarangire Game Reserve, Tanganyika," *East African Wildlife Journal*, vol. 1: 63–92.

Lamprey, H. F., 1964, "Estimation of the Large Mammal Densities, Biomass, and Energy Exchange in the Tarangire Game Reserve and the Masai Steppe in Tanganyika," *East African Wildlife Journal*, vol. 2: 1–46.

Lancaster, J. B., 1978, "Carrying and Sharing in Human Evolution," *Human Nature*, February, pp. 82–89.

Landau, M., D. Pilbeam, and A. Richard, 1982, "Human Origins a Century after Darwin," *Bioscience*, vol. 32: 507–512.

Laws, R. M., 1968, "Dentition and Ageing of the Hippopotamus," *East African Wildlife Journal*, vol. 6: 19–52.

Leakey, L. S. B., 1951, *Olduvai Gorge*, Cambridge Univ. Press, Cambridge (U.K.).

Leakey, L. S. B., 1959, "A New Fossil Skull from Olduvai," *Nature*, vol. 184: 491–493.

Leakey, L. S. B., 1965, *Olduvai Gorge 1951–1961*, vol. 1, Cambridge Univ. Press, Cambridge (U.K.).

Leakey, L. S. B., 1968, "Bone Smashing by Late Miocene Hominidae," *Nature*, vol. 218: 528–530.

Leakey, L. S. B., P. V. Tobias, and J. R. Napier, 1964, "A New Species of the Genus Homo from Olduvai Gorge," *Nature*, vol. 202: 7–9.

Leakey, M. D., 1966, "A Review of the Oldowan Culture from Olduvai Gorge, Tanzania," *Nature*, vol. 210: 462–466.

Leakey, M. D., 1967, "Preliminary Survey of the Cultural Material from Beds I and II, Olduvai Gorge, Tanzania" in W. W. Bishop and J. D. Clark, eds., *Background to Evolution in Africa*, Univ. Chicago Press, Chicago, pp. 417–442.

Leakey, M. D., 1971, *Olduvai Gorge*, vol. 3, Cambridge Univ. Press, London.

Leakey, M. D., 1976, "The Early Stone Industries of Olduvai Gorge" in *Les plus anciennes industries en Afrique*, Union Internationale des Sciences Prehistoriques et Protohistoriques, 9th Congress, Nice, pp. 24–41.

Leakey, M. D., 1978, "Olduvai Gorge 1911–75: A History of the Investigations" in W. W. Bishop, ed., *Geological Background to Fossil Man*, Scottish Academic Press, Edinburgh.

Leakey, M. G., and R. Leakey, 1976, "Further Cercopithecinae (Mammalia, Primates) from the Plio–Pleistocene of East Africa" in R. Savage and S. Coryndon, eds., *Fossil Vertebrates of Africa*, vol. 4, Academic Press, London, pp. 121–146.

Leakey, R. E., and R. Lewin, 1978, *People of the Lake: Mankind and Its Beginnings*, Anchor Press, Garden City, New York.

Lee, R. B., 1979, *The !Kung San*, Cambridge Univ. Press, Cambridge (U.K.).

Lee, R. B., and I. DeVore, eds., 1968, *Man the Hunter*, Aldine Publishing Co., Chicago.

Lee, R. B., and I. DeVore, eds., 1976, *Kalahari Hunter–Gatherers*, Harvard Univ. Press, Cambridge (Mass.).

Leechman, D., 1951, "Bone Grease," *American Antiquity*, vol. 16: 355–356.

Lewin, R., 1987, "Debate Over Emergence of Human Tooth Pattern," *Science*, vol. 235: 748–750.

Lovejoy, C. O., 1981, "The Origin of Man," *Science*, vol. 211: 341–350.

Lyman, R. L., 1979, "Available Meat from Faunal Remains: A Consideration of Techniques," *American Antiquity*, vol. 44: 536–546.

Lyon, P. J., 1970, "Differential Bone Destruction: An Ethnographic Example," *American Antiquity*, vol. 35: 213–215.

MacArthur, R., and E. Pianka, 1966, "On the Optimal Use of a Patchy Environment," *American Naturalist*, vol. 100: 603–609.

McGrew, W. C., 1979, "Evolutionary Implications of Sex Differences in Chimpanzee Predation and Tool Use" in D. A. Hamburg and E. R. McCown, eds., *The Great Apes*, Benjamin/Cummings, Menlo Park, pp. 441–464.

Maglio, V. J., 1975, "Pleistocene Evolution in Africa and Eurasia" in K. Butzer and G. Isaac, eds., *After the Australopithecines*, Mouton, The Hague, pp. 419–476.

Mann, A., 1972, "Hominid and Cultural Origins," *Man*, vol. 3: 381–386.

Mann, A., 1975, *Paleodemographic Aspects of the South African Australopithecines*, Univ. Pennsylvania Publication in Anthropology, No. 1, Philadelphia.

Mann, A., 1981, "Diet and Human Evolution" in R. Harding and G. Teleki, eds., *Omnivorous Primates*, Columbia Univ. Press, New York, pp. 10–36.

Margaria, R., P. Cerretelli, P. Aghemo, and G. Sassi, 1963, "Energy Cost of Running," *Journal of Applied Physiology*, vol. 18: 367–370.

Marks, S. A., 1976, *Large Mammals and a Brave People: Subsistence Hunters in Zambia*, Univ. Washington Press, Seattle.

Marshall, F., 1986, *Aspects of the Advent of the Pastoral Economics in East Africa*, Ph.D. Dissertation, Univ. of California, Berkeley.

Matthiesen, D., 1982, "The Contribution of the Avifauna to the Study of the Early

Pleistocene Hominids from Olduvai Gorge, Tanzania," Paper presented at ICAZ Fourth International Conference, London.

Mayr, E., 1974, "Behavior Programs and Evolutionary Strategies," *American Scientist*, vol. 62: 650–659.

Meadow, R., 1981, "Animal bones—Problems for the Archaeologist Together with Some Possible Solutions," *Paleorient*, vol. 6.

Mellett, J. S., 1974, "Scatological Origins of Micro-vertebrate Fossil Accumulations," *Science*, vol. 185: 349–350.

Melton, D. A., and C. L. Melton, 1982, "Condition and Mortality of Waterbuck *(Kobus ellipsiprymnus)* in the Umfolozi Game Reserve," *African Journal of Ecology*, vol. 20: 89–103.

Menzel, E. W., and E. J. Wyers, 1981, "Cognitive Aspects of Foraging Behavior" in A. C. Kamil and T. D. Sargent, eds., *Foraging Behavior*, Garland Press, New York, pp. 355–377.

Miller, G. J., 1975, "A Study of Cuts, Grooves, and Other Marks on Recent and Fossil Bone II. Weather Cracks, Fractures, Splinters, and Other Similar Natural Phenomena" in E. H. Swanson, ed., *Lithic Technology*, Mouton, The Hague, pp. 211–226.

Milligan, K., S. S. Ajayi, and J. B. Hall, 1982, "Density and Biomass of the Large Herbivore Community in Kainji Lake National Park, Nigeria," *African Journal of Ecology*, vol. 20: 1–12.

Mills, M. G. L., and M. E. J. Mills, 1977, "An Analysis of Bones Collected at Hyaena Breeding Dens in the Gemsbok National Park," *Ann. Transvaal Museum*, vol. 30: 145–155.

Mills, M. G. L., and M. E. J. Mills, 1978, "The Diet of the Brown Hyaena *Hyaena brunnea* in the Southern Kalahari," *Koedoe*, vol. 21: 125–149.

Morris, D., 1969, *The Human Zoo*, McGraw-Hill Publishing Co., New York.

Morrison, D. W., 1978, "On the Optimal Searching Strategy for Refuging Predators," *The American Naturalist*, vol. 112: 925–934.

Mulvaney, D. J., 1969, *A Prehistory of Australia*, Thames and Hudson, London.

Murray, M., 1967, "The Pathology of Some Diseases Found in Wild Animals in East Africa," *East African Wildlife Journal*, vol. 5: 37–45.

Myers, T. P., M. R. Voorhies, and R. G. Corner, 1980, "Spiral Fractures and Bone Pseudotools at Paleontological Sites," *American Antiquity*, vol. 45: 483–490.

Napier, J., 1962, "The Evolution of the Hand," *Sci. American*, vol. 207: 56–62.

Noe-Nygaard, N., 1977, "Butchering and Marrow Fracturing as a Taphonomic Factor in Archaeological Deposits," *Paleobiology*, vol. 3: 218–237.

Oakley, K. P., 1961, *Man the Tool Maker*, Univ. Chicago Press, Chicago.

Oliver, J. S., 1984, "Bone Damage Morphologies from Shield Trap Cave, Carbon County, Montana" in R. Bonnischen and M. Sorg, eds., *First International Conference on Bone Modification:* Abstracts, p. 27, Center for the Study of Early Man, Orono.

Olton, D. S., G. E. Handelmann, and J. A. Walker, 1981, "Spatial Memory and Food Searching Strategies" in A. C. Kamil and T. D. Sargent, eds., *Foraging Behavior*, Garland Press, New York, pp. 333–354.

Orians, G. H., 1981, "Foraging Behavior and the Evolution of Discriminatory Abilities" in J. R. Krebs and N. B. Davies, eds., *Behavioral Ecology: An*

*Evolutionary Approach*, Sinauer Ass., Inc., Sunderland, Mass., pp. 389–405.

Orians, G. H., and N. P. Pearson, 1979, "On the Theory of Central Place Foraging" in D. Horn, R. Mitchell, and G. Stairs, eds., *Analysis of Ecological Systems*, Ohio State Univ. Press, Columbus, Ohio.

Owens, M. J., and D. D. Owens, 1978, "Feeding Ecology and Its Influence on Social Organization in Brown Hyenas (*Hyaena brunnea*, Thunberg) of the Central Kalahari Desert," *East African Wildlife Journal*, vol. 16: 113–135.

Parker, S. T., and K. R. Gibson, 1979, "A Developmental Model for the Evolution of Language and Intelligence in Early Hominids," *Behavioral and Brain Sciences*, vol. 2: 367–408.

Parmalee, P. W., 1965, "The Food Economy of Archaic and Woodland Peoples at the Tick Creek Cave Site, Missouri," *Missouri Archaeologist*, vol. 27, no. 1.

Payne, S., 1972, "On the Interpretation of Bone Samples from Archaeological Samples" in E. S. Higgs, ed., *Papers in Economic Prehistory*, Cambridge Univ. Press, Cambridge (U.K.).

Payne, S., 1975, "Partial Recovery and Sample Bias" in A. T. Clason, ed., *Archaeozoological Studies*, American Elsevier, New York, pp. 7–17.

Petter, G., 1973, "Carnivores Pleistocenes du Ravin d'Olduvai (Tanzanie)" in L. Leakey, R. Savage, and S. Coryndon, eds., *Fossil Vertebrates of Africa*, vol. 3, Academic Press, London, pp. 43–100.

Pettijohn, F. J., P. E. Potter, and R. Siever, 1972, *Sand and Sandstone*, Springer-Verlag, New York.

Pfeiffer, J. E., 1985, *The Emergence of Humankind*, Harper and Row, New York.

Pianka, E. R., 1983, *Evolutionary Ecology*, Harper and Row, New York.

Pielou, E. C., 1975, *Ecological Diversity*, Wiley, New York.

Pienaar, U. de V., 1969, "Predator–Prey Relationships amongst the Larger Mammals of the Kruger National Park," *Koedoe*, vol. 12: 108–187.

Potts, R., 1980, *Lower Pleistocene Home Bases*, presented at the American Anthropological Association Annual Meeting, Washington, D.C.

Potts, R., 1982, *Lower Pleistocene Site Formation and Hominid Activities at Olduvai Gorge, Tanzania*, Ph.D. Dissertation, Harvard University, Cambridge, Mass.

Potts, R., 1983, "Foraging for Faunal Resources by Early Hominids at Olduvai Gorge, Tanzania" in J. Clutton-Brock and C. Grigson, eds., *Animals and Archaeology: 1. Hunters and Their Prey*, BAR International Series 163, Oxford, pp. 51–62.

Potts, R., 1984a, "Hominid Hunters? Problems of Identifying the Earliest Hunter-Gatherers" in R. Foley, ed., *Hominid Evolution and Community Ecology: Prehistoric Human Adaptation in Biological Perspective*, Academic Press, London, pp. 129–166.

Potts, R., 1984b, "Home Bases and Early Hominids," *American Scientist*, vol. 72: 338–347.

Potts, R., 1986, "Temporal Span of Bone Accumulations at Olduvai Gorge and Implications for Early Hominid Foraging Behavior," *Paleobiology*, vol. 12: 25–31.

Potts, R., 1987, "Reconstructions of Early Hominid Socioecology: A Critique of Primate Models" in W. G. Kinzey, ed., *The Evolution of Human Behavior: Primate Models*, S.U.N.Y. Press, Albany, pp. 28–47.

Potts, R., in press, "New Excavations at Olorgesailie and Kanjera, Kenya," *Journal of Human Evolution*.

Potts, R., and P. Shipman, 1981, "Cutmarks Made by Stone Tools on Bones from Olduvai Gorge, Tanzania," *Nature*, vol. 291: 577–580.

Potts, R. B., and A. Walker, 1981, "Production of Early Hominid Archaeological Sites," *American Journal of Physical Anthropology*, vol. 54: 264 (abstract).

Richard, A. F., 1981, "Changing Assumptions in Primate Ecology," *American Anthropologist*, vol. 83: 517–533.

Richard, A. F., 1985, *Primates in Nature*, W. H. Freeman and Company, New York.

Richardson, P., 1980, "Carnivore Damage to Antelope Bones and Its Archaeological Implications," *Palaeont. Afr.*, vol. 23: 109–125.

Rood, J. P., 1975, "Population Dynamics and Food Habits of the Banded Mongoose," *East African Wildlife Journal*, vol. 13: 89–112.

Rose, J. J., 1983, "A Replication Technique for Scanning Electron Microscopy: Applications for Anthropologists," *Amer. J. Phys. Anthro.*, vol. 62: 255–261.

Rudnai, J. A., 1973, *The Social Life of the Lion*, Washington Sq. East, Wallingford (Penna.).

Sadek-Kooros, H., 1966, *Jaguar Cave: An Early Man Site in the Beaverland Mountains of Idaho*, Ph.D. Dissertation, Harvard University, Cambridge, Mass.

Sadek-Kooros, H., 1972, "Primitive Bone Fracturing: A Method of Research," *American Antiquity*, vol. 37: 369–382.

Sadek-Kooros, H., 1975, "Intentional Fracturing of Bone: Description of Criteria" in A. T. Clason, ed., *Archaeozoological Studies*, American Elsevier, New York, pp. 139–150.

Savage, R., 1978, "Carnivora" in V. Maglio and H. B. S. Cooke, eds., *Evolution of African Mammals*, Harvard Univ. Press, Cambridge, Mass.

Schaller, G. B., 1967, *The Deer and the Tiger*, Univ. of Chicago Press, Chicago.

Schaller, G. B., 1970, "This Gentle and Elegant Cat," *Natural History*, vol. 79, no. 6, pp. 30–39.

Schaller, G. B., 1972, *The Serengeti Lion*, Univ. Chicago Press, Chicago.

Schaller, G. B., 1976, *The Mountain Gorilla*, Univ. Chicago Press, Chicago.

Schaller, G. B., and G. R. Lowther, 1969, "The Relevance of Carnivore Behavior to the Study of Early Hominids," *Southwestern Journal of Anthropology*, vol. 25: 307–341.

Schenkel, R., and L. Schenkel-Hulliger, 1969, *Ecology and Behavior of the Black Rhinoceros*, Verlag Paul Parey, Hamburg.

Schiffer, M. B., 1975, "Archaeology as Behavioral Science," *American Antiquity*, vol. 77: 836–848.

Schiffer, M. B., 1976, *Behavioral Archeology*, Academic Press, New York.

Schiffer, M. B., 1978, "Methodological Issues in Ethnoarchaeology" in R. A. Gould, ed., *From Tasmania to Tucson: New Directions in Ethnoarchaeology*, Univ. New Mexico Press, Albuquerque.

Schoener, T. W., 1971, "Theory of Feeding Strategies," *Annual Review of Ecology and Systematics*, vol. 2: 369–404.

Sept, J. M., 1984, *Plants and Early Hominids in East Africa: A Study of Vegetation in Situations Comparable to Early Archaeological Site Locations*, Ph.D. Dissertation, Univ. of California, Berkeley.

Sept, J., 1986, "Plant Foods and Early Hominids at Site FxJj 50, Koobi Fora, Kenya," *Journal of Human Evolution*, vol. 15: 751–770.

Service, E. R., 1962, *Primitive Social Organization: An Evolutionary Perspective*, Random House, New York.

Shipman, P., 1975, "Implications of Drought for Vertebrate Fossil Assemblages," *Nature*, vol. 257: 667–668.

Shipman, P., 1977, *Paleoecology, Taphonomic History, and Population Dynamics of the Vertebrate Fossil Assemblage from the Middle Miocene Deposits Exposed at Fort Ternan, Kenya*, Ph.D. Dissertation, New York Univ.

Shipman, P., 1981, *Life History of a Fossil*, Harvard Univ. Press, Cambridge, Mass.

Shipman, P., 1982, *Reconstructing the Paleoecology and Taphonomic History of Ramapithecus Wickeri at Fort Ternan, Kenya*, Museum Brief: #26, Univ. of Missouri-Columbia, Columbia.

Shipman, P., 1983, "Early Hominid Lifestyle: Hunting and Gathering or Foraging and Scavenging?" in J. Clutton-Brock and G. Grigson, eds., *Animals and Archaeology: 1. Hunters and Their Prey*, BAR International Series 163, Oxford, pp. 31–49.

Shipman, P., 1984, "Scavenger Hunt," *Natural History*, vol. 4/84: 20–27.

Shipman, P., 1986a, "Scavenging or Hunting in Early Hominids: Theoretical Framework and Tests," *American Anthropologist*, vol. 88: 27–43.

Shipman, P., 1986b, "Studies of Hominid–Faunal Interactions at Olduvai Gorge," *Journal of Human Evolution*, vol. 15: 691–706.

Shipman, P., in press, "Diet and Subsistence Strategies at Olduvai Gorge," Proceedings of Conference on "Diet and Subsistence in Prehistory," Univ. of Calgary.

Shipman, P., and J. Phillips, 1976, "Scavenging by Hominids and Other Carnivores," *Current Anthropology*, vol. 17: 170–172.

Shipman, P., and J. Phillips-Conroy, 1977, "Hominid Tool-making versus Carnivore Scavenging," *American Journal Physical Anthropology*, vol. 46: 77–87.

Shipman, P., A. J. Johnson, and S. Stahl, 1981a, "Hydraulic Behavior of Bones and the Fossil Record," *American Journal of Physical Anthropology*, vol. 54: 277 (abstract).

Shipman, P., A. Walker, J. van Couvering, P. Hooker, and J. Miller, 1981b, "The Fort Ternan Hominoid Site, Kenya: Geology, Age, Taphonomy and Paleoecology," *Journal of Human Evolution*, vol. 10: 49–72.

Siegel, S., 1956, *Nonparametric Statistics for the Behavioral Sciences*, McGraw-Hill Kogakusha, Tokyo.

Simons, J. W., 1966, "The Presence of Leopard and a Study of the Food Debris in the Leopard Lairs of the Mount Suswa Caves, Kenya," *Bulletin of the Cave Exploration Group of East Africa*, vol. 1: 51–69.

Skinner, J. D., 1976, "Ecology of the Brown Hyaena *Hyaena brunnea* in the Transvaal with a Distribution Map for Southern Africa," *South African Journal of Science*, vol. 72: 262–269.

Skinner, J. D., S. Davis, and G. Ilani, 1980, "Bone Collecting by Striped Hyaenas, *Hyaena Hyaena*, in Israel," *Paleont. Afr.*, vol. 23: 99–104.

Smith, B. H., 1986, "Dental Development in *Australopithecus* and Early *Homo*," *Nature*, vol. 323: 327–330.

Smith, E. A., 1979, "Human Adaptation and Energetic Efficiency," *Human Ecology*, vol. 7: 53–74.

Smith, E. A., and Winterhalder, B., 1981, "New Perspectives on Hunter–Gatherer Socioecology" in B. Winterhalder and E. A. Smith, eds., *Hunter–Gatherer Foraging Strategies*, Univ. Chicago Press, Chicago, pp. 1–12.

Speth, J. D., and D. D. Davis, 1976, "Seasonal Variability in Early Hominid Predation," *Nature*, vol. 192: 441–445.

Soule, R., K. Pandolf, and R. Goldman, 1978, "Energy Expenditure of Heavy Load Carriage," *Ergonomics*, vol. 21: 373–381.

Spiess, A. E., 1979, *Reindeer and Caribou Hunters*, Academic Press, New York.

Stewart, D., and I. Stewart, 1966, "The Use of Sex and Age Ratios in Estimating Abundance and Productivity of Impala," *Lammergeyer*, vol. 6: 9–19.

Strum, S. C., 1975, "Primate Predation: An Interim Report on the Development of a Tradition in a Troop of Olive Baboons," *Science*, vol. 187: 755–757.

Strum, S. C., 1981, "Processes and Products of Change: Baboon Predatory Behavior at Gilgil, Kenya," in R. Harding and G. Teleki, eds., *Omnivorous Primates*, Columbia Univ. Press, New York, pp. 255–302.

Sugiyama, Y., 1981, "Observations on the Population Dynamics and Behavior of Wild Chimpanzees at Bossou, Guinea, in 1979–1980," *Primates*, vol. 22: 435–444.

Sugiyama, Y., and J. Koman, 1979, "Tool-Using and -Making Behavior in Wild Chimpanzees at Bossou, Guinea," *Primates*, vol. 20: 513–524.

Sussman, C., 1986, "Early tools from Olduvai Gorge," *AnthroQuest*, no. 34.

Sutcliffe, A. J., 1970, "Spotted Hyena: Crusher, Gnawer, Digester and Collector of Bones," *Nature*, vol. 227: 1110–1113.

Sutcliffe, A. J., 1973, "Caves of the East African Rift Valley," *Trans. Cave Res. Group of Great Britain*, vol. 15: 41–65.

Tague, R. G., and C. O. Lovejoy, 1986, "The Obstetric Pelvis of A. L. 288-1 (Lucy)," *Journal of Human Evolution*, vol. 15: 237–255.

Talbot, L., and M. Talbot, 1963, "The Wildebeest in Western Masailand, East Africa," *Wildlife Monograph*, vol. 12: 1–88.

Tanner, N. M., 1981, *On Becoming Human: A Model of the Transition from Ape to Human and the Reconstruction of Early Human Social Life*, Cambridge Univ. Press, New York and London.

Teaford, M. F., and A. Walker, 1984, "Quantitative Differences in Dental Microwear between Primate Species with Different Diets and a Comment on the Presumed Diet of *Sivapithecus*," *American Journal of Physical Anthropology*, vol. 64: 191–200.

Teleki, G., 1973, *The Predatory Behavior of Wild Chimpanzees*, Bucknell Univ. Press, Lewisburg, Penna.

Teleki, G., 1975, "Primate Subsistence Patterns: Collector–Predators and Gatherer–Hunters," *Journal of Human Evolution*, vol. 4: 125–184.

Teleki, G., 1981, "The omnivorous diet and eclectic feeding habits of chimpanzees in Gombe National Park, Tanzania," in R. Harding and G. Teleki, eds., *Omnivorous Primates*, Columbia University Press, New York, pp. 303–343.

Thackeray, J. F., 1980, "New Approaches in Interpreting Archaeological Faunal Assemblages with Examples from Southern Africa," *South African Journal of Science*, vol. 76: 216–224.

Thomas, D. H., 1969, "Great Basin Hunting Patterns: A Quantitative Method for Treating Faunal Remains," *American Antiquity*, vol. 34: 392–401.

Toots, H., 1965a, "Sequence of Disarticulation in Mammalian Skeletons," *Contrib. Geol.*, vol. 4: 37–38.

Toots, H., 1965b, "Random Orientation of Fossils and Its Significance," *Contrib. Geol. Univ. Wyoming*, vol. 4: 59–62.

Toth, N., 1982, *The Stone Technologies of Early Hominids at Koobi Fora, Kenya: An Experimental Approach*, Ph.D. Dissertation, Dept. of Anthropology, Univ. of California, Berkeley.

Toth, N., 1985, "The Oldowan Reassessed: A Close Look at Early Stone Artifacts," *Journal of Archaeological Science*, vol. 12: 101–120.

Toth, N., and K. Schick, 1986, "The first million years: The archaeology of protohuman culture," *Advances in Archaeological Method and Theory*, vol. 9: 1–96.

Turnbull-Kemp, P., 1967, *The Leopard*, Howard Timmins, Cape Town.

Turner, M., and M. Watson, 1964, "A Census in Ngorongoro Crater," *East African Wildlife Journal*, vol. 2: 165–169.

van Couvering, J. A. H., 1980, "Community Evolution in East Africa During the Late Cenozoic" in A. K. Behrensmeyer and A. Hill, eds., *Fossils in the Making*, Univ. Chicago Press, Chicago, pp. 272–298.

Vehik, S. C., 1977, "Bone Fragments and Bone Grease Manufacturing: A Review of Their Archaeological Use and Potential," *Plains Anthrop.*, vol. 22: 169–182.

Villa, P., 1982, "Conjoinable Pieces and Site Formation Processes," *American Antiquity*, vol. 47(2): 276–290.

Villa, P., 1983, *Terra Amata and the Middle Pleistocene Archaeological Record of Southern France*, Univ. of California Press, Berkeley.

Voorhies, M. R., 1969, "Taphonomy and Population Dynamics of an Early Pliocene Vertebrate Fauna, Knox County, Nebraska," *Contrib. Geol. Univ. Wyoming*, Special Paper No. 1.

Vrba, E. S., 1975, "Some Evidence of Chronology and Paleoecology of Sterkfontein, Swartkrans, and Kromdraai from the Fossil Bovidae," *Nature*, vol. 254: 301–304.

Vrba, E. S., 1980, "The Significance of Bovid Remains as Indicators of Environment and Predation Patterns." In A. K. Behrensmeyer and A. Hill, eds., *Fossils in the Making*, Univ. Chicago Press, Chicago, pp. 247–271.

Walker, A., 1980, "Functional Anatomy and Taphonomy" in A. K. Behrensmeyer and A. Hill, eds., *Fossils in the Making*, Univ. Chicago Press, Chicago, pp. 182–196.

Walker, A., 1981, "Dietary Hypotheses and Human Evolution," *Phil. Trans. Royal Soc. London*, vol. 292: 56–64.

Walker, A., 1984, "Extinction in Hominid Evolution" in M. H. Nitecki, ed., *Extinctions*, Univ. Chicago Press, Chicago, pp. 119–152.

Walker, A., H. Hoeck, and L. Perez, 1978, "Microwear on Mammalian Teeth as an Indicator of Diet," *Science*, vol. 201: 908–910.

Walker, P., and J. C. Long, 1977, "An Experimental Study of the Morphological Characteristics of Tool Marks," *American Antiquity*, vol. 42: 605–618.

Washburn, S. L., 1960, "Tools and Human Evolution," *Scientific American*, September.

Washburn, S. L., and I. DeVore, 1961, "Social Behavior of Baboons and Early Man" in S. L. Washburn, ed., *Social Life of Early Man*, Viking Fund Publ. in Anthropology, New York, vol. 31: 91–105.

Washburn, S. L., and C. S. Lancaster, 1968, "The Evolution of Hunting" in R. B. Lee and I. DeVore, eds., *Man the Hunter*, Aldine Publ. Co., Chicago, pp. 293–303.

Watson, R. M., 1965, "Observations of the Behaviour of Young Spotted Hyaena (Crocuta crocuta) in the Burrow," *East African Wildlife Journal*, vol. 3: 122–123.

Watson, R. M., A. D. Graham, and I. Parker, 1969, "A Census of the Large Mammals of Loliondo Controlled Area, Northern Tanzania," *East African Wildlife Journal*, vol. 7: 43–60.

Western, D., 1973, *The Structure, Dynamics and Changes of the Amboseli Ecosystem*, Ph.D. Dissertation, Univ. Nairobi.

Western, D., 1980, "Linking the Ecology of Past and Present Mammal Communities" in A. K. Behrensmeyer and A. Hill, eds., *Fossils in the Making*, Univ. Chicago Press, Chicago, pp. 41–54.

Western, D., and D. M. Sindiyo, 1972, "The Status of the Amboseli Rhino Populations," *East African Wildlife Journal*, vol. 10: 43–57.

White, R., 1982, "Rethinking the Middle/Upper Paleolithic Transition," *Current Anthropology*, vol. 23: 169–192.

White, T. D., and J. M. Harris, 1977, "Suid Evolution and Correlation of African Hominid Localities," *Science*, vol. 198: 13–21.

White, T. E., 1954, "Observations on the Butchering Techniques of Some Aboriginal Peoples: 3, 4, 5, and 6," *American Antiquity*, vol. 19: 254–264.

Wiens, J. A., 1976, "Population Responses to Patchy Environments," *Ann. Rev. Ecol. Syst.*, vol. 7: 81–120.

Wiens, J. A., 1983, "Competition or Peaceful Coexistence?," *Natural History*, vol. 92: 30–34.

Wilson, E. O., 1975, *Sociobiology*, Harvard Univ. Press, Cambridge, Mass.

Wilson, E. O., 1978, *On Human Nature*, Harvard Univ. Press, Cambridge (Mass.).

Wilson, E. O., and W. H. Bossert, 1971, *A Primer of Population Biology*, Sinauer Ass., Inc., Sunderland, Mass.

Winterhalder, B., 1980, "Environmental Analysis in Human Evolution and Adaptation Research," *Human Ecology*, vol. 8: 135–170.

Wood, B. A., 1974, "Olduvai Bed I Post-cranial Fossils: A Reassessment," *Journal of Human Evolution*, vol. 3: 373–378.

Wrangham, R. W., 1983, "Ultimate Factors Determining Social Structure" in R. A. Hinde, ed., *Primate Social Relationships*, Sinauer Ass., Inc., Sunderland, Mass., pp. 255–262.

Wrangham, R. W., 1987, "The Significance of African Apes for Reconstructing Human Social Evolution" in W. G. Kinzey, ed., *The Evolution of Human Behavior*, S.U.N.Y. Press, Albany, pp. 51–71.

Yellen, J. E., 1976, "Settlement Patterns of the !Kung: An Archaeological Perspective" in R. Lee and I. DeVore, eds., *Kalahari Hunter–Gatherers*, Harvard Univ. Press, Cambridge, pp. 48–72.

Yellen, J. E., 1977a, "Cultural Patterning in Faunal Remains: Evidence from the !Kung Bushmen" in D. Ingersoll, J. Yellen, and W. MacDonald, eds., *Experimental Archeology*, Columbia Univ. Press, New York, pp. 271–331.

Yellen, J., 1977b, *Archaeological Approaches to the Present*, Academic Press, New York.

Zihlman, A., and N. Tanner, 1978, "Gathering and the Hominid Adaptation" in L. Tiger and H. Fowler, eds., *Female Hierarchies*, Beresford Books, Chicago, pp. 163–193.

Zuckerman, S., 1933, *Functional Affinities of Man, Monkeys, and Apes*, Harcourt, Brace and Co., New York.

# Appendix A: Site DK

Number of stone artifacts (all levels) = 1163
Number of Level 3 faunal remains = 2433[a]
Number of Level 2 faunal remains = 5422[a]
Depth of deposit = approximately 1.3 m for Levels 1–3.
   (Level 3 = 9 cm, Level 2 = 68 cm)
Area excavated = 345 m² (estimated average over all 3 levels)
Density of excavated remains = 32.4 per m³

## Level 3 Fauna

*Number of Specimens = 2433*[a]

Mammals identified to taxon and skeletal part = 518 (21%)
Crocodile = 814 (33%)
Chelonia = 253 (10%)
Indeterminate fragments = 848 (35%)

*Mammalian Macrofauna*

Tables A.1–9 provide data describing the mammalian macrofaunal assemblage. Tables A.3–6 provide details on the bovids according to size class, since bovids comprise the most abundant taxon and since numerous taphonomic effects are size-related. These tables highlight taxonomic representation, skeletal element frequencies, and the completeness of bones in the assemblage.

*Crocodilia*

Crocodilidae indeterminate: $N$ = 534 (422 teeth, 20 vertebrae, 10 ribs, 2 scapulae, 2 chevron, 3 humeri, 2 metacarpals, 3 metatarsals, 2 femora, 2 tibiae, 1 fibula, 1 scaphoid, 8 phalanges, 45 scutes, 12 indet. frags.)

*Crocodylus niloticus:*   $N$ = 108 (107 teeth, 1 mandible frag.)

*Crocodylus sp.:*   $N$ = 217 (175 teeth, 16 vertebrae, 10 ribs, 2 chevron, 4 ilia, 1 radius, 1 metatarsal, 1 femur, 2 carpals, 4 phalanges)

[a]Excludes microvertebrate, avian, and fish remains.

*Chelonia*

246 carapace/plastron pieces
3 innominate fragments
1 limb bone
3 indet. fragments

## Indeterminate Fragments

This term refers to specimens that were broken or otherwise modified (e.g., abraded) such that they were not assigned to one of the major taxonomic groups. Most of these specimens, however, were identified to skeletal element. Further, many of these fragments were identified as mammal bone and had enough preserved to be classified to body size category. Detailed data were recorded for over 70% of the 848 indeterminate fragments. Long bone shaft fragments represent slightly over half of this sample (310 out of 615).

Indeterminate: $N = 124$ (23 skull frags., 2 vertebra frags., 28 limb shafts, 1 podial, 70 indet.)
Small-sized indet.: $N = 3$ (3 vertebra frags.)
Medium-sized indet.: $N = 6$ (2 rib shafts, 4 limb shafts)
Large-sized indet.: $N = 2$ (1 vertebra frag., 1 limb shaft)
Very large indet.: $N = 6$ (1 mandible ramus, 1 ilium, 1 limb shaft, 1 distal femur, 2 indet.)
Small–medium indet.: $N = 26$ (3 vertebra frags., 2 rib shafts, 17 limb shafts, 4 indet.)
Medium–large indet.: $N = 10$ (3 vertebra frags., 1 rib shaft, 6 limb shafts)
Medium–very large indet.: $N = 73$ (2 rib shafts, 23 limb shafts, 48 indet.)
Mammal indet.: $N = 100$ (11 skull frags., 1 gnathic, 3 mandible frags., 14 tooth frags., 2 vertebra frags., 1 caudal vertebrae, 1 scapula frag., 1 acetabulum frag., 51 limb shafts, 1 proximal ulna, 1 femur shaft, 13 indet.)
Large microfauna: $N = 1$ (rib shaft)
Small mammal: $N = 9$ (1 tooth frag., 1 caudal vertebra, 1 ilium, 5 limb shafts, 1 proximal radius)
Medium mammal: $N = 57$ (3 vertebra frags., 1 proximal rib, 7 rib shafts, 1 scapula frag., 38 limb shafts, 2 epiphysis frags., 1 proximal radius, 2 metapodial shafts, 1 tibia shaft, 1 distal phalanx)
Large mammal: $N = 16$ (1 vertebra frag., 1 proximal rib, 13 limb shafts, 1 distal phalanx)
Very large mammal: $N = 15$ (1 vertebra frag., 8 limb shafts, 6 indet.)
Small–medium mammal: $N = 58$ (6 vertebra frags., 5 rib shafts, 44 limb shafts, 3 indet.)

Medium–large mammal: $N$ = 74 (1 skull frag., 2 tooth frags., 6 vertebra frags., 1 proximal rib, 7 rib shafts, 1 scapula frag., 2 innominate frags., 42 limb shafts, 2 humerus shafts, 1 ulna shaft, 2 metapodial shafts, 2 tibia shafts, 1 distal tibia, 1 podial, 3 phalanges.)

Medium–very large mammal: $N$ = 35 (1 mandible frag., 4 tooth frags., 1 proximal rib, 1 acetabulum frag., 11 limb shafts, 17 indet.)

Other indet. frags.: $N$ = 233 (mostly mammal, some crocodile frags., a few bird bones)

## Level 2 Fauna

*Number of Specimens ~ 5422*

Mammals identified to taxon and skeletal part = 832 (15%)
Crocodile = 2916 (54%)
Chelonia = 614 (11%)
Indeterminate fragments ~ 1000 (18%)

*Mammalian Macrofauna*

See Tables A.10–A.18.

*Crocodilia* (Postcranial specimens are fragmented in general)

Crocodilidae indet.: $N$ = 1814 (1565 teeth, 2 skull frags., 2 maxillae, 5 mandibles, 45 vertebrae, 1 chevron, 33 rib frags., 4 scapulae, 1 ant. coracoid, 1 ischium, 4 limb bone frags., 2 humeri, 2 radii, 4 ulnae, 2 metapodials, 5 metacarpals, 4 metatarsals, 5 femora, 3 tibiae, 3 fibulae, 3 carpals, 2 calcanea, 22 phalanges, 74 scute frags., 19 indet. frags.)

*Crocodylus niloticus:*    $N$ = 332 (331 teeth, 1 mandible frag.)

*Crocodylus* sp.:    $N$ = 780 (660 teeth, 2 mandibles, 26 vertebrae, 12 ribs, 1 ilium, 1 limb frag., 3 humeri, 3 radii, 1 ulna, 2 metacarpals, 2 metatarsals, 1 carpal, 1 astragalus, 8 phalanges, 29 scute frags., 25 indet. frags.)

*Chelonia*

522 carapace/plastron pieces
78 postcranial bones (limb and axial)
14 indet. fragments

*Indeterminate Fragments*

Very few of the specimens in this category were studied. Every trench had bone splinters. Most of these were fairly large, greater than 2 cm. A small size fraction among indeterminate fragments was not well represented, such as occurred in other Bed I levels. Otherwise, these fragments from DK resemble those from other levels quite well, especially in showing numerous long bone shaft pieces and a wide range of identifiable skeletal parts (cranial and tooth fragments; rib, vertebra, and pelvic pieces; foot bones and larger limb bone fragments were observed).

## DK Artifacts (Levels 1–3)

Tables A.13–15 present data of some basic features of the artifact assemblage: artifact types, the descriptive modifications to stones of various forms, and raw materials.

**TABLE A.1.** DK–3: Number of Specimens, MNE, MNSU, and MNI for Mammalian Taxa

| Taxon | Specimens | MNE | MNSU | MNI | | |
|---|---|---|---|---|---|---|
| | | | | Adult | Immature | MNI total |
| Bovid | 356 (69%) | 196 (62%) | 45 (54%) | 11 | 7 | 17 (48%) |
| Suid | 65 (13%) | 23 ( 8%) | 10 (12%) | 3 | 2 | 5 (14%) |
| Equid | 22 ( 4%) | 15 ( 6%) | 6 ( 7%) | 1 | 1 | 2 ( 5%) |
| Carnivore | 11 ( 2%) | 6 ( 2%) | 4 ( 5%) | 1 | — | 2 ( 5%) |
| Proboscidean | 15 ( 3%) | 6 ( 2%) | 4 ( 5%) | — | — | 2 ( 5%) |
| Rhino | 12 ( 2%) | 5 ( 2%) | 4 ( 5%) | 1 | 1 | 2 ( 5%) |
| Hippo | 20 ( 4%) | 9 ( 3%) | 4 ( 5%) | 1 | 1 | 2 ( 5%) |
| Giraffid | 12 ( 2%) | 8 ( 3%) | 4 ( 5%) | 1 | — | 3 ( 8%) |
| Primate | 5 ( 1%) | 4 ( 1%) | 3 ( 4%) | 1 | — | 1 ( 3%) |
| Total | 518 | 272 | 84 | 20 | 12 | 36 |

**TABLE A.2.** DK–3: Mammalian Taxa Identified and MNI Represented by Each[a]

| Taxon | MNI | Taxon | MNI |
|---|---|---|---|
| Small bovidae (1) | | Carnivora (2) | |
| *Antidorcas recki* | 4 | *Crocuta crocuta* | 1 |
| Medium bovidae (4) | | Canidae indet. | 1 |
| *Kobus sigmoidalis* | 1 | Proboscidean (2) | |
| *Parmularius altidens* | 3 | *Deinotherium bozasi* | 1 |
| *Tragelaphus strepsiceros maryanus* | 1 | Elephantidae indet. | 1 |
| Smaller species than *T. s. maryanus* | 1 | Rhinoceros (2) | |
| Hippotragini indet. | 1 | *Ceratotherium simum* | 1 |
| Large bovidae (4) | | *Diceros* sp. | 1 |
| Bovini indet. | 2 | Hippopotamus (1) | |
| Large Tragelaphini | 1 | *H. gorgops* | 1 |
| Hippotragini indet. | 1 | *H.* sp. indet. | 1 |
| *Megalotragus kattwinkeli* | 2 | Giraffidae (3) | |
| Suidae (2) | | *Giraffa jumae* | 1 |
| *Mesochoerus–Kolpochoerus limnetes* | 3 | *G. stillei* | 1 |
| *Phacochoerus* sp. | 1 | *Sivatherium* sp. | 1 |
| Suid indet. | 1 | Primates (1) | |
| Equidae (1) | | Cercopithecidae indet. | 1 |
| *Equus oldowayensis* | 2 | | |

[a]The number of taxa within any major taxonomic group is given in parentheses.

**TABLE A.3.** DK–3: Number of Specimens, MNE, and MNI for Bovid Size Classes

| Bovid size class | Specimens | MNE | MNI Adult | Immature | MNI total |
|---|---|---|---|---|---|
| Small | 44 (12%) | 33 (17%) | 3 | 1 | 4 (24%) |
| Small/medium | 27 ( 8%) | 19 (10%) | — | — | — |
| Medium | 88 (25%) | 42 (21%) | 4 | 3 | 7 (41%) |
| Medium/large | 22 ( 6%) | 11 ( 6%) | — | — | — |
| Large | 59 (17%) | 39 (19%) | 3 | 3 | 6 (35%) |
| Unclassified | 116 (33%) | 53 (27%) | — | — | — |
| Total | 356 | 197 | 11 | 7 | 17 |

**TABLE A.4.** DK–3: Minimum Number of Bovid Bones According to Skeletal Element and Size Class

| Element | Small | Small/medium[a] | Medium | Medium/large[a] | Large | Unclassified[a] |
|---|---|---|---|---|---|---|
| Braincase | | | 1 | | | |
| Maxilla | 2 | | 5 | | 4 | |
| Basicranium | | | | | | 1 |
| Mandible | 4 | | 6 | | 1 | |
| Hyoid | | | | | | 1 |
| Vertebra | | 1 | 3 | | 3 | |
| Rib | | | | | | 3 |
| Innominate | | 2 | | 1 | | 1 |
| Scapula | | | 4 | | 6 | |
| Humerus | 2 | 3 | 5 | | 2 | |
| Radius | 2 | | 1 | | | 1 |
| Ulna | | 1 | 1 | 1 | 1 | |
| Metacarpal | 2 | 1 | 2 | 1 | 2 | |
| Carpals | 1 | 3 | 3 | 2 | 3 | 2 |
| Femur | 2 | 1 | 1 | | 6 | |
| Tibia | 3 | 1 | 2 | 1 | 3 | |
| Fibula | 1 | | | | | 1 |
| Metatarsal | 4 | 1 | 3 | 1 | 2 | 1 |
| Tarsals | 6 | 3 | 5 | 3 | 2 | 8 |
| Patella | | | | | | |
| Metapodial | 2 | 2 | 1 | 1 | 1 | 3 |
| Podials | | | | | | |
| Sesamoid | | | | | | 13 |
| Phalanx | 2 | | | | 3 | 18 |
| Other | | | | | | |
| Total | 33 | 19 | 42 | 11 | 39 | 53 |

[a]Only those elements not represented under small, medium, or large bovids.

**TABLE A.5.** DK–3: MNSU for Bovid Size Classes

| Unit | Small | Small/medium | Medium | Large | Total |
|------|-------|--------------|--------|-------|-------|
| Cranial | 4 | 0 | 6 | 4 | 14 |
| Axial | 0 | 0 | 1 | 1 | 2 |
| Forelimb | 3 | 2 | 5 | 2 | 12 |
| Hindlimb | 5 | 0 | 6 | 6 | 17 |

**TABLE A.6.** DK–3: Frequency of Limb Bone Epiphyses for Bovid Size Classes

| Element/ epiphysis | Small | Small/ medium | Medium | Medium/ large | Large | Unclassified | Total |
|------|-------|-------|--------|-------|-------|--------------|-------|
| Humerus | | | | | | | |
| Proximal | 0 | 1 | 0 | 1 | 1 | 0 | 3 |
| Distal | 2 | 3 | 5 | 0 | 1 | 0 | 11 |
| Radius/ulna | | | | | | | |
| Proximal | 2 | 1 | 2 | 1 | 1 | 1 | 8 |
| Distal | 2 | 1 | 0 | 0 | 0 | 0 | 3 |
| Metapodial | | | | | | | |
| Proximal | 4 | 3 | 4 | 3 | 3 | 3 | 20 |
| Distal | 6 | 4 | 4 | 3 | 4 | 4 | 25 |
| Tibia | | | | | | | |
| Proximal | 1 | 3 | 2 | 0 | 2 | 0 | 8 |
| Distal | 3 | 1 | 2 | 0 | 2 | 0 | 8 |
| Femur | | | | | | | |
| Proximal | 2 | 0 | 0 | 1 | 1 | 0 | 4 |
| Distal | 2 | 1 | 1 | 0 | 4 | 0 | 8 |

**TABLE A.7.** DK–3: Minimum Number of Bones for Nonbovid Taxa According to Skeletal Element

| Element | Suid | Equid | Carnivore | Proboscidean | Rhino | Hippo | Giraffid | Primate |
|---|---|---|---|---|---|---|---|---|
| Braincase | | | | | | | | |
| Maxilla | 5 | 1 | | | 1 | 2 | 2 | 1 |
| Basicranium | | | | | | | | |
| Mandible | 5 | 2 | 1 | 2 | 1 | 1 | | |
| Hyoid | | | | | | | | |
| Vertebra | 3 | 1 | 1 | | | | | |
| Rib | | | | 1 | | 3 | | |
| Scapula | 2 | | | | | | 2 | |
| Humerus | 1 | 1 | | | | | 1 | |
| Radius | 1 | 1 | | | | | | |
| Ulna | | | | | | | | |
| Metacarpal | | 4 | 1 | | | | | |
| Carpals | 1 | 2 | 1 | | 2 | | | |
| Femur | | | | | | | | 2 |
| Tibia | 2 | | | | | | | |
| Fibula | 1 | | | | | | | |
| Metatarsal | 1 | 1 | | | 1 | | 1 | |
| Tarsals | | 1 | 1 | | | | | |
| Patella | | | | | | | | |
| Metapodial | | | | | | | 1 | |
| Podials | | | 1 | 2 | | 1 | | |
| Sesamoids | | | | | | | | |
| Phalanx | 2 | 1 | | | | 2 | 1 | 1 |
| Other | | | | 1 | | | | |
| Total | 23 | 15 | 6 | 6 | 5 | 9 | 8 | 4 |

340

**TABLE A.8.** DK–3 MNSU for Nonbovid Taxa

| Unit | Suid | Equid | Carnivore | Proboscidean | Rhino | Hippo | Giraffid | Primate |
|------|------|-------|-----------|--------------|-------|-------|----------|---------|
| Cranial | 5 | 2 | 1 | 2 | 2 | 2 | 1 | 1 |
| Axial | 1 | 1 | 1 | 1 | — | 1 | — | — |
| Forelimb | 2 | 2 | 1 | — | 1 | — | 2 | — |
| Hindlimb | 2 | 1 | 1 | — | 1 | — | 1 | 2 |
| Limb indet. | — | — | — | 1 | — | 1 | — | — |

**TABLE A.9.** DK–3: Frequency of Complete (Undamaged) Bones Relative to Total MNE; Frequency of Complete Long Bones Relative to Minimum Number of Long Bones for Each Major Taxon

| Taxon | Complete bones/ MNE | Percentage | Complete long bones/ MNE long bones | Percentage | Elements |
|---|---|---|---|---|---|
| Bovid | 76/196 | 39 | 10/70 | 14 | 4 metatarsals 3 femora 2 tibia 1 humerus |
| Suid | 6/23 | 26 | 2/6 | 33 | humerus, tibia |
| Equid | 3/15 | 20 | 1/7 | 14 | metacarpal |
| Carnivore | 1/6 | 17 | 0/1 | 0 | |
| Proboscidean | 2/6 | 33 | 0/0 | — | |
| Rhino | 1/5 | 20 | 0/0 | — | |
| Hippo | 1/9 | 11 | 0/0 | — | |
| Giraffid | 1/8 | 12 | 0/3 | 0 | |
| Primate | 1/4 | 25 | 0/2 | 0 | |
| Total | 92/272 | 34 | 13/89 | 15 | |

**TABLE A.10.** DK–2: Number of Specimens, MNE, MNSU, and MNI for Mammalian Taxa

| Taxon | Specimens | MNE | MNSU | MNI Adult | MNI Immature | MNI total |
|---|---|---|---|---|---|---|
| Bovid | 602 (72%) | 329 (79%) | 64 (59%) | 13 | 6 | 19 (46%) |
| Suid | 113 (14%) | 22 ( 5%) | 10 ( 9%) | 3 | 2 | 6 (15%) |
| Equid | 17 ( 2%) | 12 ( 3%) | 6 (5.5%) | 2 | — | 3 ( 7%) |
| Carnivore | 11 (1.3%) | 5 (1.2%) | 3 ( 3%) | 1 | 1 | 2 ( 5%) |
| Proboscidean | 11 (1.3%) | 4 ( 1%) | 4 ( 4%) | — | 1 | 2 ( 5%) |
| Rhino | 7 (0.8%) | 5 (1.2%) | 4 ( 4%) | 1 | 0 | 1 ( 2%) |
| Hippo | 12 (1.4%) | 6 (1.4%) | 4 ( 4%) | 0 | 1 | 1 ( 2%) |
| Giraffid | 9 ( 1%) | 7 ( 2%) | 5 (4.5%) | 2 | 1 | 3 ( 7%) |
| Primate | 50 ( 6%) | 28 ( 7%) | 9 ( 8%) | 3 | — | 4 (10%) |
| Total | 832 | 418 | 109 | 25 | 12 | 41 |

**TABLE A.11.** DK–2: Mammalian Taxa Identified and MNI Represented by Each[a]

| Taxon | MNI | Taxon | MNI |
|---|---|---|---|
| Small bovidae (1) | | Carnivora (1) | |
| *Antidorcas recki* | 4 | Indet. | 2 |
| Medium bovidae (5) | | Proboscideans (2) | |
| *Kobus sigmoidalis* | 2 | *Deintherium bozasi* | 1 |
| *Parmularius altidens* | 4 | Elephantidae indet. | 1 |
| Hippotragini indet. | 2 | Rhinoceros (1) | |
| *Tragelaphus strepsiceros maryanus* | 2 | *Ceratotherium simum* | 1 |
| Species smaller than *T. s. maryanus* | 1 | Hippotamus (1) | |
| Large bovidae (2) | | *H. gorgops* | 1 |
| Bovini indet. | 1 | Girrafidae (2) | |
| *Megalotragus kattwinkeli* | 2 | *Giraffa* sp. | 1 |
| Indet. | 1 | *Sivatherium* sp. | 2 |
| Suidae (3) | | Primates (4) | |
| *Mesochoerus–Kolpochoerus limnetes* | 3 | *Papio* sp. | 1 |
| *Phacochoerus* sp. | 1 | *Theropithecus* sp. | 1 |
| *Metridiochoerus andrewsi* | 1 | *Cercocebus* sp. | 1 |
| Indet. | 1 | *Galago* sp. | 1 |
| Equidae (3) | | | |
| *Equus oldowayensis* | 2 | | |
| *Equus burchelli* | 1 | | |
| *Hipparion* sp. | 1 (?) | | |

[a]The number of taxa within any major taxonomic group is given in parentheses.

**TABLE A.12.** DK–2: Number of Specimens, MNE, and MNI for Bovid Size Classes

| Bovid size class | Specimens | MNE | MNI Adult | Immature | MNI total |
|---|---|---|---|---|---|
| Small | 71 (12%) | 49 (15%) | 3 | 1 | 4 (21%) |
| Small/medium | 4 (0.6%) | 4 ( 1%) | — | — | — |
| Medium | 168 (28%) | 83 (25%) | 7 | 4 | 11 (58%) |
| Medium/large | 3 (0.4%) | 3 ( 1%) | — | — | — |
| Large | 60 (10%) | 46 (14%) | 3 | 1 | 4 (21%) |
| Unclassified | 296 (49%) | 144 (44%) | — | — | — |
| Total | 602 | 329 | 13 | 6 | 19 |

**TABLE A.13.** DK–2: Minimum Number of Bovid Bones According to Skeletal Element and Size Class

| Element | Small | Small/medium[a] | Medium | Medium/large[a] | Large | Unclassified[a] |
|---|---|---|---|---|---|---|
| Braincase | | | 2 | | 1 | |
| Maxilla | 2 | | 6 | | 1 | |
| Basicranium | | | | | | |
| Mandible | 3 | | 10 | | 1 | |
| Hyoid | | | | | | |
| Vertebra | 3 | | 5 | 1 | 7 | 2 |
| Rib | 1 | | | | 1 | 8 |
| Innominate | 4 | | 4 | 1 | 3 | |
| Scapula | 1 | | 6 | | | 5 |
| Humerus | 1 | | 8 | | 4 | 4 |
| Radius | 2 | | 5 | | 5 | |
| Ulna | | | 4 | | 5 | 4 |
| Metacarpal | 3 | | 7 | | 3 | |
| Carpals | 5 | | 1 | | | 19 |
| Femur | 1 | 1 | 3 | | 1 | |
| Tibia | 3 | 1 | 8 | | 5 | 4 |
| Fibula | 2 | | | | | 4 |
| Metatarsal | 1 | | 6 | | 4 | |
| Tarsals | 7 | 2 | 5 | 1 | 2 | 18 |
| Patella | 2 | | | | | 2 |
| Metapodial | 3 | | | | | |
| Podials | | | | | | |
| Sesamoid | | | | | | 33 |
| Phalanx | 5 | | 4 | | 4 | 41 |
| Other | | | | | | |
| Total | 49 | 4 | 83 | 3 | 46 | 144 |

[a]Only those elements not represented under small, medium, or large bovids.

**TABLE A.14.** DK–2: MNSU for Bovid Size Classes

| Unit | Small | Medium | Large | Total |
|------|-------|--------|-------|-------|
| Cranial | 3 | 10 | 2 | 15 |
| Axial | 3 | 3 | 2 | 8 |
| Forelimb | 3 | 11 | 6 | 20 |
| Hindlimb | 4 | 12 | 5 | 21 |

**TABLE A.15.** DK–2: Frequency of Limb Bone Epiphyses for Bovid Size Classes Based on Minimum Number

| Element/ epiphysis | Small | Small/ medium | Medium | Large | Unclassified | Total |
|--------------------|-------|---------------|--------|-------|--------------|-------|
| Humerus | | | | | | |
| Proximal | 0 | 0 | 1 | 0 | 1 | 2 |
| Distal | 1 | 0 | 8 | 3 | 5 | 17 |
| Radius/ulna | | | | | | |
| Proximal | 1 | 0 | 8 | 8 | 7 | 24 |
| Distal | 1 | 0 | 6 | 4 | 1 | 12 |
| Metapodial | | | | | | |
| Proximal | 3 | 0 | 13 | 5 | 2 | 23 |
| Distal | 6 | 0 | 10 | 8 | 5 | 29 |
| Tibia | | | | | | |
| Proximal | 0 | 0 | 2 | 2 | 0 | 4 |
| Distal | 3 | 1 | 8 | 3 | 7 | 22 |
| Femur | | | | | | |
| Proximal | 1 | 1 | 1 | 0 | 0 | 3 |
| Distal | 0 | 0 | 3 | 1 | 2 | 6 |

**TABLE A.16.** DK–2: Minimum Number of Bones for Nonbovid Taxa According to Skeletal Element[a]

| Element | Suid | Equid | Carnivore | Proboscidean | Rhino | Hippo | Giraffid | Primate |
|---|---|---|---|---|---|---|---|---|
| Braincase | 3 | | 1 | | | | 1 | 3 |
| Maxilla | 3 | 1 | 1 | | | | 1 | 3 |
| Basicranium | | | | | | 1 | | |
| Mandible | 4 | 2 | 1 | 2 | 1 | 1 | 1 | 3 |
| Hyoid | | | | | | | | |
| Vertebra | 2 | | 1 | | 1 | | | |
| Rib | | | | 1 | | | | |
| Innominate | | | | | 1 | | | |
| Scapula | | | | | | | | |
| Humerus | 1 | 1 | 1 | | | | | 3 |
| Radius | 2 | 1 | | | | | | |
| Ulna | | | | | | 1 | | |
| Metacarpal | | 1 | 1 | | 1 | | | 1 |
| Carpals | 1 | | | | 1 | | | 4 |
| Femur | 1 | | | | | 1 | | 1 |
| Tibia | | | | | | 1 | 1 | 1 |
| Fibula | | | | | | | | |
| Metatarsal | | | | | | | | 1 |
| Tarsals | 3 | 3 | | 1 | | 1 | | |
| Patella | | | | | | | | 2 |
| Metapodial | | | | | | | | |
| Podials | | | | | | | | 4 |
| Sesamoids | | 1 | | | | | 1 | |
| Phalanx | 5 | 2 | | | | | 3 | 5 |
| Other | | | | | | | | |
| Total | 22 | 12 | 5 | 4 | 5 | 6 | 7 | 28 |

[a]Specific taxon, size, age, and surface weathering were variables used to calculate the minimum number.

**TABLE A.17.** DK–2: MNSU for Nonbovid Taxa

| Unit | Suid | Equid | Carnivore | Proboscidean | Rhino | Hippo | Giraffid | Primate |
|------|------|-------|-----------|--------------|-------|-------|----------|---------|
| Cranial | 6 | 2 | 1 | 2 | 1 | 1 | 2 | 4 |
| Axial | 1 | 0 | 1 | 1 | 1 | 0 | 0 | 0 |
| Forelimb | 2 | 2 | 1 | 0 | 2 | 2 | 0 | 3 |
| Hindlimb | 1 | 2 | 0 | 1 | 0 | 1 | 1 | 2 |
| Limb indet. | 0 | 0 | 0 | 0 | 0 | 0 | 2 | 0 |

**TABLE A.18.** DK–2: Frequency of Complete (Undamaged) Bones Relative to Total MNE; Frequency of Complete Long Bones Relative to Minimum Number of Long Bones for Each Major Taxon

| Taxon | Complete bones/ MNE | Percentage | Complete long bones/ MNE long bones | Percentage | Elements |
|---|---|---|---|---|---|
| Bovid | 137/329 | 42 | 15/96 | 16 | 2 humeri<br>6 metacarpals<br>5 radii<br>1 femur<br>1 metatarsal |
| Suid | 7/22 | 32 | 0/4 | 0 | |
| Equid | 3/12 | 25 | 0/3 | 0 | |
| Carnivore | 1/5 | 20 | 0/1 | 0 | |
| Proboscidean | 1/4 | 25 | 0/0 | — | |
| Rhino | 2/5 | 40 | 0/0 | — | |
| Hippo | 2/6 | 33 | 0/2 | 0 | |
| Giraffid | 3/7 | 43 | 0/1 | 0 | |
| Primate | 13/28 | 46 | 0/14 | 0 | |
| Total | 169/418 | 40 | 15/121 | 12 | |

**TABLE A.19.** Site DK: Frequencies of Artifact Types Based on Leakey's Original Classification and on Current Study, Based on Leakey's Types (Leaky, 1971)

| Type | Original classification | Current study |
|---|---|---|
| Chopper | 47 | 56 |
| Protobiface | | 1 |
| Polyhedron | 32 | 18 |
| Discoid | 27 | 26 |
| Subspheroid | 7 | 4 |
| Spheroid | — | 1 |
| Small scraper | 17 | 21 |
| Large scraper | 10 | 3 |
| Burin | 3 | 4 |
| Awl | — | 1 |
| Laterally trimmed flake | — | 3 |
| Sundry tool | 8 | 4 |
| Casual core/tool indet. | — | 15 |
| Utilized material | 158 | 87 |
| Whole flake | 254 | 236 |
| Broken flake | 477 | 444 |
| Core fragment | 118 | 112 |
| Other *debitage* | 4 | 10 |
| Manuport | — | 3 |
| Artifact/manuport indet. | — | 13 |
| ?Artifact | — | 99 |
| Other | 1 | 2 |
| Total | 1163 | 1163 |

**TABLE A.20.** Site DK: Types of Stone Modification and Size/Form of Raw Material Used

| Material | Whole unflaked | Broken unflaked | Core | Incidental core | Flake/ flake fragment | Flake core | Incidental flake core | Indet. | Total |
|---|---|---|---|---|---|---|---|---|---|
| Cobble | 25 | 25 | 79 | 10 | 4 | 7 | 1 | 40 | 191 |
| Pebble | 2 | 3 | 33 | 2 | — | — | — | 12 | 52 |
| Slab | 3 | 1 | 5 | — | — | — | — | 1 | 10 |
| Broken fragment indet. | — | 252 | 2 | 5 | — | — | — | 5 | 264 |
| Indet. | — | — | 12 | — | 610 | 12 | 3 | 9 | 646 |
| Total | 30 | 281 | 131 | 17 | 614 | 19 | 4 | 67 | 1163 |

**TABLE A.21.** Site DK: Representation of Stone Artifact Raw Materials by Number of Specimens and by Weight

| Material | Specimens | Weight (grams) |
|---|---|---|
| Basalt | 10 | 2,978 |
| Trachyandesite | 7 | 1,166 |
| Basalt/trachyand. indet. | 189 | 14,916 |
| Nephelinite | 264 | 11,823 |
| Vesicular basalt | 207 | 35,927 |
| Lava indet. | 211 | 22,153 |
| Quartzite | 271 | 4,819 |
| Chert | 1 | 17 |
| Feldspar | 1 | 56 |
| Indeterminate | 1 | 3 |
| Total | 1162 | 93,858 |

# Appendix B: Site FLKNN–3

Number of stone artifacts = 72
Number of faunal remains = 2261[a]
Depth of deposit = 9 cm
Area excavated = approximately 209 m$^2$
Density of excavated remains = 124 per m$^3$

## Fauna

*Number of Specimens = 2261[a]*

Mammals identified to taxon and skeletal part = 390 (20%)
Crocodile = 14 (0.7%)
Chelonia = 1564 (79%)
Indeterminate fragments = 293[b]

### Mammalian Macrofauna

Tables B.1–9 provide data on the mammalian macrofaunal specimens. Tables B.3–6 present details about the bovids according to size class, since bovids form the most abundant taxon and since numerous taphonomic effects are size-related. These tables highlight taxonomic representation, skeletal part frequencies, and the completeness of bones in the assemblage.

### Crocodilia

Crocodilidae indet.: $N$ = 14 teeth

### Chelonia

1293 carapace/plastron plate pieces (mostly articulated)
1 complete shell
270 postcranial pieces (43 innominate, 6 vertebra, 1 scapula, 1 humerus, 1 ulna, 3 femur, 24 indet. limb bones, and 191 indet. frags.)

[a]Excludes microvertebrate, avian, and fish remains.
[b]Numerous indeterminate fragments come from the sieved Level 2/3 sample; see end of Appendix C.

*Indeterminate Fragments*

These broken pieces were not identified to any major taxonomic group. Many, however, were assigned to skeletal element and body size category. Shaft fragments from unknown long bones comprise 29% of this sample. Details of those fragments known to derive from Level 3 follow. More fragments undoubtedly occur in the sieved sample from Levels 2/3 combined.

Indeterminate: $N = 58$ (1 premaxilla frag., 1 tooth, 1 radius frag., 55 indet. frags.)

Small-sized vertebrate: $N = 3$ (1 vertebrae frag., 2 indet. frags.)

Mammal indet.: $N = 34$ (4 cranial frags., 2 mandible frags., 3 tooth frags., 1 vertebra frag., 1 rib shaft frag., 3 innominate frags., 13 limb shaft frags., 7 indet. frags.)

Small mammal: $N = 49$ (13 cranial frags., 1 mandible frag., 16 vertebra frags., 1 proximal rib, 3 rib shaft frags., 1 scapula frag., 6 limb shaft frags., 1 humerus shaft frag., 1 distal radius, 1 proximal femur frag., 2 phalanges, 3 indet. frags.)

Medium mammal: $N = 49$ (2 vertebra frags., 24 rib shaft frags., 2 rib distal ends, 18 limb shaft frags., 1 humerus shaft frag., 1 proximal tibia, 1 calcaneus)

Large mammal: $N = 5$ (4 limb shaft frags., 1 proximal femur)

Small–medium mammal: $N = 50$ (6 cranial frags., 1 mandible frag., 1 hyoid frag., 7 vertebra frags., 3 proximal ribs, 7 rib shaft frags., 3 sternum segments, 2 innominate frags., 15 limb shaft frags., 1 podial, 1 phalanx, 3 indet. frags.)

Medium–large mammal: $N = 44$ (1 mandible frag., 1 thoracic vertebra, 1 proximal rib, 3 rib shaft frags., 33 limb shaft frags., 1 humerus shaft frag., 2 radius shaft frags., 1 metapodial shaft frag., 1 phalanx)

Medium–very large mammal: $N = 1$ (limb shaft frag.)

## Stone Artifacts

$N = 72$

Tables B.10–12 provide some basic data about this artifact assemblage.

**TABLE B.1.** FLKNN–3: The Number of Specimens, MNE, MNSU, MNI for Mammalian Taxa

| Taxon | Specimens | MNE | MNSU | MNI Adult | MNI Immature | MNI total |
|-------|-----------|-----|------|-----------|--------------|-----------|
| Bovid | 252 (65%) | 155 (64%) | 39 (59%) | 9 | 9 | 18 (53%) |
| Suid | 35 (9%) | 20 (8%) | 9 (14%) | 3 | 2 | 5 (15%) |
| Equid | 10 (3%) | 9 (4%) | 4 (6%) | 0 | 1 | 1 (3%) |
| Carnivore | 54 (14%) | 26 (11%) | 7 (11%) | 4 | 3 | 7 (21%) |
| Primate[a] | 39 (10%) | 33 (14%) | 7 (11%) | 2 | 1 | 3 (9%) |
| Total | 390 | 243 | 66 | 18 | 16 | 34 |

[a]Includes hominid remains. Nonhominid primate remains: 8 specimens, MNI = 1.

**TABLE B.2.** FLKNN–3: Mammalian Taxa Identified and MNI Represented by Each[a]

| Taxon | MNI |
|-------|-----|
| Small bovidae (1) | |
|   Antilopini indet. | 1 |
|   Indet. | 3 |
| Medium bovidae (3) | |
|   *Kobus sigmoidalis* | 10 |
|   *Parmularius altidens* | 1 |
|   Tragelaphini indet. | 1 |
| Large bovidae (1) | |
|   Indet. | 2 |
| Suidae (1) | |
|   *Mesochoerus–Kolpochoerus limnetes* | 1 |
|   Indet. | 4 |
| Equidae (1) | |
|   *Equus oldowayensis* | 1 |
| Carnivora (5) | |
|   *Protocyon recki (Canidae)* | 1 |
|   *Galerella primitivus* (Viverridae) | 1 |
|   *Mungos minutus* (Vivveridae) | 3 |
|   *Hyaena hyaena* (Hyaenidae) | 1 |
|   Felidae indet. | 1 |
| Primates (2) | |
|   Cercopithecidae indet. | 1 |
|   Hominidae | 2 |

[a]The number of taxa within any major taxonomic group is given in parentheses.

**TABLE B.3.** FLKNN–3: Number of Specimens, MNE, and MNI for Bovid Size Classes

| Bovid size class | Specimens | MNE | MNI Adult | Immature | MNI total |
|---|---|---|---|---|---|
| Small | 34 (13%) | 25 (16%) | 3 | 1 | 4 (22%) |
| Medium | 199 (79%) | 115 (74%) | 5 | 7 | 12 (67%) |
| Large | 12 (5%) | 11 (7%) | 1 | 1 | 2 (11%) |
| Unclassified | 7 (3%) | 4 (3%) | — | — | — |
| Total | 252 | 155 | 9 | 9 | 18 |

**TABLE B.4.** FLKNN–3: Minimum Number of Bovid Bones According to Skeletal Element and Size Class

| Element | Small | Medium | Large | Unclassified[a] |
|---|---|---|---|---|
| Braincase | 1 | 4 | 1 | |
| Maxilla | | 4 | | |
| Basicranium | | | | |
| Mandible | | 13 | | |
| Hyoid | | 1 | | |
| Vertebra | 1 | 33 | | |
| Rib | 3 | 9 | | |
| Innominate | | 3 | | |
| Scapula | 2 | 4 | | |
| Humerus | 1 | 3 | | |
| Radius | | 5 | | |
| Ulna | 3 | 3 | | |
| Metacarpal | 2 | 4 | 1 | |
| Carpals | 1 | 5 | | |
| Femur | | | 1 | |
| Tibia | 1 | 3 | 1 | |
| Fibula | 1 | 2 | | |
| Metatarsal | 1 | | 2 | |
| Tarsals | 2 | 7 | | |
| Patella | | 1 | 2 | |
| Metapodial | | 1 | | |
| Podials | | | | 2 |
| Sesamoid | | 4 | | 2 |
| Phalanx | 6 | 6 | 3 | |
| Other | | | | |
| Total | 25 | 115 | 11 | 4 |

[a]Only those elements not represented in small, medium, or large bovids.

**TABLE B.5.** FLKNN–3: MNSU for Bovid Size Classes

| Unit | Small | Medium | Large | Total |
|------|-------|--------|-------|-------|
| Cranial | 1 | 13 | 1 | 15 |
| Axial | 1 | 2 | 0 | 3 |
| Forelimb | 4 | 7 | 1 | 12 |
| Hindlimb | 2 | 4 | 3 | 9 |

**TABLE B.6.** FLKNN–3: Frequency of Limb Bone Epiphyses for Bovid Size Classes Based on Minimum Number

| Element/<br>Epiphysis | Small | Medium | Large | Total |
|-----------------------|-------|--------|-------|-------|
| Humerus | | | | |
|   Proximal | 1 | 2 | 0 | 3 |
|   Distal | 0 | 3 | 0 | 3 |
| Radius/ulna | | | | |
|   Proximal | 3 | 8 | 0 | 11 |
|   Distal | 0 | 2 | 0 | 2 |
| Metapodial | | | | |
|   Proximal | 2 | 4 | 2 | 8 |
|   Distal | 3 | 6 | 1 | 10 |
| Tibia | | | | |
|   Proximal | 1 | 0 | 0 | 1 |
|   Distal | 1 | 2 | 1 | 4 |
| Femur | | | | |
|   Proximal | 0 | 0 | 1 | 1 |
|   Distal | 0 | 0 | 0 | 0 |

**TABLE B.7.** FLKNN–3: Minimum Number of Each Skeletal Element for Major Mammal Taxa[a]

| Element | Suid | Equid | Carnivore | Primate[b] |
|---|---|---|---|---|
| Braincase | | | 1 | 1 |
| Maxilla | 3 | | 1 | 1 |
| Basicranium | | | | |
| Mandible | 2 | 1 | 5 | 2 |
| Hyoid | | | | |
| Vertebra | 1 | 3 | | |
| Rib | | 2 | 1 | |
| Innominate | | | 1 | |
| Scapula | 1 | | | |
| Humerus | 4 | | | |
| Radius | 1 | | | |
| Ulna | 1 | | | |
| Metacarpal | | | | 1 |
| Carpals | | 1 | | 3 |
| Femur | | | | |
| Tibia | | | 1 | 1 |
| Fibula | | | | |
| Metatarsal | | | 3 | 5 |
| Tarsals | 1 | 1 | 3 | 7 |
| Patella | | | | |
| Metapodial | | | 2 | |
| Podials | | | | |
| Sesamoid | | 1 | | |
| Phalanx | 6 | | 6 | 11 |
| Other | | | 2 | 1 |
| | | | | (Clavicle) |
| Total | 20 | 9 | 26 | 33 |

[a]Specific taxon, side, age, and surface weathering were variables used to calculate the minimum number.

[b]Includes hominid material. Nonhominid remains are 1 maxilla, 1 mandible, and 1 tibia.

**TABLE B.8.** FLKNN–3: MNSU for Nonbovid Taxa

| Unit | Suid | Equid | Carnivore | Primate |
|---|---|---|---|---|
| Cranial | 3 | 1 | 5 | 2 |
| Axial | 1 | 1 | 0 | 1 |
| Forelimb | 4 | 1 | 0 | 2 |
| Hindlimb | 1 | 1 | 1 | 2 |
| Limb indet. | 0 | 0 | 1 | 0 |

**TABLE B.9.** FLKNN–3: Frequency of Complete (Undamaged) Bones Relative to Total MNE; Frequency of Complete Long Bones Relative to Minimum Number of Long Bones for Each Major Taxon

| Taxon | Complete bones MNE | Percentage | Complete long bones MNE long bones | Percentage | Elements |
|---|---|---|---|---|---|
| Bovid | 29/155 | 19 | 3/32 | 9 | 2 metacarpals 1 radius |
| Suid | 4/20 | 20 | 0/6 | 0 | |
| Equid | 2/9 | 22 | 0/0 | — | |
| Carnivore | 11/26 | 42 | 0/1 | 0 | |
| Primate | 15/33 | 45 | 0/1 | 0 | |

"Includes hominid remains; ratio for complete bones for nonhominid remains = 0/3.

**TABLE B.10.** FLKNN–3: Frequencies of Artifact Types Based on Leakey's Original Classification and on Current Study, Based on Leakey's Types (Leaky, 1971)

| Type | Original classification | Current study |
|---|---|---|
| Chopper | 2 | 2 |
| Protobiface | | |
| Polyhedron | 1 | 1 |
| Discoid | | |
| Subspheroid | | |
| Spheroid | | |
| Small scraper | | |
| Large scraper | 1 | 1 |
| Burin | | |
| Awl | | |
| Laterally trimmed flake | | |
| Sundry tool | | |
| Casual Core/tool indet. | | |
| Utilized material | 8 | 9 |
| Whole flake | 7 | 6 |
| Broken flake | 21 | 22 |
| Core fragment | 8 | 8 |
| Other *debitage* | | |
| Manuport | 24 | 23 |
| Artifact/manuport indet. | | |
| ?Artifact | | |
| Other | | |
| Total | 72 | 72 |

**TABLE B.11.** FLKNN–3: Types of Stone Modification and Size/Form of Raw Material Used

| Material | Whole unflaked | Broken unflaked | Core | Incidental core | Flake/ flake fragment | Flake core | Incidental flake core | Indet. | Total |
|---|---|---|---|---|---|---|---|---|---|
| Cobble | 24 | 1 | 4 | 2 | | 1 | | | 32 |
| Pebble | | | | | | | | | 0 |
| Slab | 2 | | | | | | | | 2 |
| Broken fragment indet. | | | | | | | | | 0 |
| Indet. | | | | | 38 | | | | 38 |
| Total | 26 | 1 | 4 | 2 | 38 | 1 | 0 | 0 | 72 |

**TABLE B.12.** FLKNN–3: Representation of Stone Artifact Raw Materials by Number of Specimens and by Weight

| Material | Specimens | Weight (grams) |
|---|---|---|
| Basalt | 1 | 247 |
| Trachyandesite | 16 | 4677 |
| Basalt/trachyand. indet. | 8 | 2964 |
| Nephelinite | 3 | 411 |
| Lava indet. | 9 | 4078 |
| Quartzite | 33 | 1378 |
| Total | 70 | 13,755 |

# Appendix C: FLKNN–2

Number of stone artifacts $= 0$
Number of faunal remains $= 478$
Depth of deposit $= 24$ cm
Area excavated $=$ approximately 186 m$^2$
Density of excavated remains $= 10.7$ m$^{3a}$

## Fauna

*Number of Specimens $= 478$*

Mammals identified to taxon and skeletal part $= 324$ (68%)
Indeterminate fragments $= 154$ (32%)[b]

### Mammalian Macrofauna

Tables C.1–9 present data for the mammalian macrofaunal specimens that summarize taxonomic representation, skeletal part frequencies, and completeness of bones in the assemblage.

### Indeterminate Fragments of Bone

Most of these broken pieces belong to mammals of medium body size. Long bone fragments, both shafts and various parts of identified long bones, make up 34% of these pieces. Thirty-nine fragments of unrecognizable body parts apparently were associated with suid bones and may belong to them. More fragments from this level undoubtedly occur in the sieved sample from Levels 2/3 combined.

Indeterminate: $N = 3$ (1 braincase frag., 2 indet. frags.)
Medium-sized vertebrate: $N = 1$ (limb shaft frag.)

[a]This figure is a minimum density (1) since the bones were concentrated in the central portion of this level, and (2) since this figure does not include possibly thousands of bone fragments that derive from this level but were found in the Levels 2/3 sieving.
[b]Numerous indeterminate fragments come from the sieved Levels 2/3 combined sample; see end of this appendix.

Large-sized vertebrate: $N = 1$ (occipital condyle)

Mammal indet.: $N = 5$ (2 vertebral and 3 limb shaft frags.)

Large micromammal: $N = 1$ (rib shaft frag.)

Small mammal: $N = 2$ (1 humerus, 1 limb shaft frag.)

Medium mammal: $N = 76$ (2 vertebra frags., 2 rib heads, 27 rib shaft frags., 5 limb shafts, 1 metapodial frag., 39 indet. frags.)

Large mammal: $N = 7$ (2 rib shaft frags., 1 innominate frag., 4 limb shaft frags.)

Small–medium mammal: $N = 29$ (3 vertebra frags., 1 rib, 1 proximal rib, 14 rib shaft frags., 9 limb shaft frags., 1 tibia shaft frag.)

Medium–large mammal: $N = 28$ (3 thoracic spines, 10 rib shaft frags., 1 proximal rib epiphysis, 10 limb shaft frags., 2 metapodial shaft frags., 1 proximal tibia, 1 middle phalanx)

Medium–very large mammal: $N = 1$ (indet. frag.)

## FLKNN Levels 2/3: Combined Sample from Sieving

*Number of Faunal Specimens = 36,500+*

Bovid = 12 vertebrae, medium-sized species, juvenile

Equid = 2 (1 maxilla, 1 manus cuneiform frag.)

Chelonia = (Pelomedusid carapace scute)

Indeterminate fragments = approximately 33,000

Mixed fauna = approximately 3800[c]

A few of the indeterminate fragments are recognized to body part or body size category. Most of those that are identified belong to small/medium- or medium-sized mammals. The main faunal difference between Levels 2 and 3 at this site is the abundance of Chelonia in Level 3, while none occurs in Level 2. This sieved sample yielded only one recognized turtle shell scute, suggesting that much of the sample is characteristic of Level 2. However, an abundance of microfaunal remains mixed with indeterminate fragments of (probably) larger mammals occurs in this sample and in Level 3. The majority of pieces from this combined set are 1 cm or less in length; the sample, on the whole, represents a very small size fraction of bone from probably both levels.

[c]Indeterminate fragments, microvertebrates, and avian remains.

**TABLE C.1.** FLKNN–2: The Number of Specimens, MNE, MNSU, and MNI for Mammalian Taxa

| Taxon | Specimens | MNE | MNSU | MNI Adult | MNI Immature | MNI total |
|---|---|---|---|---|---|---|
| Bovid | 156 (48%) | 107 (52%) | 37 (65%) | 9 | 5 | 14 (61%) |
| Suid | 145 (45%) | 78 (38%) | 13 (23%) | 3 | 2 | 5 (22%) |
| Equid | 18 (5.5%) | 18 (9%) | 5 (9%) | 2 | 1 | 3 (13%) |
| Carnivore | 5 (1.5%) | 3 (1.5%) | 2 (3.5%) | 1 | 0 | 1 (4%) |
| Total | 324 | 206 | 57 | 15 | 8 | 23 |

**TABLE C.2.** FLKNN–2: Mammalian Taxa Identified and MNI Represented by Each[a]

| Taxon | MNI |
|---|---|
| Small bovidae indet. | 1 |
| Medium bovidae (3) | |
| *Kobus sigmoidalis* | 6 |
| *Parmularius altidens* | ?1 |
| Tragelaphini indet. | 1 |
| Large bovidae (2): | |
| *Hippotragus gigas* | 2 |
| Large Alcelaphini | 2 |
| Indet. | 1 |
| Suidae (1) | |
| *Mesochoerus–Kolpochoerus limnetes* | 4 |
| Indet. | 1 |
| Equidae (1) | |
| *Equus oldowayensis* | 3 |
| Carnivora (1) | |
| *Galerella debilis* (Viverridae) | 1 |

[a]The number of taxa within any major taxonomic group is given in parentheses.

**TABLE C.3.** FLKNN–2: Number of Specimens, MNE, and MNI for Bovid Size Classes

| Bovid size class | Specimens | MNE | MNI | | MNI total |
|---|---|---|---|---|---|
| | | | Adult | Immature | |
| Small | 7 (4%) | 5 (5%) | 0 | 1 | 1 (7%) |
| Small/Medium | 5 (3%) | 2 (2%) | — | — | — |
| Medium | 111 (71%) | 71 (66%) | 4 | 3 | 7 (50%) |
| Large | 31 (19%) | 28 (26%) | 5 | 1 | 6 (43%) |
| Unclassified | 2 (1%) | 1 (1%) | — | — | — |
| Total | 156 | 107 | 9 | 5 | 14 |

**TABLE C.4.** FLKNN–2: Minimum Number of Bovid Bones According to Skeletal Element and Size Class

| Element | Small | Small/Medium | Medium | Large | Unclassified[a] |
|---|---|---|---|---|---|
| Braincase | | | 1 | | |
| Maxilla | | | 2 | | |
| Basicranium | | | | | |
| Mandible | | | 7 | | |
| Hyoid | | | | | |
| Vertebra | | 1 | 4 | 1 | |
| Rib | | | 3 | | |
| Innominate | | | 1 | | |
| Scapula | 1 | | 6 | 3 | |
| Humerus | 1 | 1 | 7 | 4 | |
| Radius | 1 | | 7 | 3 | |
| Ulna | | | 5 | 3 | |
| Metacarpal | | | 7 | 4 | |
| Carpals | | | 2 | | 1 |
| Femur | | | 1 | 2 | |
| Tibia | | | 4 | 3 | |
| Fibula | | | | | |
| Metatarsal | 1 | | 7 | | |
| Tarsals | | | 1 | | |
| Patella | | | 1 | | |
| Metapodial | 1 | | | | |
| Podials | | | | | |
| Sesamoid | | | 3 | | |
| Phalanx | | | 2 | 5 | |
| Other | | | | | |
| Total | 5 | 2 | 71 | 28 | 1 |

[a]Only those elements not accounted for by small, medium, or large bovids.

**TABLE C.5.** FLKNN–2: MNSU for bovid size classes

| Unit | Small | Medium | Large | Total |
|------|-------|--------|-------|-------|
| Cranial | 0 | 7 | 0 | 7 |
| Axial | 0 | 2 | 1 | 3 |
| Forelimb | 2 | 11 | 5 | 18 |
| Hindlimb | 1 | 7 | 2 | 10 |

**TABLE C.6.** FLKNN–2: Frequency of Limb Bone Epiphyses for Bovid Size Classes Based on Minimum Number

| Element/ Epiphysis | Small | Medium | Large | Unclassified | Total |
|--------------------|-------|--------|-------|--------------|-------|
| Humerus | | | | 0 | |
| Proximal | 0 | 0 | 1 | 1 | 1 |
| Distal | 1 | 7 | 4 | | 13 |
| Radius/ulna | | | | 0 | |
| Proximal | 1 | 12 | 5 | 0 | 18 |
| Distal | 0 | 3 | 1 | | 4 |
| Metapodial | | | | 1 | |
| Proximal | 0 | 15 | 4 | 0 | 20 |
| Distal | 2 | 9 | 4 | | 15 |
| Tibia | | | | 0 | |
| Proximal | 0 | 0 | 2 | 0 | 2 |
| Distal | 0 | 4 | 2 | | 6 |
| Femur | | | | 0 | |
| Proximal | 0 | 1 | 0 | 0 | 1 |
| Distal | 0 | 1 | 2 | | 3 |

**TABLE C.7.** FLKNN–2: Minimum Number of Each Skeletal Element for Major Mammal Taxa[a]

| Element | Suid | Equid | Carnivore |
|---|---|---|---|
| Braincase | | | 1 |
| Maxilla | 2 | | |
| Basicranium | | | |
| Mandible | 4 | | 1 |
| Hyoid | | | |
| Vertebra | 1 | | |
| Rib | 1 | | |
| Innominate | 3 | | |
| Scapula | 1 | | |
| Humerus | 1 | 1 | |
| Radius | | 1 | |
| Ulna | | | |
| Metacarpal | 4 | 4 | |
| Carpals | 2 | 6 | |
| Femur | 2 | | |
| Tibia | 2 | 1 | |
| Fibula | 2 | 1 | |
| Metatarsal | 3 | | |
| Tarsals | 4 | | 1 |
| Patella | | | |
| Metapodial | 3 | 1 | |
| Podials | | | |
| Sesamoid | 12 | | |
| Phalanx | 31 | 3 | |
| Total | 78 | 18 | 3 |

[a]Specific taxon, side, age, and surface weathering were variables used to calculate the minimum number.

**TABLE C.8.** FLKNN–2: MNSU for Nonbovid Taxa

| Unit | Suid | Equid | Carnivore |
|---|---|---|---|
| Cranial | 4 | 0 | 1 |
| Axial | 2 | 0 | 0 |
| Forelimb | 3 | 3 | 0 |
| Hindlimb | 4 | 2 | 1 |

**ABLE C.9.** FLKNN–2: Frequency of Complete (Undamaged) Bones Relative to Total MNE; Frequency of Complete Long Bones Relative to Minimum Number of Long Bones for Each Major Taxon

| Taxon | Complete bones MNE | Percentage | Complete long bones MNE long bones | Percentage | Elements |
|---|---|---|---|---|---|
| ovid | 23/107 | 21 | 16/62 | 26 | 9 metacarpals<br>3 radii<br>1 metatarsal<br>1 tibia<br>1 humerus<br>1 radioulna |
| ⅃id | 48/78 | 62 | 0/5 | 0 | |
| quid | 9/18 | 50 | 1/8 | 12 | metacarpal |
| arnivore | 0/3 | 0 | 0/0 | — | |

# Appendix D: Site FLK–22

Number of stone artifacts = over 2,647
Number of faunal remains = approximately 40,172
Depth of deposit = 9 cm
Area excavated = approximately 290 m²
Density of excavated remains = at least 1539 per m³

## Fauna

*Number of Specimens = approximately 40,172*

Mammals identified to taxon and skeletal part = 614
Chelonia = 54
Crocodile = 14
Indeterminate fragments = approximately 15,247
Mixed fauna = approximately 24,243[a]

*Mammalian Macrofauna*

Tables D.1–9 present data for the mammalian macrofaunal specimens that summarize taxonomic representation, skeletal part frequencies, and completeness of bones in the assemblage.

*Crocodilia*

13 teeth
1 middle phalanx

*Chelonia*

53 carapace/plastron pieces
1 ilium

[a]Includes indeterminate fragments, microvertebrates, and avian remains.

369

*Indeterminate Fragments*

The following list details information about a sample of bone fragments that was not assigned to any major taxon. The sample consists of 1363 specimens, less than 10% of all indeterminate fragments from this site. Most of these specimens from this sample and the total set of indeterminate fragments come from small- and medium-sized mammals. Out of the sample described here, 54% were fragmented long bone pieces; most of these were diaphysis fragments.

Indeterminate: $N = 123$ (12 cranial frags., 1 caudal vertebra frag., 1 proximal rib, 5 limb shaft frags., 1 sesamoid, 103 indeterminate frags.)

Small-sized vertebrate: $N = 5$ (1 vertebra, 1 limb shaft frag., 3 indet. frags.)

Small/medium-sized vertebrate: $N = 1$ (vertebra frag.)

Mammal indet.: $N = 634$ (30 cranial frags., 1 maxilla, 10 gnathic pieces, 14 mandible frags., 48 tooth frags., 12 vertebrae frags., 150 rib shaft frags., 4 scapula frags., 158 limb shaft frags., 207 indet. frags.)

Small mammal: $N = 161$ (2 mandibular rami, 17 vertebra frags., 3 proximal ribs, 10 rib shaft frags., 108 limb shaft frags., 1 humerus shaft frag., 5 metapodial shaft frags., 1 femur shaft frag., 1 tibia shaft frag., 1 calcaneus frag., 12 indet. frags.)

Medium mammal: $N = 148$ (2 mandibular condyles, 5 vertebra frags., 7 proximal ribs, 26 rib shaft frags., 1 scapula frag., 1 innominate frag., 101 limb shaft frags., 2 radius shaft frags., 2 metapodial shaft frags., 1 pisiform)

Large mammal: $N = 19$ (1 thoracic vertebral spine, 2 proximal ribs, 5 rib shaft frags., 10 limb shaft frags., 1 tibia shaft frag.)

Very large mammal: $N = 5$ (2 rib shaft frags., 3 limb shaft frags.)

Small–medium mammal: $N = 244$ (1 cranial frag., 2 mandible frags., 2 tooth frags., 14 vertebra frags., 7 proximal ribs, 11 rib shaft frags., 1 sternum segment, 1 scapula frag., 178 limb shaft frags., 1 humerus shaft frag., 1 radio–ulna shaft frag., 2 metapodial shaft frags., 4 tibial shaft frags., 1 astragalus, 1 calcaneus, 2 phalanges, 15 indet. frags.)

Medium–large mammal: $N = 187$ (6 mandible frags., 2 tooth frags., 4 vertebra frags., 5 proximal ribs, 25 rib shaft frags., 1 sternum segment, 2 scapula frags., 1 innominate frag., 129 limb shaft frags., 1 radius frag., 3 metapodial frags., 3 tibia shaft frags., 2 sesamoids, 1 phalanx, 2 indet. frags.)

Medium–very large mammal: $N$ = 25 (1 maxilla frag., 1 vertebra frag., 19 limb shaft frags., 1 phalanx, 3 indet. frags.)

The following list estimates the number of small bone fragments and fragments plus microfauna in each excavation area:

*Balk:*
- Approximately 1290 bone fragments, mostly mammalian; small to medium-sized animal bones especially well represented
- Approximately 690 microfaunal remains and bone fragments of small mammals

*Cutting B:*
- Approximately 7016 bone fragments, mostly mammalian
- Approximately 4886 bone fragments and bird and fish remains

*Cutting C:*
- 125 mammalian indeterminate fragments, though thousands of such fragments occurred on the border between Cuttings B and C (included in Cutting B count)

*Cutting D:*
- 69 mammalian indeterminate fragments
- Approximately 4250 microfaunal remains and bone fragments belonging mostly to medium and small mammals but including a few pieces from large animal bones

*Cutting E:*
- 89 bone fragments, mostly mammalian

*Cutting F:*
- 37 bone fragments, mostly mammalian
- Approximately 1000 bone fragments, mostly microfaunal remains

*Cutting G:*
- Approximately 266 mammalian bone fragments, especially long bone shaft fragments from small animals
- Approximately 1580 comminuted bone fragments mainly from small mammals and bones from micromammals, birds, and fish

*Cutting K:*
- Approximately 677 indeterminate bone fragments, mostly mammalian

*No cutting specified:*
- Approximately 3968 bone fragments, mostly mammalian
- Approximately 11,827 microvertebrate remains, some bird and fish specimens, and mammal bone fragments

## Stone Artifacts

$N = 2647+$

The count of artifacts includes an estimate of the number of stone flakes (mostly quartzite) incorporated in several slabs of hard tuff from the top surface of Level 22, which were stored in the National Museums of Kenya. This count does not include 100 or more tiny quartzite flakes that were noted among the thousands of tiny bone splinters and microvertebrates obtained by sieving. Tables D.10–12 provide data about the main part of the artifact assemblage: artifact types, descriptive modifications to stones of various forms, and raw materials.

**TABLE D.1.** FLK "Zinj": Number of Specimens, MNE, MNSU, and MNI for Mammalian Taxa

| Taxon | Specimens | MNE | MNSU | MNI Adult | Immature | MNI total |
|-------|-----------|-----|------|-----------|----------|-----------|
| Bovid | 509 (83%) | 302 (83%) | 71 (70%) | 16 | 4 | 20 (56%) |
| Suid | 33 (5%) | 17 (5%) | 11 (11%) | 3 | 2 | 5 (14%) |
| Equid | 35 (6%) | 28 (8%) | 11 (11%) | 4 | 1 | 5 (14%) |
| Carnivore | 23 (4%) | 10 (3%) | 4 (4%) | 1 | 1 | 2 (6%) |
| Giraffid | 2 (0.3%) | 1 (0.3%) | 1 (1%) | 0 | 1 | 1 (3%) |
| Primate | 11 (2%) | 4 (1%) | 3 (3%) | 2 | 1 | 3 (8%) |
| Total | 613 | 362 | 101 | 26 | 10 | 36 |

**TABLE D.2.** FLK "Zinj": Mammalian Taxa Identified and MNI Represented by Each[a]

| Taxon | MNI |
|---|---|
| Small bovidae (1): | |
|   *Antidorcas recki* | 7 |
| Medium bovidae (3): | |
|   *Kobus sigmoidalis* | 4 |
|   *Parmularius altidens* | 4 |
|   Tragelaphini indet. | 2 |
| Large bovidae (3): | |
|   Bovini indet. | 1 |
|   *Oryx* sp. | 1 |
|   Large Alcelaphini | 1 |
| Suidae (3): | |
|   *Mesochoerus–Kolpochoerus limnetes* | 1 |
|   *Metridiochoerus andrewsi* | 2 |
|   *Notochoerus* sp. | 1 |
|   Indet. | 1 |
| Equidae (2): | |
|   *Equus oldowayensis* | 4 |
|   *Hipparion* sp. | 1 |
| Carnivora (1): | |
|   *Canis mesomelas* | 1 |
|   Indet. | 1 |
| Giraffidae (1): | |
|   *Giraffa stillei* | 1 |
| Primates (2): | |
|   Cercopithecidae indet. | 1 |
|   *Australopithecus boisei* | 1 |
|   Hominidae indet. | 1 |

[a]The number of taxa within any major taxonomic group is given in parentheses.

**TABLE D.3.** FLK "Zinj": Number of Specimens, MNE, and MNI for Bovid Size Classes

| Bovid size class | Specimens | MNE | MNI Adult | Immature | MNI total |
|---|---|---|---|---|---|
| Small | 157 (31%) | 119 (39%) | 6 | 1 | 7 (35%) |
| Small/medium | 14 (3%) | 5 (2%) | — | — | — |
| Medium | 239 (47%) | 125 (41%) | 8 | 2 | 10 (50%) |
| Medium/large | 12 (2%) | 8 (3%) | — | — | — |
| Large | 27 (5%) | 20 (7%) | 2 | 1 | 3 (15%) |
| Unclassified | 61 (12%) | 25 (8%) | — | — | — |
| Total | 510 | 302 | 16 | 4 | 20 |

**TABLE D.4.** FLK "Zinj": Minimum Number of Bovid Bones According to Skeletal Element and Size Class

| Element | Small | Small/medium[a] | Medium | Medium/large[a] | Large | Unclassified[a] |
|---|---|---|---|---|---|---|
| Braincase | | | 2 | | 1 | |
| Maxilla | 2 | | 3 | | | |
| Basicranium | | | | | | |
| Mandible | 7 | | 8 | | 2 | |
| Hyoid | | | | 1 | | 1 |
| Vertebra | 10 | 3 | 8 | 4 | 5 | 1 |
| Rib | 4 | | | | 2 | 17 |
| Innominate | 6 | | 4 | | 3 | |
| Scapula | 3 | | 8 | | | |
| Humerus | 6 | | 12 | | | |
| Radius | 4 | | 12 | | 1 | 2 |
| Ulna | 3 | | 5 | 1 | | |
| Metacarpal | 5 | | 8 | | | 1 |
| Carpals | 12 | | 12 | 1 | 1 | |
| Femur | 2 | | 6 | | | |
| Tibia | 6 | | 5 | | 1 | |
| Fibula | 1 | | 1 | | | |
| Metatarsal | 11 | | 5 | | | |
| Tarsals | 13 | 1 | 9 | | 1 | |
| Patella | 1 | | 1 | | | |
| Metapodial | | | | | | 1 |
| Podials | | | | | | |
| Sesamoid | 6 | | 14 | | | |
| Phalanx | 17 | 1 | 3 | 1 | 3 | 2 |
| Other | | | | | | |
| Total | 119 | 5 | 125 | 8 | 20 | 25 |

[a]Only those elements not accounted for by small, medium, or large bovids.

**TABLE D.5.** FLK "Zinj": MNSU for Bovid Size Classes

| Unit | Small | Medium | Large | Total |
|---|---|---|---|---|
| Cranial | 7 | 8 | 3 | 18 |
| Axial | 5 | 3 | 2 | 10 |
| Forelimb | 8 | 16 | 2 | 26 |
| Hindlimb | 9 | 7 | 1 | 17 |

**TABLE D.6.** FLK "Zinj": Frequency of Limb Bone Epiphyses for Bovid Size Classes Based on Minimum Number

| Element/Epiphysis | Small | Small/medium | Medium | Medium/large | Large | Unclassified | Total |
|---|---|---|---|---|---|---|---|
| Humerus | | | | | | | |
| Proximal | 3 | 0 | 1 | 1 | 1 | 0 | 6 |
| Distal | 6 | 0 | 12 | 0 | 1 | 0 | 19 |
| Radius/ulna | | | | | | | |
| Proximal | 7 | 0 | 17 | 1 | 0 | 2 | 27 |
| Distal | 0 | 1 | 2 | 0 | 0 | 0 | 3 |
| Metapodial | | | | | | | |
| Proximal | 15 | 1 | 13 | 0 | 0 | 1 | 30 |
| Distal | 10 | 0 | 10 | 0 | 0 | 0 | 20 |
| Tibia | | | | | | | |
| Proximal | 5 | 0 | 2 | 0 | 0 | 0 | 7 |
| Distal | 5 | 0 | 2 | 1 | 1 | 2 | 11 |
| Femur | | | | | | | |
| Proximal | 2 | 0 | 5 | 1 | 0 | 0 | 8 |
| Distal | 2 | 0 | 4 | 0 | 0 | 0 | 6 |

**TABLE D.7.** FLK "Zinj": Minimum Number of Each Skeletal Element for Major Mammal Taxa[a]

| Element | Suid | Equid | Carnivore | Giraffid | Primate[b] |
|---------|------|-------|-----------|----------|-----------|
| Braincase | | | | | 1 |
| Maxilla | 1 | 1 | 1 | | 1 |
| Basicranium | | | | | |
| Mandible | 4 | 5 | | 1 | 1 |
| Hyoid | | | | | |
| Vertebra | | 1 | | | |
| Rib | 2 | 9 | 4 | | |
| Innominate | | | 1 | | |
| Scapula | 1 | 3 | | | |
| Humerus | 1 | | | | |
| Radius | | | | | |
| Ulna | 1 | | 1 | | |
| Metacarpal | | | | | |
| Carpals | | | | | |
| Femur | | 1 | | | 1 |
| Tibia | | 1 | | | 1 |
| Fibula | | | | | |
| Metatarsal | 3 | 3 | | | |
| Tarsals | 4 | 4 | 1 | | |
| Patella | | | | | |
| Metapodial | | | 2 | | |
| Podials | | | | | |
| Sesamoid | | | | | |
| Phalanx | | | | | |
| Other | | | | | |
| Total | 17 | 28 | 10 | 1 | 4 |

[a]Specific taxon, side, age, and surface weathering were variables used to calculate the minimum number.

[b]Hominid material includes 1 cranium (braincase and maxilla), 1 tibia, and 1 fibula.

**TABLE D.8.** FLK "Zinj": MNSU for Nonbovid Taxa

| Unit | Suid | Equid | Carnivore | Giraffid | Primate |
|------|------|-------|-----------|----------|---------|
| Cranial | 5 | 5 | 1 | 1 | 2 |
| Axial | 1 | 1 | 1 | 0 | 0 |
| Forelimb | 2 | 3 | 1 | 0 | 0 |
| Hindlimb | 2 | 2 | 1 | 0 | 1 |

**TABLE D.9.** FLK "Zinj": Frequency of Complete (Undamaged) Bones Relative to Total MNE; Frequency of Complete Long Bones Relative to Minimum Number of Long Bones for Each Major Taxon

| Taxon | Complete bones MNE | Percentage | Complete long bones MNE long bones | Percentage | Elements |
|---|---|---|---|---|---|
| Bovid | 96/302 | 32 | 10/97 | 10 | 4 metatarsals 2 metacarpals 2 tibiae 1 humerus 1 radius |
| Suid | 6/17 | 35 | 0/2 | 0 | |
| Equid | 5/28 | 18 | 0/2 | 0 | |
| Carnivore | 1/10 | 10 | 0/1 | 0 | |
| Giraffid | 0/1 | 0 | 0/0 | — | |
| Primate | 0/4 | 0 | 0/2 | 0 | |

**TABLE D.10.** FLK "Zinj": Frequencies of Artifact Type Based on Leakey's Original Classification and on Current Study, Based on Leakey's Types (Leaky, 1971)

| Type | Original classification | Current study |
|---|---|---|
| Chopper | 17 | 17 |
| Protobiface | | |
| Polyhedron | 9 | 5 |
| Discoid | 2 | 3 |
| Subspheroid | | 1 |
| Spheroid | | |
| Small scraper | 18 | 9 |
| Large scraper | 6 | 1 |
| Burin | 4 | 4 |
| Awl | | |
| Laterally trimmed flake | | |
| Sundry tool | | |
| Casual core/tool indet. | | 5 |
| Utilized material | 135 | 69 |
| Whole flake | 257 | 204 |
| Broken flake | 1865 | 1875 |
| Core fragment | 155 | 140 |
| Other *debitage* | 1 | 154 |
| Manuport | 91 + | 99 + |
| Artifact/manuport indet. | | 47 |
| ?Artifact | | |
| Other | 1 | 14 |
| Total | 2561 + | 2647 + |

**TABLE D.11.** FLK "Zinj": Types of Stone Modification and Size/Form of Raw Material Used[a]

| Material | Whole unflaked | Broken unflaked | Core | Incidental core | Flake/ flake fragment | Flake core | Incidental flake core | Indet. | Total |
|---|---|---|---|---|---|---|---|---|---|
| Cobble | 47 | 68 | 15 | — | — | — | — | 11 | 141 |
| Pebble | 5 | 4 | 2 | — | — | — | — | — | 11 |
| Slab | 9 | 13 | 1 | 1 | 3 | — | — | 2 | 29 |
| Broken fragment indet. | — | 195 | 8 | 2 | — | — | — | 5 | 210 |
| Indet. | — | 3 | 2 | — | 681 | 6 | 2 | 6 | 700 |
| Total | 61 | 283 | 28 | 3 | 684 | 6 | 2 | 24 | 1091 |

[a]Numerous broken flakes and core fragments are not included; almost all such pieces would be classified under "flake fragment" or "broken fragment indet.", as are the majority sampled here.

**TABLE D.12.** FLK "Zinj": Representation of Stone Artifact Raw Materials by Number of Specimens and by Weight

| Material | Specimens | Weight (grams) |
|---|---|---|
| Basalt | 5 | 55 |
| Basalt/trachyandesite indet. | 16 | 846 |
| Nephelinite | 18 | 4892 |
| Vesicular basalt | 125 | 32,349 |
| Lava indet. | 89 | 14,186 |
| Quartzite | 2387 | ~20,000 |
| Gneiss | 2 | 45 |
| Feldspar | 5 | 30 |
| Total | 2647 | 72,403 |

# Appendix E: Site FLK North–6

Number of stone artifacts = 130
Number of faunal remains = 2258[a]
Depth of deposit = 50 cm
Area excavated = approximately 37 m$^2$
Density of excavated remains = approximately 64.5 per m$^3$

## Fauna

*Number of Specimens = 2258[a]*

Mammals identified to taxon and skeletal part = 740 (33%)
Crocodile = 2 teeth
Indeterminate fragments = 1516 (67%)

### Mammalian Macrofauna

Tables E.1–9 present data for the mammalian macrofaunal specimens. This information summarizes taxonomic representation, skeletal part frequencies, and the completeness of bones in the assemblage. Data for bovids is broken down by body size category since this family represents a wide range of body sizes.

### Indeterminate Fragments

These fragments, for the most part, were ones not recognized to belong to any major taxonomic group, although skeletal part was often identified. Several hundred pieces, however, were associated spatially with particular skeletal elements from the main *Elephas recki* carcass. These pieces were not included in the count of *E. recki* specimens since that would serve merely to inflate artificially the number of specimens assigned to this taxon relative to other taxa. The summary of these fragments is presented under indeterminate fragments for convenience sake. Fragments from medium-sized mammal bones predominate. One-third of these specimens are long bone fragments, especially from diaphyses.

[a]Excludes microvertebrate, avian, and fish remains.

381

Indeterminate: $N = 16$ (1 mandibular ramus, 8 vertebra frags., 1 rib shaft
    frag., 1 distal humerus, 1 proximal tibia, 4 indet. frags.)
Mammal indet.: $N = 64$ (8 cranial frags., 1 mandible frag., 13 tooth frags.,
    6 caudal vertebrae, 1 sternum frag., 2 innominate frags., 5 limb shaft
    frags., 28 indet. frags.)
Large micromammal: $N = 7$ (1 cranial frag., 3 vertebra frags., 1 innominate
    frag., 1 distal metapodial, 1 indet. frag.)
Small mammal: $N = 26$ (1 cranial frag., 4 vertebra frags., 1 proximal rib, 1
    rib shaft frag., 2 innominate frags., 11 limb shaft frags., 2 femur frags.,
    1 calcaneus, 1 phalanx, 1 indet. frag.)
Medium mammal: $N = 21$ (2 mandible frags., 5 vertebra frags., 2 proximal
    ribs, 2 rib shaft frags., 5 limb shaft frags., 2 metapodial frags., 1 distal
    femur, 1 carpal indet.)
Large mammal: $N = 1$ (thoracic vertebra frag.)
Very large mammal: $N = 1$ (tooth fragment—a flake with a bulb of force
    and an enamel platform from a very large tooth; specimen measures 26
    $\times$ 16 $\times$ 6 mm)
Small-medium mammal: $N = 22$ (1 cranial frag., 1 mandible frag., 1 premolar
    frag., 4 vertebra frags., 1 proximal rib, 1 rib shaft frag., 8 limb shaft
    frags., 1 splint, 1 carpal, 1 calcaneus epiphysis, 2 indet. frags.)
Medium–large mammal: $N = 21$ (1 cranial frag., 14 vertebra frags., 1 proximal
    rib, 1 innominate frag., 4 limb shaft frags.)
Medium–very large mammal: $N = 40$ (1 rib shaft frag., 26 limb shaft frags.,
    13 indet. frags.)
Other mammal fragments (various sizes): $N = 726$

*Elephas recki:*      $N = 471$ (12 vertebral epiphyses, 12 rib proximal epiphyses, 140 innominate frags., 160 frags. of left scapula, 11 frags. of left radius,
66 frags. of right radius, 70 skull frags.)


## Stone Artifacts


$N = 130$
Tables E.10–12 present data on this artifact assemblage.

**TABLE E.1.** FLK North–6: Number of Specimens, MNE, MNSU, and MNI for Mammalian Taxa

| Taxon | Specimens | MNE | MNSU | MNI Adult | MNI Immature | MNI total |
|---|---|---|---|---|---|---|
| Bovid | 262 (35%) | 168 (46%) | 31 (51%) | 7 | 3 | 10 (45%) |
| Suid | 71 (10%) | 18 ( 5%) | 8 (13%) | 2 | 2 | 4 (18%) |
| Equid | 1 (0.1%) | 1 (0.2%) | 1 ( 2%) | 1 | 0 | 1 ( 5%) |
| Carnivore | 10 (1.3%) | 7 ( 2%) | 4 ( 7%) | 1 | 1 | 2 ( 9%) |
| Proboscidean | 357 (52%) | 159 (44%) | 10 (16%) | 0 | 2 | 2 ( 9%) |
| Rhino | 5 (0.6%) | 5 (1.3%) | 2 ( 3%) | 0 | 1 | 1 ( 5%) |
| Hippo | 1 (0.1%) | 1 (0.2%) | 1 ( 2%) | — | — | 1 ( 5%) |
| Giraffid | 3 (0.4%) | 3 (0.8%) | 3 ( 5%) | 1 | — | 1 ( 5%) |
| Total | 740 | 362 | 60 | 12 | 9 | 22 |

**TABLE E.2.** FLK North–6: Mammalian Taxa Identified and MNI Represented by Each[a]

| Taxon | MNI |
|---|---|
| Small bovidae (1): | |
|   *Antidorcas recki* | 2 |
|   Indet. | 1 |
| Medium bovidae (3): | |
|   *Parmularius altidens* | 3 |
|   Tragelaphini indet. | 2 |
|   Hippotragini indet. | ?1 |
| Large bovidae (1): | |
|   *?Syncerus acoelotus* | 1 |
| Very large bovidae (1): | |
|   Indet. | 1 |
| Suidae (1): | |
|   *Mesochoerus–Kolpochoerus limnetes* | 4 |
| Equidae (1): | |
|   *Equus oldowayensis* | 1 |
| Carnivora (1): | |
|   Canidae indet. | 2 |
| Proboscidean (1): | |
|   *Elephas recki* | 2 |
| Rhinoceros (1): | |
|   *Ceratotherium simum* | 1 |
| Hippopotamus (1) | |
|   *Hippopotamus* sp. indet. | 1 |
| Giraffidae (1): | |
|   *Giraffa jumae* | 1 |

[a]The number of taxa within any major taxonomic group is given in parentheses.

**TABLE E.3.** FLK North–6: Number of Specimens, MNE, and MNI for Bovid Size Classes

| Bovid size class | Specimens | MNE | MNI Adult | MNI Immature | MNI total |
|---|---|---|---|---|---|
| Small | 83 (32%) | 64 (38%) | 2 | 1 | 3 (30%) |
| Small/medium | 16 ( 6%) | 8 ( 5%) | — | — | — |
| Medium | 92 (35%) | 59 (35%) | 3 | 2 | 5 (50%) |
| Medium/large | 17 ( 6%) | 8 ( 5%) | — | — | — |
| Large | 5 ( 2%) | 4 ( 2%) | 1 | 0 | 1 (10%) |
| Very large | 3 ( 1%) | 3 ( 2%) | 1 | 0 | 1 (10%) |
| Unclassified | 46 (18%) | 22 (13%) | — | — | — |
| Total | 262 | 168 | 7 | 3 | 10 |

**TABLE E.4.** FLK North–6: Minimum Number of Bovid Bones According to Skeletal Element and Size Class

| Element | Small | Small/medium[a] | Medium | Medium/large[a] | Large | Very large | Unclassified[a] |
|---|---|---|---|---|---|---|---|
| Braincase | | | 1 | | 1 | | |
| Maxilla | 2 | | 2 | | | | |
| Basicranium | | | | | | | |
| Mandible | 1 | | 4 | | | | |
| Hyoid | | | | | | | |
| Vertebra | 2 | 4 | 4 | 6 | 1 | | 1 |
| Rib | | 3 | | 1 | 1 | 2 | 2 |
| Innominate | 1 | | 3 | | | | |
| Scapula | | | 2 | | | | |
| Humerus | 3 | | 4 | | | | |
| Radius | 3 | | 5 | | | | |
| Ulna | 4 | | 2 | | | | |
| Metacarpal | 1 | | 3 | | | | |
| Carpals | 5 | | 6 | 1 | | | |
| Femur | 1 | | 3 | | | | |
| Tibia | 2 | | 4 | | | 1 | |
| Fibula | 1 | | 2 | | | | |
| Metatarsal | 2 | | 1 | | | | |
| Tarsals | 9 | | 4 | | | | |
| Patella | 3 | | 2 | | | | 1 |
| Metapodial | 3 | | | | | | |
| Podials | | | | | | | |
| Sesamoid | 2 | 1 | 2 | | | | 8 |
| Phalanx | 19 | | 6 | | 1 | | 10 |
| Total | 64 | 8 | 59 | 8 | 4 | 3 | 22 |

[a]Only those elements not represented by small, medium, or large bovids.

**TABLE E.5.** FLK North–6: MNSU for Bovid Size Classes

| Unit | Small | Medium | Large | Very large | Total |
|------|-------|--------|-------|------------|-------|
| Cranial | 2 | 4 | 1 | 0 | 7 |
| Axial | 1 | 2 | 1 | 1 | 5 |
| Forelimb | 5 | 5 | 0 | 0 | 10 |
| Hindlimb | 3 | 4 | 0 | 1 | 8 |
| Limb indet. | 0 | 0 | 1 | 0 | 1 |

**TABLE E.6.** FLK North–6: Frequency of Limb Bone Epiphyses for Bovid Size Classes

| Element/ Epiphysis | Small | Medium | Medium/large | Total[a] |
|--------------------|-------|--------|--------------|----------|
| Humerus | | | | |
|   Proximal | 1 | 1 | 0 | 2 |
|   Distal | 2 | 4 | 0 | 6 |
| Radius/ulna | | | | |
|   Proximal | 6 | 6 | 0 | 12 |
|   Distal | 2 | 5 | 0 | 7 |
| Metapodial | | | | |
|   Proximal | 2 | 4 | 0 | 6 |
|   Distal | 6 | 2 | 0 | 8 |
| Tibia | | | | |
|   Proximal | 2 | 1 | 1 | 4 |
|   Distal | 2 | 3 | 0 | 5 |
| Femur | | | | |
|   Proximal | 1 | 0 | 0 | 1 |
|   Distal | 1 | 3 | 0 | 4 |

[a] No data are applicable for other size classes.

**TABLE E.7.** FLK North–6: Minimum Number of Each Skeletal Element for Major Mammalian Taxa[a]

| Element | Suid | Equid | Carnivore | Proboscidean | Rhino | Hippo | Giraffid |
|---|---|---|---|---|---|---|---|
| Braincase | | | 1 | 1 | | | |
| Maxilla | 4 | | 1 | 1 | | | |
| Basicranium | | | | 1 | | | |
| Mandible | 4 | | | 1 | | | 1 |
| Hyoid | | | | | | | |
| Vertebra | 4 | | 1 | 47 | 2 | 1 | |
| Rib | 1 | | | 36 | | | |
| Innominate | | | | 2 | | | |
| Scapula | 1 | 1 | 1 | 2 | | | |
| Humerus | 1 | | | 2 | | | |
| Radius | | | | 2 | | | 1 |
| Ulna | 1 | | 1 | 2 | | | |
| Metacarpal | | | | 7 | 1 | | |
| Carpals | | | | 13 | 1 | | |
| Femur | | | 1 | 4 | | | |
| Tibia | 1 | | 1 | 2 | | | |
| Fibula | | | | 2 | | | |
| Metatarsal | | | | 6 | | | |
| Tarsals | 1 | | | 11 | | | |
| Patella | | | | 1 | | | |
| Metapodial | | | | | 1 | | |
| Podials | | | | | | | |
| Sesamoid | | | | 5 | | | |
| Phalanx | | | 1 | 13 | | | |
| Other | | | | | | | 1 |
| | | | | | | | (sternum) |
| Total | 18 | 1 | 7 | 159 | 5 | 1 | 3 |

[a]Specific taxon, side, age, and surface weathering were variables used to calculate the minimum number.

**TABLE E.8.** FLK North–6: MNSU for Nonbovid Taxa

| Unit | Suid | Equid | Carnivore | Proboscidean | Rhino | Hippo | Giraffid |
|------|------|-------|-----------|--------------|-------|-------|----------|
| Cranial | 4 | 0 | 1 | 1 | 0 | 0 | 1 |
| Axial | 1 | 0 | 1 | 2 | 1 | 1 | 1 |
| Forelimb | 2 | 1 | 1 | 3 | 1 | 0 | 1 |
| Hindlimb | 1 | 0 | 1 | 4 | 0 | 0 | 0 |

**TABLE E.9.** FLK North–6: Frequency of Complete (Undamaged) Bones Relative to Total MNE; Frequency of Complete Long Bones Relative to Minimum Number of Long Bones for Each Major Taxon

| Taxon | Complete bones/ MNE | Percentage | Complete long bones/ MNE long bones | Percentage | Elements |
|-------|---------------------|------------|-------------------------------------|------------|----------|
| Bovid | 73/168 | 43 | 9/42 | 21 | 2 radii<br>2 humeri<br>1 metacarpal<br>2 metatarsals<br>1 femur<br>1 tibia |
| Suid | 3/18 | 16 | 1/3 | 33 | tibia |
| Equid | 0/1 | 0 | 0/0 | — | |
| Carnivore | 1/7 | 14 | 0/3 | 0 | |
| Proboscidean | 67/159 | 42 | 7/14 | 50 | 2 humeri<br>2 femora<br>2 tibiae<br>1 fibula |
| Rhino | 2/5 | 40 | 0/0 | — | |
| Hippo | 0/1 | 0 | 0/0 | — | |
| Giraffid | 0/3 | 0 | 0/1 | 0 | |
| Total | 146/362 | 40 | 17/63 | 40 | |

**TABLE E.10.** FLK North–6: Frequencies of Artifact Types Based on Leakey's Original Classification and on Current Study, Based on Leakey's Types (Leaky, 1971)

| Type | Original classification | Current study |
|------|-------------------------|---------------|
| Chopper | 4 | 1 |
| Protobiface | 1 | 0 |
| Polyhedron | | |
| Discoid | | 1 |
| Subspheroid | | |
| Spheroid | | |
| Small scraper | | |
| Large scraper | | |
| Burin | | |
| Awl | | |
| Laterally trimmed flake | | |
| Sundry tool | | |
| Casual Core/tool indet. | | 3 |
| Utilized material | 24 | 13 |
| Whole flake | 22 | 17 |
| Broken flake | 62 | 68 |
| Core fragment | 10 | 10 |
| Other *debitage* | | 1 |
| Manuport | 7 | 16 |
| Artifact/manuport indet. | | |
| ?Artifact | | |
| Other | | |
| Total | 130 | 130 |

**TABLE E.11.** FLK North–6: Types of Stone Modification and Size/Form of Raw Material Used

| Material | Whole unflaked | Broken unflaked | Core | Flake/ flake fragment | Indet. | Total |
|----------|----------------|-----------------|------|-----------------------|--------|-------|
| Cobble | 5 | 9 | 3 | | | 17 |
| Slab | 5 | | 1 | | | 6 |
| Indet. | | 2 | 11 | 88 | 1 | 102 |
| Total | 10 | 11 | 15 | 88 | 1 | 125 |

**TABLE E.12.** FLK North–6: Representation of Stone Artifact Raw Materials by Number of Specimens and by Weight

| Material | Specimens | Weight (grams) |
|---|---|---|
| Basalt | 2 | 893 |
| Trachyandesite | 3 | 1297 |
| Basalt/trachyandesite indet. | 6 | 1410 |
| Nephelinite | 6 | 2283 |
| Lava indet. | 3 | 1671 |
| Quartzite | 93 | 4436 |
| Chert | 2 | 20 |
| Indet. | 1 | 2 |
| Total | 116 | 12,012 |

# INDEX